CHINA'S MILITARY MODERNIZATION

CHINA'S MILITARY MODERNIZATION

Building for Regional and Global Reach

Richard D. Fisher Jr.
Foreword by Arthur Waldron

STANFORD SECURITY STUDIES
An Imprint of Stanford University Press
Stanford, California

Stanford University Press
Stanford, California

First published in paperback in 2010.

China's Military Modernization: Building for Regional and Global Reach, by Richard D. Fisher, Jr., was originally published in hardcover by Praeger Publishers, an imprint of ABC-CLIO, LLC, Santa Barbara, CA. Copyright 2008 by Richard D. Fisher, Jr. Paperback edition by arrangement with ABC-CLIO, LLC, Santa Barbara, CA. All rights reserved.

Special discounts for bulk quantities of Stanford Security Studies are available to corporations, professional associations, and other organizations. For details and discount information, contact the special sales department of Stanford University Press. Tel: (650) 736-1782, Fax: (650) 736-1784

Printed in the United States of America on acid-free, archival-quality paper.

Library of Congress Cataloging-in-Publication Data
Fisher, Richard D., 1959–
 China's military modernization : building for regional
and global reach / Richard D. Fisher Jr. ; foreword by
Arthur Waldron.
  p. cm.
 Originally published: Westport, Conn. : Praeger
Security International, 2008.
 Includes bibliographical references and index.
 ISBN 978-0-8047-7195-5 (pbk. : alk. paper)
 ISBN 978-0-8047-7194-8 (cloth bound : alk. paper)
 1. China—Armed Forces. 2. China—Armed Forces—
Weapons systems. 3. China—Military policy. I. Title.
 UA835.F57 2010
 355′.033551—dc22   2010014978

CONTENTS

Foreword by Arthur Waldron   vii

Preface   xv

Acknowledgments   xxi

CHAPTER 1   China's Strategic Challenge   1

CHAPTER 2   The Party Army: Pillar of China's Government   15

CHAPTER 3   Foreign Security Policy   40

CHAPTER 4   China's Military Transformation   66

CHAPTER 5   Military-Technical Sector Transformation   80

CHAPTER 6   Building for Local War Dominance   123

CHAPTER 7   Building for Future Power Projection   169

CHAPTER 8   How the CCP-PLA Challenges America and Its Allies   213

Notes   253

Index   301

Foreword

China's dramatic military buildup over the last several decades is perhaps the single most important challenge in strategic affairs today, not only for China's neighbors from Russia and Japan and the Koreas and Taiwan to India and Central Asia, but also for world strategic affairs in places seemingly remote from China, from the Middle East and Europe to Africa and Latin America.

Before choosing policies to deal with this Chinese challenge, however, we must first be sure we know what it is. Richard Fisher's great contribution in this volume is to give us the facts and to do so in a way that is fundamentally empirical and rich in informative descriptions of China's systems and capabilities—all informed by an expertise in military analysis that is serious, original, and illuminating.

Fisher has been doing this sort of work since he discovered a fascination with aviation as a small child. He has followed all available open sources on China's military with great care, supplementing that research with regular visits, numbering in the many dozens by now, to air shows and other venues where he talks shop with the representatives both of China and of countries that provide technology and equipment to China. Fisher draws his broader perspective from an impressive knowledge of military technology in general and aircraft in particular, from World War I to the present. He is, in my opinion, the world's leading authority on the Chinese military not in government service—and probably better than many who have spent decades in the intelligence community. Certainly he is the first person I consult about any report of a new Chinese capability.

For these reasons, this is the book with which to begin if you want to think for yourself about the Chinese military, for it will give you the information you

need. It will also give you interpretation and opinion, but no answers, as is so
common in publications of this type, *prêt à pénser*. Some, I think, will not be
pleased with the facts Fisher presents here, for reasons I will survey briefly
below. When they take issue, however, I hope very much that such people will
engage Fisher first of all on the facts: is the information he presents sound and
accurate? Correction of factual error is always a fundamental contribution. Only
after the facts have been thoroughly discussed, disagreements about them
flagged, and methods identified for resolving disagreements identified, can the
equally important evaluation begin of what is to be inferred from these facts.

Fisher's record on factual accuracy is enviable. In 2004 I was invited by the
Aspen Institute in Berlin to make a presentation about China. To provide some
starting point for this I distributed copies to the Germans around the table—
government officials, journalists, academics, and others—of a few pages Fisher
had prepared listing the chief dual-use technologies that Germany and other
European countries had provided to China: such things as engines that had civilian uses but could also solve for China some otherwise formidable difficulties
with submarine propulsion.

I circulated that list with some trepidation. The Germans reading my hand-
out were in some cases people who had been involved in the very sales decisions
Fisher documented. But after about five minutes of silence, during which the
pages were scrutinized, the signal came: yes, we agree this is an accurate, comprehensive and fair description of what we have sold. What followed then was
a remarkable conversation, for it was not with me. Rather it was among the
Germans themselves about the wisdom, or lack thereof, of such sales. I sat back
and listened with interest, for the reactions of that German group, and the questions they raised are essentially those that should be in the mind of any reader
of this important book.

First, the Chinese military buildup has clearly caught the world by surprise
and unprepared. This fact is not owing to some extraordinary Chinese success
in concealment and deception. Rather it is the result of foreign unwillingness to
recognize the intelligence and resourcefulness of the government in Beijing, as
well as reluctance to accept that China was seeking not local or regional, but
global great power status. Dual-use technologies, for example, were not being
procured in an impulsive or unsystematic way. Rather, somewhere in the Chinese
military, a plan or set of plans had been drawn up for comprehensive military
modernization, to be self-sufficient when possible, based on dual-use purchases
from when feasible, and otherwise on direct military purchases from Europe,
Israel, Russia, and other countries. Espionage was also extensively employed. By
such means China was able to leap over decades of costly internal research and
development and move far more rapidly toward state-of-the-art military technology than anyone had expected.

Today China has near top-of-the-line fighter jets in substantial numbers; she
possesses a robust nuclear and ballistic missile capability that includes stage separation and multiple independently targeted re-entry vehicle (MIRV) technologies

that have been acquired from the West by irregular means, as well as antisatellite and growing space warfare capabilities. Her submarine fleet is growing, and along with her aircraft, they regularly violate the territorial air and sea space of such neighbors as Korea and Japan. Perhaps half a dozen aircraft carriers are on the drawing boards. Such capabilities are quite different to what received opinion expected perhaps two decades ago, when serious discussion of China's military future got under way.

Twenty years ago specialists on the People's Liberation Army began to hold informal, privately funded gatherings under shifting auspices, some of the proceedings of which were published by the American Enterprise Institute, whose then Senior Fellow James Lilley sponsored them. I was among the first participants and remember well how, whenever I suggested that Chinese history indicated an overriding concern with military power, I was met with the most excruciatingly patient of explanations that my concerns had no foundation. China's military was obsolete. She sought to modernize it a bit and reach a threshold of minimal deterrence. But beyond that her government's primary concern was to raise living standards and the welfare of the population. We and our friends had nothing to fear, provided of course we did not somehow "provoke" China, "forcing" her to react by seeking military capabilities she would otherwise not have wanted.

An argument went on for a good decade between a handful of specialists who expected a major Chinese bid for military power, and the consensus of the field, which saw China as having economic and not strategic goals. Now, as Fisher's book makes clear, that argument is over, the then-conventional wisdom has been proven false, and the handful of concerned specialists vindicated. This brings us to a second question, also asked that evening in Berlin: namely, how could (almost) everyone had gotten things so wrong?

The answer to this question has more to do with how one analyzes the Chinese regime than with anything specifically military. It hearkens back to complex debates among scholars of the history of Germany, which has also made massive attempts to achieve military leadership over the past little more than a century. Some German scholars explain her military buildups—for example, that of her fleet in the years before World War I—as driven from outside. It was a matter of *Aussenpolitik*—foreign policy—above all, and could have been moderated, whether in the years before World War I or in the period leading up to World War II, by more forthcoming policies on the part of the then great powers. This argument contains truth and it applies, to a degree, to China, which has always conceived of herself as the leading civilization and polity in the world, and seeks to regain it.

Other German scholars, however, stress that military buildups in that country were decided not by foreign but rather by domestic challenges—by *Innenpolitik* or internal politics. One recalls that Bismarck, who launched the wars of German unification in the 1860s, was called to be chancellor only when a deadlock in parliament prevented the passage of the military budget. Bismarck realized that he could split the liberal bloc by making visible progress toward the universally shared goal of national unity—which he did, defeating Austria, the logical candidate as leader of a united Germany—and then France, in short, low-cost, and decisive wars that culminated with the spectacle of a Prussian king—his power incomparably augmented by the wars, as Emperor of a German empire that was the largest state in Europe—at the Hall of Mirrors at Versailles. In less than ten years Bismarck and the great general Moltke had utterly overturned the long-prevailing pattern of European power—and furthermore (perhaps this was the real purpose?) firmly installed the Hohenzollerns of Prussia as rulers of the *Kaiserreich*, at which the former great powers—England, France, Austria and Russia—blinked their eyes in surprise, disbelief, and apprehension.

The idea that domestic political considerations—*Innenpolitik*—might drive China's military development is by and large rejected by students of that country, though widely accepted by Chinese analysts—not necessarily in writing—and by certain scholars such as James Polachek, whose *Inner Opium War* (Cambridge, MA: Harvard University Press, 1991) is a neglected classic, and the present author, who makes such a case for the Ming dynasty (1368–1644) in *The Great Wall of China: From History to Myth* (Cambridge, UK: Cambridge University Press, 1989) as well as others. The general concept goes back at least to the Greek Isocrates (436–338 B.C.), who counseled that the fractious city-states of his country could best be unified if a small-scale war was maintained constantly with Persia—big enough to stimulate a sense of national interest greater than regionalism, but not so big as actually to get out of control and pose an existential threat to Greece.

Fisher is concerned above all with documenting the Chinese military buildup; understandably he therefore devotes little attention to considering the fundamental forces driving it; the same can be said of my German audience, for most observers and commentators on the buildup, and even of government officials charged with formulating long-term policy. The fact is that motivation is difficult to explain; more than a century later, historians of Germany are still debating the proportions of inner and outer policy in that country's series of wars since the late nineteenth century. Like the Germany of which Bismarck became chancellor, however, today's China is essentially an autocracy, in which survival of a nonrepresentative and self-perpetuating ruling class (nobles, Junkers, and the military in one case, the Communist Party in the other) counts for more than national interest. In both countries, too, that ruling class was aware of its own obsolescence. Twenty years ago in China the party army essentially sacked its own capital city, Beijing, on the night of June 4, 1989, killing a still unknown number of peaceful democracy demonstrators and sending to prison large numbers of people, who remain there. In the years since, unequal and corrupt economic development, often involving outright confiscation of farmers' land, for example, or misappropriation of public funds and property, has created both a wealthy urban upper class that depends on the state, and an increasingly impoverished rural underclass. Violence against the government has become common.

Foreign observers discount the possibility that discontent could destabilize the tightly buttoned-down Communist regime; the regime itself does not. It maintains large military forces devoted exclusively to quelling civil unrest, the People's Armed Police; it regularly arrests and detains whom it pleases, in violation of its own laws; and it engages in pervasive surveillance and censorship, of print and broadcast media (already state-owned), the Internet, cell phone traffic, and so forth. Most importantly, the government actively seeks to use officially inculcated nationalism and xenophobia to rally a population that no longer has much use for Communist doctrine.

China has no obvious enemies, however. Japan and Taiwan seek good relations, as do Russia and India and everyone else. Finding the sort of threat Isocrates identified in the Persians is therefore difficult and tricky. If, for example, official China stirs up demonstrations against French-owned department stores, or against Japanese visitors, or rattles sabers against Taiwan or India, the result is, as will be seen, the gradual ratcheting up of the military capabilities of the countries threatened, a result unfavorable to China's desire for preeminence. If, on the other hand, the Chinese government accepts a peaceful international environment, it destroys the rationale for military buildup and opens the way to the outcry from the people that, with the military threat passed, the time has come for an end to one-party dictatorship.

The debate about the reasons for the German buildup provide, then, a framework for considering the fundamental question of the reason for China's rapid rearmament. Is Beijing chiefly interested, as Bismarck was, in defeating liberalism and uniting his country (in the Chinese case, keeping it united, unless one insists that somehow Taiwan must be forced to submit)? Or is China actually seeking the sort of capability to intervene all over the world without challenge, such as Britain once possessed and the United States still barely maintains? And doing so because she genuinely wishes to rearrange the current distribution of world military power in her favor?

If the former answer is correct: that China's military buildup is primary to strengthen the Party's domestic grip, then the rest of the world can do very little about it. Change will come only if and when China's political system changes. In a free election China would form a parliament dominated by poor farmers. That they would favor ignoring the countryside and pouring tens of billions of dollars a year into nuclear submarines, space exploration, and so forth seems highly unlikely. Confrontation with Russia has by no means ended with the disintegration of the Soviet Union, but what remains is nowhere near so dangerous or on such a scale as what was taken for granted from the 1950s to the 1980s. Why the change? Regime change in Russia; no more, no less. The same could happen in China.

If the latter answer is better, however—that China is genuinely seeking hegemonic military power in Asia and globally—then the world faces potentially serious problems. Bear in mind before plumping for this answer that, throughout their history, Chinese states have been overwhelmingly land-based and that their wars have chiefly been wars of succession and overland conquest. To be sure, China attempted at various times to intervene in the domestic affairs of so-called tributary states, such as Korea and Vietnam, but usually with unhappy results. So if China has now decided to become a world military power, that is a shift from her historical tradition. It is a shift, moreover, that is fraught with risks.

Military actions elicit reactions. In the past twenty years we have seen India enter the club of thermonuclear powers, largely owing to the threats posed by China and Pakistan. We have seen the Koreas, between them, develop nuclear weapons, a formidable fleet of stealthy conventional submarines capable of cutting off all sea access to north China by closing the narrows between Shandong and the Liaodong peninsula. Japan, responding to constant Chinese provocations and the Korean missile and nuclear program, is upgrading her intelligence and military capabilities—and of course a Japan that turned its attention to things military would quickly become the dominant power in Asia. Russia views with suspicion a Chinese buildup that could threaten the anchor of the Russian Pacific position at Vladivostok. Taiwan has made herself self-sufficient in a range of missiles and warheads that would make any actual military excursion across the Strait well-nigh impossible. Vietnam is developing nuclear capabilities.

On land, China's increasing military presence in the ethnically non-Chinese western territories of Tibet and East Turkestan (Xinjiang), the latter of which was annexed by the non-Chinese Qing dynasty in the eighteenth century, worries large but underpopulated states such as Mongolia, as well as India and others. When one adds the ripples spreading from the recent revelation of China's major submarine base on the island of Hainan (to the east of the Vietnamese coast and worryingly close to the Philippines, Malaysia, Singapore, and Indonesia) and from her bolstering of air power in the Paracel Islands (seized from Vietnam), the area of reaction to Chinese military expansion itself expands to include much of Southeast Asia.

Finally, China's search for energy and strategic depth has drawn her deep into Islamic Central Asia. One may wonder how robust the current alliance will prove between the "godless Chinese" (as some other Asians call them), who swill alcohol and eat pork—deeply offensive to Muslims—and such states as Iran, Pakistan, Kazakhstan, and others.

As China takes stakes in more and more places, she may appear to be gaining strength, but she is also becoming overextended, creating hostages to fortune and putting in place the makings of a two-front or multifront war that would be difficult to handle.

Fisher documents the Chinese military advances that have prompted these countervailing developments around China's periphery, but he does not survey what the various countries affected are doing. That is an important topic, however, one that demands its own book.

The reader who takes aboard the information Fisher provides will be forced to ask what, if anything, the United States should do. This is a question that is only now beginning to come into prominence. For decades the United States has systematically ignored the Chinese developments Fisher documents, or has rationalized them away as either a matter of routine force modernization or a narrow program targeted on Taiwan, but has never considered them as a single entity having many aspects and manifestations.

At present the United States is the security guarantor for South Korea and Japan explicitly, and implicitly for Taiwan. American forces, however, have proved incapable of coping with the relatively minor military challenge of Iraq; our numbers of combatants and platforms are steadily moving downward, and one suspects that after Iraq, overseas military operations will be so unpopular that undertaking them—even those required by binding treaty—will be politically impracticable. I find it inconceivable, for example, that Washington would go into a major war, let alone a nuclear war, to defend Japan against China.

By the same token, the United States is singularly unenthusiastic about genuine military self-sufficiency on the part of her allies. Washington has prevented Seoul from developing nuclear weapons, while China has acquiesced and most likely aided Pyongyang in the same pursuit. Washington has twice prevented Taiwan from developing nuclear weapons, though the island state now has sufficient nuclear know-how to become operational within six months. If and when Japan develops nuclear weapons, as she must unless she is willing to be coerced by the nuclear states around her, Washington is likely to exert powerful negative pressure (as in the Korean and Taiwanese cases) even though the United States is no longer capable of ensuring the security of those states.

The United States navy and air force will continue to be decisive weights in Asian security. So too will American strategic and intelligence cooperation with countries such as India, Australia, Taiwan, the Koreas, and Japan. But the United States by itself cannot and should not attempt to take on the task of deterring China single-handed.

Ultimately such deterrence can be accomplished only by states who will clearly take whatever measures are necessary for their own defense. Japan or Taiwan would use weapons of mass destruction, if necessary, to defeat a Chinese attack, as would Vietnam or India. But the United States would not, whatever the treaties may say. And short of that sort of robust and credible capability China will not be deterred. The United States, then, has a largely offshore and cooperative role in the maintenance of peace in Asia. The danger, ironically enough, is that she will become so convinced that China can be controlled absent military deterrent that she will undermine the attempts of her own allies to become strong—as in the Korean and Taiwanese cases mentioned.

Time was when major wars began in Europe and spread to Asia. The failure to deter Japan in the 1930s led to the first all-out Pacific War. Today the danger is that failure to deter China may have the same effect. But if so, the result will be far worse, for Japan attacked a weak China and even weaker colonial Southeast Asia. Only her ill-conceived attempt to bring the United States to the bargaining table by destroying the fleet at Pearl Harbor led to massive escalation. Today massive escalation can be achieved without American involvement. A war that pitted China against Japan, either of the Koreas, India, or even Taiwan would be massive and destructive to a degree difficult to imagine.

Avoiding such a war is an imperative. To carry out that imperative requires, as Sun Zi teaches, precise knowledge of all circumstances—above all, of the capabilities of one's possible adversary. Richard Fisher does a great service by making available in this volume authoritative knowledge about today's Chinese military. This is a book that should be pondered by all. The next step, deciding on how to respond (or not), will then be made in an informed and deliberate way. Proceeding thus is the best way to be sure that none of the formidable Chinese order of battle is ever used in combat.

Arthur Waldron
Lauder Professor of International Relations
University of Pennsylvania

Vice President
International Assessment and Strategy Center

Washington, D.C., June 4, 2008

PREFACE

This book is intended to be a resource for students and analysts seeking to measure the current and future dimensions of China's strategic military growth. Its primary focus is on the political and military dimensions of China's strategic growth. Although economic and cultural, or "soft power," dimensions are important, they are not the main focus here. This is an attempt to look at the medium-term future of the People's Liberation Army, but the information limitations dictate that it is not a definitive description, which will require constant reassessment.

It is important to acknowledge that a full understanding of China's political-military strategic development is not possible, because of the nature of military and strategic information in China. Its government denies essential information to Chinese citizens and foreigners, requiring diligent researchers to go to great lengths—literally—to find needed data. In China such information is broadly classified and carefully compartmentalized and protected. There is also a historic and military culture dimension: Chinese leaders reflect and venerate the wisdom of their ancient strategists such as Sun Zi, who, nearly 2,500 years ago, explained, "All war is deception." To its credit the U.S. government, especially under the Bush administration, has sought to impress upon Chinese officials the many reasons why it is in their self-interest to become more transparent militarily. While there has been progress, it has been minuscule and at a glacial pace, which only serves to sustain doubts about China's intentions.

Like other recent academic assessments of China's modern military, this book is largely an examination of open sources, with the addition of unique interview data gathered over the course of a decade. There are a variety of methods to approach this subject. Some view analysis of China's military doctrine as essential to providing key answers. There is a great deal of Chinese military literature on questions of general or even nuclear doctrine. But there is no access by foreigners to official documents that provide definitive explanations or outline future doctrine or equipment choices. So analysts must devise their best guesstimates based on literature, official statements, actions, interview data, and assessment of modernization decisions.

This analyst acknowledges the need for an examination of all aspects of China's military trajectory but has chosen to put a special emphasis on China's military-technical capabilities. Whereas even a capabilities-based analysis is fraught with uncertainties, technologies and weapons are to some extent easier to define, and their inherent choices can also help form conclusions about China's military strategic direction. In an effort to limit some of these uncertainties, since 1996 this analyst has sought to surface new data about China's military modernization by directly interviewing those involved in this process. Doing so has involved attending twenty-two military exhibitions from 1996 through 2008 in Russia, India, Pakistan, the United Arab Emirates, Singapore, Japan, and, up until 2004, China's Zhuhai Airshow. In addition to interviews with officials from Chinese military companies or foreign companies doing business with them, there have been numerous opportunities to interview government officials in Taiwan, Japan, India, and Singapore, who have provided additional insights.

This approach has yielded a broad database about the PLA's modernization as well as specific new "stories" to which the author has made decisive or significant contributions. A sample of ten major stores would include

- Zhuhai 1996: First indication that the PLA was developing a terminally guided MRBM
- Moscow 1997: First indication that Russia was selling radar satellite technology to the PLA
- Zhuhai 1998: First indication that China was developing anti-tactical ballistic missiles
- Moscow 2001: China's "theft" of Russian counter-stealth radar technology
- Zhuhai 2002: First indications of a family of Chinese antisatellite missiles
- Zhuhai 2004: China's progress in developing new generation land attack cruise missiles
- IDEX 2005: Ukrainian involvement in China's naval phased array radar program
- Moscow 2005: China's broad interest in Russian aircraft technology for aircraft carriers
- DEFEXPO 2006: New directions in China's effort to build large transport aircraft
- IMDEX 2007: China's intention to develop new helicopter amphibious assault ships

The unfortunate reality of this period is that these are stories that the Chinese government did not want published. For example, Chengdu's J-10 fighter has been known of since the early 1990s and Internet photos began appearing in 1998, but it was not legally permissible in China to write about this aircraft until its official declassification in January 2007. As of May 2008 the official J-10 performance specifications had not been made public. Reports emerged that some Chinese were jailed for posting early Internet pictures of the J-10, but that has not stopped hundreds of pictures from emerging, from 1998 to the fighter's partial declassification in late 2006.

The penalties to Chinese for disclosing sensitive information was made clear to the author in late 1998, when a Chinese source sought me out to say that the individual who had explained China's development of terminal missile guidance technologies at the 1996 Zhuhai show had been punished. The reason for China's anger became clearer by 2002 to 2003, when additional disclosures started to unveil China's intention to build a revolutionary terminally guided antiship ballistic missile. The United States had no real defense against such a weapon, and the Chinese government clearly preferred that U.S. understanding of this program be delayed as long as possible, to prevent the development of countermeasures.

So it is with much of the subject area covered in this book. The Chinese government would rather there not be a critical focus on their new and future weapon systems and how they increase PLA capabilities versus Taiwan, Japan, India, or even the United States. Various experts and observers started commenting on China's ambitions and actions to acquire aircraft carriers starting in the mid-1980s. But China regularly denied such ambitions, and its officials began issuing (grudging) admissions only in 2006. China's visible efforts to acquire space weapon systems and long-range power projection capabilities also follow decades of denials or obfuscation.

Understanding the sensitivity of these subjects, this analyst decided that engaging officials of the People's Liberation Army was not going to yield the same level of information as engaging engineers and military company officials. In contrast to democracies, top PLA officials do not need to hold regular press conferences with freewheeling questions, issue detailed press briefings on their actions or budgets, or engage a large community of journalists and analysts, in order to attract funding or policy support. Foreign analysts and journalists, much less Chinese, cannot make short-notice visits to key officials or defense companies and inquire about their latest programs, as is often taken for granted in the West.

In early 2005 I was able to ask a Chinese aerospace company official what it would take for a foreign reporter to gain permission to visit their fighter assembly line. The chuckled reply, which I took to be serious, was, "A Politburo decision," or the top leadership level of the ruling Communist Party. This would be like waiting for a U.S. Cabinet-level decision, an indication of the level of protection China accords such information. Only in 2006 and 2007 did the PLA begin to allow top U.S. military leaders to get close to new Chinese weapon systems, although PLA officers had been visiting U.S. aircraft carriers and many other modern systems for almost three decades.

Instead, the PLA maintains a large number of officials and scholars who "handle" visiting foreigners, but their job is largely to limit information and to shape perceptions. Nevertheless, there are many U.S. and other scholars and analysts who have benefited greatly from this community, and they are to be credited for having devoted professional energy to sustaining relationships that continue to yield insights. My single formal encounter with the PLA was to accept an invitation to attend the 2004 Sun Zi Conference in Guangzhou. While the academic treatment of Sun Zi Bingfa by PLA officers varied widely, the principal reason for attending was that this was one of the only "sanctioned" events in which foreign experts could interact with PLA officers.

While this invitation is gratefully acknowledged, it followed a period in which this author, in addition to several others, had been increasingly lumped into the Chinese propaganda bureaucracy's creation of the "China Threat Theory." This is a classic propaganda ploy of autocratic states: to demonize the critics rather than engage them or refute the substance of their claims by revealing a greater truth. This effort sometimes borders on comical, but the goal is most serious: to destroy the credibility of the target and to delegitimize him in his field. It is a form of "soft assassination" employed by China, which, Ralph Sawyer has aptly noted, draws from a long and harsher history. My reporting on the specific details of China's military modernization, combined with its increasing propensity to threaten democratic Taiwan, Japan, India, and U.S. forces qualified me for inclusion in the "China Threat School."

Consequently it was not surprising when in 2004 the Chinese Foreign Ministry sought to deny my visa to visit the 2004 Zhuhai Airshow, but it was dissuaded by the timely intercession of U.S. government officials and, perhaps, by my existing invitation to the Sun Zi conference. The Zhuhai show, while a tightly controlled exercise in releasing information, constitutes one of the most generous Chinese exercises in "transparency," in which one can ask real questions and sometimes get straight answers. In 2006 the Chinese Foreign Ministry did deny my visa necessary to attend the Zhuhai show. No explanation was offered other than a cryptic comment by a Consular official: "I think you know why."

This analyst is not alone; China has long used such denials of access to chasten and control the work of foreign journalists and academics critical of its actions. But in 2006 and 2007 the PLA has opened slightly, allowing top U.S. Army, Air Force, and Navy commanders access to units with new equipment as well as access to some key leaders. In August 2007 a delegation from the House Armed Services Committee visited a Second Artillery missile base, an unprecedented gesture. But this does not begin to equate the access the PLA has had to the U.S. side since the 1980s. The Chinese understand, however, that democracies rely on facts to fuel vital debates, which they can try to manipulate even with such crude tactics as access denial. In time, one can only hope that the Chinese government will embrace a level of transparency that truly enables other countries to seek assurance, a process those countries must accomplish for themselves, for which the words of officials or experts chosen by China's government cannot be substituted. But until the Chinese government embraces transparency, refusing to allow it to control, manipulate, or designate those who describe the People's Liberation Army becomes a matter of self-defense.

Other sources have also figured prominently in this volume. The governments of the United States and Taiwan provide regular public assessments of China's military capabilities and intent. In 1997, in part as a reaction to the alleged timidity of the Administration of President Bill Clinton, the Republican Party–controlled Congress mandated an annual Department of Defense report on China's military power. Although it has not risen to the detail level of the former *Soviet Military Power* series initiated by President Ronald Reagan, the vigorous interagency process that results in this document has ensured that it is the world's most credible statement by any government on China's military direction—a statement that the Chinese government would be loath to produce itself. However, this document is also conspicuous by what it does not address, to include potential rapid PLA progress in the areas of multiple-warhead missiles, missile defense, and fifth-generation fighters, which are explored in this volume.

In addition, the Internet, which the PLA and China's security services have long fashioned into a weapon against other countries and against their own people, has in turn yielded amazing insights into China's military modernization. Despite a gauntlet of Internet censors, patriotic Chinese Web posters are often the first to make available new images of PLA naval ships under construction or of new, previously unknown weapon systems. But the Internet is also a playground for Chinese government deceptions, and the knowledge of Chinese netizens is often wrong or incomplete.

A late source that has contributed to this volume has been the partial access to Chinese data bases that offer cross references to a vast collection of Chinese military-technical literature. Partial access to the Chinese National Knowledge Infrastrucure (CNKI) is available (though expensive) at the Library of Congress, but the number of articles that can be obtained are far smaller than identified in the data base. However, Web-based access to CNKI (http://www.cnki.com.cn/) and to competitors such as "Wanfang Data" (http://www.wanfangdata.com.cn/), "ilib" (http://www.ilib.cn/), and "VIP" (http://www.cqvip.com/) can yield a large number of abstracts of relevant journal articles. Also impressive is the large body of Western military-technical research included in these data bases that is aiding Chinese engineers. On the other hand, not having access to whole articles is one weakness of these data bases; another is that Chinese censorship rarely allows Chinese authors to relate their work to specific Chinese weapons programs. There is also the danger that these data bases are manipulated for deception purposes. In the main, citation of these articles is meant to offer partial proof or to offer a useful indications of potential PLA technical developments. The former Foreign Broadcast Information Service (FBIS), now called the World News Connection, a U.S. government service responsible for foreign media translations, used to feature this critical Chinese military-technical literature heavily, but the flow has fallen to a trickle, much to the detriment of the open source–dependent analytical community.

ACKNOWLEDGMENTS

There are many to whom the author owes unending thanks for assistance that has, in ways major or minor, contributed to this volume. First, it would not have been possible without the encouragement and support of my colleagues at the International Assessment and Strategy Center. Arthur Waldron has provided much needed encouragement for the research contributing to this work, has coached this book from its inception, and has been a valued mentor for many years. Thor Ronay has provided essential leadership for the IASC, my work in it, and support for realizing this project. In many ways this book is the product of a collective effort, and I cannot begin to express my gratitude. I would also like to thank the Earhart Foundation and the Institute for International Relations at the National Chengchi University for supporting my previous research which has contributed to this volume.

The insights provided by government and corporate officials from Taiwan, Russia, and China must be gratefully acknowledged. Chinese military company officials and, on a few occasions, officers of the PLA have provided many answers to questions. In Taiwan, understandably, many more government officials have provided deeper levels of insight, because they are on the front line. However, it is not possible to credit individuals in Taiwan, Russia, and China, out of consideration for their position or safety. I also thank colleagues on the military show circuit, professional journalists Rob Hewson, Wendell Minnick, Reuben Johnson, Yihong Chang, and Doug Barrie, who have diligently tracked many of the same stories and developments, and whose insights are regularly cited. A special debt is owed to Bill Gertz of the *Washington Times*, who has used his unrivaled sources to provide the nation with a unique warning of China's military and strategic challenge. However, the conclusions herein are my own.

Although this book only rarely cites unique U.S. government sources, many close to government have provided inspiration and guidance over many years. Special thanks is owed to Bill Triplett, who worked tirelessly for the truth, first in government and then as author, and who has been a generous friend. Thanks is also due to Ambassador James R. Lilley, first for a long career of contributions to American security and then as a mentor to many of the community of academics and analysts concerned with the PLA. His encouragement and that of Chuck Downs regarding an earlier work on the PLA helped create a template for my subsequent work. Thanks is also due to the late William G. Geimer, founder of the Jamestown Foundation, who hired me as the first editor of the *Jamestown China Brief.* From late 1999 to early 2000 I had the privilege to work for former Congressmen Christopher Cox, who had just led what remains the most comprehensive U.S. government review of China's espionage and broad threat to the security of the United States. His devotion to principle and detail set a very high standard for my work.

Thanks is also due to friends and colleagues who have provided encouragement and a sounding board on many occasions. Such include June Teufel Dreyer, John Copper, Mark Stokes, Gordon Chang, John Tkacik, David Murphy, Jason Bruzdzinski, Carlo Kopp, and Richard Pawloski. I would also like to thank the team at Greenwood Publishing Group, Alicia Merritt for her original interest and encouragement, and Nicole Azze for her editing advice and support. I would also like to thank Lisa Connery for her valuable editing support.

Finally, words cannot express my thanks for the critical support and encouragement provided on the homefront by my wife, Nancy, and my three children, Ben, Sam, and Hillary. I will always remain grateful for their patience and understanding over the long journey leading to this book, that time lost with a husband and father was for a noble purpose.

CHAPTER 1

CHINA'S STRATEGIC CHALLENGE

In 2008 America and its coalition partners find themselves engaged in a costly and protracted war against the terrorist forces of Islamic extremism. This struggle handily predates Osama bin Laden's September 11, 2001, attacks against the United States, but it became an intense U.S. priority as the George W. Bush administration sought to confront Islamist terrorist strongholds, first in Afghanistan and then in Iraq after the 2003 U.S. toppling of Saddam Hussein. This will be a lengthy and costly struggle, given that the Islamists are driven by a religious-ideological justification to wage war against liberal democracy and the inability of military force alone to defeat them. American preoccupation with this war caused a sharp change in President George W. Bush's formerly critical approach to the People's Republic of China (PRC) prior to September 1991,[1] leading to an increasing "reliance" on Chinese strategic support. China's acquiescence is essential for United Nations acceptance of the war in Iraq and Afghanistan; China is now regarded as a "partner" in the War on Terror; and Washington increasingly accedes to Chinese leadership in resolving North Korea's nuclear weapons challenges and in turn follows China's wishes to contain legitimate democratic expressions on Taiwan for recognition and independence.

At the same time China is pursuing a broad quest for global influence and access to resources and markets and is building common cause with most of the world's antidemocratic regimes. China is doing so having benefited from the greatest period of economic growth and transformation in its 5,000-year history, made possible by the West's welcoming of trade and investment with China. Furthermore, China is making no contribution in terms of lives or treasure to arrest the spread of Islamist terror. Instead China is accelerating its military buildup, whose consequences, absent a U.S. commitment to deter and provide leadership, may be the unraveling of the U.S.-led alliance system in Asia, perhaps leading to arms races and new unforeseen threats to Americans. When the Nixon Administration began its dialogue with China's Communist leadership in the early 1970s, the United States was assured of its own strategic superiority and was confident in the knowledge that a weak China needed the United States to counter a much stronger Soviet Union. At that time there was little concern or fear that, within forty years, power balances could shift so much that China could begin to pose a serious military challenge to the United States. And while China expended great energy seeking to quell concerns and to conceal its gathering strength, it has made occasional demonstrations.

Rapidly Advancing Military Technology and Global Ambitions

For example, on January 11, 2007, China's People's Liberation Army (PLA) destroyed a Chinese weather satellite with a direct-ascent antisatellite (ASAT) missile. While China's two previous attempts to destroy the satellite in July 2005 and February 2006 were known to a small number of intelligence and military personnel in the United States and perhaps a few other countries,[2] the successful test was a shock to the world when revealed about six days later. It took the Chinese government twelve days even to acknowledge what the world had already long known. This event illustrates several aspects of China's accelerating military challenge:

- China's military action in space signals that, when its interests dictate, China will not be bound by U.S. or Western conventions, in space or on Earth, and that it will not cede the strategic "high ground" to another power.
- China has cloaked its military growth in denial and secrecy and will continue to do so. Since the 1980s China has loudly championed the idea of a treaty to ban weapons in space, but since that same period it has been developing missile and laser space weapons. Former Chinese paramount leader Deng Xiaoping once told Richard Nixon that China "is against whoever goes in for development of outer space weapons."[3]
- China is making very rapid progress in applying high technology to gain new military capabilities, and future demonstrations in the areas of energy weapons, nanoweapons, unmanned weapons, and cyberwarfare are very possible.
- China is able to gather and assimilate advanced foreign military technology rapidly. The DF-21 intermediate range ballistic missile (IRBM), which forms the basis for the PLA's SC-19 ASAT and its new antiship ballistic missile, was perfected after China obtained U.S. missile motor technology.
- China is focusing on attacking key "asymmetric" vulnerabilities of the U.S. military, such as its growing dependence on space information systems, without which the U.S. military cannot wage war.

China's construction of a military capability in outer space is but one dimension of China's future military-strategic challenge. For most of the years since 1992 China's official military budget has grown by double digits, or more than 10 percent, per year. In 2007 the official defense spending figure grew 17.8 percent, to an official total of $44.9 billion. The U.S. Department of Defense has long disputed China's bookkeeping and estimates the total is closer to $125 billion. China strongly disputes this, and in mid-2007 former PLA intelligence chief Lt. General Zhang Qinsheng stated that the annual increase "is mostly used to make up the retail price, improve welfare of the military personnel, and for better logistical support." Yet China's military spending is also paying for the following programs:

- *Space warfare:* Missile, space plane, and laser-based space weapons
- *Space information architecture:* Surveillance, navigation, communications, and electronic intelligence (ELINT) satellites
- *Anti-ballistic missile (ABM) defenses:* China is most likely developing an ABM system which could be deployed after 2020.
- *Manned moon presence:* To secure China's potential military and economic interests
- *Nuclear missiles:* Three types of new solid-fuel intercontinental and submarine-launched ballistic missiles (ICBMs/SLBMs) in or near deployment
- *Energy weapons:* High-power microwave weapons now deployed (lasers to follow?)
- *Fifth-generation combat jets:* Two, possibly three fifth-generation programs under way
- *Unmanned combat and surveillance jets:* Three air companies have active programs.
- *Nuclear submarines:* New nuclear attack and ballistic-missile subs now being built
- *Aircraft carriers:* Chinese naval officers, informally, say four to six may be built.
- *Antiship ballistic missiles:* A revolutionary weapon that only China is building
- *Large amphibious assault ships:* 20,000-ton LPDs being built and an LHD in development
- *Large (60-ton capacity) airlifters:* Proposals from both of China's air consortia
- *Airmobile army forces:* developing new family of airmobile wheeled combat vehicles.

In 2007 China was the only country that was pursuing all of these expensive military construction and development programs. Each program requires an extensive research, development, and production base, plus generations of engineers to develop follow-on systems. In many cases the United States and Russia developed these capabilities only after several decades of effort, while China in most cases is able to compress its development-production cycle into two decades, thanks to access to foreign technologies. Russia has more money for its military after energy price spikes and, in 2007, announced plans for six nuclear aircraft carriers and a manned moon program, though there is considerable reason to doubt these will succeed. But Russia does not have plans for a long range amphibious projection fleet. The United States, by choice, has no active space weapons program. Furthermore, the United States is modernizing only one solid-fuel ICBM (which will be armed with only one warhead) and is not building any nuclear ballistic-missile submarines.

Each of these programs listed above also represents an aspiration to global, not just regional military power. Although a permanent Chinese manned moon presence may not happen until 2020 to 2030, most of these PLA programs either are being realized now, or could be by the end of the next decade. The aspects of China's military buildup that can be identified in 2007 may constitute only the beginning of a military competition that could severely challenge Asia and the United States sooner rather than later. When realized, the PLA programs listed above may only allow China to approach an American level of military capability circa 2007 to 2010. But China is accumulating this similar spread of capabilities, with depth in some areas, at a breakneck pace. Chinese, U.S., and other universities have trained a new generation of Chinese military engineers, many of whom are responsible for current military-technical break-throughs for China and have long careers ahead of them. American policy makers should consider that, increasingly, it may be China that first develops the next-generation weapon system, not the United States or Russia.

Internal Weakness

An additional concern is that what China may or may not do with its acceler-ating military and political power will be determined by the very few Chinese who lead the Chinese Communist Party (CCP). In 2007 all 1.3 billion citizens of the PRC were beholden to only 73.36 million CCP members.[4] The CCP, in turn, is ultimately controlled by about 300 people selected from its ranks: the 300 or so members of the Central Committee, who produce a twenty- to twenty-five-member Politburo, which is dominated by its eight- or so-member Standing Committee, which is in turn usually dominated by its single Chairman. The CCP tolerates no political competition and ruthlessly employs internal police and security services in cooperation with organs of the CCP to search out, co-opt, or destroy political opposition.

Such resistance to political reform may be accelerating China's path to a series of internal crises. Looming crises such as a potential collapse of a weak financial system, deepening resentments from endemic corruption, a mounting burden from environmental disasters, a growing economic and social disparity between the prosperous coastal regions and the majority, who do not share in this wealth, plus outright opposition as demonstrated by Tibetans in March and April 2008, or the insistence of the majority of Taiwanese to be governed by their own democracy and not by Beijing, may eventually spur events that could overwhelm a CCP regime with thin legitimacy. In April and May 2008 Chinese at home and abroad demonstrated a resentful and at times threatening nationalist anger in response to Western protests against Chinese behavior in Tibet and the Sudan, organized around the China's global Olympic Torch relay. This anger was abruptly arrested by the need to respond to the devastating May 12 earthquake in Sichuan. While the government and the PLA won respect for their rapid response to the disaster, and there was a rare openness in media reports, it is not clear that openness will grow following these incidents. In the months prior to the November 2007 Party Congress, current CCP Secretary Hu Jintao made clear he would tolerate neither calls from the left for imposing Maoist like discipline or calls for internal CCP reforms toward representative democracy.

Ultimately the power position of the CCP depends on the loyal support of the 2.25 million members of the PLA, the 1.5 million People's Armed Police (PAP), and 800,000 other internal security forces. In short, the CCP maintains a political dictatorship enforced by security services, police, and the armed forces. This will require that the CCP maintain its largely martial character and pay increasing heed to the priorities of the PLA and the security services. This means, most likely, that the CCP will continue to strengthen policies designed to control Chinese, while giving the PLA the means to obtain greater global military influence.

Threatening Foreign Policy Choices

The aforementioned circumstances also mean that China's military and foreign policies will proceed without the potentially moderating influences of countervailing institutions, such as legislatures or a free press. Indeed, China has a large press, and there are many government-sponsored and academic institutions, which have voluminous output on foreign affairs and military subjects, and individual Chinese do express a wide range of views on their Internet. But there is little to suggest that there are major identifiable opinion centers that offer fundamentally different choices to those made by the CCP. China's penchant for secrecy and deception stratagems, based on venerated historic treatises of statecraft such as that of Sun Zi, dating back to the sixth century B.C., further compound the task of analysis of Chinese actions. Such a lack of honest debate is at least in part responsible for China's pursuit of policies or actions that can only be viewed as counterproductive for most Chinese:

- Preparing for a war against democratic Taiwan, thus also risking war with the United States, possibly resulting in long-term hostility between China and the West, even though such a war may fail and still imperil China's political stability and continued economic growth
- Pursuing political-military hegemony in Asia, specifically trying to push out American influence, with little regard to the potential to spur an Asian arms race that ultimately may force non-nuclear states such as Japan, Taiwan, and Australia to seek nuclear weapons or other major deterrent capabilities

- Proliferating nuclear weapon and missile technology to Pakistan, North Korea, and Iran, with no regard for their potential to give this same technology to terrorist groups who, in turn, may well attack Israel, the West, and eventually China too
- Resisting efforts by the United States and its allies to mobilize decisive political and economic pressures against North Korea's and Iran's nuclear weapons programs, indicating China's potential to "protect" future nuclear weapons programs undertaken by its friends
- Making common cause with and becoming an increasing source of support to belligerently antidemocratic dictatorial regimes such as North Korea, Cuba, Venezuela, Iran, Burma, Zimbabwe, and Sudan—all of which fuel suspicion of China's future goals and prompt resentment against China as seen during its 2008 Olympic Torch relay.
- Pursuing an increasingly active military entente with an increasingly authoritarian Russia while also leading the countries of Central Asia in its Shanghai Cooperation Organization down the path to an eventual military alliance designed to preserve dictatorships, exclude Western influences from the Eurasian heartland, and further isolate India
- Undertaking a massive program of global cyberespionage and surveillance that has resulted in growing alarm in capitols around the world, in which China has wrecked cyber networks in Taiwan, has likely caused power outages in the United States, and has likely positioned its cyber forces to launch instant and devastating attacks against the American electronic infrastructure.

This list indicates that China is making quite disturbing choices regarding its use of global influence. There is of course, much that appears positive. China has created new institutions and regulations that appear to signal a greater interest in stopping its own nuclear and missile proliferation, yet the proliferation continues. China's leadership in helping to convince North Korea to end its nuclear weapons program is praised by many in Washington, yet the material effect of the Six-Party Talks China has led since 2005 has been minimal—North Korea even tested nuclear weapons in 2006. China professes a willingness to forge a peaceful future with the people of Taiwan, yet it ignored Taiwan's democratically elected government from 2000 to 2008, works to divide Taiwan politics between the older sympathetic Kuomintang Party from the "independence" leaning Democratic Progressive Party, and shows no interest in slowing its accelerating military buildup near Taiwan.

Most commercially oriented countries, which include most of Asia, greatly value their economic ties with China, which contribute increasingly to their growth. Yet for Asians, China's military buildup causes fear, and they are wary of China's subtle but increasing push that they choose between Chinese and American leadership. Beijing has long sought to convince Japan and Australia to end missile defense cooperation with the United States. However, both continue this pursuit, and Japan and the United States have sought to deepen strategic relations with India in the hopes of balancing China. In July 2007 an Australian defense strategy paper noted, "China's emergence as a major market and driver of economic activity both regionally and globally has benefited the expansion of economic growth in the Asia-Pacific and globally. But the pace and scope of its military modernisation, particularly the development of new and disruptive capabilities such as the anti-satellite missile (tested in January 2007), could create misunderstandings and instability in the region."[5]

China's Assurances Versus Its Historic Character

Despite its growing military and foreign policy choices, which pose threats to its neighbors and to American interests, Chinese leaders are quick to assure the world of their peaceful intentions. Until recently, China advanced the "theory" created by CCP theoretician Zheng Bijan of China's "peaceful rise." Chinese leaders routinely describe their foreign policies as one of "noninterference" and that China will never seek "hegemony." Furthermore, China adheres to a "no first use" policy regarding nuclear weapons, and it routinely opposes "militarization of space" and destabilizing "missile defense." But one can question the sincerity of such pronouncements in the face of China's rich domestic and foreign martial heritage and its veneration of strategies of deception, subterfuge, and, when necessary, "total war." In addition, China actually was the "hegemon" of its region for many centuries, and many Chinese believe that China should resume its rightful place.[6] This alone could set the stage for a long period of conflict with Japan, India, and the United States.

The *Art of War* by Sun Zi (596–544 B.C.), one of the first texts on the universal arts of war (Table 1.1), is revered and studied intently by China's civil and military leaders as a superior Chinese contribution to the history of strategic thought. It was produced during the late Spring and Autumn Annals period, one of constant intrigue, assassination, and warring among competing feudal kingdoms. For Sun Zi, the highest morality was the survival and expansion of the state, which required a vigorous embrace of war as an essential art that demanded constant preparation and consideration, "War is a matter of vital importance to the state; a matter of life or death; the road either to survival or ruin. Hence it is imperative that be studied thoroughly."[7]

Shock and consternation greeted the publication of *Unrestricted Warfare* by two PLA colonels in 1999, in which they praised cyberwarfare and the tactics of terrorist Osama bin Laden, which was remembered after his attacks against the United States on September 11, 2001.[8] While some analysts have noted that *Unrestricted Warfare* does not represent PLA doctrine and that its authors are political officers, not strategists,[9] it is also clear that their version of "total war" is but the latest in a long tradition of Chinese strategic literature on the use of all means of power to obtain objectives. Texts such as the *Shi Chi* and *Tso Chuan* became textbooks on the employment of deception, infiltration, bribes, and sex to undermine enemies.[10] Former Chinese Defense Minister Chi Haotian is reported to have said in a speech, "In Chinese history, in the replacement of dynasties, the ruthless have always won and the benevolent have always failed."[11]

Table 1.1 Sun Zi's Axioms

Sun Zi's treatise *The Art of War,* along with many other ancient writings on statecraft, are studied intently and guide China's current political and military leaders in their personal as well as national approach to gaining power. Sun Zi's advice includes such points as the following:

Statagems

All warfare is based on deception.

Be so subtle that you are invisible. Be so mysterious that you are intangible. Then you will control your rival's fate.

Warfare

Hence to fight and conquer in all your battles is not supreme excellence; supreme excellence consists in breaking the enemy's resistance without fighting.

Hold out baits to entice the enemy. Feign disorder, and crush him.

Attack him where he is unprepared, appear where you are not expected.

Security against defeat implies defensive tactics; ability to defeat the enemy means taking the offensive.

In war, then, let your great object be victory, not lengthy campaigns.

Espionage

Thus, what enables the wise sovereign and the good general to strike and conquer, and achieve things beyond the reach of ordinary men, is foreknowledge.

Knowledge of the enemy's dispositions can only be obtained from other men.

Current PLA preparations for cyberwarfare that could cripple the U.S. economy, for space warfare that could eliminate the U.S. military's primary means of surveillance and communication, as well as for a high-casualty war to conquer Taiwan, therefore, are not historic aberrations. Given China's record of proliferation to regimes with terrorist connections, it is also necessary to ask, How would China respond to a nuclear terrorist attack against the United States? Would China join those hunting the terrorists or instead seize the moment to attack Taiwan?

The recent record also shows that China has been willing to engage in offensive wars that entail great risk and sacrifice.[12] China is also willing to define "victory" in geostrategic as well as operational results. Estimates that Mao Zedong lost over 250,000 troops during the Korean War demonstrated his willingness to take great risks and sacrifice lives. During World War II Mao had waged a lackluster war against the Japanese invaders, hoping to waste and exhaust his greater foe, the Kuomintang, but barely a year after winning his revolution he moved to commit hundreds of thousands of troops to invade North Korea, in order to impress Stalin, deliver a "defeat" to the Americans, and reassert China's authority over Korea. Deng Xiaoping's 1979 war against Vietnam cost China about 20,000 lives, yet did little damage to Vietnam's defenses. Yet this war advanced Deng's domestic political power consolidation, embarrassed Hanoi's allies in Moscow, and encouraged the United States and its NATO allies to join China in an anti-Soviet entente.

Would Hu Jintao be willing to use the PLA in a similar large-scale offensive manner, perhaps against Taiwan? It is reported that Deng's decision to select Hu to succeed Jiang Zemin was influenced by Hu's willingness to lead police forces and up to 170,000 troops from the Chengdu Military Region to suppress political protests in Tibet violently in March 1989.[13] One unconfirmed report notes that as a Red Guard during the Cultural Revolution, Hu may have led students to burn down the British Embassy in August 1967.[14] Thirty-two years later, in May 1999, just after Chinese students attacked the U.S. embassy in Beijing and burned down the consulate in Chengdu following the mistaken U.S. bombing of the Chinese embassy in Belgrade, Yugoslavia, it was Hu, then vice president, who gave the first Chinese government comment, saying, "The Chinese government firmly supports and protects, in accordance with the law, all legal protest activities."[15] While it is possible that China's leaders will resort to external wars to deflect internal strife, others argue that the final decision depends more on a leader's calculation of strategic opportunity versus cost.[16] Nevertheless, it appears that in Hu Jintao the PLA has a leader who is not afraid to use force. Thus, there are compelling reasons to consider that Chinese leaders may conclude that attacking Taiwan is worth risking international opprobrium, economic and political boycotts, and even large-scale loss of life, if it could secure a "victory" that would in any way force an end to Taiwan's democratic era and thus reshape the geostrategic balance of power in Asia against the United States.

This should serve as a warning. The Chinese Communist Party–led government is not satisfied with a world order in which the United States is the dominant power. While Chinese leaders acknowledge their growing dependence upon global good will for vital commercial and resource access, recent experience shows that CCP leaders will seize opportunities to alter power relationships and power balances. Their actions will very likely include the calculated but decisive use of military force. A Chinese decision to use force will depend on numerous factors, but perhaps among the most important is whether Chinese political and military leaders believe they possess the raw military power to prevail.

Can We Engage the PLA and Create Confidence?

Since the 1980s successive U.S. administrations have tried to engage China in hopes of developing a basis for "confidence" that might in the future help prevent conflict. The PLA and U.S. shows of force surrounding China's threatening military exercises near Taiwan in March 1996 and the April 2001 collision that saw the destruction of a PLA Navy jet fighter and the compromise of a U.S. Navy EP-3 electronic intelligence aircraft point to the need for some level of communication. The Clinton Administration did make substantial efforts to reach out to the PRC, which did not result in a greater PLA interest in "transparency."[17] But the PLA did accept all that, in the hope of fostering "confidence," the United States would reveal about its forces. For its part, the George W. Bush administration has repeatedly expressed its frustration with China's lack of transparency.[18] In June 2005 at the annual Singapore Shangri La Conference hosted by the International Institute of Strategic Studies, former U.S. Secretary of Defense Donald Rumsfeld stated:

> China appears to be expanding its missile forces, allowing them to reach targets in many areas of the world, not just the Pacific region, while also expanding its missile capabilities within this region. China also is improving its ability to project power, and developing advanced systems of military technology. Since no nation threatens China, one must wonder: Why this growing investment?; Why these continuing large and expanding arms purchases? Why these continuing robust deployments?[19]

With Rumsfeld's October 2005 visit to China, his first as Secretary of Defense, the latest uptick in U.S.-China military exchanges began. In 2006 and 2007 the PLA even decided to allow U.S. representatives to visit some new and modern weapons. However, American frustration continues. In June 2007 then–Undersecretary of Defense Richard Lawless commented, "As a consequence of what we see as a deliberate effort on the part of China's leaders to mask the nature of Chinese military capabilities, the outside world has limited knowledge of the motivations, decision-making, and key capabilities of China's military or the direction of its modernization."[20]

The first real opening in military-military contacts occurred during the late Carter administration, when the anti-Soviet entente was sealed with the beginning of intelligence cooperation. This cooperation grew to include CIA listening posts in northern China, directed against the Soviet Union, and covert U.S. shipments of Chinese arms to the Afghan mujahedeen fighting Soviet occupation. President Ronald Reagan approved a limited sharing of military technologies judged as "defensive," leading to sales of artillery radar, fighter radar, torpedoes, and civil Lockheed-Martin C-130 transport aircraft. However, Reagan also maintained consistent support for Taiwan, to Beijing's consternation. Technology cooperation, however, was largely halted after an arms embargo imposed on China following the Tiananmen massacre, an embargo that remains in force as of early 2008.

From the late George H. W. Bush administration to the second George W. Bush administration, U.S.-PLA exchanges have waxed and waned in response to respective internal political pressures.[21] The early moves by Secretary of Defense William Perry to revive contacts in 1993 and 1995 were stopped by the

Chinese side in response to the Clinton administration's early 1995 decision to allow Taiwan President Lee Teng Hui to visit Cornell University and other U.S.-Taiwan exchanges, which led to China's decision to conduct threatening military exercises around Taiwan in July 1995 and March 1996. Military exchanges did not really resume until the December 1996 visit of Chinese Defense Minister Chi Haotian. There was a further hiatus following the May 1999 accidental U.S. bombing of the Chinese Embassy in Belgrade. But in late 1998 the Republican-led Congress expressed opposition to what it perceived was a dangerous increase in U.S.-PLA interactions that threatened to reveal too much to the PLA.

At the beginning of the George W. Bush administration, there was a drop off in enthusiasm for U.S.-PLA exchanges, largely because of perceptions that during its later years the Clinton administration went overboard, allowing greater PLA access to the U.S. side, and thus learning more about U.S. capabilities and not reciprocating by allowing useful U.S. access to the Chinese side. After many U.S. complaints, exchanges resumed in 2005 and 2006. In early 2006, Chairman of the Joint Chiefs of Staff Peter Pace visited China, was shown an Su-27 unit, and was able to visit a new ZTZ-99 tank and its crew. In July 2007 Pacific Command Commander Timothy Keating was able to have a semi-candid conversation during which the Chinese side confirmed what had been increasingly clear since 2002: that they intended to build aircraft carriers. Then, in August 2007, future Chairman of the Joint Chiefs Admiral Mike Mullen visited China and was able to view PLA Navy maneuvers involving a Type 039 *Song* class submarine, a first. And later that month the House Armed Services Committee for the first time sent a delegation that was allowed to visit a Second Artillery office building and tour a *Luhu* class destroyer.

As encouraging as these new visits may appear, they still do not approach the level of openness shown to the PLA during its visits to U.S. facilities (see Table 1.2). On a broader level the open character of the United States, with its overproductive defense press and competitive legislative process, allows the PLA to achieve a far more rapid and deeper understanding of current to medium-term U.S. capabilities and intentions. One cannot obtain the same from the PLA. As the chart above indicates, the United States has allowed the PLA to attend many more complex military exercises and demonstrations that would allow the PLA to gain an understanding of vulnerabilities. The United States has been refused requests to send observers to the two "Peace Mission" exercises, the most complex undertaken by the PLA. The PLA, arguably, has had access to more advanced U.S. weapons systems, especially to U.S. aircraft carriers, which the PLA intently desires to defeat and emulate. American requests to inspect new PLA weaponry have been rebuffed until late 2006 and 2007.

It is not possible to read actual PLA military doctrine documents, as one can view U.S. official doctrinal documents. While there is a large body of Chinese-language secondary literature on these subjects, it can only assist educated guesses. The Chinese defense press is allowed to provide details about historic

Table 1.2 Highlights of Reciprocal Military Access Compared, PLA and U.S.

	China	United States
Military exercises	PLA refused U.S. requests to send observers to its "Peace Mission" multinational combined arms exercises in 2005 and 2007. U.S. officials have been allowed to see various unit-level demonstrations. In 2007 a U.S. admiral was allowed to view PLA Navy (PLAN) maneuvers, and a U.S. attache attended the "Warrior 2007" army exercise in September.	PLA observers attended RIMPAC multinational combined arms exercise in 1998, Cope Thunder advanced air force exercise in 1998, and the large Valiant Shield combined-arms exercises near Guam in 2006. PLA officers have observed U.S. Army airborne and tank gunnery exercises.
Aircraft carriers	PLA has yet to allow U.S. or Western inspection of the ex-Ukrainian carrier *Varyag* and only started acknowledging its carrier ambitions to U.S. military officials in 2007.	The United States has allowed PLA officers to tour U.S. aircraft carriers in 1980, 1997, 2006, and 2007. PLA officers have had a catapult takeoff and an arrested landing on a U.S. carrier.
Submarines	PLA has not allowed U.S. officials to tour PLAN nuclear submarines and allowed only outside viewing of the new Type 039 SSK in 2007.	PLA officers toured a U.S. SSN in Pearl Harbor in 1997, a move that was "unauthorized" by civilian leaders at the time.
Destroyers	PLA has used old *Luhu* and *Luhai* class DDGs to visit U.S. ports and for tours, but has not let U.S. officials tour its new Aegis radar-equipped *Luyang 2* DDGs.	Chinese officials tour U.S. Aegis radar-equipped DDGs when they visit Chinese ports.
Combat aircraft	U.S. officials have visited H-6, J-7E, J-8I, J-8II, and Q-5 units, all obsolete aircraft. In 2007 U.S. officials were able to inspect fourth-generation Su-27 and JH-7As for the first time. A request to visit a J-10 unit was refused in 2007. A potential PLA stealth fighter remains secret. No test flights have been made by U.S. pilots.	PLA groups have visited at least four U.S. F-15 bases, then the most modern U.S. fighter. In 1998 a PLA general was able to inspect a U.S. F-117 stealth fighter. Before that, PLA pilots likely have test flown U.S. F-16s in the Pakistan Air Force.

weapons and even some military policies, but it cannot report in depth about current and, especially, future military policies and weapon systems. Even at arms shows where China is trying to sell weapons systems, security restrictions limit what sales personnel can say about the latest weapons for the PLA and about future systems. When questioned on the BBC in mid-2006 about U.S. concerns about China's military spending and transparency, China's UN Ambassador to Geneva Sha Zukang said "It's better for the U.S. to shut up and keep quiet."[22] At least Dr. Shen Dingli of Shanghai's Fudan University, an oft-cited unofficial "spokesman" for the Chinese government, offered an honest reason for Chinese reticence: "We have to keep certain secrets in order to have a war-fighting capability. . . . We can't let Taiwan and the U.S. know how we are going to defeat them if the U.S. decides to send forces to intervene in a conflict over Taiwan."[23]

After his June 2007 visit to China, U.S. Pacific Command Commander Admiral Timothy Keating recounted one of his conversations: "Our Chinese guests said, 'Here's what we'll do. You take care of the Eastern Pacific, we'll take care of the Western Pacific, and we'll just communicate with each other.'"[24] Did such a statement constitute China's real intention: to destroy the U.S.-led alliance system in Asia? And consequently, when China achieves even greater military power and global prominence, will it become more hostile to the West and especially, to the United States and its allies?

The U.S. Navy did not have to wait long for a more "formal" demonstration of Chinese displeasure at its presence. Just before the aircraft carrier U.S.S. *Kitty Hawk* was to dock in Hong Kong to allow many crew members to have family reunions for the November 2007 Thanksgiving holiday, China informed the United States that the *Kitty Hawk* group was not welcome. Even though the U.S. Navy makes about fifty port calls in Hong Kong a year, which are arranged by diplomatic procedures months in advance, the Bush Administration chose to respond to an apparent message from China's visiting Foreign Minister Yang Jeichi and call the incident a "misunderstanding."[25] But then China's Foreign Ministry angrily retorted there was no misunderstanding and that China had acted to protest American military sales to Taiwan and the recent Washington, DC, reception for the Dalai Lama, the spiritual leader of Tibet.[26]While China often and sometimes loudly protests American military and diplomatic support for Taiwan and the deep political sympathies shown to the Tibetan spiritual leader, the *Kitty Hawk* snub was a rare demonstration of that displeasure. Because American support for Taiwan is grounded in laws such as the 1979 Taiwan Relations Act and because sympathy for the Dalai Lama also runs deep, these policies are unlikely to change in reaction to Chinese snubs or even more forceful action. Once China had revealed plainly that it deliberately snubbed the U.S. Navy and had denied Hong Kong visit to other U.S. ships, protests were delivered, and the *Kitty Hawk* made a rare transit of the Taiwan Strait, a show of force veiled by the fact that adverse weather made that route necessary. Despite nearly two years of intense Bush Administration efforts to "engage" the PLA, the *Kitty Hawk* incident came as a painful reminder that "peace" with the

PLA will require that Washington surrender strategic friends and compromise core political values.

In January 2008 Admiral Keating made another visit to China, with a clear effort to get beyond the *Kitty Hawk* incident and to try to advance the long-standing goal of U.S. military leaders of building "relationships" with their PLA counterparts so as to build "confidence." Keating even suggested that the PLA could participate in the regular U.S.-Thai Cobra Gold joint-service exercises, which would constitute a major upgrade in political acceptance of the PLA and a facilitation of PLA military activities in Southeast Asia.[27] After long urging by Washington, at the end of January 2008 China agreed to set up a "Hotline," which, the United States hopes, will facilitate better communication between the U.S. government, the U.S. military, and the PLA. Another hopeful pause emerged in the aftermath of the horrific May 12, 2008, earthquake in Sichuan, when China made a rare allowance for many countries, including the United States, Japan, and Taiwan, to send relief supplies.

But after nearly three decades of U.S. attempts at "engagement," it is just not possible to say that U.S. military and PLA leaders can ever be "friends" as long as China embraces strategic ambitions such as the conquest of democratic Taiwan and displacing American strategic relationships in Asia. The *Kitty Hawk* incident also demonstrates that China's hostility toward the U.S. military presence in Asia is not due to the U.S. military per se, but to deeper ideological issues such as basic challenge of democracy to the Chinese Communist Party dictatorship. The PLA, despite some recent progress in allowing foreigners to visit more units, does not intend to become anywhere near as transparent as any military from a democratic country. And behind their smiles, it is likely that Chinese leaders will keep their military and strategic intentions very much a mystery. It is not likely that the PLA itself will fully explain the goals of its current military buildup and the future capabilities it seeks.

China's frustrating penchant for secrecy or refusal to be "transparent" finds ample justification in Sun Zi. As noted by Ralph Sawyer, Sun Zi's stress on secrecy was a "force multiplier," quoting his formulation, "The pinnacle of military employment approaches the formless . . . If I determine the enemy's disposition while I have no perceptible form, I can concentrate my forces while the enemy is fragmented." A modern corollary would be former paramount CCP leader Deng Xiaoping's constant advice to "bide our time and hide our ambitions."[28] The remainder of this book is one analyst's attempt to lift some veils and produce an open-source assessment of China's near- to medium-term military capabilities. The following chapters will examine how the PLA supports Communist Party ambitions, how the PLA is arming for Asian regional conflict, and how the PLA is also beginning to build capabilities to project real military power far beyond Asia.

CHAPTER 2

THE PARTY ARMY: PILLAR OF CHINA'S GOVERNMENT

On August 1, 2007, in Beijing's Great Hall of the People, the man who represents the two most important centers of power in China was at the center of a celebration. Hu Jintao, who is the Chinese Communist Party (CCP) Secretary General and Chairman of the Central Military Commission of the Communist Party, and thus ultimate leader of China's People's Liberation Army (PLA), was leading a festive program celebrating the eightieth anniversary of the founding of the PLA. Covered extensively on Chinese television, the event featured speeches by Communist Party and military officials and programs of song and dance by military performers. While Hu's speech was not published in its entirety, the Chinese state media reported extensively on its important aspects. Hu's speech serves to sum up the essential political alliance that forms the basis for the Chinese political system today: the alliance between the CCP and the PLA.

Hu made clear the essential direction of the CCP-PLA relationship: "The PLA is forever at the Chinese Communist Party's command. . . . To follow the CPC's command is the overriding political requirement that the Party and Chinese people have placed on the PLA and is the unshakable and fundamental principle for the PLA."[1] In turn, Hu stated the Party's obligation to the PLA: "We will gradually increase spending on national defense as the economy grows and continue to modernize national defense and the armed forces.[2] . . . [T]he Communist Party of China (CPC) and governments at all levels should support the enhancement of military capabilities. . . . Party committees and governments at all levels should do a good job in supporting the army and giving preferential treatment to families of servicemen."[3] In addition, as reported by *Xinhua*, Hu explained how much progress the PLA has made since the CCP began making its modernization and buildup a key national priority in the early 1990s:

> The PLA is "no longer a small, single-service force, but a strong and multiple-service force, which has made progress in modernization and is stepping toward an information technology-based army," he said. "By putting in place a comprehensive scientific, technological and industrial structure for national defense, the PLA is increasingly better positioned to defend the nation," Hu said. It has cleared a path of development that suits China's realities, improved its own organizations and structures, enhanced logistic and equipment support capabilities, and cultivated many competent military professionals for the new era, he said. "All these have strengthened the PLA's capability to better perform its mission and provided a solid foundation for the basic realization of defense and military modernization," he added.[4]

Military and Economic Power

While Hu's statements did not approach the detail of the United States Department of Defense's annual *China Military Power* report, he gave what Chinese generals would consider a positive assessment of growing military power. Hu essentially described the result so far of a massive fifteen-year under-taking to jump two to three generations of military technology, transforming an obsolete force mired mainly in 1950s technologies into a modern force that is now poised for more rapid developments. At 2.25 million men, China's armed forces are the world's largest, though not all can be considered "modern." But just getting to this point has taken enormous resources. According to its own figures, China's military spending has increased 258 percent from 2001 to 2007. As seen in Table 2.1, Japan's military expenditures have been essentially flat, and China's spending surpassed Japan's in 2007.

For the same 2001–2007 period the U.S. Defense Intelligence Agency (DIA) estimates growth of about 83 percent (based on its high estimates of spending), as seen in Table 2.1. The DIA estimated China's 2007 military spending to be between $85 billion and $125 billion.[5] Both numbers would place China second in world military spending after the United States, which spent $532 billion in 2007 ($173 billion allocated to the War on Terror). In 2006 the DIA estimated that if Gross Domestic Product (GDP) growth rates were sustained, military spending could increase "three-fold or more by 2025," or between $210 billion and $315 billion.[6]

The DIA's estimates are viewed as exaggerated by some Western analysts,[7] and they are scorned annually by the Chinese government.[8] However, as the Pentagon explained in its 2007 report, PLA military spending estimates by U.S. and private organizations for 2003 ranged from $30 billion to $141 billion if viewed through Purchasing Power Parity (PPP), a statistical adjustment that seeks to derive a more accurate comparison of currency values based on their

Table 2.1 Chinese Military Spending: Chinese Official Figures and U.S. Estimates[a]

	2001[b]	2002[b]	2003[b]	2004[b]	2005[b]	2006	2007
DIA High	67	71	78	86	94	105	125
DIA Low	47	50	55	60	66	70	85
Chinese Official Military Budget	17.43	20.78	23.26	26.90	30.27	37.41	45
Japan's Military Budget	44.2	44.7	44.8	44.4	44.1	43.7	41.75

[a] $U.S. billions
[b] Updated numbers estimated from DIA Projection Chart, Department of Defense, Military Power of China, 2006, p. 27.
DIA: Defense Intelligence Agency Sources: U.S. Department of Defense, Military Power of China, 2006 and 2007; Jane's Sentinel 2007; Stockholm International Peace Research Institute.

purchasing power.[9] Furthermore, it has long been suspected by analysts that the Chinese government does not include large budgets that affect PLA growth in its official military spending figure, such as research and development, foreign weapons purchases, and local government support. DIA estimates for future spending gain more credibility considering that the PLA will soon be undertaking very expensive personnel, research, and production programs. These would include greater salaries, professional education and benefits, aircraft carriers plus their air wings, large amphibious projection ships, new classes of nuclear submarines, fifth-generation combat aircraft, large transport aircraft, unmanned and perhaps manned space weapons, and an expensive manned Moon program. Add to this the possibility of protracted wars of occupation on Taiwan or in Central Asia, and PLA budgets could increase even faster.

By other measures, China's growing power cannot be denied. China is the world's most populous country with an estimated 1.32 billion people in mid-2007, 4.3 times the U.S. population of 301 million.[10] According to Chinese figures, growth in Gross Domestic Product (GDP) has averaged 9.7 percent from 1979 to 2005, a stellar accomplishment.[11] When measured in terms of PPP, one estimate holds that China's GDP could exceed that of the United States by 10 percent in 2015 ($22 trillion vs. $20 trillion) and exceed it by 58 percent by 2025 ($57.1 trillion vs. $35.9 trillion).[12] The U.S. Department of Commerce estimated that China's industrial production grew by 22.9 percent in 2006 alone. As an indicator of future industrial potential, a 2005 Duke University study concluded that China conferred over 351,000 four-year engineering degrees in 2004, compared to over 134,000 in the United States.[13]

In 2004 China surpassed Japan as the world's third largest trading country (after the United States and the European Union), though over half of China's foreign trade is conducted by foreign companies. For the United States, China is the second largest trading partner and second largest source of imports. In 2006

China was the fourth largest destination for U.S. exports; its status could rise to third in 2007.[14] The United States' largest trade deficit is with China; in 2006 Americans imported $232.6 billion more than they exported to China (U.S. exports $55.2 billion, U.S. imports $287.8 billion).[15] To be fair, much of this is total cost of parts made elsewhere but assembled in China. But its trade surpluses have allowed China to build up the world's largest reserve of foreign currency, at $1.33 trillion in August 2007, of which $405.1 billion was in U.S. Treasury bonds, the second largest U.S. Treasury holding after Japan.[16] This reserve could grow to $2 trillion by 2010. While holding such an amount of U.S. "money" allows China to undervalue the price of its currency, subsidizing its exports and promoting job growth, it also amounts to a huge potential to invest and buy tangible items in the future.[17]

China is the largest trading partner for Japan and Australia, and it is expected to become India's largest trading partner in 2008, surpassing the United States. China is Africa's third largest trading partner. In 2006 China became Iran's largest trading partner, surpassing Japan.[18]

Chinese are expected to become ever more important consumers as well, which will further enhance China's economic power. China's middle class, with income of about $5,000/year, amounted to about 100 million people in 2007, but by one estimate it may to grow to 700 million people by 2020.[19] If its growth continues, China's consumer market may become the world's second largest by 2015. According to one report, in 2007 Chinese consumed 32 percent of the world's rice, used 47 percent of its cement, and smoked every third cigarette.[20]

Leadership of the PLA

The PLA's loyalty to the Communist Party is ensured by the PLA's complete subordination to the Party, policed by a system of political commissars, who report directly to the Party. In turn, the Party sees that the PLA has the authority and resources that it requires. PLA authority is cemented in the Party's Central Military Commission (CMC), which puts the PLA directly under the command of the Party Politburo Chairman, currently Hu Jintao (Table 2.2). Comparable to a Standing Committee of the Politburo of the CCP, the CMC is one of the most powerful Party organs in peacetime; in wartime, the CMC becomes the principal command authority for the Party over the PLA, with the General Staff as the principal executive body. Former Vice Chairman Liu Huaqing was the last CMC member to be a member of the pinnacle CCP Politburo Standing Committee. After Liu, PLA membership on key CCP organs has stabilized at two CMC members on the larger Politburo and one on the Central Committee Secretariat, seen as an effort to balance various constituencies.[21] A number of CMC officers have also served as generals, having both political commissar experience and operational command experience.[22]

According to the December 2002 PRC National Defense White Paper, the CMC also controls the PLA's nuclear weapons. However, the reality is more

Table 2.2 Central Military Commission, November 2007

Member	Age/Background	Current Position/ Date	Concurrent Positions
Hu Jintao	65; CMC Vice Chairman, 1998–2004	Chairman, CMC/2004	Secretary General CCP; President of PRC
General Guo Boxiong	66; Most of career in Lanzhou Military Region, General Staff Department	Vice Chairman/ 2002; joined CMC in 1999	Politburo member
General Xu Caihou	64; General Political Department, Shenyang and Jilin Military Regions	Vice Chairman/ 2004; joined CMC in 2000	Secretary, CCP Central Committee Secretariat
General Liang Guangli	67; former Commander, Shenyang andNanjing Military Regions ; 1979 Vietnam War veteran	Member/2002	Minister of Defense; Politburo member
General Chen Bingde	66; former Commander, Nanjing Military Region during 1996 exercises against Taiwan; armaments expert	Member/2004	Chief of General Staff Department; CC member
General Li Jinai	65; General Armament Department; General Political Department; COSTIND; Second Artillery	Member/2002	Director, General Political Department, CC Member
General Liao Xilong	67; Most of career in Chengdu Military Region, 1979 Vietnam War veteran	Member/2002	Director, General Logistics Depart- ment; CC member
General Chang Wanquan	59; former Commander, Shenyang Military Region	Member/2007	Director, General Armament Department; director of China's space program; CC member
General Xu Qiliang	57; Deputy Chief of Staff General Staff Dept; Commander, Peace Mission 2007; former Shenyang MR-AF Commander; pilot	Member/2007	Commander, PLA Air Force; CC member
General/ Admiral Wu Shengli	Deputy Chief of General Staff Department, former Commander, South Sea Fleet, Deputy Commander, East Sea Fleet	Member/2006	Commander, PLA Navy; CC member

Table 2.2 *(Continued)*

Member	Age/Background	Current Position/ Date	Concurrent Positions
General Jing Zhiyuan	63; Career in Second Artillery, former Commander, Base 56, MRBMs and testing	Member/2004	Commander, Second Artillery; CC member

likely that control of nuclear weapons resides in the Chairman of the CMC and the Chairman of the Standing Committee of the Politburo. These offices were previously unified in the person of Jiang Zemin prior to 2002. That year these offices separated when Hu Jintao rose to become Secretary General of the CCP. It is possible that anxiety over control of nuclear weapons was one of several issues that resulted in Hu's assumption of the CMC in 2004, cutting short what was expected to be a longer tenure by Jiang.

Although there is a duplicate CMC that is subordinate to the State President and the National People's Congress, the Party's CMC is different in that has a General Office, which serves as a central coordinating unit. The General Office facilitates and supervises personal interaction among senior members of the PLA leadership and manages the external activities of the Ministry of Defense. It also coordinates interaction among the core military bureaucracies and oversees CMC ad hoc subcommittees that address policy issues.

A Red Army leadership body that existed during China's Revolutionary War, the CMC fell out of use late in the revolution. It was revived by Mao in 1954 when he also created other Soviet-style state structures to regularize control over the PLA. The CMC has largely been dominated by PLA Army generals, and as a consequence, the PLA stressed an Army perspective in its doctrine and equipment. A notable exception occurred under Deng Xiaoping, who in 1989 elevated PLA Navy Commander (1982–1988) Liu Huaqing to the CMC. Liu emerged as principal Vice Chairman in 1992, retiring in 1997. Liu had credentials as a veteran of the Long March and critical experience in technology development, which was in demand by Deng to shake up the PLA. Liu was in large part responsible for shifting the PLA's focus toward high-technology services such as the Navy, Air Force, and Second Artillery missile force; shopping abroad for new weapons and technology; and advancing the construction of aircraft carriers.

The most important recent evolution in the CMC occurred in 2004, when the commanders of the PLA Navy, PLA Air Force, and Second Artillery were all admitted as CMC members. This move reflected the PLA's previous decision to implement modern "Joint Forces" doctrines by allowing these high-technology services to have a direct impact on key decisions. The decision to make Air Force General and Deputy General Staff Department Director Xu Qiliang the commander of the deployed force for the August 2007 "Peace Mission 2007" exercises in Russia further affirmed the PLA Army's increasing willingness to defer to leadership from its high-tech sister services, as well as implementing the PLA's doctrinal emphasis on "jointness." Xu's quick rise to command of the PLA Air Force in September 2007 also serves to emphasize the PLA Air Force's rise in prominence in the PLA high command.

Despite the importance of its last major reform, the CMC does not have many members with actual combat experience, a factor shared throughout most of the PLA. At the top levels, notable exceptions include GSD Director General Liang Guanglie and GLD Director General Liao Xilong, both veterans of the 1979 punitive war against Vietnam—the last major conflict undertaken by the PLA. Younger CMC members such as Generals Liang Guanglie, Chen Bingde, and possibly Jing Zhiyuan have had some experience leading major exercises directed against Taiwan, but these exercises did not involve actual combat. While planning and preparing for war may be the focus of their professional lives, it cannot be predicted how they will perform once the "fog of war" increases the chances for mistakes that could lead to disaster.

The other major departments of the CMC include the following:

General Staff Department (GSD) The General Staff Department is the key department of the PLA: it commands PLA forces during wartime and oversees policy implementation of behalf of the CMC. It is also heavily responsible for military and weapons procurement, operational planning, training, and human and electronic/signals intelligence. All major Army units and the Second Artillery, Air Force, Navy, and Marines are subordinate to the GSD. In 2004, to help implement new joint forces doctrines, generals from the PLA Navy and the PLA Air Force were made Deputy Directors of the GSD.

General Political Department (GPD) The influence of the CCP in the PLA is enforced by the General Political Department. The GPD oversees the PLA system of political commissars, who run CCP units down to the company level. The GPD controls ideological indoctrination, ensures political loyalty, manages personal records and cultural activities, and oversees military justice matters.

General Logistics Department (GLD) The General Logistics Department is responsible for the well-being of PLA personnel. This include management of supplies, transportation, housing, medical services, and pay. In 1997 the GLD led a modernization of logistic functions.

General Armaments Department (GAD) Formed in 1998 as part of a broader set of reforms designed to reduce the PLA's role in the economy, the General Armaments Department was formed to put the PLA in control of the PRC's military-industrial complex. The GAD took over most of the weapons development and production roles of the Commission for Science, Technology, and Industry for National Defense (COSTIND). The GAD also plays a key role in the sale of weapons, including nuclear and missile technologies. Arms-selling firms such as Norinco, Poly, China Xinshidai, and many smaller firms also have espionage responsibilities. The Director of the GAD is also the director of China's manned and unmanned space programs.

The Ministry of Defense exercises authority mainly through the person of the Defense Minister, who is usually one of the current CMC Vice Chairmen and usually has also served on the Politburo. The Ministry itself does not exercise formal command over the PLA but the Defense Minister has been a high-profile political position: Lin Biao, who served under Mao Zedong, is a prominent example. Former Defense Minister Chi Haotian's political power drew from his key role under Deng, leading the forces that put down the peaceful Tiananmen protesters in June 1989. Former Defense Minister Cao Gangchuan, who retired in early 2008, appears to have risen on the strength of his key role in high-technology development and in the lucrative weapons import and export business, some of the profits of which are a "perk" for high CCP leaders. Cao had kept a high diplomatic profile and was involved in negotiations for key weapons deals from Russia. Cao also joined Hu Jintao to observe the Peace Mission 2007 exercises in Russia, sharing the limelight of this first major PLA foreign deployment. The elevation of Liang Guanglie in 2007 to the Defense Minister position marked a change: his career has been far more associated with troop leadership than with PLA modernization or key turns in the CCP-PLA relationship.

The Enduring CCP-PLA Alliance

The main reason why a Communist Party–led China has been able to reach such heights of military and economic achievement, while also retaining its power position for close to sixty years, has been its enduring alliance with its armed forces. Perhaps the most salient aspect of this relationship is that the CCP commands the PLA. When Mao Zedong was leading his revolution in Yan'an Province in 1938, he wrote, "Every Communist must grasp the truth, 'Political power grows out of the barrel of a gun.' Our principle is that the Party commands the gun, and the gun must never be allowed to command the Party."[23] But on the eve of the PLA's eightieth anniversary, Hong Kong's *Ping Kuo Jih Pao (Apple Daily)* trumped Mao's dicta, offering perceptibly, "However in truth, it is the 'gun that commands the party.' Whoever controls the right to command the army is the supreme leader of the [CCP]."[24] It is this deeper truth that accounts for the CCP's longevity, but it also reveals perhaps its most fundamental weakness: the armed forces that give power to the Party have the potential to take it away.

From the Party's beginning through the brutal suppression of the peaceful Tiananmen protests in June 1989, it has been repeatedly demonstrated that "control of the gun" determines who commands the Party. In 1929 Mao was able to consolidate his early control over the Party, and remove it from its early Soviet benefactors, when he was able to force Red Army leaders Zhu De and then Peng

De Hui to submit to his authority.[25] In the late 1960s, after the Mao-inspired Red Guards had launched their "Cultural Revolution," which had eliminated many of Mao's enemies, but then had begun to push much of China into chaos, Mao had to resort to the PLA to establish martial law and assert his authority over the Party. By 1971 PLA officers controlled 50 percent of civilian leadership positions and up to 60 to 70 percent of provincial leadership positions.[26]

In the power struggle that followed Mao's death on September 9, 1976, the decisive move was made within a month by the PLA's top official, Marshal Ye Jianying. Mao had given Ye control of the PLA, and as Vice Chairman of the pinnacle Central Military Commission (CMC) and Minister of Defense, Ye ordered the arrest of the radical "Gang of Four" led by Mao's wife, Jiang Qing.[27] Ye and Marshal Nei Rongzhen were then able to help then-Premier Hua Guofeng to consolidate his control over the Party. The lesson of PLA control as the route to power was likely not lost on Deng Xiaoping, a veteran of the early revolutionary struggle and the Long March and a member of the first CMC created in 1954. Ousted from his positions of Vice Chairman of the CMC and Chief of the General Staff following Premier Zhou Enlai's death in January 1976, Deng was able to regain these positions in July 1977. From there Deng was able to consolidate his power over the Party from late 1978 to June 1981, when he replaced Hua as Chairman of the CMC, becoming the paramount "Second Generation" leader of the CCP. The last formal position Deng held was CMC Chairman; this position was given to his chosen successor Jiang Zemin in November 1989.

Tiananmen Massacre

But Deng would again require the PLA's aid to keep the Party in power. Deng's key achievement was his ability to shift China's focus to economic revival and reconstruction, as exemplified by his policy of the "Four Modernizations": agriculture, industry, science and technology, and defense. Deng was successful because he increased economic freedoms, first to empower farmers to end chronic food shortages and later to empower entrepreneurs to start China's continuing impressive economic growth. But these moves, plus the ongoing example of Soviet leader Mikhail Gorbachev's example of limited political reform, or "Glasnost," inspired demands for greater political freedom and democracy, or what dissident Wei Jingsheng famously called the "Fifth Modernization."[28] By the late 1980s demands for political reform, anger at the economic disparities resulting from successful economic reforms, and anger at official corruption culminated in massive protests in Beijing, centering in Tiananmen Square, the historic heart of the Chinese government.

Deng and other Party elders decided the protesters posed a threat to the continuation of Communist Party rule and ordered PLA and police units to prepare for a crackdown. Deng ordered military preparations starting on April 25, 1989, and declared martial law on May 20. By the time operations commenced, the PLA had gathered about 50,000 troops. These troops came from fourteen of the PLA's then-twenty army groups, plus two airborne brigades, but mainly from Beijing area units such as the 38th and 27th Group Armies. The most violent military operations in Beijing took place June 3–4, 1989. Chinese government sources place the number of deaths in the hundreds, while the International Red Cross estimated 2,700 civilian deaths, and NATO Intelligence later estimated that 6,000 to 7,000 civilians and 1,000 soldiers died over several days of fighting.

This event not only strengthened the CCP-PLA alliance; it also profoundly influenced China's domestic and foreign political directions. The Party's principal objective has been to root out and destroy any attempt to foment opposition to its pervasive rule of China. In the PLA and in broader society there was an immediate crackdown on democracy activists. According to PLA documents, as many as 3,500 PLA commanders were investigated after Tiananmen.[29] There have also been successive crackdowns on other democracy activists and a militant response to any other large-scale social grouping. Varying degrees of violence have been used against the Tibetans seeking to regain independence, Muslims in Xinjiang who at times have attacked the government, nonviolent religious groups and sects including Catholic and Protestant churches, and the moral-civic group the Falun Gong. Contrary to expectations in the West that the Internet would undermine Party control,[30] China has managed to keep the Internet from becoming a medium of organized protest, instead turning it into a weapon of political control and military attack.

Political and military leaders who supported the Tiananmen crackdown profited, as did the PLA in general. Jiang Zemin was elevated from Shanghai Party boss to the Politburo as a result of his rapid support for the crackdown. Deng's decision to anoint Hu Jintao to be Jiang's successor is said to have been influenced by Hu's leadership in imposing martial law and facilitating a similar military crackdown in Tibet in March 1989. General Chi Haotian, who led the military operations, would become Minister of Defense, and General Zhang Wannian, leader of the airborne troops who were particularly zealous killers, would later rise to First Vice Chairman of the CMC.[31] The October 1992 Fourteenth Party Congress selected a Central Committee with a record 23.3 percent soldiers, while Deng and Jiang broadly increased the PLA's role in government affairs; this included allowing eight top PLA officers to attend Politburo meetings as nonvoting members.[32] After Tiananmen, the United States and the EU imposed military embargoes, to which China responded by becoming increasingly hostile toward the United States while re-embracing post-Soviet Russia and then commencing what remains a very high national priority to fund and build a modern and increasingly capable PLA.

Third and Fourth Generation

Under the "Third Generation" leadership of Jiang Zemin (1989–2004) and the "Fourth Generation" and current leadership of Hu Jintao, the PLA has become an increasingly "professional" armed force in the sense of gaining an officer corps with higher levels of education, the creation of a new technically proficient Non-commissioned Officer corps in 1997, and an increasing trend toward basing promotions on merit. But the PLA is not "professional" in the Western sense that it is loyal to a Constitution or body of law as opposed to a single Party and its paramount leader. This plus the end of a Party leadership with direct revolutionary and thus military experience—Deng was the last— has created an even greater need for the Party's paramount leader to have control of the PLA to affirm his position as Party leader and to be perceived as a military leader to affirm his control of the PLA. In the far less violent Party factional politics between Hu, who was actually selected by Deng to be Jiang's successor, and Jiang, control of the PLA became the final confirmation of a transfer of power. In 2002, as Hu assumed the Chairmanship of the Party, Jiang wanted to rule, as did Deng, with a long lingering hold on the Chairmanship of the CMC. However, the PLA became increasingly uncomfortable with having to divide its loyalties and actually became part of the pressure that led to Jiang's yielding this last power position to Hu in 2004.[33]

For Jiang and Hu, who had never served in the PLA, "military leadership" has revolved around the heaping of resources on the PLA while attending to a gradual but intensive process of building personal loyalties through the granting of top-level officer promotions, accommodating PLA foreign policy priorities, and running an active propaganda campaign to burnish the image of their military leadership. In all but two years since the early 1990s, the PLA has received double-digit annual military budget increases (based on its official budget numbers). Jiang quietly ended Deng's fourth-place priority for military modernization in the early 1990s and allowed CMC Vice Chairman Liu Huaqing to commence an accelerated foreign military technology "shopping spree," mainly with Russia, that exceeded the smaller outreach to the West before Tiananmen. In 2002 Jiang acknowledged the PLA's leadership of the politically high-profile manned space program. Hu shows little indication he will reduce the PLA's high budgetary priority, and has focused on increasing training, troop pay and benefits, and investments in new power-projection weapons systems. In contrast to Mao's purges, Jiang and Hu have sought to cultivate personal loyalties by controlling top military promotions. Before the Seventeenth Party Congress in October 2007, Hu pushed forward a rotation in the major Military Region commands, about which one Chinese report noted, "In the covert rule of the CPC, this is seen as a sign of the leader's true hold of military powers."[34]

Both Jiang and Hu have undertaken a constant series of keynote speeches before PLA formations, photo opportunities with troops, and visits to key military factories and design bureaus to review new military-technical developments. In 1999 Jiang led the massive military parade in Beijing that the Party uses to celebrate tenth anniversaries. With extensive Chinese media coverage, Hu traveled to Russia in August 2007 to join Russian leader Vladimir Putin in viewing the final stages of the Peace Mission 2007 exercises, which were the largest PLA deployment to a foreign country to date. In contrast, at the same time the United States was holding its far larger 2007 Valiant Shield combined arms exercises near Guam. The Valiant Shield exercises received minimal coverage in the U.S. press, and there was little expectation that President George Bush would alter his vacation to go witness them.

This period has also seen the PLA create a strong "lobby" that has become adept at conveying its desires to the Party leadership while maintaining its fervent loyalty to the Party. Although PLA generals are no longer part of the CCP Politburo pinnacle Standing Committee, two generals are usually on the larger Politburo. PLA generals also comprise a significant portion of the CCP Central Committee and the annual pro-forma National People's Congress. In terms of national policies, the PLA has been consistently credited for insisting on hardline policies toward Taiwan even as military pressures and threats have had the effect of deepening the Island's creation of a nationalist identity and increasing its desire for "independence." Policies insisting on "reunification" with Taiwan at any cost also serve to justify greater military expenditures. But all of this also may create a new "corporate identity" within the PLA, which, like broader Chinese society, may soon insist on solutions to vast economic and social challenges the Party is unable to resolve.

Is PLA Loyalty Eternal?

While the arrest of the Gang of Four can be considered an adroit move amid a key CCP power struggle, perhaps the closest the PLA ever came to being party to a coup was in 1971, when Defense Minister Lin Biao, who was then Mao's most trusted subordinate and designated successor, became suspect by Mao. In response, Lin's son Li Guo "Tiger," with his father's approval, led an assassination conspiracy with a small group of friends. Amid increasing fears of arrest by Mao, Lin decided, along with his son, to flee to Hong Kong or Russia, but Tiger had recruited a young PLA Air Force general to try to kill Mao. The attempt was thwarted. Lin's plans were revealed by his daughter, forcing Lin, his wife, and his son to board a jet airliner before fueling was complete, and it crashed in Mongolia early on the morning of September 13, 1971, killing all aboard.[35] The plot devastated an already paranoid Mao, saw the elevation of Marshal Ye Jianying to PLA commander, and cast a pall of political suspicion over the PLA Air Force that may still linger today.[36] Though largely a defensive response to Mao, Lin's "coup" caused his being castigated as a traitor. But Lin's reputation has seen a rehabilitation in recent years. In 2007 the CCP was confident enough to acknowledge Lin's contributions to the Revolutionary War in a major museum display commemorating the PLA's eightieth anniversary.[37]

However, the CCP does not take the PLA's loyalty for granted. In addition to regular exhortations of Party control over the PLA, the Party maintains a large apparatus of political commissars through the General Political Department under the Central Military Commission. Commissars are present at almost every level of command and some have been known to jump between political and troop command positions. The role of the commissar has also grown from one of ensuring strict political loyalty to the Party to include responsibilities for monitoring the welfare of the troops. But despite this level of political and personnel control over the PLA, the Party has led a political campaign since 2004 against the idea of a "professional army" that would owe its loyalty to the state instead of the Party.[38] Such concerns by the Party may have been prompted by unreported internal PLA reactions to the 2002 reforms in Taiwan. These reforms formalized Taiwan's armed forces' loyalty to the state, whereas their allegiance had been to the Kuomintang Party during the rule of Chiang Kai-shek. Continuing this theme in July 2007, Defense Minister Cao Gangchuan wrote in the CCP journal *Qiushi* (Seeking Truth) , "Some hostile forces have made it their priority to westernize the Chinese military and have preached the non-politicalization and nationalization of the military in an attempt to separate the military from the Party leadership."[39] This campaign could be designed to "smoke out" sympathizers, but as James Mulvenon has noted, it also "has an overall cumulative effect opposite to that intended, raising more questions and eyebrows about the actual loyalty of the PLA to the party."[40]

One indication of possible "thinking beyond the CCP" in the PLA is the example of Deputy Political Commissar of the Air Force Lt. General Liu Yazhou. Yazhou is a 56-year old writer, educator, son-in-law of the late Chinese President Li Xiannian and thus a "Princeling," and one of the few PLA officers allowed to visit Taiwan and study in the United States.[41] A maverick who apparently enjoys some degree of support and protection, he gained prominence in 2001 with an essay on Mao's humiliating 1949 defeat while trying to take the island of Quemoy. This essay was widely viewed as a "call to senses" against top-level political sentiments that China had to take military action against Taiwan. Liu is a nationalist with a clear sense that China's military power must grow to protect more distant interests. But he is said to favor an accommodation with Taiwan, a relationship with the United States that is not necessarily hostile, and closer relations with radical Middle Eastern regimes, though he is harsh toward Japan. However, while bowing to the need to "consolidate the Party's ruling position," he has also strongly criticized corruption and advocates greater political reform, even democratic reform, lest there be widespread popular revolt in China.[42] It is not clear how far his career will progress, though his accompanying Defense Minister Cao on a trip to Pyongyang in April 2006 may be a positive sign.[43]

While a crisis sufficient to cause the PLA to unite for the purpose of overthrowing the CCP has yet to pass, it would be unwise to dismiss such a possibility. The PLA and the People's Armed Police, while structured and programmed to serve the Party, are very likely the only forces in the current period in China that could also take power away from the CCP if they could unite sufficiently around that purpose. To be sure, military support is essential for the Party to suppress and divide all other opposition, and military loyalty to the

Party appears solid. But what if the CCP, due to an accumulation of its weaknesses, was unable to respond effectively to a widespread and sudden outburst of unorganized rebellion? Or, what if the Party were to "lose" Taiwan either by its own mistakes or by those of the PLA? The PLA is not bound by generations of institutional and statutory loyalties that bind democratic militaries, even in crises. Might the PLA have a lower crisis level threshold for action? Of course, such questions cannot be answered, but the crises that swirl around the CCP make them plausible concerns.

CCP Weakness

Despite the many clear measures of China's recent success, the Communist Party appears less and less able to overcome its many internal contradictions, to confront the many challenges to political and social stability in China, or to act with a level of justice that would build support. It is also important to remember that China's current level of success has only been realized for the last thirty or so years. For China, the previous century had been one of constant internal strife. It had seen two wars against Japan that China lost, and then a debilitating struggle between Nationalist and Communist forces beginning in the mid-1920s that ended only when Mao Zedong's Red Army/People's Liberation Army put the CCP in power in October 1, 1949, forcing Nationalist leader Chiang Kai-shek to flee to Taiwan.

Mao Zedong tried to build a socialist economy, conquered Tibet, and tried to build a military superpower that could compete with the Soviet Union for leadership of the Communist movement. But Mao also led China into his own period of violent turmoil, as he sought to physically destroy classes, caused a devastating famine by trying to force industrialization with his "Great Leap Forward," and then, from the early 1960s to his death, led his "Cultural Revolution," which wrought vengeance against all perceived opponents. Recent estimates place the number of Chinese who died as a result of Mao's barbarism between 65 and 70 million.[44] Mao remains venerated by the current Communist leadership. They wish to avoid the public anguish that the revelations of Stalin's crimes caused in the former Soviet Union. The CCP forbids a similar airing of Mao's crimes out of fear of undermining the Party's legitimacy.[45] The Chinese government "strongly protested" when U.S. President George W. Bush spoke at the June 2007 dedication of the new Victims of Communism Memorial, during which he mentioned Chinese who had died under Communism.[46]

But it is Mao's Communist Party that still rules China, though for how long? The Party has rejected Mao's ideological ambition to control economic and personal life; instead, in a new policy slogan created by Hu Jintao, the Party is offering a "Harmonious Society" based on economic growth and substantial economic freedom without political freedom. While the Party today has broadened its base to include entrepreneurs and professionals as well as military members, its refusal to distribute power damages the growth of civil society and undermines the Party's legitimacy. It is also increasingly unable to make itself accountable, so it is not able to balance or reconcile competing regional or even rural-urban demands. As did Mao and Deng, might China's current leaders face internal tumult that could once again radically alter China's direction? Might they also try to stave off instability by resorting to military activism, particularly against Taiwan? A recent body of literature suggests that China's continued rapid and "peaceful" rise is not assured for a number of serious reasons.[47] These are discussed in the following paragraphs.

Population-Employment Pressures

China's large population of 1.3 billion creates unique pressures. About 40 percent of Chinese live in urban areas, and China plans to have half its population in urban areas by 2020. But this will create new employment pressures requiring China to generate 20 to 25 million new jobs a year, resulting in great pressure to maintain high rates of economic growth. While unemployment has fallen from 11 percent in 2004 to under 5 percent in 2007, there is also the new problem of finding jobs for college graduates. In 2005 about 25 percent of college graduates could not find jobs. Unemployment plus an increasing withdrawal of government services such as health care could also undermine support for the government.

There is already a growing disparity between urban and rural incomes. Chinese statistics for 2006 indicate an average urban disposable income of $750 and $250 for rural residents.[48] The 800 million who live beyond the prosperous coastal regions do not share in China's new wealth. In addition, China's aging population—11 percent over age 60 in 2006, expected to climb to 30 percent by 2015—will increasingly strain China's pension systems, which do not even cover rural residents.[49] In addition, Chinese preferences for sons are creating a dangerous imbalance in male-female ratios, which some call the "Bachelor Bomb," a future in which unfulfilled males feed domestic and foreign policies of violence.

Weak Financial Institutions

Though the CCP's gambit for job creation and stability rests on a continually growing economy, that in turn rests on a foundation of weak financial institutions. Banks, in particular, have a high percentage of "bad loans," or loans upon which they will never collect because they were made to state-owned or failed companies. In mid-2006 the China Banking Regulatory Commission estimated that bad loans amounted to $163 billion, or a "manageable" 7.5 percent of total loans, while the independent Fitch Ratings estimated the total to be closer to $460 billion, more than one-fifth of total loans. To keep its banks solvent, since 1998 China has spent $400 billion to cover bad loans.[50] As a consequence, banks have little incentive to reform and become solvent, especially when Party officials apply pressure to issue more bad loans, lest unprofitable state firms fail and create more destabilizing unemployment.

Environmental Deterioration

A further lack of government accountability, especially at the local level, sees cities and regions competing pell-mell for new investments to create export and cash-generating enterprises, resulting in serious damage to China's environment. In mid-2007 a Dutch government–funded NGO declared that China had exceeded the United States in the production of "greenhouse gases" threatening the environment.[51] The major culprit is China's excessive dependence on high-pollutant coal, which accounts for 65 percent of all China's energy consumption.[52] According to the World Health Organization, China has sixteen of the world's twenty most polluted cities, and out of concerns of promoting "social unrest," China tried to suppress data that it suffers 750,000 premature deaths a year due to pollution.[53] About one-third of the Chinese population does not have access to clean drinking water, about 70 percent of lakes and rivers are polluted, and groundwater tables are declining—a threat to agriculture and water supplies.[54] Lack of safety in the separation of humans and poultry industries is thought to have been a major contributor to the late 2003 outbreak of a new Corona virus, later known as SARS, although the Chinese government first sought to suppress this information rather than help people defend themselves.

Restive Peoples

Like the former Soviet Union, China is an empire of nationalities, many of whom would choose autonomy or independence were it not for the intensive efforts of the Party and the Police organs to find, isolate, and, if necessary, destroy opposition to CCP rule. The regions inhabited by restive Tibetans and the Muslim Uighur areas constitute 60 percent of China's territory, contain many critical resources, and are the location for critical railroads and pipelines. Chinese Muslim Uighurs undertake occasional terrorist attacks in Beijing and in the Xinjiang area, with many harboring resentments due to CCP-led suppression, which was particularly harsh during the Cultural Revolution.[55] Despite intense efforts by the CCP, the attraction of radical Muslim ideologies appears to be increasing.

In 1950 the PLA invaded and conquered Tibet and has since sought to suppress its unique Buddhist religion/culture by forcing the Tibetans' spiritual leader, the Dalai Lama, to flee, trying to control the religion by selecting compliant leaders, and reportedly killing up to 1.5 million Tibetans.[56] Despite long efforts by Beijing to move Han Chinese to Tibet and dominate the local economy and society, Tibetans are still willing to protest against religious persecution by Beiing.[57] Violent Tibetan protests and attacks against Chinese shop owners in many cities across Tibet in early March 2008 came as a shock to the Chinese government and to many around the world. Beijing was forced to deploy troops and undertake a wide crackdown, but Tibetans proved their ability to sustain a nationalist unity, and a minimal capacity to resist, in spite of decades of Chinese suppression. Tibetan anger may persist should Chinese officials follow through on plans to select the next Tibetan spiritual leader, a gross violation of Tibetan religious practice. China also seeks to control other religions such as the Catholic Church, Protestant churches, and even the Falun Gong spiritual group—all of which resist CCP control.

Weakening Political Legitimacy

The weight of China's problems, compounded by government corruption and a lack of accountability, especially at local levels, feeds widespread anger fueling increasing numbers of protests, all of which point to a crumbling legitimacy for the CCP. According to Chinese police statistics, popular protests rose to 74,000 incidents or 3.67 million participants in 2004, compared to only 730,000 protest participants in 1994.[58] The number of protest incidents grew to 80,000 in 2005. Though most incidents go unreported, a riot over water access in the village of Bo Mei, in Guangdong Province, in April 2005 saw 10,000 farmers and villagers battle about 1,000 police and government officials.[59]

These protests grow but do not threaten Party control because the Party works hard to make sure disaffected groups do not coordinate or unite. Yet despite massive Chinese investments to control the Internet and other kinds of connectivity, a mobile phone text message on June 1 and 2, 2007, caused thousands of people in Xiamen to brave the wrath of employers by attending a near-spontaneous rally to protest the construction of a chemical plant near residential areas. Chinese officials fear these media.[60] In September 2007 there were reports that "thousands" of demobilized soldiers staged "coordinated" riots to protest poor treatment at government-run training schools.[61] In September 2007 Vice Minister of Information Industry Lou Qinjian stated, "As soon as a major social situation occurs, Internet opinion makes waves and it becomes extremely easy for street politics to break out, directly threatening social stability."[62]

The CCP's declining legitimacy boils down to its unwillingness to allow political reforms that would increase accountability and guarantee popular rights; or, to be blunt, it will not permit democratic evolution. CCP corruption reaches staggering heights and even affects the PLA. In 2006, only after a mistress would not keep quiet did the PLA fire a Deputy Commander of the East Sea Fleet and other officers over corruption that could not be hidden. The central government is unable to make local governments enforce pollution standards, and these localities expropriate farmers' land to fuel economic development and growth, both of which fuel protests. While there appears to have been some pressures building within the CCP for many years to undertake some kind of "democratic" reform, this pressure is also resisted by hard-liners in the Party and the PLA. In 2003 and again in 2007 there appears to have been noticeable agitation within the Party about the necessity for reforms, but in both cases the debate appears to have been turned off.[63] Signaling the end of a burst of debate in early 2007, Premier Wen Jiabao, while admitting the need for reforms, also declared, "We must keep a firm grasp on the basic principles of the Party in the initial stage of socialism, without wavering, for 100 years."[64]

The Party may believe that it can keep power for another 100 years, but competing democratic examples that flourish in Taiwan, and in the democratic reform movement in Hong Kong, further undermine the Party's legitimacy. In the face of widespread popular support for "universal suffrage" promised in the 1997 Basic Law that Britain negotiated for its return of Hong Kong to Chinese sovereignty, the Party has instead created very limited legislative institutions, which they pack with Party supporters. In 2003, on the anniversary of the Tiananmen Massacre, one million Hong Kong residents protested political restrictions, and dismay will likely grow the longer the Party resists real democratic reform. Over 50 percent of Taiwanese support a peaceful "de jure" independence from China, and most would never willingly accept Communist Party rule. But there are apparently many in the Party who see they are headed toward a cliff. Since 2004 there has been a vigorous "hardliners versus reformers" debate within Party theoretical circles about the causes for the fall of the Soviet Communist Party, with some willing to admit the Soviet Communist Party was doomed to failure, implying the CCP will suffer the same fate.[65]

Protecting the Party

In 2007, however, the CCP remains firmly in power. While the CCP differs greatly from the Soviet Party regarding its willingness to allow growing economic freedoms, it maintains a very Soviet-like security apparatus (Table 2.3) to ensure that the Party can suppress any potential challenge to its power, while it builds up its formal military forces to aid its ability to obtain greater global power. The CCP views all who would oppose its rule as enemies, and it actively prosecutes enemies domestically and abroad. Before the Seventeenth Party Congress in October 2007, CCP Politburo member and Public Security Minister Zhou Yongkang was quoted warning police at all levels of the "arduous task of maintaining social harmony," saying, "Our country is in a period of outstanding conflict among the people, high crime rates and complex struggles against enemies. . . . We should safeguard the leadership of the Communist Party, the socialist system and the state regime of people's democratic dictatorship with real actions."[66]

The Ministry of Public Security is the main police force; it deals with conventional law enforcement as well as prosecuting political crimes. Instead of allowing debate or democracy, the Party maintains a large United Front Department (UFD) with branches throughout China and overseas. The UFD seeks to dissuade opposition and gather support among otherwise rebellious minorities and to mobilize overseas Chinese citizens to support the CCP. If the UFD cannot co-opt active-minded individuals to support the CCP or stay out of the political arena, then it helps to mark them for attention from security organs. The Ministry of Propaganda tries to maintain strict censorship of all domestic media, and even foreign media that is widely distributed in China. The

Table 2.3 Protecting the Party: China's Security Services

Service	Size	Authority/ Command	Primary Mission	Secondary Mission
PLA	2.25 million	Military/CMC	National defense	Internal defense
People's Armed Police	1.5 million	Paramilitary/ CMC and State Council	Internal defense	National defense
Militia	10 million (2004)	Paramilitary/ CMC and State Council	National defense	Internal defense
Ministry of Public Security (MPS)	800,000	Civilian/State Council	Law enforcement/ Internal defense	
Ministry of State Security (MSS)	100,000 (estimate)	Civilian/State Council	Internal counter-intelligence and external espionage	Internal defense
United Front Department (UFD)	n/a	CCP/Central Committee	Mobilize support for the CCP from diverse domestic groups and overseas Chinese, or help to defeat them.	The UFD has a secondary role in organizing espionage, such as on foreign universities
Foreign Liaison Department	n/a; small	CCP/Central Committee	Gather foreign intelligence for the CCP; serve as a covert liaison with foreign radical groups	

Sources: International Institute of Strategic Studies, *Military Balance, 2006–2007*; Federation of American Scientists; *China's National Defense, 2004.*

Propaganda Ministry and the Ministry of Public Security are two of the largest groups that seek to control China's rapidly growing Internet culture, seeking to ensure that it does not become a medium for organizing future revolt. This often involves pressure on foreign software and Internet companies to surrender inside data so that China's "Internet police" can effectively block unwanted outside data or find Chinese using the Internet for activities judged to be subversive.

People's Armed Police

The People's Armed Police (PAP) was created in 1983, but it was vastly strengthened after the Tiananmen Massacre to create a new internal army to fight large-scale political movements, such as the pro-democracy protesters of 1989, that might again rise against the CCP. Out of the 500,000-man PLA reduction of the late 1990s the PAP received fourteen divisions. Today, its 1.5 million-man force is organized much like the PLA. They are assigned to a number of internal protection duties including border protection, forest protection, and protection of leadership officials. One trend visible within the PAP and, to a lesser degree, other police forces is that of increasing mechanization. The PAP and other police forces utilize heavy armored personnel carriers based on the WZ551 design and also use a variety of other vehicles, some produced under license in China of Ford and Iveco designs. A 2006 Chinese exhibition of police technologies saw displays from Ford and the Segway Company, which displayed its personal transporters. Some PAP units can function as light infantry in support of regular PLA units. The PAP and the police have also created many specialized units to counter terrorist attacks or respond rapidly to urban insurrections. These teams are highly trained, can scale buildings and rappel from helicopters, and are armed with a variety of special weapons, including crossbows for silent operations. In September 2007 an 87-man PAP team went to Moscow for counterterrorism exercises with Russian Interior Ministry forces.[67]

Domestic and Foreign Espionage

In addition to sustaining large formal intelligence organizations, the Chinese government seeks to enlist a variety of groups and individuals in a pervasive global espionage campaign. For the two principle intelligence organizations, the Ministry of State Security (MSS) and the Second Department of the PLA General Staff Department, counterintelligence appears to be the most important function, with the most important goal being the protection of the Party. But both groups also focus heavily on foreign intelligence gathering. China has a long history of effective employment of espionage and agents of influence preceding the era of Sun Zi. Today espionage is a viewed as essential for the PLA to prepare for future challenges, not just to understand enemies, but also to gather foreign military and civilian technology to accelerate the growth of China's economic strength. In July 2007 Federal Bureau of Investigation (FBI) Director Robert Mueller remarked, "China is stealing our secrets in an effort to leap ahead in terms of its military technology, but also the economic capability of China. It is a substantial threat that we are addressing in the sense of building our program to address this threat."[68] As indicated in the chart below, China has had a remarkable string of successes against the United States in terms of penetrating the U.S. government and stealing critical technologies (Table 2.4).

Table 2.4 Military Damage to U.S. Security from Chinese Espionage

Target	Time Frame	Means of Access	Impact
U.S. Nuclear Weapon Designs	1970s–1990s	Open sources; contact with U.S. nuclear lab engineers; possible spies	Based on U.S. Intelligence Community data the Cox Commission reported in 1999 that the PRC had gained information on the W-88, W-87, W-78,W-76, W-70, W-62, and W-56 nuclear warheads, plus some warhead casing designs, which likely helped the PLA design new smaller warheads for its DF-31 and JL-2 missiles.
FBI Counterintelligence Operations	1980s to 2000	Katrina Leung, FBI informant and double agent	Compromised two top FBI counterintelligence officials handling her; suspected of having passed along great knowledge of U.S. operations and methods; may have compromised past operations and assets.
Stealth: F-117	1999	F-117 downed by Serbia in 1999	PRC reported to have obtained parts of stealth coating outer skin, engine radiation suppression area, and guidance systems. These would have helped China design its own stealth systems.
Stealth: B-2	1999–2002	Noshir Gowadia, Northrop Grumman engineer	Gowadia pioneered new technology IR suppression on B-2 bomber; was recruited to give lectures in China; convicted of selling stealth technology that helps PLA develop new stealthy cruise missiles. USAF's B-2 bombers may now face new dangers from PLA countermeasures.
Combat Aircraft, Shuttle, and Missile Technology	Late 1970s to 2006 (?)	Dongfan "Greg" Chung	Former engineer for Rockwell and Boeing cooperated with AVIC-1 officials and provided data on the Space Shuttle, C-17, F-15, B-70, Delta IV rocket, and up to 24 manuals for the B-1 bomber. He also gave many lectures in China on the Shuttle and aircraft stress analysis issues, which would have aided the PLA's space shuttle and aircraft programs.

Table 2.4 *(Continued)*

Target	Time Frame	Means of Access	Impact
Cruise Missile Technology	1998–2000	Taliban	China reportedly paid $10 million to former Taliban regime for U.S. Tomahawk cruise missile pieces, a deal that almost led to diplomatic relations with Taliban.
Patriot SAM	1990–1992	Diversion reported from Israel or Germany	Israel vehemently denied leaking Patriot SAM technology to China; U.S. source strongly confirmed to author that "China has the Patriot"; this helped the PLA to develop advanced SAMs in the first decade of the twenty-first century.
Terfenol-D	Prior to 2002	PRC students in U.S.	Terfenol-D is an advanced conductive material developed by the U.S. Navy and used to improve the performance of submarine sonar. This has likely improved PLA submarine and ship sonar.
Anti-Submarine Technology	1985–1997	Peter Lee	Former Los Alamos nuclear lab engineer Peter Lee shared advanced radar technology useful in tracking submarines, and he shared nuclear testing data that could help the PLA develop modern nuclear warheads.
Navy Advanced Electric Drive	1983–2005	Chi Mak and associates	Apparently passing data to China since 1983; electrical engineer for Power Paragon; when caught he was preparing to ship data on U.S. Navy's Quiet Electric Drive, a key technology for stealthier warships and submarines. Mak was also tasked to find technology on electric catapults, which would have helped development of new rail gun weapons.

Sources: Report of the Select Committee On U.S. National Security and Military/Commercial Concerns With The People's Republic of China, Volume 1, Submitted by Mr. Cox of California, Chairman (Washington DC: U.S. Government Printing Office, 1999); Jeff Gerth and James Risen, "Reports Show Scientist Gave U.S. Radar Secrets to China," *New York Times*, May 10, 1999; Terrence P. Jeffery, "The Spy Who Got Away," *Human Events*, April 21, 2000, p. 1; "Noshir Gowadia," CI Center, http://cicentre.com/Documents/DOC_Noshir_Gowadia_Case.htm; Chitra Ragavan, "China Doll," *U.S. News and World Report*, November 2, 2003; Department of Justice press release, February 11, 2008.

China's premier intelligence organization is the Ministry of State Security (MSS), created in 1983 to conduct both domestic counterintelligence duties and foreign espionage. It has regional and functional offices, and its main think tank is the Chinese Institute for Contemporary International Relations (CICIR), which also sends its "scholars" abroad. In late August 2007 Vice Minister for State Security Geng Huichang replaced the long-serving Xu Yongyue as the head of MSS. Geng is reportedly an international relations specialist who is an expert on the United States, Japan, and industrial espionage and was the former head of the CICIR.[69] The MSS has had notable success in penetrating the U.S. Central Intelligence Agency (CIA) and the FBI. For thirty of his nearly forty years working for the U.S. government, Harry Wu-Tai Chin was a translator and analyst with the CIA, but he had been recruited by Chinese intelligence in 1944. He was able to pass data to Chinese intelligence services that gave them insights into the U.S. level of knowledge about China, its methods, and even its assets.[70] A second but more damaging penetration saw MSS double agent Katrina Leung sexually compromise two top FBI counterintelligence agents. For over a decade Leung passed unknown amounts of data to the MSS on U.S. knowledge of Chinese espionage, which would have been of enormous use to its spies.[71]

The PLA also defends the Party by playing a major role in the gathering of foreign intelligence. It does so along with the MSS, which gathers intelligence against both domestic and foreign enemies. Under the PLA's General Staff Department there are two bureaus that gather and analyze intelligence, plus one organ under the General Armaments Department:

General Staff Second Department (Er Bu) The Second Department, whose director is Major General Chen Xiaogong, is responsible for gathering and analyzing military and political intelligence on foreign countries. The Er Bu runs agent networks and gathers open source data. The head of the Er Bu has also at times had a high international profile, attending conferences and giving speeches, as a sort of PLA spokesman. This would also be consistent with the Er Bu's counterintelligence function in that it actively seeks to shape perceptions of the PLA in hopes of reducing negative efforts directed against it.

General Staff Third Department (San Bu) The Third Department, whose director is Major General Qui Rulin, is responsible for maintaining and analyzing the output of a large electronic intelligence (ELINT) and signals intelligence (SIGINT) network around the PRC's border, and with foreign facilities in Burma and Cuba. The San Bu is also sometimes tasked with overseas clandestine targeted data-gathering missions. One source has told this author that a Third Department team was found in the middle of a desert of a Middle Eastern country monitoring electronic traffic on the eve of the 1991 Gulf War.

China Defense Science and Technology Information Center (CDSTIC) Under the control of the General Armament Department since 1998, the CDSTIC orchestrates overt (and likely some covert) technology collection

undertaken by the PRC's vast military-industrial complex. This organization published a manual for intelligence collection[72] that noted there are
roughly 4,000 individual intelligence organizations operating in the PRC,
many being associated with defense related companies, institutes, and
academies.[73]

PLA intelligence organs are, like the MSS, apparently capable of highly targeted
intelligence operations. For example, it is likely that PLA played a substantial
role in Iran's network of theft and smuggling to maintain its U.S.-made arsenal.
In 1995 Iran expert Ken Timmerman reported that U.S. Customs officials told
him that "Chinese middlemen and front companies [were] deeply involved in a
vast military aircraft spare parts pipeline to Iran."[74] In 1999 the Cox Commission
reported that between 1996 and 1997 the Los Angeles U.S. Customs Service
seized over 500 electron tubes for the F-14A on their way to Hong Kong.[75] These
were probably for the fighter's AN/AWG-9 radar. In February 2003 the U.S.
Department of Justice indicted Jinghua Zhuang and Xiuwen Liang, of the
California-based Maytone International, for seeking export parts for the F-14,
AIM-9 Sidewinder air-to-air missile, Hawk surface-to-air missile, and TOW antitank missile.[76] While the Department of Justice only hinted that Iran might be
the final destination for F-14 parts, Iran would also be seeking parts for these
missiles, which were purchased from the United States before 1979.

A unique aspect of China's approach to intelligence is that its breadth and
depth appear unlimited. China's intelligence services are complex in a vertical
sense. They all have regional and city-based units, which often run both foreign
and domestic operations, sometimes separate from higher-level knowledge or
control. China uses all manner of contact with target individuals with privileged
information, not "so much [to] try to steal secrets as to try to induce foreign
visitors to give them away by manipulating them into certain situations."[77] It is
difficult to determine the limits of what China considers to be intelligence assets.
In addition to a range of government employees, Chinese intelligence services
use diverse groups such as students, businessmen, business delegations, cultural
delegations, and overseas Chinese[78] largely to gather massive amounts of unclassified data, but on occasion, these groups are enlisted to penetrate governments
and companies to retrieve very sensitive information. According to one U.S.
government assessment, "The FBI has stated that virtually all Chinese allowed
to leave the PRC for the United States are given some type of collection requirement to fulfill."[79] These Chinese "assets" may only operate once and not communicate with handlers until they return to China, complicating detection and
defenses. As will be explored in chapter 5, the PLA and intelligence services are
also making increasing use of the Internet as an offensive weapon for gathering
intelligence.

Cooptation and control of overseas Chinese is another important function for
China's intelligence services. They may also help to monitor and control
Chinese students as well as penetrate and persecute groups and individuals

opposed to the CCP regime. The MSS think tank CICIR deploys "scholars" to U.S. universities. One such scholar in residence at the University of Maryland once told the author that, in addition to his formal project of producing an analysis of President George W. Bush's reading list for the Chinese leadership, he would also write opinion articles for Chinese American newspapers.[80] It is also apparent that the Chinese government exerts control though a global network of "Chinese Students and Scholars Associations" (CSSAs), which exist at many U.S. and European universities.[81] CSSAs have helped organize and fund demonstrations against Taiwanese leaders in New York City and have been accused of aiding Chinese industrial espionage in Europe.[82] Chinese diplomat-defector Chen Yonglin has stated that foreign Chinese student groups are coordinated by Chinese embassies and are used to recruit future CCP members.[83] China made another demonstration of its ability to mobilize nationalist overseas Chinese when it helped organize counter-protests to the Olympic Torch relay in Australia and the United States, following the wounded pride caused by protests against the Torch relay in Europe.[84]

Furthermore, recent defectors from the Chinese Ministry of Foreign Affairs have noted that China uses a large number of "spies" in Australia and Canada to monitor and even physically harass opposition groups such as the Falun Gong.[85] On Feburary 8, 2006, Falun Gong computer expert Li Yuan was severely beaten in his Atlanta, Georgia, home, and the group blamed Chinese government agents.[86] Should China decide to violently suppress democrats in Hong Kong, or undertake a difficult war to conquer Taiwan, it can be expected that the CCP will dispatch intelligence operatives to infiltrate, harass, and suppress remaining Hong Kong democracy supporters or Taiwan independence activists, especially if they flee abroad to lead governments in exile.

An additional danger is that any number of these intelligence assets and China-controlled groups could potentially be mobilized by the PLA to perform military missions. Furthermore, China's intelligence organs may also seek to enlist other radical groups or even radical states to perform military missions that would aid Chinese objectives. For many years, the Central Committee's Foreign Liaison Department was responsible for aiding and training Maoist revolutionary groups, until such activities were curtailed after Mao's death. According to some sources the Foreign Liaison Department was the main conduit for China's relations with the Taliban before 9/11.[87] In addition, Chinese intelligence organs and the PLA likely have cooperative relations with Chinese Triads and other criminal networks.

CHAPTER 3

FOREIGN SECURITY POLICY

This chapter examines the significant influence of China's People's Liberation Army (PLA) on China's foreign policy. The PLA is likely to play a greater role as China builds up its military forces to, in Hu Jintao's 2004 formulation, "provide a security guarantee for the national interests," which is usually interpreted to mean defending more distant interests.[1] China has fought both "defensive" and "offensive" wars for the purpose of shaping its security environment to its advantage. China's attack against the United Nations in North Korea in 1950 and its 1979 offensive against Vietnam are examples of the latter. Future offensive battles or wars could be fought to secure Chinese control over territories disputed with South Korea and Japan, and to achieve the "sacred mission" of "reunification" with Taiwan. The PLA is a key lobby for hard-line policies against Taiwan, Japan, and the U.S.-led alliance system in Asia. It is also a key lobby for military power projection, from the sale of nuclear and missile technologies to strategic partners to the building of new weapons needed to defend China's increasingly distant interests. These interests include the need to secure access to petroleum and other resources, and the need to protect the sea-lanes that transport resources to China and carry Chinese products abroad. This commerce is directly responsible for sustaining China's continued economic growth, and thus, is also responsible for maintaining the Communist Party's power position.

Regarding its formal influence, the PLA participates in foreign policy coordination bodies under CCP auspices, lobbies CCP leaders, and makes decisions that do not require Foreign Ministry approval. The CCP maintains several "Leading Groups," which combine Party, civilian, and even NGO participants to guide area-specific policies. The Taiwan Leading Group is led by Hu Jintao. It is also said to include Jia Qinglin, the highest ranking Politburo member involved in political work; United Front Department (UFD) Director Liu Yandong; State Councilor Tang Jiaxuan; Central Committee General Office Director Wang Gang; Ministry of State Security Director Geng Huichang; and either the Director of PLA Intelligence or the Director of the Second Department of the General Staff Department.[2] From the early 1990s until the Taiwan Straits crisis of 1995–1996, the PLA was a steady source of pressure on Party leaders to adopt hard-line policies toward the United States, and in a further act of Party deference, the PLA was even reported to have received the "self-criticism" of Jiang Zemin and Foreign Minister Qian Qichen in the wake of Washington's decision to allow Taiwanese President Lee Teng Hui to visit the United States.[3]

Occasionally the PLA seems to have the power to overrule Foreign Ministry authority over foreign policy. The January 2007 antisatellite (ASAT) shoot-down provides an example. Some analysts have questioned whether the Chinese Foreign Ministry's seeming shock and surprise at the January 2007 PLA satellite shoot-down might indicate rogue behavior by the PLA, or at least a dangerous lack of coordination.[4] However, given that the January ASAT demonstration was likely preceded by two other attempts,[5] and that those attempts were preceded by a decades-long R&D effort, it is far more likely that Hu Jintao was fully aware of the PLA's ASAT test program and had overarching security reasons for not informing his diplomats.[6] As the Foreign Ministry had been promoting a treaty to ban the "weaponization" of outer space since the 1980s, it would appear logical that the PLA would prevail on Hu Jintao to keep the diplomats unaware. Hu and the PLA likely decided that there was more to gain from demonstrating this power to the Americans. China still insists that it supports a treaty banning weapons in space, but this campaign now appears to have been a deception to prevent outside pressure from affecting its space weapons quest.

The PLA does not regard the fourteen countries on China's border to be a friendly neighborhood. Countries such as Korea, Japan, and Vietnam harbor resentments from recent Chinese attacks or pressure during China's Imperial Era. Since World War II, China has fought—from minor skirmishes to major battles—with six of its neighbors: Korea (1950–53), India (1962), Russia (1969), Vietnam (1979 and 1988), the Philippines (1995) and Taiwan (1949, 1956, 1958, 1995, and 1996). Whatever the strength of their current relationships, Russia, India, Japan, Korea, and Vietnam are all wary of China's growing power. India's bitter rival Pakistan was made a nuclear missile power by Beijing. China is engaged in territorial disputes over islands and economic zones that could flare up into military clashes, such as in the East China Sea with Japan, South Korea, and Taiwan. China insists on legal claims to most of the South China Sea, major areas of which are also contested by Vietnam, Malaysia, the Philippines, and Taiwan. On China's eastern horizon, democratic Taiwan sits squarely in the middle of major sea-lanes that feed Shanghai and northern ports. And to its south, China's anxiety is growing over its increasing reliance on access to the

Straits of Malacca, currently controlled by Malaysia and Singapore. About 80 percent of China's total energy imports pass through the Straits of Malacca.

It is against this collection of historic adversaries that China is seeking to once again assert its dominance of Asia as well as to compete with the United States for global power. Under the guise of multilateralism, Beijing is seeking to weaken the United States and outflank Japan, India, and Taiwan while the United States is preoccupied with fighting Islamist terrorism.[7] The PLA has played a critical part in projecting CCP power, first by proliferating nuclear and missile technologies to key partner states that serve to shift regional balances in China's favor and undermine U.S. and Indian security interests. The PLA is also playing a role in promoting hostility toward American-led security networks in Asia, as it also seeks to create Chinese-led security networks that help ensure access to resources and create a basis for future protection of critical maritime routes. But looming over all of these is China's ongoing preparation to wage war against democratic Taiwan, which could lead to war with the United States. Whether China will do so remains unknown, but its aggressive stance since 2007 on the Taiwan Strait and elsewhere has forced Australia, India, Japan, and the United States to seek greater strategic cooperation. This would further increase the potential for arms races or even clashes, for which China could pay a steep political, economic, or even military price.

Taking Taiwan

Since 1949, when the defeated Chiang Kai-shek and his Kuomintang (KMT) followers fled to Taiwan and took control, Taiwan has developed a political system, political culture, and national identity quite apart from those of China. More to the point, Taiwan is well into consolidating a transition to democracy started in the 1980s, and the vast majority of Taiwan's twenty-three million people show no inclination to surrender their freedoms to CCP rule. A late 2006 poll of Taiwanese indicated that 62 percent would opt for immediate "independence" if allowed by Beijing, while 54 percent supported it without waiting for Chinese approval.[8] However, Chinese leaders want the world to believe that Taiwan is an "integral part of China"[9] and often declare that "reunification" with Taiwan is a "sacred mission"[10] for the Chinese people. They occasionally declare that a formal Taiwanese declaration of independence would be "cause for war."[11] What they want the world to believe is that controlling Taiwan is so important that the CCP regime might fall if Taiwan were to become formally independent. After all, who would then stop Tibet or Xinjiang from following Taiwan's example? Whether true or not, as former Deputy Assistant Secretary of State for East Asia Susan Shirk has noted, the myth linking Taiwan to CCP regime survival "is so pervasive that it creates its own political reality, especially in Communist Party headquarters."[12]

But there is also another imperative motivating the CCP leadership. As Ross Munro has noted, "In the eyes of PRC leaders, Taiwan is first and foremost a strategic target that must soon be subjugated if China is to realize its goal of becoming Asia's dominant and unchallenged power."[13] The PLA National Defense University (NDU) textbook *The Science of Military Strategy* explains further:

> The reunification of China's mainland and Taiwan not only is something that concerns China's national sovereignty and territorial integrity . . . but also will exert impact upon the survival and development of the Chinese nation and the rejuvenation of the great nation of China in this century. . . . If Taiwan should be alienated from the mainland, not only our maritime defense system would lose its depth, opening a sea gateway to the outside forces, but also a large water area and rich reserves of ocean resources will fall into the hands of others. What's more, our line of foreign trade and transportation, which is vital to China's opening up and economic development will be exposed to the surveillance threats of separatist and enemy forces, and China will be forever locked on the west side of the first chain of islands of the West Pacific. . . . "The independence of Taiwan" means the start of war. . . . Although this is something undesirable for China, we have to face it. The Taiwan issue is the largest and the last obstacle which we must conquer in the Chinese people's path to rejuvenation in the 21st Century.[14]

From the PLA perspective, control of Taiwan would "rejuvenate" Chinese power by causing a geostrategic shift in China's favor. Far more important than the territorial or resource benefits to be gained, it would also give the PLA an "unsinkable aircraft carrier" astride the sea-lanes vital to the economic security of South Korea, Japan, Australia, India, and the Southeast Asian economies that depend on unhindered commerce. For sure, these sea-lanes are just as important to China's economy, and the PLA Navy (PLAN) could be almost as disruptive from its current bases. But Taiwan's East Coast offers one advantage not allowed by bases on the mainland: immediate access to deep-water patrol areas for nuclear ballistic missile submarines. The PLAN's new nuclear submarine base on Hainan Island is not optimal because it is in a confined sea.[15] Furthermore, missiles and bombers based on Taiwan are that much closer to U.S. forces on Guam, and they are far better placed to monitor and interdict Japanese and U.S. forces based in Japan, blocking their access to the South China Sea and beyond to the Persian Gulf. Without even turning Taiwan into a nuclear weapons base, China's mere control of Taiwan would serve to shift the geopolitical balance and would make military relationships that Beijing would oppose, such as with Washington, less desirable for its neighbors.

What likely deters the PLA and CCP leadership is their consideration of the cost of "taking" Taiwan, that is, their calculation of their raw military ability to do the job. This cost is related to their perception of Washington's willingness to fulfill long-standing indirect and stated assurances to defend Taiwan. The PLA's military superiority on the Taiwan Strait is increasing because of its accelerating buildup, examined more fully in Chapter 6, and because of Taiwan's

political stalemate, which blocked meaningful defense modernization investments from 2004 to 2007. A 2005 Japanese report noted that the PLA and CCP
leadership was sobered by its own estimates that the conquest of Taiwan would
cost 20,000 to 30,000 Chinese lives over the course of a twenty-seven-day
campaign.[16] This figure might assume continuous Taiwanese military resistance
but might not account for Taiwanese "retaliation." Either way it is unlikely the
PLA would get away with a brief campaign, as it would have to support an occupation garrison of hundreds of thousands for the balance of a generation, or until
the CCP could exterminate Taiwan's democratic aspirations, both literally and
politically, by bloody purges and years of indoctrination. There is also the issue
of the estimated one million Taiwanese who reside in China[17]—would they be
unaffected by a war against their compatriots?

Then there would be the possibility of having to also fight U.S. armed forces
and perhaps those of Japan. Although Washington ended its military alliance
with Taiwan in 1975 and switched its diplomatic recognition to Beijing at the
end of 1978, the U.S. Congress quickly passed the Taiwan Relations Act (TRA)
in April 1979, which states: "[T]he Congress finds that the enactment of this
Act is necessary—"

> (3) to make clear that the United States decision to establish diplomatic relations
> with the People's Republic of China rests upon the expectation that the future of
> Taiwan will be determined by peaceful means;
> (4) to consider any effort to determine the future of Taiwan by other than peaceful
> means, including by boycotts or embargoes, a threat to the peace and security of the
> Western Pacific area and of grave concern to the United States.

This language is commonly assumed to be a strong assurance, just short of a
treaty, that the United States will help defend Taiwan if the latter is attacked by
China. The United States sells Taiwan most of its "defensive" weapons and since
the late 1990s has increased its interaction with Taiwan's defense forces to aid
the transfer of new doctrines and tactics to advance the modernization of
Taiwan's armed forces. Washington is also upgrading its forces in the Asian
theater and increasing its forces on Guam, in part to deter a Chinese attack on
Taiwan. The Bush administration's mantra, repeated to Taiwan and China, is
that the United States will not accept any "unilateral changes" on the Taiwan
Strait. A conflict, whether the United States was on the winning or losing side,
would likely also result in Washington leading and enforcing a global economic
embargo against China. The 2005 Pentagon PLA Report noted, "Chinese leaders also calculate that a conflict over Taiwan involving the United States would
give rise to a long-term hostile relationship between the two nations—a result
that would not be in China's interest."[18]

While Chinese leaders often state they "cannot give up the use of force"
regarding Taiwan, they have also embarked on a multifaceted strategy that com-
bines political, economic, cultural, and psychological elements, first to prevent

Taiwan from declaring "de jure independence" and then to maneuver Taiwan into accepting "unification" with China over the long term.[19] China has encouraged significant Taiwanese investment in China and has tolerated a large Taiwanese trade surplus, both to calm popular fears among Taiwanese and to build supporters in Taiwan's business community. China has also worked hard to divide Taiwanese by appealing to the Kuomintang Party while isolating and refusing to talk to the Democratic Progressive Party (DPP)-led government. This outreach and the manipulation of thousands of individual actors are ultimately coordinated by the Taiwan Leading Group, within which the United Front Work Department plays a major role.

Perhaps the most important Chinese nonmilitary attack on Taiwan has been its constant battle to diminish U.S. strategic support for the island. Derecognition was followed by an attempt in the U.S.-China Joint Communiqué in August 1982 to have the United States commit to gradually reducing its arms sales to Taiwan, but then-president Ronald Reagan secretly assured Taiwan that if China became hostile, the United States would sell sufficient weapons. However, in 1998 President Clinton for the first time publicly stated that the United States "would not support" Taiwan's independence or Taiwanese membership in international organizations requiring "statehood." This new policy by Clinton would come to bedevil U.S.-Taiwan relations after the election in March 2000 of President Chen Shui-bian, a supporter of Taiwan's "independence." Chen's Democratic Progressive Party was committed to forging a separate Taiwanese identity apart from China and increasing Taiwan's diplomatic recognition. The old U.S. policy of the 1970s of "not recognizing" Taiwan would open the United States to pressure from Beijing.

Although Clinton was criticized by Republicans and other supporters of Taiwan for making this concession to Beijing, the Bush administration has taken them further. Bush began his term seeking to show strong support for Taiwan by offering an arms sales package in April 2001 consisting of four *Kidd*-class destroyers, twelve P-3C anti-submarine aircraft, eight conventional submarines, and Patriot PAC-3 missile interceptors—all systems the Clinton administration would not sell to Taiwan. But by 2004 the United States became deeply committed to wars in Iraq and Afghanistan. China saw this as an opportunity to put pressure on Bush over Taiwan, as China became slightly more helpful to the United States over the challenge of North Korea's nuclear weapons and the War on Terror. Following Chinese Premier Wen Jiabao's visit to Washington in December 2003, President Bush became increasingly critical of actions by President Chen perceived as altering the "status quo" in favor of "Independence." In prompting Bush, Beijing had succeeded in putting pressure on Washington to help rein in the "independence" tendencies of Taiwanese President Chen Shui-bian. By late 2007 a real conflict had erupted between Taipei and Washington over Chen's intention to press for a national referendum on whether "Taiwan," not the "Republic of China" should be admitted to the United Nations. It was a populist democratic issue for DPP supporters, but because Beijing and the Bush administration viewed it as a move toward a formal name change for Taiwan, it was interpreted by the Bush administration as a move to alter the status quo and led to public calls that Chen withdraw the referendum.[20] While the tiff did not threaten a rupture in Taipei-Washington relations, it did represent a new low point in that Washington and Beijing were on a parallel course in seeking to limit democratic expression in Taiwan.[21] The tiff also caused Washington in late 2007 to "refuse to consider" Taipei's request for sixty-six new F-16 fighters.[22]

At the close of 2007, tensions remained high. At the Asia Pacific Economic Cooperation (APEC) summit in Sydney, Australia, Hu Jintao "told President Bush that the next two years will be a highly dangerous period for the Taiwan issue."[23] Indeed, the balance of military power on the Taiwan Strait will increasingly favor the PLA until Taiwan can make substantial corrective improvements in its armed forces. In late August 2007 the PLA held a surprise combined arms exercise at a new Joint Forces training area on the Shandong Peninsula, an area north of Taiwan. Taiwan responded in mid-September with its own military exercises.

Following the U.S. House of Representatives Armed Services Committee trip to China to meet and tour PLA ships and facilities in late August 2007, committee chairman Representative Ike Skelton (D-IN) expressed his fears that China might attack Taiwan over the issue of the U.N. referendum in Taiwan. Skelton noted that an attack would stress U.S. capabilities, saying, "Right now, we've bitten off a lot in the Middle East. Our military, especially our Army and Marines, are stretched thin. We're on the verge of having a broken Army. To take on anything else would be very difficult."[24] While many might doubt that China would risk an attack on Taiwan in 2008, the year it hosts the politically vital Summer Olympics, the following year and afterward might produce a tide of national pride. If the United States were dissuaded or diverted, many in the PLA might assess they have an opportunity to attack.

Very little is known about how China would "rule" Taiwan. In a January 1995 speech former paramount leader Jiang Zemin offered Taiwan the following:

[Taiwan's] **social and economic** systems will not change. . . . As a special administrative region, Taiwan will exercise a high degree of autonomy and enjoy legislative and independent judicial power, including that of final adjudication. It may also retain its armed forces and administer its party, governmental and military systems by itself. The Central Government will not station troops or send administrative personnel there.[25]

Jiang's speech, however, does not offer any clear statement that Taiwan can keep its existing *political* system. One only has to look at the example of the "peaceful unification" with the Special Administrative Region of Hong Kong to note that the CCP has little desire to allow its citizens to implement a full representative democracy. While Britain managed to negotiate "autonomy" for Hong Kong for fifty years in its 1984 handover agreement, there is no guarantee that it will continue after 2047. By that time, Hong Kong might be wholly controlled from Beijing and lose its economic competitiveness vis-à-vis Shanghai. Should China have to forcibly invade Taiwan to effect "reunification," it can be expected that none of the 1995 Jiang promises would be allowed. Instead, there would be a harsh occupation featuring massive purges of independence and democracy activists, refugee flows to Japan and the Philippines, and a comprehensive national reeducation campaign. Finally, within a short time, Taiwan would be made a base for PLA strike aircraft, naval forces, nuclear missiles, and nuclear ballistic missile submarines.

Even if the United States were preoccupied with conflicts in Iraq and Afghanistan, it is likely that the United States and Japan would make some kind of military response, as well as a diplomatic and economic response, to an all-out PLA attack or invasion of Taiwan. As will be explored in Chapter 5, a U.S. move to help defend Taiwan would likely result in great loss of U.S. life at sea and in the air. Washington and Tokyo would also likely seek to organize punitive economic and financial embargoes on China, which it is not certain that Europe, Australia, or India would support for long. Key to easing the post–Taiwan War shock and hostility from the West, especially from the United States, would be to conclude the war as quickly and with as little violence as possible. This would be aided tremendously by complicit politicians in Taipei, but perhaps even more so by a catastrophe affecting the United States.

Proliferation

Should the horrific tragedy of a rogue nuclear terrorist attack occur in an American, Israeli, European, or even Chinese city, the victim state and the world would seek to identify and hunt down the perpetrators. There would be a first circle of suspects, perhaps terrorists linked to either a Sunni Muslim terrorist faction (possibly related to Osama bin Laden) or a radical terrorist Shiite faction with ties to Hezbollah and/or Iran. This would lead to a second circle of suspect sources for the nuclear device: Iran, Pakistan, North Korea, and, in the future, perhaps Syria, all of which have ties to terrorists. But when accounts are settled, due credit should be given to a third circle of countries: China and Russia.[26] Far exceeding what Russia has done, China has attempted to practice what John Mearsheimer termed "managed proliferation,"[27] hoping to use nuclear and missile exports to create power balances that protect its security interests. China also proliferates nuclear and missile technologies to undermine American security interests and those of its allies.[28] China's actions, however, have not created a new basis for stability but have instead created threats that could endanger its own people. By arming Pakistan, Iran, and North Korea with nuclear weapon and missile technologies, the CCP regime has lit several fuses of secondary proliferation that may eventually lead to tragedy. Tables 3.1 and 3.2 summarize China's nuclear and missile proliferation activities.

First Tier

China has proliferated nuclear and missile technologies to two tiers of states. The first tier (Table 3.1) consists of strategic partners that China has sought to

Table 3.1 China's Nuclear and Missile Proliferation Matrix: First-Tier "Strategic Partner" States

	Risk Profile	PRC Strategic Interests	Nuclear Weapon Technology	Nuclear Energy Technology	Missile Technology
Pakistan	Danger: secondary. Proliferation: very high. Nuclear weapon technology to Libya; nuclear technology to North Korea and Iran; unstable state	Counter India with indirect nuclear threat; undermine U.S. power in South Asia; be seen a nuclear benefactor to Sunni Muslim world; provide indirect aid to Saudi Arabia; SCO observer.	Direct aid: sold Pakistan 1960s' and 1980s' vintage nuclear bomb designs; provided engineering and material assistance with nuclear bomb manufacturing; key partner for A. Q. Khan.	Direct aid: one reactor sold; 12/06 agreement to explore selling up to six nuclear power reactors to Pakistan	Direct/indirect aid: sold Pakistan the means to make Shaheen 1 and Shaheen 2 solid fuel ballistic missiles; sold M-11 SRBMs; likely help with new Babur cruise missile; aided North Korean transfer of NK/PRC liquid fuel missiles and technology.
Iran	Danger: secondary. Proliferation: very high. Cruise missile tech to Hezbollah; weapons to Taliban; unstable state.	Attain greater influence in Shiite Muslim world; increase energy relations; undermine U.S. power in Middle East; SCO observer.	Direct/indirect aid: nuclear reprocessing technology; nuclear training; continued sale of precursors and dual-use technologies that contribute to weapons program; possible access to PRC nuclear weapon design from Pakistan; diplomatic protection.	Direct aid: small research reactors; uranium mining, uranium conversion, and possible uranium enrichment technology	Direct/indirect aid: Missile technology and training; cruise missile manufacturing technology sale; some PRC technology in North Korean Nodong/Shahab missiles; member, Asia Pacific Space Cooperation Organization.

| North Korea | Danger: secondary. Proliferation: very high. Threatens to transfer nuclear technology; ballistic missile technology to Pakistan, Iran, Syria; unstable state. | Keep Communist regime in power; undermine U.S. influence; create indirect threat to Japan. | Direct/indirect aid: training of nuclear scientists in 1970s; allowed Pakistan to transfer uranium reprocessing technology in the late 1990s; extensive diplomatic protection. | Direct aid: training of nuclear scientists in 1970s. | Direct/indirect aid: technical help with SCUD and Nodong missiles; aided staging on Taepodong; potential for solid fuel tech aid from Pakistan. |

use as "proxies" by building up their power to confront common enemies; this usually has the added bonus of enhancing China's stature with the common target state. China's nuclear aid to Pakistan extends back to the 1960s and followed India's nuclear program, which was in turn a response to China's nuclear program. By arming Pakistan with nuclear and then missile technologies, China fueled a South Asian arms race that redoubled India's intense preoccupation with Pakistan while "surrounding" India with hostile states. In addition, China gained great prestige in the larger Sunni Muslim world by providing them with "the bomb." Saudi Arabia is reportedly a major funder of Pakistan's nuclear and missile programs, and it likely expects to have access to them if needed. China has transferred at least two generations of nuclear weapon designs to Pakistan. China also aided Pakistan's ability to produce highly enriched uranium (HEU), which is the basis for uranium-based bombs. In this effort, China joined forces with A. Q. Khan, a nuclear engineer who helped start Pakistan's nuclear program when, in the 1970s, he stole the technology for Dutch centrifuges used to make HEU. Khan subsequently led the development of Pakistan's HEU-based weapons. China has also provided assistance with plutonium reprocessing.

To deliver its nuclear weapons, China sold Pakistan an estimated thirty-six M-11 short-range ballistic missiles, each of which could carry a small nuclear warhead. In 1993 the Clinton administration reluctantly sanctioned Chinese companies for this sale, but that did not stop China from training Pakistani engineers and transferring missile-manufacturing equipment to make the 700-km range Shaheen 1 and 1,500-km range Shaheen 2 solid-fuel ballistic missiles.[29] China was certainly party to Pakistan's trade of uranium reprocessing for North Korean Nodong missiles in the late 1990s, inasmuch as the Pakistan Air Force C-130s conducting this traffic had to refuel at Chinese airbases. Pakistan's 2005 development of its Babur land attack cruise missile (LACM) was also a cooperative effort in which A. Q. Khan organized the 2001 sale of Russian-designed Kh-55 LACMs in the Ukraine to China, Iran, and Pakistan. China is then believed to have developed the DH-10 LACM, a version of which became the Babur.[30] Pakistan's cruise missiles will likely benefit from China's future surveillance and navigation satellite networks. Pakistan is also a member of the Chinese-led Asia Pacific Space Cooperation Organization, and thus it could receive additional long-range missile technologies under the guise of space science cooperation.

North Korea

China's nuclear aid to North Korea extends back to the 1960s and 1970s. This aid was a product of Cold War competition with the Soviets and Beijing's desire to sustain its influence in Pyongyang. Whatever their differences, Korea's Kim regime has had strong and consistent support from the PLA. Today North Korea is a de facto nuclear state: in October 2006 it tested a nuclear weapon. In 2007 North Korea had an unknown number of plutonium- and uranium-based nuclear weapons. These are likely small enough to be fitted on North Korea's growing arsenal of long-range missiles, which eventually will be able to reach targets in the United States. A nuclear-armed North Korea serves to create a "proxy" threat against Japan, especially as it has moved closer to the United States following the end of the Cold War. But such a threat also helped to divide South Koreans and help accelerate a generational ambivalence toward their traditionally strong military alliance with the United States, steadily undermining its strength. South Koreans who are willing to make enormous sacrifices to live in "peace" with North Korea—including the current South Korean government of President Roh Moo Hyun—have also been willing to sacrifice their alliance with the United States.

China's record of enabling North Korea's nuclear capability outweighs its more recent efforts to rein them in. When the world became alarmed at North Korea's accumulating nuclear weapons potential in the early 1990s, China consistently opposed U.S. efforts to lead the United Nations to sanction North Korea for its refusal to allow international inspectors as stipulated by Pyongyang's joining the Nuclear Nonproliferation Treaty.[31] China's "protection" for Pyongyang continued as it became more belligerent, even after Pyongyang was discovered to have secretly created a secondary uranium bomb program to circumvent the plutonium bomb program the Clinton administration tried but failed to halt with its 1993 Agreed Framework. At their October 25, 2002, summit CCP leader Jiang Zemin told George W. Bush, "We are completely in the dark,"[32] apparently regarding North Korea's uranium weapon program; the United States had invalided the 1993 U.S.-North Korean "Agreed Framework" over this program just five days before. Jiang was surely dissembling, as China had allowed Pakistani Air Force C-130s to use Chinese bases for refueling and transit to trade North Korean missile cargo for Pakistani uranium reprocessing technology.[33] Furthermore, China provided discreet assistance to North Korea's Scud missile program. And during the 1990s China provided engineering training,[34] missile-making material,[35] and assistance to help Pyongyang develop and attach a solid-fuel third stage of its Taepodong IRBM,[36] assistance that would be useful in developing later ICBMs.

Following North Korea's provocative 2003 declaration that it had nuclear weapons, and then following the 2003 U.S. invasion of Iraq, China became nervous enough to become engaged. By 2004 China was helping to organize the Six-Party Talks, which the Bush administration has patiently continued in the hopes that China would help pressure North Korea to give up its nuclear weapons. After three years of ups and downs, on February 13, 2007, this process produced a North Korean agreement to "eliminate" its nuclear weapons and the capacity to produce them by the end of 2007. This process dragged on and was vociferously defended by the Bush administration principal negotiator, Ambassador Christopher Hill. At the end of August 2007, former U.S. Ambassador to the United Nations John Bolton wrote, "There is still simply no evidence that Pyongyang has made a decision to abandon its long-held strategic objective to have a credible nuclear-weapons capability."[37] By January 2008 North Korea had indeed reneged on finally ending its nuclear capabilities. Once again, the result of China's actions was to give North Korea vital time to build up its nuclear arsenal, as reports surfaced that it could be seeking to subcontract its nuclear weapons work to others.[38]

Iran

China has also been indispensible to Iran's nuclear and nuclear missile ambitions. This relationship has accelerated since the Iranian Revolution and the 1980–1988 Iran-Iraq war, when China came to sell weapons to both sides. China's provision of nuclear and missile assistance serves to ensure the survival of the radical Shiite regime, helping it stand up to its Sunni neighbors and to the United States, as it wages proxy conflicts against Israel and the United States through Hezbollah and other groups. For its part, China is Iran's largest trading partner and receives an increasing amount of Iran's petroleum resources. China's transfer of nuclear technology to Iran has included engineer training started in the mid-1980s; research reactors; possible assistance with large power reactors; and uranium mining, reprocessing, and possibly enrichment technology.[39] China is apparently not concerned that Iran is providing Chinese-made weapons to Hezbollah, which has been waging war against Israel, or that Iran has been aiding radical Shiite terrorists in Iraq and Afghanistan. There is a very real fear that once Iran is able to manufacture working nuclear weapons, it will give them to its allied terrorist network.[40]

Despite an October 1997 promise to Washington to halt its nuclear technology sales to Iran, there are continuing reports of such assistance. In 2005 the Iranian Council for National Resistance accused China of selling Iran beryllium (useful for nuclear triggers), maraging steel (twice as hard as stainless steel and critical for fabricating bomb casings), and centrifuges (to reprocess uranium into bomb-grade material).[41] China has also provided critical diplomatic cover to Tehran. In early 2006, as Iran was violating its last commitments to the Nuclear Nonproliferation Treaty and the United States was seeking to organize a reaction and sanctions through the UN Security Council, China was there to delay strong action and make sure they did not have teeth. The result is that by the end of 2007 both Israel and the United States, for reasons of punishing Iranian support for terrorists in Iraq, were looking more closely at options for military strikes to stop Iran's nuclear weapons program.

China is also a major direct and indirect source of missile technology for Iran. China has sold Iran missile-making materials, provided discreet assistance to produce some Scud-based missiles, and sold the means to make a range of tactical missiles from the C-802 anti-ship cruise missile and smaller. Iran's part in the 2001 A. Q. Khan purchase of Ukrainian/Russian Kh-55 LACMs raises the possibility of Chinese assistance in production of Iran's own LACM, reportedly named *Ghadr*.[42] Such missiles would give Iran or its terrorist allies the ability to conduct long-range missile strikes, perhaps against U.S. and European targets.

Furthermore, the PLA may be increasing direct cooperation with Iran's military forces. In 2005 the Commander of the Nanjing Military Region visited Iran.[43] This visit was important because of the Region's intense focus on building sophisticated defenses of the type Iran would need to repel air attacks by the United States and its allies.

Second-Tier States/Secondary Proliferation

China has also had a direct and indirect impact on the nuclear and missile ambitions of many other states: a second tier (Table 3.2). Some of these states, such as Saudi Arabia, are of critical importance to Chinese interests now. Were China to assist other states such as Brazil or Turkey, Beijing would gain a strategic partner in two strategically pivotal locations. Others including Egypt, Syria, and Bangladesh have long-standing relationships with China, but they also have nuclear weapon ambitions of their own. Some in this second tier have managed to advance their nuclear or missile ambitions via secondary proliferation of Chinese nuclear and/or missile technologies. Secondary proliferation has been advanced mainly by Pakistan's A. Q. Khan network and by North Korea. Khan sold China's initial nuclear bomb design, given to Pakistan in the 1980s, to Libya. When Libya turned over this document and, one hopes, the rest of its nuclear weapons effort to the United States in 2005, some sources reported that the Chinese bomb designs had penciled on them the names of the Chinese officials who either were involved in or who profited from the original sale to Pakistan. Did Libya share the bomb design with others, perhaps terrorists? It is not known.

In early September 2007 Israeli fighters bombed a site in Syria that had nuclear and/or missile related items shipped from North Korea. In late August 2007 former U.S. Ambassador to the United Nations John Bolton told the Wall Street Journal:

> We know that both Iran and Syria have long co-operated with North Korea on ballistic missile programmes and the prospect of co-operation on nuclear matters is not far-fetched. Whether and to what extent Iran, Syria or others might be "safe havens" for North Korea's nuclear weapons development, or may have already participated with or benefited from it, must be made clear.[44]

If these reports prove true, then North Korea, having benefitted from China's nuclear aid and protection, would be advancing China's interest in strengthening the Iran-Syria-Hezbollah axis' efforts to surround Israel and undermine U.S. influence in the Middle East. The world may be just starting to realize the dangers created by China's initial proliferation of nuclear and missile technologies to Pakistan, North Korea, and Iran. Through secondary proliferation of Chinese technologies between the members of the first tier and into the second tier, China's proliferation actions have made the highest

Table 3.2 China's Nuclear and Missile Proliferation Matrix: Second-Tier States

	Risk Profile	PRC Strategic Interests	Nuclear Weapon Technology	Nuclear Energy Technology	Missile Technology
Saudi Arabia	Danger of secondary proliferation: medium. Has nuclear missile ambitions; unstable state.	Assure access to Saudi petroleum; become eventual strategic guarantor to Saudi Royal Family.	Indirect aid: Saudis are believed to have access to PRC–aided Pakistani nuclear weapons if needed.		Direct/indirect aid: sale of DF-3 IRBMs in 1988; likely access to Pakistan's PRC-assisted nuclear missiles if desired.
Syria	Danger of secondary proliferation: high. Links to Hezbollah; nuclear weapon ambitions; unstable state.	Strengthening long-standing relationship with Syrian dictatorship; strengthening its ability to undermine U.S. influence.		Direct aid: by 2001 a small PRC-made research reactor was in operation. Indirect aid: possible centrifuge sale by A. Q. Khan.	Direct aid: attempts to sell M-9 missiles in 1990s. Indirect aid: NK missiles sold may have PRC technology; PRC and NK helping larger Iran-Syria missile production program.
Egypt	Danger of secondary proliferation: medium. Has nuclear weapon ambitions; unstable state.	Leader in Islamic world; military technical partner.		Direct Aid: 11/06 nuclear power cooperation agreement.	Indirect aid: may benefit from PRC tech in North Korean missiles sold to Egypt.
Bangladesh	Danger of secondary proliferation: medium. Islamist elements strong; some nuclear weapon ambitions.	Building influence in Dacca to help surround India with hostile states, aiding Beijing's leverage over Delhi.		Direct aid: 2005 Nuclear Cooperation Agreement; talk of a power reactor project; training for nuclear engineers.	Direct aid: sale of C-802 antiship cruise missiles.

Turkey	Danger of secondary proliferation: low.	Muslim country with great appeal to Chinese Uighurs; in NATO and may join EU.	Direct/indirect aid: mid-1990s sale of SRBM and artillery rocket manufacturing technology; possible interest in Pakistan/PRC cruise missile.
Brazil	Danger of secondary proliferation: low. Has latent nuclear weapon ambitions.	Latin American leading state; may diminish U.S. influence and divert U.S. attention if armed with strategic weapons.	Direct aid: reports of enriched uranium sale in 1984; Brazil requests nuclear energy cooperation with PRC in 2004, PRC response positive. Indirect aid: through the process of developing and launching four surveillance satellites, Brazil has likely increased its understanding of large missiles.

contribution to the possibility that terrorists will someday possess and use nuclear weapons.[45]

Irresponsibility Continues

China responded to increasing American complaints during the 1990s about its proliferation by gradually joining nonproliferation regimes and making halfway attempts to "adopt" (rather than join and enforce) international standards such as the Missile Technology Control Regime (MTCR). A 2005 Chinese white paper states, "China firmly opposes the proliferation of WMD and their means of delivery and has actively participated in international non-proliferation process."[46] But China's proliferation activities with radical countries continued despite continued U.S. entreaties. In July 2007 a Pentagon official stated, "[T]here remain serious gaps between China's official rhetoric and its achievements" on nonproliferation. Furthermore, he stated:

> We have repeatedly approached the PRC Government at all levels with our concerns about the activities of Chinese entities. We have provided specific instances and information about actual or potential transfers. China's mixed record of success in responding, particularly regarding entities and individuals that are serial proliferators, leads to questions about China's commitment to fully halt such proliferation activities.[47]

Furthermore, China refused to join the 2003 U.S.-led Proliferation Security Initiative, intended to create a global alliance of national enforcement agencies that would develop new rules to halt the spread of weapons of mass destruction. Instead, China played a key role in gutting a critical U.N. Security Council resolution that would have led to the creation of new rules to help prevent such proliferation.[48]

China's refusal to stem its current proliferation, not to mention reversing its previous proliferation or arresting the secondary proliferation it has enabled, raises the question whether China might actually believe it can profit from being the enabler of nuclear tragedies. Apparently, China's top leaders profit personally from their sale of nuclear and missile technology. Former Secretary of State James Baker related in his memoirs that China would not stop missile sales to Pakistan in the early 1990s because Chinese leaders gain a share of the profits.[49] To be sure, China has tried to cynically use U.S. fears of its proliferation activities to force concessions from Washington. During the controversy over China's sale of M-9 missiles to Pakistan in the 1990s, Beijing responded by trying to create a linkage to U.S. sales of advanced weapons to Taiwan.[50] More recently the Bush administration has had to directly deny Taiwanese fears that post-2003 U.S. criticism of Taiwan's "independence" tendencies was done in part to ensure China's help with North Korea's nuclear threats. Nuclear attacks in the United States might provide the kind of opportunity that PLA leaders need to take

Taiwan. Chinese leaders may believe they can avoid the same scourge, but China has its own challenge of growing pro-Islamist sympathies in Xinjiang. The forces of Islamist terror that would attack the West with nuclear weapons, if they could, might also someday attack China.

Friend of Other Dictatorships

An adjunct to China's active proliferation has been its embrace and increasing support for nondemocratic and antidemocratic regimes. While George W. Bush has stopped using the term "axis of evil," which he coined in his 2001 State of the Union address, China has become the chief ally of the countries that make up the "Axis of Evil": Cuba, North Korea, Iran, and Iraq (under Saddam Hussein).

China's support for Saddam Hussein rose to the level of barely covert military support, constituting an undeclared military campaign against the United States. In late 2002, as the Bush administration was preparing for its 2003 war to topple Saddam, a report emerged that revealed China's military aid for Saddam. It seems that the Bush administration had to tell China to remove its nationals who were helping Saddam to build fiber-optic communication links between Iraqi gun and missile antiaircraft sites for the purpose of improving their ability to conduct attacks against U.S. aircraft imposing a U.N. "no-fly zone." The Chinese company Huawei, which has close ties to the PLA, was doing this work for Saddam. The Bush administration did not want to bomb and kill the Chinese working for Saddam. Such an attack could prompt a repeat of China's vicious nationalist riots that ruined the U.S. Embassy in Beijing following the accidental bombing of the Chinese Embassy in Belgrade, Serbia, in 1999.

But according to one U.S. source, in 1999 the United States had to conduct at least a dozen bombing attacks against Chinese-built fiber-optic communication nodes in order to hinder Iraqi antiaircraft weapons targeting U.S. aircraft.[51] The source, who was close to this action at the time, described a deadly "cat and mouse game" in which China's role was apparently well known to the U.S. side. This source acknowledged that in addition to this direct aid to help Saddam withstand U.N. sanctions, China was also able to observe American military reactions and assess the strengths and weaknesses of U.S. intelligence operations. An understanding of how the United States can detect and respond to changes on the battlefield would be of particular interest to the PLA as it prepares for a possible war against Taiwan.

China's drive for ever-greater resources is also driving a "value-free" foreign policy in which Beijing is proud to let business trump principle. Because much of the world's petroleum is developed and exported by U.S. and other Western firms, China has had to aggressively seek alternative sources, and it has not been inhibited by the nature of the potential source regime. In addition to being a key nuclear and military partner for Iran, in 2006 China edged out Japan as Iran's largest trading partner. Iran accounts for 12 percent of China's oil imports and in late 2006 signed a $100 billion deal to develop Iran's oil fields. China buys

60 percent of Sudan's oil and has invested heavily in its oil industry. For both Iran and Sudan, petroleum revenues from China help sustain repressive regimes. In the Western Hemisphere, Venezuela's socialist strongman Hugo Chavez is trying to forge a deeper strategic partnership with China and devise ways to sell it more oil. In most cases China's effort to seal resource relationships with noxious regimes is aided by the sale of Chinese weapons. Sudan uses Chinese A-5 fighter-bombers and many other small arms to wage war on its minorities.

Undermining American Alliances

The PLA's not-so-casual offer to U.S. Commander in Chief Pacific Command (CINCPAC) Admiral Keating in June 2007 that "we'll take care of the Western Pacific, and we'll just communicate with each other" belies the PLA's post-Taiwan conquest agenda: dismantling the U.S.-led security network in Asia so that China can resume its place as the preeminent power in that region. This campaign is represented by China's long campaign against U.S.-led missile defenses in Asia, which has had notable success in South Korea, and China's efforts to create an alternate security structure in Southeast Asia.

Anti-missile Defense

In 1980 China apparently shelved its first anti-ballistic missile and ASAT program.[52] After nearly twenty years of effort, the program had yielded few successes, and Deng Xiaoping needed its budget for more important goals. However, President Ronald Reagan's 1983 announcement of the Strategic Defense Initiative of missile defenses led Deng to make two decisions. The first was to agree to recommendations of top Chinese scientists and weapons engineers to create the 863 Program of intensive basic high-technology research for military applications: this led to the SC-19 ASAT that was demonstrated in January 2007. There is a strong possibility that this demonstrated ASAT program is linked to an ongoing anti-ballistic missile (ABM) program (explored in Chapter 6). The second decision was to mount a political-diplomatic campaign against the "militarization" of outer space and against missile defenses. From the mid-1980s until the late 1990s there was little to no knowledge of China's early interest in ABM systems. But to say the least, from the mid-1990s[53] until the mid-2000s, Chinese diplomats and other officials have been vociferous in their opposition to American missile defense initiatives. They have also strongly criticized Japan and Australia for joining the United States in missile defense endeavors.

Chinese officials claim that missile "defense" is nothing but an excuse to secure an offensive advantage against China. This claim is spurious in that Japan, Australia, and Taiwan really have little to no capability to actually strike China. What these nations and their U.S. allies really seek is a defense against Chinese short- and medium-range ballistic missiles, and this is what truly threatens China's leaders. With missile defenses, China's ability to threaten Japan, Taiwan, or (perhaps in the future) India, diminishes. It is the loss of this "leverage of fear" which Chinese leaders themselves fear the most. The PLA also understands that missile defense is a transformative technology that helps those militaries to modernize in other important respects. And perhaps just as serious for China, missile defense provides a political justification for U.S. allies to continue their alliances with Washington. To their credit, successive Japanese, Australian, and Taiwanese governments have withstood China's pressure and threats. American-led missile defense is now advancing significantly with Japan, and tri-lateral cooperation with Australia may be possible. Taiwan has the U.S. Patriot PAC-2 and an indigenous missile interceptor, and after four years of political argument, it appears ready to buy better Patriot PAC-3 missile interceptors.

China has had better results with its efforts to undermine the strategic rela-tionship between the United States and the Republic of Korea (ROK). Seoul has become increasingly beholden to China's influence over Pyongyang to moderate Kim Chong Il's behavior and to China's increasing clout as a key trading part-ner. In addition, the government of Roh Moo Hyun (February 2003–February 2008) came to power with an anti-American nationalist predisposition that was also hostile toward Japan and sympathetic toward China. While Roh did agree to send contingents to help in Iraq and Afghanistan, he also bowed to national-ist pressures which have accelerated the U.S. military withdrawal from South Korea. A wild card, however, is China's dispute with South Korea over outcrop-pings in the East China Sea such as Suyan Rock, which inflame South Korean nationalist passions when China asserts its claims.[54]

China has had better luck using its increasing influence in Seoul to block U.S.-South Korean missile defense cooperation and to keep U.S. forces in South Korea from aiding Taiwan. In the late 1990s, amid fears of North Korea's drive to build nuclear weapons and its growing missile arsenal, South Korean diplomats would enumerate the reasons why they could not cooperate with the United States in the area of missile defense. After listing issues of cost and questionable utility given other North Korean threats such as its massive artillery, they would then note, "it will harm our relations with China."[55] In 2006 Seoul changed its posi-tion slightly by seeking to purchase used Patriot missiles with anti-missile capa-bility from Germany as a means of acquiring some degree of missile defense.[56] But Seoul has not elected to join the United States in a deep missile-defense rela-tionship to include joint research and tactical cooperation, as has Japan. This asymmetry is likely due to issues of cost, but it also likely includes a continued fear of offending China as well as resentment against the United States over its deepening strategic relationship with Japan.

South Korea's trajectory is to become even more estranged from Washington and Tokyo, and perhaps closer to Beijing. In early 2005 Roh stated, "We will not be embroiled in any conflict in Northeast Asia against our will. This is an absolutely firm principle we cannot yield under any circumstance." This was viewed at the time as his attempt to forbid U.S. forces in South Korea from going to Taiwan's assistance in the event of a Chinese attack.[57] The United States now bases seventy-two F-16s in Korea, which would be sorely needed in the event of a Chinese attack on Taiwan. Such moves serve to increase PLA confidence that it can attack Taiwan, further undermine U.S. confidence in its alliance with South Korea, and raise fear in Japan that it could face the twin threats of a belligerent South Korea and a Taiwan under Communist Chinese control. South Korea's military modernization, which includes large aircraft-carrying ships, Boeing F-15E medium weight fighter-bombers, AIP submarines, and (in the future) fifth-generation fighters, appears aimed as much at democratic Japan as at North Korea or China.

Southeast Asia

Southeast Asian states have traditionally been wary of China because of its imperial history, its support for revolutionary groups in the 1960s and then for the genocidal Khmer Rouge in Cambodia, its 1979 attack against Vietnam, and its gradual predation of the disputed territories of the South China Sea in the 1980s and 1990s. The last decade has seen a sea change in China's approach, but its goal of extending its dominance over Southeast Asia remains the same. China has used its increasing commercial impact on Southeast Asian economies and its ties to ethnic Chinese communities to greatly increase its influence. China's approach has been appealing compared to Washington's preoccupation with Islamic terrorism, a point of controversy in the largely Muslim states of Malaysia and Indonesia and in the Philippines. While Singapore, Thailand, and the Philippines do appreciate their adjusted post–Cold War military relationships with Washington, they, along with Malaysia and even Indonesia, are now willing to consider new military relationships with Beijing. Such a prospect would have been considered a distant one in the mid-1990s.

After taking the Paracel Islands from Vietnam in the waning days of the Vietnam War, and then taking several of their possessions in the Spratly group in 1988, Beijing has settled for alternating periods of "gab or grab," with its last overt move being the occupation of Mischief Reef about 150 miles off the Philippine island of Palawan in early 1995. Despite occasional police-level skirmishes that have seen shots fired by Chinese, Philippine, and Vietnamese patrol vessels, often targeted at fishermen, China has generally promoted joint development of ocean resources over assertions of sovereignty. Beijing has the luxury to do so now that it holds the commanding heights in the South China Sea. It has an airfield on Woody Island, which is adjacent to the South China Sea's main commercial sea-lane. Furthermore, its islets in the Spratly group have been steadily built up during this decade to include radar and electronic intelligence equipment, larger docking facilities, and helicopter pads.

At least one major reason for China's seemingly counterproductive campaign to assert control over the South China Sea started to become apparent in the early 2000s, when it became clear that Hainan Island would eventually host perhaps the PLA Navy's most important naval base, intended for its next-generation nuclear-powered ballistic missile submarines (SSBNs).[58] It is likely that the Paracel and Spratly bases will eventually serve as links in a chain of sensors to secure the South China Sea as a "bastion" for PLAN SSBN patrols. When this happens, China's tolerance of U.S. and Japanese naval activities in this region may diminish. One potential flashpoint may be Taiwan's Spratly possession of Itu Aba, on which the Chen government is planning to build an airfield. A PLA strike could mark the start of a more aggressive defense of its "territory." As the PLA looks to move SSBNs, nuclear-powered fast-attack submarines (SSNs), and future aircraft carriers to its new base in Hainan, few in Southeast Asia seem to remember that China in 1999 pledged to sign protocols to the 1995 Southeast Asian Nuclear Weapons Free Zone Treaty (SEANWFZT) that oblige it "not to use or threaten to use nuclear weapons within the Southeast Asia Nuclear Weapon-Free Zone." Washington traditionally has not recognized any of the competing claims to the South China Sea and has wisely decided not to sign protocols to the SEANWFZT.

As the PLA prepares to move nuclear forces into Southeast Asia it has also begun a charm campaign of military engagement, with the intention that this will lead to cooperative exercises and arms sales. Philippine Professor Renato Cruz De Castro has noted, "While the United States remains Southeast Asia's most important military actor, its power and influence are being gradually eroded by China's soft-power diplomacy and hard-power buildup."[59] In December 2005, with Malaysian inspiration, China helped form the East Asian Summit, for the purpose of creating a forum that excluded the United States. In the mid- to late 1990s the PLA began to increase its engagement of Southeast Asian counterparts, moving to a point in late 2005 where the PLA started to suggest that the PLA and militaries of the Association of Southeast Asian Nations (ASEAN) began multilateral military exercises. According to one source, Burma, the Philippines, and Malaysia were in favor, while Singapore, Indonesia, Vietnam, and Brunei were less enthusiastic.[60] Thailand, which had a long-standing close relationship with the PLA including army and naval weapon sales, held their first joint military exercise with the PLA in Guangzhou in July 2007.[61] China is also marketing major weapons: Type 071 LPDs and J-10 fighters to Malaysia, Type 039 submarines to Thailand, Z-9 helicopters to the Philippines, and possibly missiles to Indonesia.

While Beijing and many Southeast Asians would not like to view China's increasing military activity and presence as coming at the expense of U.S. influence, inevitably that will happen. One key indicator is their respective willingness to stand up to Beijing regarding Taiwan. Singapore has been under Chinese pressure to end its military training relationship with Taiwan. The Philippines, just to the south of Taiwan and a long-standing military treaty ally of Washington, would seem a likely active ally, but it probably will not be. Since the U.S. military departure from Philippine bases in 1992, Manila has shown little willingness to be as active a defense partner as Japan or Australia. In mid-2007 one recently retired top-level Philippine officer told this author there was "no chance" that the Philippines would offer strategic assistance in the event of a Chinese attack on Taiwan.

China's pressure also extends to the South Pacific, where it has been in competition with Taiwan for political recognition and has been seeking to winnow the deep and long-standing U.S.-Australian military alliance.[62] Australia has been a strong and dependable U.S. ally, joining the United States in the Korean, Vietnam, and both Iraq Wars. China has consistently opposed Australian cooperation with the United States in the area of missile defense, which has grown under the leadership of Prime Minister John Howard and was opposed early in the decade by the opposition Labor Party. Nevertheless in mid-2007 Australia was studying whether to join the deeper U.S.-Japan missile defense cooperative efforts.[63] China has had more success in scaring Australians away from cooperating with the United States under the ANZUS Treaty should China attack Taiwan. In early 2005 a visiting Chinese Foreign Ministry official publicly warned Australia not to assist the United States should there be a Taiwan War.[64] For its part, the United States has had to remind Australia that the ANZUS Treaty would oblige Australia to help in the event the United States is attacked in the event of a war over Taiwan. Nevertheless, China has become Australia's most important market for natural gas, iron ore, and other commodities, and China's growing economic power creates great pressure in Canberra to get along with the rising power. For the September 2007 APEC meeting Hu Jintao spent a week in Australia, receiving rave reviews, while President Bush only spent a day, having to return home to confront critical Iraq War issues.

Chinese pressure on America's defense network is only likely to increase as the PLA increases its overall power, especially its power-projection capabilities, into the next decade. China's isolation of Taiwan and its pressure on U.S. allies to stop missile defense cooperation and potential cooperation in the event of a Chinese attack on Taiwan are but the early phases of this effort. China's ensuring the survival of a nuclear-armed North Korea creates additional pressures. What China either does not expect, or believes it can overcome, is the arms race that will occur should American military leadership be trumped by either a successful conquest of Taiwan or a gradual erosion of Taiwan's independence over time. Japan and South Korea are both building large air-capable ships and both have space launch vehicles that could easily form the basis for intermediate range ballistic missiles. Furthermore, Japan, South Korea, and Australia have the technical ability to build nuclear weapons if they chose.[65] By undermining the Americans and hastening their potential exit from the region, China hopes to establish a new order, but they should not expect that Japan, India, and others would fall in line.

Securing Resources and Shaping Central Asia

China's growing dependence on foreign energy and commodity resources is becoming acute and has been driving its foreign policies. Such interdependence is thought by many to be a likely moderator of Chinese behavior, but this must be balanced by its "value-free" embrace of many dictatorial regimes in pursuit of resources, relationships that usually involve military aid. One critical Chinese enterprise has been the Shanghai Cooperation Organization, which since its inception in has increasingly taken on the character of a military alliance. Furthermore, as explained further in Chapter 5, China is building military capabilities that eventually may be able to protect or assert its access to critical distant resources.

In 2006 China imported about 45 percent of the total oil it consumed: this grew to 48 percent in July 2007[66] and could reach 50 percent by 2008.[67] One estimate notes this reliance on imported oil could grow to 62 percent by 2011[68] and another predicts 84-percent dependence by 2030.[69] Regarding natural gas, which is gaining favor because it yields less pollutants, it is estimated by 2010 that China will be importing 20 percent of its annual 100 billion cubic meters of natural gas consumption. This rate of consumption could double by 2020, at which time 50 percent would have to be imported.[70] Also increasing is China's dependence on foreign sources for the many commodities that sustain its economic growth. China is now the world's largest consumer of aluminum, copper, lead, nickel, tin, zinc, iron ore, coal, wheat, rice, palm oil, cotton, and rubber.[71] In a 2007 report the United Nations Conference on Trade and Development noted, "China is now the world's largest steel producer, steel consumer, steel exporter, iron ore importer and the second largest iron ore producer."[72] In 2006 China consumed 43 percent of global iron imports.[73] According to one Chinese expert, China's self-sufficiency ratio for corn could fall from 94.7 percent in 2000 to 74 percent in 2020, and for soybeans could fall from 46.1 percent to 20.6 percent over the same period.[74]

Surmounting the Malacca Dilemma

Eighty percent of China's imported oil passes through the Straits of Malacca, and the volume of petroleum that passes though this strait to China is only set to grow. For this reason, Beijing is taking an increasing interest in securing its passage and defending its critical sea-lanes to the Persian Gulf. According to a Singaporean official, Singapore and Malaysia are becoming favorably inclined to joint Malacca Strait naval patrols that include PLA Navy warships.[75] But China is also investing in port construction along the way, in Burma and in Gwadar, Pakistan, which may be able to host PLA Navy forces in the future. China is also building an airfield near Gwadar. Gwadar has been the location of attacks against Chinese engineers by Baluchistani separatists. There are currently plans to link Gwadar to Western China by rail and pipeline. In addition, China is interested in supporting pipelines from Burma and pipelines that cut across Malaysia to ease China's reliance on Malacca.

Shanghai Cooperation Organization

Securing energy sources and energy routes is also a main reason for China's creation of the Shanghai Cooperation Organization (SCO), which, in addition to the East Asia Summit, is the most ambitious Chinese project to create a security structure that excludes the United States. Extended from the "Shanghai Five" (China, Russia, Kazakhstan, Kyrgyzstan, and Tajikistan) with the addition of Uzbekistan in 2001, in 2004 and 2005 the Shanghai Cooperation Organization also included Mongolia, India, Pakistan, and Iran as "observers." Should the observers become full members, the SCO would then encompass the world's two largest armies and four (soon to be five) nuclear weapon states. Central Asia is rich in resources, especially oil and gas, and China is building pipelines there to ease its dependence on the Straits of Malacca. Economic cooperation is a high priority for the SCO, which may form a free-trade area in the future. The region is also vulnerable to the sway of radical Muslim ideologies.

While Russian and Chinese spokesmen have emphasized repeatedly that the SCO is not a "military alliance" or "directed" at any one country, it is obvious that its unstated mission is to make its region safe for authoritarian governments. The SCO Charter declares their opposition to "terrorism, separatism and extremism." "Extremism" is often interpreted to mean both Islamist radicalism and democracy. In July 2007 the SCO decided to organize a collective list of proscribed organizations, including deserving terrorists, but Western NGOs fear the list might also include democracy advocates. Then, on the eve of its major 2007 "Peace Mission" military exercise, at a Chief of Staff's conference in Urumqi, China, Russian Chief of the General Staff General Yuri Baluyevsky attacked "certain Western states" that advocate "the formation of the so-called 'true democratic' institutions of state and public management . . . which causes destabilization of the situation in the states of the region."[76] Russia and China share a fear of democratic movements such as the 2004–2005 "Orange Revolution" that advanced democracy in Ukraine. In May 2005 the Uzbekistan government suppressed a largely peaceful revolt that it blamed on Islamists.

The SCO's highest-profile accomplishment has been in the area of advancing military cooperation. In 2004 the SCO formed its Regional Anti-Terrorism Structure (RATS), but in 2005 it held it first major military exercise between Russia and China in the latter's Shandong Peninsula training area, and then in August 2007 it held a second exercise with all six SCO members in Russia. The 2005 exercise simulated air interdiction, naval blockade, and amphibious and airborne assault skills that the PLA would need to attack Taiwan. In 2007 China, for the first time, sent airborne, light mechanized armor and air forces long distances to Russia to practice skills needed to suppress a democratic revolution within one of the SCO member states.[77] Should Iran and Pakistan join the SCO, it is likely that both will also host major SCO-member exercises, which would assist the training of their armed forces. This anticipated mission is likely helping to justify the PLA's current investment in power-projection capabilities.

The SCO's growth into a full alliance, however, is not assured. In 2007 Russia tried to cosponsor the Peace Mission exercise with the Moscow-led Central States Treaty Organization, which China rejected. Chinese forces also had to deploy a far greater distance because Russian-leaning Kazakhstan did not allow the Chinese forces to pass through the country. Should the SCO make full members of all of its observers, its contradictions will increase. A nuclear-armed and terrorist-inclined Iran will embroil the organization in one direction, while a nuclear-armed Pakistan beset with Islamist internal insurrection could present the SCO with dangers whether or not it decided to intervene. China and Russia would like to attract India deeper into the SCO to pull it away from Washington's orbit, but India's raucous democratic politics will challenge any external suitor's designs. India, however, is hedging its bets by improving its strategic relations with the U.S. and Japan. In September 2007 twenty-five Indian, Australian, Japanese, Singaporean, and U.S. naval warships held exercises,[78] following former Japanese Prime Minister Abe Shinzo's late August call for an "arc of freedom" democratic alliance during a visit to Delhi.[79]

CHAPTER 4

CHINA'S MILITARY TRANSFORMATION

Chapter 1 outlined China's strategic challenges, and Chapter 2 explored how China's military supports the continuation of Chinese Communist Party rule. Chapter 3 also described how China's expanding strategic economic and security interests are putting China on a trajectory toward becoming a global military power. This chapter and the next will begin to examine the ongoing transformation of China's military capabilities. This chapter will examine the People's Liberation Army's (PLA) revolution in doctrine and operations, and Chapter 5 will examine the reform of China's high-technology and military-industrial sectors, and the PLA's embrace of the information revolution and its substantial progress toward waging wars under "informationized" conditions.

China's military growth and modernization is determined by the Communist Party leadership's interaction with the PLA, contingent upon the Party's determination of national priorities and budgetary constraints. The goals of PLA modernization are reflected in the PLA's military doctrine and then the "software" and "hardware" programs it undertakes to fulfill its doctrine. In a seemingly innocuous manner, the 2006 Defense White Paper describes People's Liberation Army modernization goals as follows:

> The first step is to lay a solid foundation by 2010, the second is to make major progress around 2020, and the third is to basically reach the strategic goal of building informationized armed forces and being capable of winning informationized wars by the mid-21st century. [1]

One might interpret this conception as meaning that China's leaders are not planning to build a military capable of *winning* wars against a modern military like that of the United States until 2050. But such a task would require not only a military with global reach, but also one that succeeds in developing and incorporating new generations of weapons technology far beyond today's concepts. It is also important to consider that China could gain military ascendance over most other countries well before 2050, which is already causing for deep disquiet in Asia. For example, in February 2007 Taiwanese President Chen Shui-bian stated, "This year, [China] will have the readiness to respond to an emergency military conflict. By 2010, it will be prepared to fight a large-scale war, and before 2015, it will achieve the decisive capability to win a war."[2]

It is perhaps more useful to view China's military modernization in the current era as having two basic phases. The first, lasting from the reign of Deng Xiaoping probably into the early 2010s, can be viewed as the "catch-up" period to prepare for large regional military contingencies, such as Taiwan and Korea, and to consolidate control over the South China Sea. The second period builds on the accomplishments of the first but is more tailored to the requirements of exercising global military influence. The beginning of the eleventh Five-Year Plan (2006–2010) marks a period of overlap. The PLA is not yet ready to decisively fight and win a Taiwan War, but it has gone far enough to begin leveraging its achievements to begin building extraregional military capabilities.

The decade of the 1990s proved pivotal for the PLA. It began the decade large and backward, making some mistakes, but it emerged from that decade with the beginning of fundamental reform in the two key areas that mattered: doctrine and its military-industrial sector. In addition, the PLA began to apply the lessons of the information revolution to meet its specific challenges. This decade has seen acceleration in PLA progress in all three areas. In addition, the PLA has undertaken large and painful personnel and structural changes. From 1985 to 2005 the PLA cut its numbers by 1.7 million men, including 170,000 officers. This cut was needed in part to pay for technical modernization but it also conformed to ongoing doctrinal changes that sought to take the PLA out of its era of manpower-intensive and defensive "People's War" doctrines.

In addition to large-scale personnel cutbacks, a second key driver for success in all three areas of transformation has been China rapid construction of a modern computer, software, communication, and broadband Internet infrastructure during the 1990s. The PLA played a key role in justifying, funding, and building this massive investment on China's part. With the help of Taiwanese investors and large companies such as IBM and Microsoft, China has become a world leader in computer and peripheral production and soon will be a world leader in software. The purchase of IBM's PC and laptop line by China's Lenovo in 2005 illustrates China's rise as a computer power. As of early 2001 the PRC had over one million kilometers of fiber optic cable, including 170,000 kilometers of long-distance fiber optic cable in nearly fifty trunk lines.[3] This means that China started this decade with one of the world's most modern broadband networks. The Chinese government has sought to control this network, not just to keep it from becoming a threat but also to exploit it to exert greater control over its citizens. For the PLA as well as for the military industry, access to modern computing power and advanced software has been a key enabler for their respective successes.

Revolution in Doctrine, Organization, and Missions

By early 1999, the end of the ninth Five-Year Plan, it was becoming apparent that the PLA had completed a new version of what in the West would be called its "Military Doctrine," or the principles that guide military operations, weapons procurement, structure, and training. The study of a country's military doctrine is crucial as it can go far to explain its strategic stance and the type of operations a country deems necessary, and thus the force structure it may seek. This can then be combined with assessments of actual military activities and equipment modernization to derive a more complete assessment. While many democracies, including the United States (through the Department of Defense), make basic doctrinal documents available to the public, there are no official Chinese military documents available to the public that definitively describe its military doctrine. These are viewed as classified information that cannot be revealed to foreigners. Conclusions about the evolution of China's military doctrine have been based on a large body of partial information that has included official Chinese government and military statements, PLA military academic books and journal articles, Chinese reports on exercises and military activities, and foreign interactions with Chinese military officials and scholars. But beginning in 1999, the PLA has published new military textbooks to assist with general education about its latest doctrinal evolution. These books have provided important insights into current PLA doctrine.[4]

Furthermore, China does not view the concept of "doctrine" in the Western sense, but divides this concept into "Operational Theory" and "Operational Practice," with the study of "Military Science" linking the two.[5] The PLA also views war as entailing three levels of conflict: wars, campaigns, and battles. These three levels are informed by strategy, campaign methods, and tactics, respectively.[6] In 1999 the new doctrine was concretized by the PLA in an official "New Generation Operations Regulation," which the PLA refers to as *gangyao*, or the highest-level operational and training guidance documents for campaigns. These *gangyao* are thought to have been issued for joint campaigns for the Army, Navy, Air Force, and Second Artillery, and for logistic operations.[7]

Active Defense to Preemptive Strike

China's primary operational strategy guideline is called "Active Defense," which stipulates, "China does not initiate wars or fight wars of aggression."[8] At the June 2007 Shangri-La Conference in Singapore, hosted by the International Institute for Strategic Studies, PLA Second Department Director (intelligence chief) Lt. General Zhang Qinsheng sought to reassure listeners by giving a standard statement of China's defensive policy: "Strategically we adhere to defence, self-defence and would win by striking only after the enemy has struck. China shall never fire the first shot. Such an approach is consistent with the ancient Chinese thought to use caution before getting into a war—use force only for a just cause, put people first, and cherish life."[9]

However, this is not what PLA officers are taught. The Pentagon noted that the PLA National Defense University textbook *The Science of Campaigns (Zhanyixue)* says, "the essence of [active defense] *is to take the initiative and to annihilate the enemy.*"[10] Another PLA NDU textbook, *The Science of Military Strategy*, notes, "Under high-tech conditions, for the defensive side, the strategy of gaining mastery by striking only after the enemy has struck does not mean waiting for the enemy's strike passively."[11] It then fundamentally transforms the definition of "first shot" by stating that if "hostile forces such as religious extremists, national separatists, and international terrorists challenged a country's sovereignty, it could be considered as 'firing the first shot' on the plane of politics and strategy."[12]

This, it would appear, provides an ongoing justification for a preemptive war, whether fought to hold on to such militarily occupied territories as Tibet and East Turkestan (Xinjiang)—it is striking that "religious extremists" are the first threat mentioned—or against the "separatists" in Taiwan. In 2007 the Pentagon concluded, "China's acquisition of power projection assets, including long-distance military communication systems, airborne command, control and communications aircraft, long-endurance submarines, unmanned combat aerial vehicles, and additional air-to-ground precision guided missiles indicate that the PLA is generating a greater capacity for military preemption."[13]

Prior to Deng Xiaoping the PLA's overarching operational strategy was known as "People's War" (Table 4.1). While often thought of as a defensive and largely guerrilla strategy, People's War envisioned a total war that was protracted in length, might have a nuclear component, and could include large offensive counterattacks as well as guerrilla operations. Key to "People's War," however, was the dedication to maintaining a large armed militia in addition to regular forces and the degree to which practically every community, economic unit, and company was given a role to play in a potential war. This aspect of "People's War" survives to inform later evolutions of PLA strategy; the militia, popular mobilization, and community mobilization, remain key components for future PLA military success.

By the mid-1980s Deng began putting his own stamp on strategy, which was given the moniker "Local War under Modern Conditions."[14] With the decline in threat from the Soviet Union, the scope of wars could be considered limited in duration and confined to regions "local" to China's territory. The main posture turned to one of "Active Defense," or striking first on the eve of an anticipated attack so as to achieve the momentum needed for victory. Until the mid- to late 1990s, however, there was little consideration of Joint Operations,

Table 4.1 Evolution of PLA Operational Doctrines and Strategies

Periods	Scale	Length	Posture	Dynamics	Manpower/ Technology	Arms/Services
Pre-1979: "People's War"	Early, total, nuclear war	Protracted	Defense-dominant	Mobile; lure the enemy in deep	Manpower-intensive, "inferior fighting superior"	Combination of regular and local militia
Post-1979: "Local War under Modern Conditions"	Major, total war	Less protracted	Defense-dominant	Positional defense of borders and cities	Less manpower-intensive	Combined arms (mainly ground forces)
Post-1985: "Local War under Modern Conditions"	Local war	"Quick battle, quick resolution"	Offensive: gain initiative by striking first	Mobile, forward deployment	"Elite forces and sharp arms"	Combined arms (mainly ground forces)
Post-1996: Local war under high-tech conditions	War zone campaign	"Quick battle, quick resolution"	Offensive-dominant	Mobile, forward deployment	Mechanized "elite forces and sharp arms"; "local and temporary superiority"	Joint services operations (Army, Air Force, Navy, Second Artillery)
Post-2002: Local war under informationized conditions	Campaign and battle	"Quick battle, quick resolution"	Offensive-dominant	Mobile power projection	Mechanized and informationized "elite forces and sharp arms"	Integrated joint operations

Source: Nan Li, "New Developments in PLA's Operational Doctrines and Strategies," in Nan Li, Eric McVadon, and Qinghong Wang, *China's Evolving Military Doctrine, Issues and Insights,* Pacific Forum CSIS, V.6, N. 20, December 2006, Honolulu, Hawaii, http://www.csis.org/media/csis/pubs/issuesinsights_v06n20.pdf. Used with permission.

a concept that was evolving in the West. The PLA was still very much an Army-dominated organization even though there was a sharp recognition of the need to modernize the PLA Air Force and Navy. During this period, under largely Army command, the PLA services would sometimes operate in "coordination," but real and deep "jointness" was not possible. The PLA's maneuvers versus Taiwan in 1995 and 1996 exposed some of the weaknesses of the PLA's strategic development. The PLA fired DF-15 missiles near Taiwan in July 1995 and March 1996, but not in rapid coordination with other weapons. The PLAAF's new Sukhoi Su-27 fighters were used to drop "dumb" munitions in a dangerous and exposed manner. The result was that Taiwanese and U.S. observers were not impressed.

In this decade (the 2000s) the major evolution in strategy and operations involves the shift from "Joint Operations" (JO) to "Integrated Joint Operations" (IJO) (Table 4.2). The PLA is beginning to incorporate the lessons learned from successive American campaigns during the 1990s and 2000s, and is beginning to realize the benefits of organizational change and the more widespread usage of information technologies. Whereas JO still placed emphasis on individual service divisions, and command chains were still largely vertical, IJO begins to accept that service divisions do not matter when command chains can be "flat" due to the leveling power of digital command, control, and sensor systems. Instead of units in individual services marching according to a plan, it is instead possible to allow groups of forces to achieve ad-hoc coordination based on the tactical needs of the moment. This is also made more possible by the PLA's development of new sensors on UAVs and aircraft, plus precision guided missiles and bombs; these tools give front-line officers the ability to call in limited but lethal strikes in a short period and produce near-immediate damage assessments to guide further decisions.

The degree of PLA success in meeting this level of integrated "jointness" cannot yet be determined from open sources. But the move toward IJO was reflected in the 2004 decision by the PLA to make the commanders of the Navy, Air Force, and Second Artillery permanent members of the Central Military Commission's high command. For a period of time, the main operational command General Staff Department included both a Navy and an Air Force deputy commander. Some evidence suggests the PLA is trying hard. In April 2007 there were reports of an experimental "army-air tactical corps," the Shenyang Military Region, led by a Group Army and the command post of the Shenyang Air Force, but involving officers from subordinate divisions and regiments.[15] It seems that real success would require even lower levels of intimate interservice cooperation.

It is likely that by the end of this decade the PLA will produce a new version of operational guidance to fit the new balance of strategy and technological capabilities. A key question to consider is whether this strategy will begin to reflect the PLA's growing capability to actually "project" power within and beyond its "local" regions. Will new guidance be required to conduct such

Table 4.2 Key Differences Between Joint Operations and Integrated Joint Operations

	Actor/Structure	Service Boundaries/ Identities	Coordination	Levels	Depth	Time	Effects
Joint operations	Individual service; vertical and tall	Clear	Plan-based	Campaign-level	Limited depth	Limited time	Unit
Integrated joint operations	Networked system; flat and short	Blurred	Action-based	All levels	All depth	All times	Systems

Source: Nan Li, "New Developments In PLA's Operational Doctrines and Strategies," in Nan Li, Eric McVadon, and Qinghong Wang, *China's Evolving Military Doctrine, Issues and Insights,* Pacific Forum CSIS, V6, N. 20, December 2006, Honolulu, Hawaii, http://www.csis.org/media/csis/pubs/issuesinsights_v06n20.pdf. Used with permission.

projection and to conduct operations at the destination? This could apply to space, air, and naval operations in addition to army operations. Furthermore, by that time will there be a new "space" service, equal to the others, that will demand its own attention in terms of operations and strategy?

Organization

While there has been some reporting in the past that the PLA was considering doing away with its long-standing seven Military Regions (MRs) as the basis for its organization, in favor of larger groupings reflecting strategic directions, this has not come to pass. The MR remains useful in terms of promoting some level of jointness. At the level of MR command, the Air Force and Navy have long held deputy command slots in the coastal Shenyang, Nanjing, and Guangzhou MRs. The MR is also proving a useful basis on which to promote greater joint training and joint logistics. Since the Logistic Reforms of 1998, when the PLA sought to divest the majority of its non-combat-related economic assets, there has been an added effort to seek greater efficiencies. Examples include combining functions across services such as hospitals, and a greater effort to contract out services such as food, laundry, and housing to the local economy.

During wartime, however, it appears that the principle strategic grouping will the War Zone, which could combine units from more than one MR and whose size and missions are determined by the campaign. It appears that the War Zone will be commanded by a member of the CMC.

Personnel

While the PLA is likely to remain a conscript-based military for many years to come, the PLA has also realized that it must attract increasing numbers of more highly educated troops in competition with a demanding civilian economy. In the less developed Western areas of China the PLA remains a great opportunity for advancement. The PLA uses appeals to patriotism, but increasingly it is also using higher pay and provision of greater job security. In the last decade the PLA has created a new Noncommissioned Officer (NCO) Corps, mainly to staff an increasing number of high-tech jobs, that provides higher pay rates and benefits. In 2006 the PLA started hiring contract civilian employees. The PLA has also placed great emphasis on "Professional Military Education" and is making greater education opportunities available to troops; for example, soldiers deployed to the far-off Spratly Islands can now take correspondence classes via broadband satellite links.

Training

The last decade has also seen a substantial improvement in military training. The 1996 joint-forces exercises intended to intimidate Taiwan were anything but "joint," and in some cases they demonstrated poor military performance. For example, modern Su-27 fighters were used to deliver "dumb" bombs in a way that would have exposed the planes to ground defenses, and operations were more "simultaneous" than "joint." The August 2005 Peace Mission joint-forces exercise with Russian forces on China's Shandong Peninsula provided a stunning contrast. The PLA conducted real joint exercises with a foreign armed force, encompassing air, sea, and ground operations. Peace Mission 2007, held August 9–17 of that year, proved even more ambitious. For the first time in its history the PLA transported 1,700 troops, airborne and train-transported armor, and nearly fifty combat and transport aircraft thousands of kilometers into Russia. These forces, in conjunction with a slightly larger Russian force and token contingents from the other members of the Shanghai Cooperation Organization (SCO), conducted combined land and air attack operations. It can now be expected that as the PLA acquires new large transport aircraft and new large amphibious assault ships, it will seek regular opportunities for more distant, even global, military exercises.

Training is now a huge business in the PLA, with all of the MRs having created areas for Joint Warfare training centers and dedicated "Tankmen" training centers. PLA exercises now stress increasing realism, especially fighting in adverse electronic environments, and make greater use of OPFOR and Aggressor units to increase realism. There has been an added emphasis on conducting difficult and complex amphibious assault exercises. All the PLA services make greater use of simulators to provide better combat training. The Air Force uses simple and advanced cockpit simulators, the Navy uses command deck simulators, and the Army uses simulators for tanks, man-launched SAMs, antitank missiles, and even soldier tactics. These have the advantage of being cheaper and allowing instructors to analyze performance in detail.

The PLA has even invested considerable resources to create modern "battle labs" that seek to give officers, and sometimes troops, experience in commanding campaigns or battles though use of simulated command posts and high-fidelity simulation. One Chinese report notes that after "several years" of development, the Second Artillery Command College created a battle lab described as follows:

> This massive battle lab group covers over 10 specializations such as strategic missile unit strategy, campaigns, tactics, command, training, engineering, communications, logistics, and equipment, and includes 43 laboratories with modern equipment. Within the lab group, a "three-dimensional battlefield" consisting of a battlefield observation module, a scene simulator, and a scene database reflects all of the important elements of the battlefield, such as the sky and sea, geography and terrain, and personnel and equipment. It can verify and assess the battle plans of a missile base and missile brigade or regiment, and can quantify and examine the results of battle and training methods. Here, students can experience what it's like to be on the scene themselves.[16]

Roles and Missions of PLA Services

As its doctrine and technology modernize, the roles and missions of the PLA services have expanded. Some missions are acknowledged in Chinese government documents such as the regular National Defense White Papers. Other potential roles and missions are not mentioned in the White Papers but can be examined based on other data. Inasmuch as there has been some discussion within the PLA about a future "Space Force," that concept is examined in this section. In addition the PLA's nuclear forces are assuming new missions as they become more capable.

Army

The 2006 Defense White Paper says, "The Army aims at moving from regional defense to trans-regional mobility, and improving its capabilities in air-ground integrated operations, long-distance maneuvers, rapid assaults, and special operations."[17] This description is indeed reflected in the organizational emphasis on decreasing the size of units from divisions to brigades, and at the same time upgrading their "mechanization" by increasing the number of trucks, tracks, and more recently, wheeled fighting vehicles. Armor systems are becoming more capable as artillery and air defenses are becoming more mobile. The PLA Army is also placing far greater emphasis on building up its Aviation Corps, Special Forces, and Information Warfare units. Although the 2006 White Paper makes unexplained mention of "long-distance maneuvers" it does not examine the relatively near-term potential for the PLA to develop long range airmobile power-projection units consisting of light but powerful armored vehicles which will be transported by new large Chinese-built airlifters. Airmobile Army projection will also be complemented by new naval power projection for Marine and Army amphibious units.

Navy

The 2006 Defense White Paper says, "The Navy aims at gradual extension of the strategic depth for offshore defensive operations and enhancing its capabilities in integrated maritime operations and nuclear counterattacks."[18] The big question the White Paper does not address is whether the PLA Navy (PLAN) is now planning for operations far beyond the "First Island Chain," now that its ambition to build aircraft carriers and long-range amphibious projection ships is being realized. The PLAN's emphasis on submarines remains for this decade, though its rapid development new classes of surface combatants during the tenth Five-Year Plan raises the prospect of further growth. In addition, the PLAN can be expected to simultaneously stress the development of "asymmetrical" capabilities such as new antiship ballistic missiles (ASBMs) and deepwater naval mines. The PLAN's potential acquisition of five to six new nuclear-powered ballistic missile submarines (SSBNs) solidifies its role in China's nuclear strategies.

Air Force

The 2006 White Paper says, "The Air Force aims at speeding up its transition from territorial air defense to both offensive and defensive operations, and increasing its capabilities in the areas of air strike, air and missile defense, early warning and reconnaissance, and strategic projection."[19] The 2004 White Paper noted: "Emphasis is placed on the development of new fighters, air defense and anti-missile weapons, and the means of information operations and automated command systems. Combined arms and multi-role aircraft combat training is intensified to improve the capabilities in operations such as air strikes, air defense, information counter-measures, early warning and reconnaissance, strategic mobility, and integrated support."[20]

This marks a great turn for a service that has been held politically suspect by the Communist Party because of its role in the Lin Biao coup attempt in 1971 and perhaps a February 1973 attempt against Deng Xiaoping. The PLA did not use its airpower during its attacks against India in 1962 or Vietnam in 1979.[21] However, in a future war it should be expected that the PLA would make extensive use of its new airpower, development of which was made a high priority beginning in the early 1990s. A mark of the rise in trust and prominence of the PLA Air Force (PLAAF) was that PLAAF General Xu Qiliang, Deputy Chief of the General Staff Department, was given the high-profile job of joint force commander for the deployed PLA units of Peace Mission 2007.

PLA Air Force officials have been glib about their new "offensive" posture which is made real by their acquisition of new fourth-generation multirole fighters. PLAAF doctrinal literature stresses coordination with missile and naval strikes. The PLAAF is also devoting considerable resources to the development of new fifth-generation combat aircraft and unmanned surveillance and combat aircraft, which could emerge in the next decade. The White Paper's mention of "missile defense" is new and unexplained, but later batches of PLAAF S-300 surface-to-air missiles (SAMs) are capable of antitactical ballistic missile defense, and the January 2007 antisatellite (ASAT) demonstration also demonstrates the PLA's potential to build strategic missile defenses. The PLAAF is now acquiring new bombers armed with land attack cruise missiles, developing a series of new Precision Guided Munitions (PGMs), and planning to build a new class of large transport aircraft, all of which will enable greater "strategic projection" in the future.

Second Artillery

Regarding the PLA's dedicated nuclear and non-nuclear missile forces, the 2006 White Paper says, "The Second Artillery Force aims at progressively improving its force structure of having both nuclear and conventional missiles, and raising its capabilities in strategic deterrence and conventional strike under conditions of informationization."[22] Indeed, the number of intercontinental ballistic missiles (ICBMs) is slated to grow this decade, but the PLA's number and variety of non-nuclear medium-range (MRBM) and short-range (SRBM) ballistic missiles and land attack cruise missiles (LACMs) may grow much faster. The Army, Navy, and Air Force will come to control an increasing number of long-range non-nuclear missiles, potentially creating organizational friction for the Second Artillery.

Nuclear Doctrine

At the end of 2006 China provided its most succinct statement of nuclear doctrine in its 2006 National Defense White Paper. It states:

> [China's] fundamental goal is to deter other countries from using or threatening to use nuclear weapons against China. China remains firmly committed to the policy of no first use of nuclear weapons at any time and under any circumstances. . . . China upholds the principles of counterattack in self-defense and limited development of nuclear weapons, and aims at building a lean and effective nuclear force capable of meeting national security needs. . . . China's nuclear force is under the direct command of the Central Military Commission. China exercises great restraint in developing its nuclear forces. It has never entered into and will never enter into a nuclear arms race with any other country.[23]

The December 2002 National Defense White Paper said much the same, though more directly:

> China consistently upholds the policy of no first use of nuclear weapons, and adopts an extremely restrained attitude toward the development of nuclear weapons. China has never participated in any nuclear arms race and never deployed nuclear weapons abroad. China's limited nuclear counterattack ability is entirely for deterrence against possible nuclear attacks by other countries.[24]

While China has repeatedly affirmed a "no first use" (NFU) policy regarding its nuclear weapons arsenal, there is good reason to believe that it seeks to promote an ambiguous stance about its nuclear doctrine in order to use its "limited" nuclear force to deter U.S. intervention should China attack Taiwan. A desire to sustain this ambiguity is likely a main reason behind General Zhu Chenghu's response to *Asian Wall Street Journal* editor Danny Gitting's July 2005 question about "possible Chinese tactics in the event of a conventional war over Taiwan." General Zhu stated: "If the Americans interfere into the conflict, if the Americans draw their missiles and precision-guided ammunition into the target zone on China's territory, I think we will have to respond with nuclear weapons." Gittings then said Zhu went on to say this could lead to the destruction of "hundreds of, or two hundreds" of American cities.[25] After these remarks were published on July 18, the Chinese Foreign Ministry issued a July 21, 2005, statement affirming its "no first use" policy regarding nuclear weapons. As China has never disclosed its true nuclear doctrine, Zhu's statement can be taken as a strong indication it contains elements that stress defensive "nuclear deterrence," but it might also envision the use of nuclear threats for blackmail and coercion.

In early 2008 additional Chinese statements cast further doubt regarding the sincerity of China's NFU pledge. Chai Yuqiu, a vice principal with the Nanjing Army Command College, told the *Ta Kung Pao* newspaper that China's no-first-use nuclear policy is not unlimited, saying, "The policy of not to use nuclear weapons first is not unlimited, without conditions, or without premises." Chai also noted, "China will never use nuclear weapons first, especially not to use nuclear weapons against non-nuclear countries. . . . When big powers equipped with nuclear arms disregard the completeness of sovereignty and territory of Chinese people and make frequent moves that are unconventional and hurt the fundamental interests of Chinese people, however, it is not impossible to break such a strategy on tactical issues."[26] Chai apparently confirmed General Zhu's 2005 threat that China will strike the United States with nuclear weapons if the United States intervenes to aid Taiwan against a Chinese military attack.

There is also reason to question whether China's dominant posture of "active defense" applies to nuclear forces, which would mean that China envisions a range of offensive to preemptive uses for its nuclear forces. In a passage concerning the use of nuclear weapons, *The Science of Military Strategy* states, "The strategy of striking only after the enemy has struck, never means taking a beating passively. The opportune moment should be seized to launch the nuclear counterattack at the earliest possible time."[27] This would justify strong doubts regarding China's "no first use" assurance. In 1996 then–Chinese arms control Ambassador Sha Zukang stated that "no first use" did not apply to Taiwan, which he considered "Chinese territory." While this statement was later retracted, the fact that the PLA may have some SRBMs with tactical nuclear warheads should justify concern that the PLA does indeed envision the use of nuclear strikes in the event of a campaign to conquer Taiwan.[28] In 2005 the Pentagon reported that "some PLA theorists" suggested using nuclear high-altitude electromagnetic-pulse attacks to "decapitate" Taiwan's leadership, believing that the United States would not view such as "crossing the nuclear threshold."[29]

The words "lean and effective" may be interpreted by some to mean "small" numbers of nuclear forces, but there is also reason to suspect that China could put multiple warheads on its newer ICBMs and submarine-launched ballistic missiles (SLBMs), which might allow the PLA to make exponential increases in the ability of a "small" nuclear force. The 2006 White Paper also makes no negative mention of "missile defenses," which in the past China has criticized vociferously, instead suggesting that missile defense might be an Air Force mission. The PLA's demonstration of a direct ascent ASAT in January 2007 raises the possibility that the PLA is simultaneously developing anti-ballistic missile (ABM) systems. Should they be developed, multiple warheads and ABMs would create great uncertainty around China's long-standing effort to promote a "defensive" nuclear strategy.

Potential Space Force

In the last decade, despite the Chinese government's high-profile efforts to ban weapons in outer space, the PLA has devoted resources to the strategic operations and technological development of space weapons.[30] Looking to the future, *The Science of Military Strategy* notes, "It seems that space warfare will be inevitable in future wars and that space offensive is likely to be a new strategic offensive pattern in the future."[31] It is also reported that Chinese military and legal scholars are examining the possible legal justifications for conducting military operations in outer space.[32] Therefore, it should not be surprising that the PLA may be considering the formation of a new service, a "Space Force," to handle military activities and operations in outer space. In 2004 a PLA officer disclosed to this author that there had been a debate within the PLA over which PLA service should dominate such a Space Force: the Air Force or the Second Artillery.[33]

Then in July 2006 the Hong Kong journal *Chien Shao* published an article, claimed to be based on PLA literature and sources, asserting that China has been secretly preparing a "space war experimental team" that could lead to the formation of a new service, a "Space Force" to be assembled from elements of the General Armament Department, the Space Agency, and the Second Artillery Corps. The Space Force might have 90,000 personnel and would be directly subordinate the Central Military Commission.[34] While the article makes clear the PLA did not yet have such a Space Force, it was actively studying the possibility. The article further noted that China's leaders "will accelerate the pace of space build-up and actively develop 'killer' weapons, including laser weapons, particle beam weapons, microwave pulse weapons, electromagnetic guided missiles, and antiradiation missiles."[35]

CHAPTER 5

MILITARY-TECHNICAL SECTOR TRANSFORMATION

Along with doctrinal and structural reforms in the PLA, the last fifteen years have seen enormous progress in overall investment, reform, and modernization of China's military-industrial sector. This chapter examines China's efforts to develop indigenous high technology, continually advance its capacity to produce advanced-technology weapons, and leverage advances from foreign military technology. The 1990s saw an intense effort in all three areas. Despite losing nearly three decades of advances due to the chaos of Mao's convulsive politics, by the middle of the first decade of this century, China was beginning to produce world-class weapons and starting to demonstrate high-technology military capabilities not even possessed by the United States.

The PRC government views its effort to promote broad high-technology research and innovation as a key to building the PRC's "comprehensive national power" into this century. It is fair to observe that the PRC's highest leadership is more personally involved in the creation of future technological break-throughs, and in ensuring their contribution to advanced military programs, than is the top government leadership of the United States. In 1997 the Chinese Communist Party formally codified its "Sixteen-Character Policy," which consists of the following components: (1) Combine the civil and the military; (2) Combine peace and war; (3) Give priority to military products; and (4) Let the civil support the military. Consistent with this policy, in mid-2000 *Xinhua* reported that Jiang Zemin said, "[The] war industry should be closely linked with other industries so that a vigorous national defense system based on science and technology can be formed."[1] By contrast, in the United States, technological innovation is led by the civilian sector and mainly serves the civilian economy. Military research benefits from U.S. government support and civil breakthroughs, but the national economy is not mobilized broadly to support military goals.

To promote military-technical advances the PRC has relied on programs such as the 863 Program, conceived in March 1986 to focus state investment in specific military and civil technologies. In part a reaction to the U.S. Strategic Defense Initiative and the European Eureka program,[2] the 863 Program targeted for development the key areas of space, lasers, automation, biotechnology, information systems, energy, and new materials. Significant products of the 863 Program have included space and airborne synthetic aperture radar, unmanned deep-diving submarines, unmanned microaircraft, gas-cooled nuclear reactors, space launch vehicles, and satellites. In 1995 the PRC started Project 909, a five-year plan to develop a world-class semiconductor industry.

The "Assassin's Mace" and High-Tech Weapons Efforts

Harnessing advanced military technology to attack a vital weakness in one's opponent is not a new concept, either to Chinese military strategy or to the strategies of other cultures. However, it is a long-standing practice in Chinese statecraft, going back thousands of years, to seek "trump card" or "assassin's mace" weapons against an enemy. Assassin's mace weapons are usually developed in secret from an unknown technology. They are used with surprise to attack a vital weakness of the enemy that helps precipitate his rapid defeat. Today the search for such weapons would be regarded as part of an "asymmetrical" strategy that seeks to build strengths to exploit the military weaknesses of an enemy.

The PLA's search for new assassin's mace weapons was given new impetus by former President Jiang Zemin. In the second half of 1999, in an undisclosed speech that was reported upon in *Liberation Army Daily* in early 2001, Jiang is reported to have called for the accelerated development of assassin's mace weapons.[3] It is possible that "Assassin's Mace" could also constitute a new PLA weapons development and acquisition program. The goal would be to find new weapons, using both low and high technology, that could be used with surprise to attack a vital weakness and accelerate Taiwan's defeat. Such weapons could be relatively simple, such as a novel type of naval mine, or very complex, such as a new supersonic missile that cannot be intercepted. However, Jiang could also be seeking weapons based on new technical principles that do not exist yet in other military forces. Such weapons would also help bring about an even more profound transformation in the PLA, as envisioned by the Revolution in Military Affairs (RMA).

The PLA has also spent a great deal of time and effort to determine the effects of high technology on military transformation. Key PRC military-intellectual institutions such as the Academy of Military Science, the PLA's National Defense University, and COSTIND are deeply analyzing the RMA and its implications for the PRC.[4] In an insightful 1988 study on future military competition, General Mi Zhenyu, former vice president of the Academy of Military Science, suggested that the PRC "plan[s] to be better, to be ahead of everyone," and noted how future militaries would rely on advances in information, stealth, and directed-energy weapons.[5] Some authors also understand that the RMA involves adoption of radical new operational concepts, such as "soft-kill" or "hard-kill" noncontact combat (described later in this chapter) that can take place at very long ranges and allows for very short chains of command. New forms of combat will include "battles" between computer networks, new forms of radiation that can disable electronics and equipment, and new robot combat systems.[6] For example, in January 2001 Major General Wang Hongguang, Commandant of the PLA Armored Forces Engineering Academy, stated:

> Extending our vision to the 21st Century, the extensive application of information technology, nano technology, new materials technology, new energy resources technology, and other high and new technologies will enable our army to be reborn. Operational space will become even wider, operational modes will become more varied, response time will become even quicker, actions will be more agile, and attacks will become more forceful. . . . All types of weapons systems and support and logistics systems will combine with the "information flow" to become one entity, implementing real coordination of high efficiency and accuracy, real-time attack and real-time support. . . . Electromagnetic artillery, kinetic bombs of high altitude and high speed, and smart weapons and high efficiency pulse weapons with laser and particle beam capabilities will through their unique capabilities release the operational capabilities and threat capacity of the ground forces. . . . The mass tactics of larger infantry operations will only remain in the people's memories.[7]

What follows is a descriptive list of major areas of PLA high-technology weapons development.

Lasers

China is developing military lasers for a range of applications, from weapons to radar and communications. Recent Chinese military technical literature may indicate the development of land-based and naval laser weapons.[8] Revelations in September 2006 that China had used ground-based high-power lasers against U.S. satellites focused new attention on the threat of Chinese laser weapons. But the U.S. intelligence sector had been providing warnings for years. In the 2000 Report to the Congress on PLA modernization, the U.S. Department of Defense noted, "China already may possess the capability to damage, under specific conditions, optical sensors on satellites that are very vulnerable to damage by lasers. Beijing also may have acquired high-energy laser equipment and technical assistance, which probably could be used in the development of ground-based ASAT [antisatellite] weapons. Given China's current level of interest in laser technology, Beijing probably could develop a weapon that could destroy satellites in the future."[9] The 2002 Department of Defense PLA Report stated, "China reportedly is focusing its laser weapon development on antipersonnel, counter-precision guided munitions air defense, and ASAT roles."[10]

China has invested heavily in its own laser programs but may also benefit from foreign technology. China has recruited Russian laser technicians, and Chinese engineers appear to be familiar with current U.S. military laser developments and with the potential for lasers to destroy or disable targets.[11] In the next decade it is possible that the PLA will field new laser weapons for antiair and ground attack missions. Lasers could arm unmanned aerial vehicles (UAVs) and satellites as well. In addition China is likely developing laser radar,[12] or "ladar," which can illuminate targets in most weather conditions; it is also developing lasers for communications, such as for submarines.[13] An unconfirmed report from 2003 noted that the PLA might have already deployed a "laser cannon" for tactical missions.[14] In early 2008 a popular Chinese military Web site suggested that basing a laser on the Moon might overcome the atmospheric distortion Earth-based lasers would face in attacking enemy satellites.[15]

Radio Frequency Weapons

In 2004 a U.S. source disclosed to this author that the PLA was nearing the deployment of a new non-nuclear Electromagnetic Pulse (EMP) warhead on a short-range ballistic missile (SRBM); this deployment was confirmed by Taiwanese sources in late 2005 and mid-2007. This is very likely a High-Power Microwave (HPM) warhead fitted to a new version of the DF-15 SRBM. The PLA is developing a family of Radio Frequency (RF) weapons including EMP and HPM as key future weapons for information warfare. These weapons all seek to use or direct a form of radiation for use in degrading or destroying microcircuits, computers, radar and other sensors, communications networks, and other electronic systems, and they are among the most highly sought-after weapons for information warfare.[16] According to one PLA analyst, EMP weapons can be used to disable an aircraft carrier. He notes, "The strong magnetic field and electromagnetic pulse caused by an explosion can destroy all important integrated circuits and IC chips . . . thus paralyzing the radar and telecommunications system of the aircraft carrier and vessels around it as well as the ship-mounted missiles and aircraft."[17]

HPM weapons have the potential to produce the same effect as EMP but without the need for a nuclear explosion. HPM also has advantages in that many counter-EMP measures do not work against HPM devices.[18] As such, they offer the means to decisively disrupt enemy forces. If miniaturized, they can be reduced to the size of an artillery shell or missile warhead. It might also be possible to develop HPM weapons that combine the functions of a radar and a weapon, capable of increasing their power output as they approach a target. RF weapons are able to direct electronic radiation at a target but at much shorter ranges.[19] Since the mid-1970s, China has sought to develop HPM weapons under the direction of an engineer who received his degree from Berkeley.[20] A 1996 PRC conference on electronic warfare stressed the need for the PRC to develop HPM weapons and defenses against them.[21] The PRC may be developing a missile that uses a burst of RF energy to disable an incoming missile or aircraft[22] and is reported to have a "radio-flash" HPM bomb for use by the PLA Air Force (PLAAF).[23]

Thermobaric Weapons

The PLA has developed a range of thermobaric weapons, which destroy by generating heat and pressure. One main advantage is their ability to create a large explosive effect for their size. Fuel-air explosives (FAEs) are one kind of thermobaric weapon. FAEs are usually missile warheads or bombs that create a cloud of atomized fuel, which is then ignited to create a great amount of heat and pressure. In the late 1990s a failed attempt at theft led the PLA to co-produce the Russian Instrument Design Bureau Shmel ("Bumblebee") shoulder-fired FAE rocket. One rocket can destroy a small house. At the 2001 IDEX show in Dubai, Russian sources relayed that Russia was helping the PRC to develop thermobaric warheads for artillery rockets.[24] China is known to have FAE bombs for aircraft and FAE warheads for its artillery rockets and SRBMs. At the 2007 IDEX show China revealed a thermobaric round for the ubiquitous Russian-designed Rocket-Propelled Grenade (RPG), which raises the possibility of it being co-produced by Iran and then being transferred to terrorist groups.

Hypersonic Vehicles

Like the United States,[25] Russia, and others, the PLA is seeking to develop hypersonic strike vehicles. These vehicles can also serve as low-earth orbit launch vehicles and could be considered the successor to the strategic bomber and intercontinental ballistic missile (ICBM).[26] The PLA has similar goals for its hypersonic research program, which has been ongoing for decades.[27] There are indications this research has included design of hypersonic vehicles and the potential military uses of hypersonic vehicles.[28] China has built a Hypersonic Propulsion Test Facility in Beijing featuring a wind tunnel that can generate velocities up to Mach 5.6.[29] For the PLA, access to Russian technology may provide shortcuts to building its own hypersonic research and development capability. At the 1997 Moscow Air Show, former Central Military Commission (CMC) Vice Chairman General Liu Huaqing was shown in *PLA Pictoral* to be viewing the Russian Raduga hypersonic test engine display.[30] This engine was designed for speeds up to Mach 6.5.[31] In early 2001 a Russian report noted that China was negotiating to contribute to a novel hypersonic suborbital program of the Leninets Holding Company called AYAKS.[32] Leninets officials at the 2001 Moscow Air Show confirmed China's interest. AYAKS proposed a novel kerosene-fueled "magnetoplasmochemical" engine that would allow the vehicle to travel from Russia to the United States in 1.6 hours.[33] In early 2007 a French report suggested that China had tested a scramjet-powered hypersonic test vehicle in late 2006.[34] Then in December 2007, Chinese Internet imagery appeared to show a model of a possible hypersonic test vehicle, having a missile shape with long tapered delta wings.[35]

Unmanned Combat Vehicles

Like the United States, the PLA is developing a range of airborne unmanned aircraft (UAV, UCAV), unmanned ship and underwater vehicles (USV, UUV), and unmanned ground combat vehicles. The PLA produced several versions of the U.S. 1960s *Firebee* drone captured during the Vietnam War. South Africa and Russia are potential sources for new UAV and UCAV technology. A South African–Chinese joint venture marketed South African target drones and UCAV concepts at the 2006 Zhuhai Air Show. Russia's revelation in mid-2007 that the MiG and Sukhoi corporations are working on subsonic attack UCAVs[36] may yield cooperative programs with China. Taiwanese sources have long been concerned that the PLA has converted about 200 older J-6 fighters to serve as unmanned combat aircraft.[37]

At successive Zhuhai air shows since 1996, the PLA has unveiled ever more sophisticated UAVs and UCAVs. At the 2006 show Chengdu unveiled a concept turbofan-powered surveillance UAV about the same size and shape as the U.S. Northrop-Grumman Global Hawk large surveillance UAV; at the same show, the Guizhou Aircraft Corporation unveiled its box-wing Soar Dragon turbofan-powered surveillance UAV. The Shenyang Aircraft Corporation also unveiled its concept supersonic Dark Sword unmanned air combat vehicle, but in three display opportunities in 2006 and 2007, it has revealed almost nothing about this program. However, there is one report that South Africa's Denel may be involved in the Dark Sword project.[38] The Zhuhai show also saw China reveal a ducted-fan hovering UAV for advanced Army surveillance, similar in size to ducted-fan UAVs being considered for the U.S. Army Future Combat System.

The 2006 Zhuhai show also revealed a new unmanned patrol/surveillance boat that a wall poster described as useful for "long-distance reconnaissance, communication relay, electronic interference, sea monitor, target strike, target damage assessment . . . as well as submarine mines search and anti-submarine combat." As part of the 863 Program, China has developed unmanned underwater vehicles (UUVs).[39] In 1997 the PRC revealed a UUV featuring artificial intelligence and automatic controls that reach depths of 6,000 meters. This UUV was developed with assistance from Russia.[40] In early 2007 Chinese television showed a PLA Navy minesweeper using a UUV for countermine operations.

Regarding unmanned vehicles for ground combat use, the PLA has revealed that it has conducted experiments with controlling multiple unmanned armored personnel carriers. This could be an indication that the PLA is investigating their use for combat support or even combat missions. At the Beijing Military Museum's PLA Eightieth Anniversary display in August 2007, the PLA also revealed a new tracked combat robot similar to several models used by the U.S. and European armed forces. The PLA's tracked vehicle was equipped to climb stairs and had two weapon stations.

Electromagnetic Weapons

A type of weapon often associated with the RMA, electromagnetic guns use magnets, or a combination of magnets and chemical propellants, to give projectiles speed and range far greater than is possible with chemical propellants alone. Electromagnetic guns offer the potential to give high fire rates to artillery-size projectiles along with the range and speed of a short-range ballistic missile, and thus they can be used for missile defense as well as strike missions. The PLA is known to have a great interest in electromagnetic guns and is researching several systems, including electromagnetic guns and combined chemical and electromagnetic ("electro-thermal") guns.[41] One 2007 report notes that China has "set up no fewer than 22 research institutes studying various aspects of electromagnetic launch (EML)."[42] This report also notes that at the Thirteenth International Electromagnetic Launch Symposium, held in May 2006 in Potsdam, Germany, the Chinese accounted for fifty-two papers, second only to the United States, which had seventy-two.[43]

The PLA is also working on applications for electromagnetic weapons. In 1996 PRC analyst Ch'en Huan noted that electromagnetic guns would be useful for space warfare.[44] A 2001 Hong Kong report noted that the PRC has been developing an "ultra-speed dynamic electric gun," or electromagnetic gun, since about 1983.[45] At least one Chinese document indicates that China began testing rail-gun systems back in 1986.[46] Although the Hong Kong report said such a weapon would be available "soon," as of early 2008 there has been no open-source confirmation that they are in PLA service. The 2001 article also noted, "There are plans to adopt them as part of the weaponry of space combat services which are being planned but have yet to be formally established."[47] In early 2008 an Asian source disclosed to this author that China was making progress not just in developing rail guns, but also in developing their hypersonic speed projectiles, which must withstand enormous stress. China is also reportedly developing electromagnetic plate armor: armor plates that can be electromagnetically fired into oncoming shells or missiles to protect armored vehicles.[48]

Nano Materials and Machines

The PLA is investing heavily in nanotechnology and appears to understand that this is a key transformational military technology. A 2005 Chinese report noted that China was investing about $100 million in nanotechnology research and had at least 100 nanotechnology-related programs employing 3,000 engineers.[49] A 2006 Chinese article lists seven military applications for nanotechnology, including potential nanodiscs with a "million times" the storage of current computers, nanotube structures "100 times stronger than steel," the ability to make "genetic weapons," superthin stealth radar-absorbing coatings, microweapons, nanosatellites, and soldier equipment such as armor cloth and laser-protection head gear. This author notes that nanotechnology will even impact operational methods:

> The entry of "nano army corps" onto the battlefield will intensify the struggle for reconnaissance and counter-reconnaissance, complicate the struggle for stealth and counter-stealth, and the struggle between sabotage and counter-sabotage will become more intense. The big combining with the small and the small consuming the big will become the new combat style. A brand new combat style and method will produce brand new combat theories. The brand new combat theories of "stealth surprise attack OPS," "micro vital point OPS," "concealed paralysis OPS," and "nano-deterrence OPS" will emerge in an endless stream.[50]

The PLA has already made some progress toward nanoweapons. In the mid-1990s Major General Sun Bailin suggested that in the future U.S. military equipment would be vulnerable to attack by armies of sound-energy-powered "ant robots."[51] At an exhibit of achievements of the 863 Program in early 2001, the PRC put on display a picture of a microhelicopter about 20 mm in length with an electromagnetic motor 2 mm in diameter.[52] General Sun also mentioned "blood vessel submarines" capable of finding diseases or fighting them.[53] The same 863 Program exhibition also featured mini robots for internal medical inspection of humans.

Biotechnical Weapons

Biotechnology was a major element of the 863 Program, though advertised accomplishments focus on genetic engineering to produce better crops and combat human disease. While little is written in the PRC about the issue of biotechnical weapons, one article in the July 2000 issue of the PRC magazine *Science Times* advised, "People with breadth of vision consider that biochemical [weapons] are an important deterrent force and they will be even more fearsome than atomic bombs in future wars."[54] It is at least possible that the PLA is conducting research in this area inasmuch as the United States is identified researching military applications for this class of technologies as well. The Chinese writers identified several possible military biotechnical applications. Bioelectronic equipment such as protein-based computers could have capabilities "several hundred million times higher" than existing computers and be similar to human brains while being immune to electromagnetic weapons. Biological bombs could result in explosives "3–6" times the power of conventional explosives. Bionavigation, such as exists in birds, could be applied to microweapons. Bioenergy sources could conceivably use chemicals to produce hydrogen, which can be combined with small amounts of petroleum fuel to give long-range capability to equipment. Bionic power could replicate the strength of human muscles. The article also notes that bioengineering can be used to create "fighting animal soldiers" or even "artificial people."[55]

Stealth and Counterstealth

In the early 1990s Chinese expert Cao Benyi stated, "[I]t is necessary for China to make every effort to develop stealth technology, to develop stealth, and to do what is necessary to enable China's stealth technology to catch up with the world's most advanced level of such technology in a short time."[56] At the 1998 Zhuhai Air Show the Chinese company Seek Optics revealed its work on coatings designed to deflect radar energy, and on computer programs for aiding the design of stealthy objects. The PLA Navy's new *Luyang* guided-missile destroyers (DDGs), Type 054 guided-missile frigates (FFGs), and *Houbei*-class fast-attack craft (FACs) use stealth shaping and stealth coatings. The Pentagon estimated the PLA would have a stealthy cruise missile operational by 2003.[57] And at the 2006 Zhuhai show an AVIC-1 calendar showed what might be the first image of an experimental Chinese stealth fighter-bomber. China's future fifth-generation multirole combat aircraft is also expected to make extensive use of stealth technology.

An early 2008 review of Chinese military technical literature indicates the likelihood of substantial Chinese research regarding stealth materials, stealth shaping, and stealth for turbfan engines. This literature may also indicate a substantial Chinese interest in "Plasma Stealth" technology,[58] in which a field of charged plasma particles (plasma) absorbs radar signals, greatly reducing the requirement for radical stealth shaping for aircraft. Russia's Keldysh Institute had pioneered research on this technology, but it has not been reported to have yielded a useful stealth system.

Due to the critical importance of stealth for future U.S. combat platforms, it is expected that China would also devote considerable energy to the development of counterstealth technology. China used former Northrop Grumman engineer Noshir Gowadia to learn some of the stealth secrets he helped develop for the Northrop Grumman B-2 stealth bomber. At the 2005 IDEX show China revealed a three-element "passive radar" detection system, similar to the Ukrainian Kolchuga, that is able to detect, locate, and identify almost all electronic emissions of concern. At the 1998 Zhuhai show the 23rd Institute of the China Aerospace Company was marketing their J-231 metric-wave radar, which its claimed had "high anti-stealth" capability.[59] Metric wave radar technology dates back to the 1930s and uses large-frequency radio wavelengths, whereas most passive stealth technology is designed to counter the far smaller wavelengths of modern radar. When combined with modern computers, metric-wave technology has great counterstealth potential. In fact, at the 2001 Moscow Air Show a Russian company marketing this type of improved metric-wave radar complained bitterly that China had stolen its technology.[60]

Supercavitating Underwater Weapons

Supercavitating underwater weapons move through water at very high velocities, sometimes faster than sound. They are able to move so quickly because they form an air bubble, or cavitation, around the structure. Once launched, there is little defense against such high-speed underwater weapons. They are envisioned for use as torpedoes, antitorpedoes, antimines, or missiles that travel underwater and then air-launch near the shore to defeat antimissile defenses.[61] Russia is the leader in supercavitation technology and in 1977 fielded the *Shkval* (Squall) rocket torpedo, which can achieve speeds up to 200 knots, or 100 meters per second (230 mph), through water. An advanced version of the *Shkval* is reportedly capable of 300-knot speeds.[62] In August 1998 the PRC was reported to have purchased forty *Shkval* rocket torpedoes from Kazakhstan.[63] This could indicate that the PLA also has programs underway to develop supercavitating underwater weapons. A source in Taiwan noted that the PLA was using these weapons to aid the development of its own supercavitating weapons that might have been in testing at the time.[64]

Leveraging Foreign Weapons and Technology

Since its inception the PLA has relied on waves of foreign weapons inputs, mainly from the former Soviet Union and Russia, even though it has been loath to depend on foreign weapons due to their unreliable availability. The former Soviet Union was generous with army, air force, and naval systems through the 1950s, until the supply was cut off following the Sino-Soviet split of the early 1960s. But this connection was resumed with a vengeance after the 1989 Tiananmen Massacre. Russian technology, ironically, supplanted European and American technologies that were made available to cement anti-Soviet cooperation during the 1980s, but this cooperation abruptly ended following the 1989 Tiananmen Massacre. Israeli weapons and technology began flowing to the PLA in the late 1970s until cut off by intense pressure from Washington after 2000. In many cases the PLA has taken a chance and created a foreign dependency

PLA backwardness and demand plus Russian economic desperation in the early 1990s served to accelerate PLA purchases, which became even more substantial following the 1995–1996 confrontation over Taiwan. Instead of seeking marginal gains from foreign weapons purchases, the PLA took the risk of relying on very large foreign weapons purchases to achieve near-term growth in capabilities. The 2002 order of eight new Russian Kilo submarines is a case in point. With this order, the PLA sought to exceed the 2001 U.S. intention to sell Taiwan eight new submarines by making sure Russia actually delivered, whereas the U.S. prospects for delivery remain unclear as of mid-2008. But this purchase increased by 200 percent the number of Kilos slated for the PLA Navy. Likewise, the purchase of nearly 1000 "triple-digit" S-300 surface-to-air missiles gives the PLA a formidable air defense capability that will be hard for even U.S. air forces to overcome. Wholesale purchases that are being used to seek major advances in capability are listed in Table 5.1.

China's sustained economic growth and sustained military spending have made it possible for the PLA to sustain its arms-buying binge. The main recipient

Table 5.1 Major PLA Weapons Purchase Packages Since 1990

300+ Sukhoi fighters by 2007, many upgraded for multirole missions

Thousands of Russian antiair and precision ground-attack weapons for aircraft

Twenty Russian Il-76 heavy transport aircraft; thirty-eight more ordered

About 1,000 Russian S-300PMU/PMU2 SAMs

Twelve Russian Kilo submarines, eight with Club long-range antiship missiles

Four Russian *Sovremenniy*-class missile destroyers

Russian weapons and electronics packages for four new classes of stealthy warships

A Russian/Ukrainian aircraft carrier to serve as a transitional platform for the PLA Navy

Russian 1-meter electro-optical and radar satellite technology

Partnership in the European Galileo navigation satellite system

Over 200 Russian Mi-17 helicopters

Co-development of an 8-ton helicopter with Europe's Eurocopter

---

of the PLA's spending has been Russia. During the December 2003 visit to Russia of PRC Defense Minister Cao Gangchuan, it was revealed by Russian sources that PRC arms purchases from Russia would exceed $2 billion in 2004.[65] This figure held about the same for 2005 and 2006, but had fallen to a trickle by 2008. While a few large weapons purchases are possible in the future, especially in the area of aircraft carrier fighters, China's high priority on building indigenous development and production, a falling attractiveness for Russian technology, plus latent Russian anxiety about China have combined to depress their once booming arms traffic. While many Russian firms have assisted China's willingness to move to weapons component purchase or co-production, China may expect a more sympathetic response in terms of military technology transfers from European firms once the controversial 1989 European Union arms embargo is lifted. A review of the main foreign sources of PLA military technology follows.

Russia

In a reversal of the late Cold War antagonism, since the collapse of the Soviet Union the new Russian Federation has emerged as the PRC's principal source for advanced military hardware, military technology, military-technical training, and advice. The most recent phase in PRC-Russian relations began in August 1986, when then-President Mikhail Gorbachev made a surprising speech that contained strong overtures towards the PRC. Among other things, Gorbachev proposed cooperation in space exploration.[66] Following Tiananmen, the West's shunning of the PRC's military accelerated a military rapprochement with a newly impoverished Russia. Early in the 1990s, the PRC was able to drive hard bargains, getting the Russians to accept substandard "barter goods" in exchange for early shipments of weapons. By the mid-1990s, Russia's pervasive need for hard currency forced a restructuring of its PRC military trade to a cash basis. Early Russian reluctance to sell its most modern technology faded continuously during the 1990s: now it is the Russians who are increasingly hard-pressed to come up with "something new" for Beijing.

In the late 1990s, the PRC started to double its annual arms purchases and they reached the $2 billion level. One 2007 estimate held that China has purchased $26 billion worth of Russian arms between 1994 and 2006.[67] This served to fund the purchase of large numbers of Sukhoi fighters, the maintenance of one and maybe two Sukhoi co-production agreements, a trebling of the number of Kilo submarines, and the eventual purchase of about 1,000 S-300 surface-to-air missiles (SAMs). In addition to purchasing advanced weapons, the PLA has been forced to learn—often the hard way—that new weapons require new doctrine, tactics, training, and maintenance practices, or "software." In many instances, the challenge of developing new "software" has been more difficult for the PLA than buying new "hardware," but the PLA is learning. For example, the PLAAF's experience with the inadequacy of the single-mission Su-27 air-superiority fighter influenced a mid-1990s decision to acquire only multirole combat aircraft in the future. To take full advantage of the advanced capabilities of the Su-27, the PLAAF had to formulate more aggressive training programs. Access to Russian technology obtained from the Su-27 has influenced domestic aircraft programs. In the early 1990s, Chengdu had to modify its J-10 fighter to take advantage of access to the Russian Saturn Alyuka AL-31 engine also used by the Su-27.

According to one report, Russia-PRC cooperation in space technologies predates the breakup of the Soviet Union, possibly beginning in 1989.[68] During a December 1992 visit to Beijing, then-Russian President Boris Yeltsin was pressed by the PRC to begin cooperation in space technologies.[69] Space cooperation was early on the agenda for growing Russia-PRC cooperation, with efforts to formalize unconnected early cooperative programs in 1995.[70] By 1999, a Russian report noted that there were eleven joint space programs being implemented.[71] Perhaps sometime in 2000, a new bilateral commission was created to coordinate multiple bilateral space cooperation programs.[72] Cooperation was expanded in 2003 to cover new areas in unmanned spacecraft.[73] In June 2005 Russia and China formed a "Moon and Distant Space Exploration" special joint working group, with meetings held in August 2005 and May 2006.[74] Key technology transfers include a Soyuz manned space capsule, space suits, astronaut training, space tracking technology, and electro-optical and radar satellite technology. The Chinese "space lab" concept looks very similar to the Russian Almaz/Salut early space station, and Chinese proposals for unmanned Moon probes look similar to Russian Lavochkin designs.

There is an increasing emphasis on broader technology development cooperation in which the PRC seeks to attract Russian technological investment in the

PRC and the PRC in turn invests in high technology in Russia. In 1993, there were 300 Russian scientists on long-term defense-related programs; by 2000, this number jumped to 1,500.[75] High-technology development contracts between Russia and the PRC jumped from $11.7 million for thirty-five contracts in 2001 to $20.7 million for thirty contracts in the first six months of 2002.[76] A 2002 PRC technology delegation visiting Moscow to advance these contracts included officials from "leading shipbuilding, nuclear energy, aerospace and defense industry companies."[77] Long seeking to shift the balance of China's military trade from hardware to technology, in December 2003 Defense Minister Cao Gangchuan made a special push to change this balance to 70 percent technology and 30 percent hardware.[78] To overcome potential European competition Russia has complied, helping China to absorb both naval weapons technology and SAM technology. Despite simmering anger since about 2004, Russia is likely to accept the painful Chinese absorption of the Sukhoi Su-27 into an "indigenized" J-11B fighter program.

This shift from outright purchases to co-production and co-development has also resulted in a decline in China's position as Russia's military customer, taking 69–70 percent of total military sales in 1996–1997 down to 40 percent in 2006; this was expected to decline to 17–19 percent in 2007.[79] Perhaps noting this change in the relationship, a *Ta Kung Pao* article on the 2007 Moscow Air Show noted, "Today, Russian enterprises are beginning to cooperate with their Chinese counterparts with a positive attitude in all areas, whether it is hypersonic missile technology or advanced phased array radar technology, advanced jet engine manufacturing technology or military aerospace."[80]

However, there remains a potential for significant future sales, to include Tu-95 and Tu-22M3 bombers, aircraft carrier technology, unmanned combat aircraft, large air transport technology, submarine technology, and space technology. President Vladimir Putin's increased military assertiveness in 2007 and his apparent commitment to build six new nuclear-powered aircraft carriers,[81] a new fifth-generation air defense system potentially capable of space intercepts,[82] and perhaps new long-range bombers[83] indicate a willingness to retain a competitive position in the China arms market. Should the European Union end its military embargo on China, Russia will face greater pressure to offer its most up-to-date technologies to China and increasingly accept subordinate co-development positions in order to retain its position as principle military-technical partner.

Nevertheless, Russians are also coming to realize they will face competition from cheaper and modern Chinese military products as well as from Beijing's ability to compete for influence in Central Asia, the Persian Gulf, and beyond. Furthermore, it is apparent that within the Russian military there has been long-standing opposition to continuous sales of high technology to China, objections which have continuously been overruled by political and military-industry leaders. In 2006 and 2007, while still seeking an "entente" with China in order to present a "united front" of "multilateralism" to the United States, it is also clear that the prosperity resulting from massive petroleum price increases has allowed Moscow the luxury of some wariness toward Beijing. In late 2007 one Russian source told this author, "[I]n time, this time of open doors to China will come to an end."[84] By early to mid-2008 Russian reports built on this anxiety, noting government hesitation to export unidentified technologies, and even expressing fears that weapons sold could be turned against them.[85] The problem is that Russia has already given China most of the technology needed to almost catch up with the West.

Ukraine

While Ukraine has probably only sold roughly $1–2 billion in military products to the PLA between 1994 and 2004, it has been useful nonetheless. Since the breakup of the Soviet Union, Russian and Ukrainian military concerns have become more competitive, and the PLA has sought to take advantage of this. Ukraine has been a source for space and missile technologies, conducting training for PLA astronauts, possibly selling the PLA advanced liquid-fuel rocket engines, and serving as a principle source for air-to-air missiles for PLA Sukhoi fighters. After much effort the PLA was able to buy the rusting hulk of the carrier *Varyag* and tow it to Dalian in 2002. There it will teach PLA Navy (PLAN) engineers about Soviet-era aircraft carrier technology. In addition, Ukraine contains specialists in top-notch electronic warfare, an area in which the PLA is stepping out and investing to create new products. If reports are to be believed, it was PLA investment that allowed Ukraine to create the feared Kolchuga passive radar.[86] The PLA has also cooperated with Ukrainian companies to develop a new naval phased-array radar for the PLAN's No. 170–class air-defense destroyers.[87] A 2006 report revealed that in 2001 Pakistan's A. Q. Khan network engineered the sale of Ukrainian-held Russian-made Kh-55 strategic cruise missiles to Pakistan, Iran, and China—all of which have now have effective analogues of this system.[88] Ukraine is also reported to have sold China the ability to make new laser systems and possibly optical guidance systems for its new GB-1 precision-guided bomb.

Israel

During the late 1970s and early 1980s, the United States encouraged Israel to develop military-technical ties with the PRC as a way to indirectly aid PRC military modernization against the former Soviet Union. During the 1980s, Israel offered the PRC its technology in the areas of tank weapons, antitank missiles, surface-to-air missiles, cruise missiles, military electronics, and aircraft design. But by the 1990s, the Israel-PLA relationship became a matter of increasing concern for Washington, not just because of the sophistication of technology sold, but because some of the technology was of U.S. origin, or made possible by access to U.S. weapons systems, and was subsidized by U.S. taxpayers.[89]

Israel has sold the PLA mainly aircraft and missile technology. The most famous PRC-Israel project has been the co-development of the Chengdu Jian-10

(J-10) fourth-generation multirole fighter. This project drew heavily on Israel's Israeli Aircraft Industries Lavi advanced fighter,[90] which was terminated after the United States withdrew its financial and political support. But the Lavi, in turn, drew heavily from U.S. technology, including some associated with the Lockheed-Martin F-16 fighter. U.S.-based technology in the J-10 may include avionics, advanced composite materials, and flight control specifications.[91] A mid-2008 report cited Russian sources, relaying information from Chinese colleagues, that China had obtained an actual prototype of the Lavi to aid the development of the J-10,[92] as had been rumored for many years. This fighter has been operational since 2004–2005 and is expected to be produced in large numbers. In 2000 the Clinton administration stopped Israel from completing a contract to provide up to four advanced IAI Phalcon phased-array airborne radar systems to the PLA for $1 billion.[93] While it appears the PLA has gone ahead and acquired this capability by other means, this marked the first time the United States caused Israel to stop a large arms sale to China. But the Bush administration sought a final end to Israel's arms sales to China following revelations in 2002 and 2003 that Israel sold a large number of its Harpy antiradar drones to the PLA and was intending to upgrade them.[94]

Israel's principal motivation for pursuing its arms relationship with the PRC was to support its own arms industries, whose independence and competitiveness Israel requires for its national security. However, some Israelis have suggested another motivation. Israeli officials claim that one benefit of its sale of Lavi fighter technology to China has been to prevent sales of surface-to-surface missiles to Israel's neighbors.[95] However, in mid-1996, the CIA reportedly disclosed that China might have shipped "missile-related components" to Syria.[96] And there is the larger question of PRC nuclear and missile proliferation and the dangers that has created for Israel. China's sale of missile technology to Iran has enabled its long-range missiles that can reach Israel. Furthermore, Iran has transferred advanced Chinese missiles such as the C-802 to the Hezbollah terrorist group in Lebanon, which used it to almost sink an Israeli corvette in July 2006. Iran has additional shorter-range Chinese antiship weapons that could also pose a threat to Israel if given to Hezbollah. Then, in October 2007, Russian reports cited Iranian sources noting that Iran had "signed a contract" worth $40 billion to purchase 24 J-10 fighters, while other sources noted the deal included 240 short- and medium-range air-to-air missiles.[97] While China almost immediately denied such a sale was happening,[98] other knowledgeable sources confirmed that the deal was being negotiated. While this exposure likely forced China to "postpone" this sale, it has long been predicted that such a danger to Israel could emerge from its sale of military technology to China.[99]

Europe

In the late 1970s and into the 1980s, the Europeans jumped into the PRC arms market to compete with the United States and Israel. France and Britain were the leaders, followed by Italy and then Germany (which sold mainly dual-use items). Sweden also began an arms relationship with the PRC. However, most of this commerce was curtailed by EU sanctions in response to the 1989 Tiananmen Massacre. After the mid-1990s, Britain, France, Spain, and Italy modified their interpretations of the 1989 sanctions to allow increasing amounts of "dual-use" technology to be sold to the PRC. Under this interpretation, Europeans have sold defense electronics and helicopter technology to the PLA.

By the late 1990s, Beijing was putting heavy pressure on many European countries to end these sanctions and resume military technology and weapons sales. Seeing that its harangue was having an effect, Beijing continued to press hard. Beijing scored by blocking a German reconnaissance satellite sale to Taiwan in 1999[100] and put sufficient pressure on Germany and Spain (in 2001–2002), to block the sale of their conventional submarine technology to Taiwan. A 2003 Chinese White Paper on PRC-EU relations said, "The EU should lift its ban on arms sales to China at an early date so as to remove barriers to greater bilateral cooperation on defense industry and technologies."[101] By the end of 2003 Germany and France were calling for the end of the embargo. In conjunction with the mid-December 2004 EU summit, major European defense and aerospace companies also called for an end to the embargo.[102] Their tone was set by EADS (European Aeronautics and Defense Company), which in early October 2003 signed a "strategic cooperation agreement" with AviChina, an investment arm of AVIC II, that would involve the "the joint development, manufacturing and modernization of helicopters, regional aircraft and training aircraft."[103]

However, by May 2005 the Bush administration had succeeded in turning the tide. First Britain decided to support the United States and not push for an end to the embargo, and then Germany followed suit, especially following the election of Angela Merkel as Chancellor. As of early 2007 France, Italy, and Spain were on record as supporting the lifting of the embargo, but Britain and Germany remained opposed. Since 2005 Japan has become increasingly active in Europe rallying support for the embargo.

Embargo relaxations during the 1990s saw the 1998 British sale to China of the 1960s Rolls Royce Spey turbofan, which allowed China to develop the Xian JH-7A fighter-bomber. Britain, Germany, and Italy have sold satellite technology to the PRC. The European space consortium Astrium has sought to sell manned-space life-support technology and has lobbied to allow the PRC to join the International Space Station.[104] A 2003 agreement to secure a PRC financial contribution to the future European Galileo navigation satellite constellation marked a new high point in space cooperation. The end of the embargo might not necessarily lead to large European weapons sales to China, but the PLA would seek far deeper military technology relationships in the areas of space, missiles, aircraft, UAVs, network electronics, electronic warfare, warships, and submarines. A number of international sources for high technology of interest to the PLA are summarized in Table 5.2.

Table 5.2 Foreign Sources for PLA High Technology[a]

	Russia	Ukraine	Israel	Europe	US
Microsatellite Technology				Yes	
Radar Satellite Technology	Yes	Possible			
Electro-Optical Satellite Technology	Yes	Possible	Possible	Possible	
Communication Satellite Technology			Yes	Yes	Yes
Missile Technology	Yes	Yes			Yes
Manned Space Technology	Yes	Yes		Possible	
Cruise Missile Technology	Yes	Yes	Yes		Yes
Laser Technology	Yes	Possible		Yes	Yes
Combat Aircraft and Related Technology	Yes	Yes	Yes	Yes	Yes
Military Aircraft Engines	Yes	Yes		Yes	
Aircraft Weapons	Yes	Yes	Yes		
Airborne Warning and Control System (AWACS)/ Synthetic Aperture Radar (SAR) Technology	Yes	Yes	Yes	Yes	Yes
Submarine Technology	Yes		Yes	Yes	
Submarine Weapons	Yes				
Aircraft Carrier Technology	Yes	Yes		Yes	
Warship Technology	Yes	Yes		Yes	
Tank Technology	Yes	Yes	Yes	Yes	
Antitank Technology	Yes	Yes	Yes	Yes	
Helicopter Technology	Yes			Yes	Yes
Advanced Communication	Yes			Yes	Yes
Electronic Warfare/ Intelligence	Yes	Possible	Yes		

[a]Foreign sources include sales, commercial cooperation, and espionage.

South Africa

Since 2000 China has also developed a military-technical cooperation relationship with South Africa. South Africa maintains a small but innovative arms
industry that has, over time, benefited from European and Israeli technical
inputs. South Africa offers competitive weapon systems in the areas of armor, air
defenses, aircraft missiles, and unmanned aerial vehicles. South Africa's large
defense firm Denel had a small display booth at the 2002 Zhuhai Air show. A

2004 report claimed China and South Africa were negotiating sales of UAV sur-veillance cameras and the advanced A-Darter antiaircraft missile (AAM).[105] By the 2006 Zhuhai show, the China New Era Company, an apparent Chinese-South African partnership, was marketing the South African Skua target drone and promoting advanced unmanned combat air vehicle (UCAV) concepts armed with the Denel Mokopa air-launched antitank missile. South African technology is reported to have contributed to Shenyang's futuristic "An Jian" supersonic UCAV.[106] At the 2007 IDEX show a South African source disclosed their sale of an intelligent-fuse 35-mm antiaircraft gun to China,[107] apparently based on Swiss-German technology from the AHEAD (Advanced Hit Efficiency and Destruction) system. An AHEAD gun is able to put a precisely timed "cloud" of tungsten subprojectiles, from a small number of rounds, in front of an oncoming target. This gun now arms a new PLA Army tracked gun-missile antiaircraft system and is able to offer greater defense against tactical ground-attack mis-siles and precision-guided weapons. Then in December 2007 and January 2008, imagery from a Chinese university and from Chinese military Web pages sug-gested that China had copied the Denel A-Darter AAM and had also produced a radar-guided missile similar to the R-Darter AAM.[108] These fifth-generation AAMs will greatly enhance the aerial combat capabilities of PLA aircraft.

Modernizing the Military Industry

Although reform has been slow and painful for China's military-industrial sector, it is yielding results. In the early 1990s the PLA was hard-pressed to produce modified versions of 1950s-era Soviet aircraft, tank, and submarine designs. By 2010 the PLA could be deploying many of its own weapons, or weapons systems based largely on foreign technology but made in China. In addition, by 2010 the PLA could be a major competitor in foreign arms markets, offering modern aircraft, ships, and even missiles without analogues in Russia or the West. Such a prospect was unthinkable in 2000.

Although the all-around absorption of foreign-made military components and technology, plus the widespread use of foreign advanced modeling and design software, have played a key role in the growing success of China's defense indus-tries, there is another important driver: competition. By a 2002 estimate there were over 10,000 firms in the PRC with some relationship to the PLA.[109] In many cases defense industries are triple or quadruple redundant, especially those concerned with the production of engines, tanks, and many missiles. This redundancy was instituted by Mao as part of his "People's War" strategies to ensure defense production would continue even if large parts of China were to become occupied. As part of the 1998 Logistics Reforms, however, there was a clear effort to promote greater competition within the defense sector. This was instituted by the breakup of the large defense consortia into smaller consortia that were then allowed to compete (Table 5.3). In addition, the PLA allowed this sector to have access to sources of funding other than state funds.

Table 5.3 PRC's Main State-Owned Military Corporations Since 1998

Old Corporation	New Corporation	Main Products
Ministry of Electronics Industry	Ministry of Information Technology and Telecom Industry (MTTI)	
China National Nuclear Corporation	China National Nuclear Corporation (CNNC)	
	China National Engineering Construction Corporation (CNEC)	
Aviation Industries of China (AVIC) (There are mid-2008 reports of a re-merger of these two groups)	China Aviation Industry Corporation 1 (AVIC 1)	Chengdu Aircraft (J-7, J-10, FC-1); Shenyang Aircraft (J-8; J-11); Guizhou Aviation (FT-7, UAVs); Xi'an Aircraft (H-6, JH-7, MA-60)
	China Aviation Industry Corporation 2 (AVIC 2)	Harbin Aircraft Industries Group (helicopters, light-transport aircraft); Shaanxi Aircraft (Y-8); Hongdu (K-8, L-15); Changhe (helicopters); Chinese Special Vehicles Research Institute (WIG); Beijing University of Aeronautics and Astronautics (UAVs, virtual flight); Xi'an ASN (UAVs)
China North Industries Corp	China North Industries Group Corporation (CNIGC)	Has about 300 associated factories, research, and marketing groups. Responsible for a broad range of Army equipment from small arms, ammo, artillery, antitank missiles, trucks, and Army support equipment. Also sells construction and transport machinery.
	China South Industries Group Corporation (CSIGC)	Has about seventy-six related organizations. Produces cars and motors and conducts research for military products.
China State Shipbuilding Corp	China State Shipbuilding Corporation (CSSC)	Controls southern shipyards and naval enterprises in Guangdong, Jiangxi, Anhui, and Shanghai. Produces destroyers, frigates, ELINT ships, and a wide range of civil ships.

Table 5.3 (*Continued*)

Old Corporation	New Corporation	Main Products
	China State Shipbuilding Industry Corporation (CSIC)	Controls northern yards in Yunnan, Dalian, Hubei, Tianjin, Shanxi, and Liaoning, along with about ninety-six associated enterprises. Produces destroyers, frigates, submarines, and a wide range of civil ships.
China Aerospace Corporation	China Aerospace Science and Industry Corp (CASIC)	Medium-range ballistic missiles (MRBMs), SRBMs, SAMs; Cruise Missiles, SC-1 ASAT (?)
	China Aerospace Science and Technology Corporation (CASC)	Long March satellite launch vehicles (SLVs); DF-5; DF-31; DF-21; reconnaissance and communication satellites; manned space systems
	China Aerospace Machinery and Electronics Corporation (CAMEC)	China Sanjiang Space Group (DF-11); Hangtian Tsinghua (micro- and nanosatellites)

The early results of these innovations could be seen at the 2002 Zhuhai Air Show, when an upstart private company proposed a new fighter, apparently in partnership with the state-owned Guizhou Aircraft Corporation. Although Guizhou later absorbed this program, it began because the PLA allowed a group of investors to pool their money to start the fighter project. By the February 2007 IDEX show, one could see even greater results as PLA-controlled trading companies marketed two competing fixed short-range air defense systems, five mobile air-defense systems, two families of Gatling gun systems, two new types of short-range ballistic missiles, and two families of precision-guided aircraft weapons. In many cases these systems were as good as or better than what Russia offered and probably less expensive, meaning they are bound to meet with greater success.

In June 2007 the Chinese leadership took steps that could further accelerate these trends, when the Commission of Science, Technology, and Industry for National Defence (COSTIND), the National Development and Reform Commission, and the state-owned Assets Supervision and Administration Commission issued new guidelines to allow domestic and foreign investment in defense firms.[110] With greater access to capital, state-owned weapons development and production concerns will be enabled to invest in riskier technologies that might yield advances and profits but might not otherwise be supported by more risk-averse government officials. Outside investment has long been a key enabler for defense innovation in the West, and it is increasingly having an impact in Russia.

There has long been tension between those in the PLA who demand new weapons as soon as possible and prefer to buy select foreign systems and those who follow the historic desire by the PRC to strengthen self-reliance, which emphasizes the interests of PLA-subordinate defense industries over foreign weapons purchases. The middle ground for the PLA has long been to try to graft various foreign components into largely indigenous weapon designs to increase their capability, or in turn to produce a new generation of weapons. From the 1970s to the mid- to late 1990s, there were many attempts to do this, usually with only marginal success. In the early 1990s, the PLA Navy acquired two *Luhu*-class destroyers, which for the first time combined U.S. and Ukrainian gas turbine engines; French SAMs, defensive electronics, and command and control systems; and an Italian CIWS. There were integration problems, and the ship's performance, while an improvement for the PLA, was obsolete compared to the ships of neighboring navies. In addition, the early 1990s saw the PLA Navy encounter serious problems trying to marry disparate technologies into its first Type 039 *Song*-class conventional submarine. For most of the 1990s, indigenous fighter programs—whether the Shenyang J-8II, Chengdu J-10, or Chengdu Super-7/FC-1—encountered delays due to arms embargoes, funding issues, and inability to decide whether to obtain a given component from a foreign source or make it themselves.

However, it must be concluded that there has been steady improvement in weapons production since 2000. One reason may be that the PLA has learned lessons on how to better use foreign expertise. A recent example of this is the seemingly happy ending to the long-running saga of the Rolls Royce Spey turbofan engine co-production deal. This project started in 1975, but the PLA was not able to co-produce this engine, which was needed to complete a much-needed fighter-bomber, the Xian JH-7. In the late-1990s, when the PLA decided that it really wanted the JH-7 to succeed, it went back to Rolls Royce, and by 1999 they cut a new deal. The PLA purchased more used Spey engines to carry forward some JH-7 production, but it also allowed Rolls Royce some co-production work. The result is the new Qinling turbofan engine, which has allowed full production of the JH-7A fighter-bomber. In the mid-1990s the PLA Navy built its *Luhai*-class destroyer using Ukrainian gas turbine engines but an unimpressive weapons outfit. In the first decade of the twenty-first century, the PLA Navy built three new classes of destroyers, based largely on Russian weapons and electronics but with significant new Chinese weapons and electronics as well. Both the Type 039 Song and the newer Yuan non-nuclear submarines are foreign-design inspired, but the Yuan represents a new and better generation. Table 5.4 illustrates the degree to which current and future Chinese weapons programs combine foreign and domestic components.

But the PLA's real goal is to build up China's defense industries to become world-class defense technology innovators rather than consumers of new ideas

Table 5.4 Providing a Bridge: Foreign Content of Future PLA Weapons

Weapon System	Foreign Content	Domestic Content
Antisatellite, Direct Ascent	British micro- and nanosatellite technology	PRC design and solid-fueled mobile launch system
Radar Satellite	Russian antenna	PRC satellite bus
Synthetic Aperture Radar (SAR) Aircraft	Russian Tu-154; U.S. SAR technology	PRC-designed SAR
Y-8 Airborne Early Warning (AEW) aircraft	British Racal/Thales *Skymaster* AEW radar	Shaanxi Y-8 transport aircraft
Chengdu J-10 Multirole Fighter	Russian engine; possible Russian radar; Israeli airframe and control system assistance	PRC designed airframe; possible PRC radar and defensive systems; PRC weapons
Shenyang J-11B Multirole Fighter	Russian-designed airframe, some avionic and electronic systems	PRC multimode radar, weapons, engine, stealth technology
SD-10 Active Air-to-Air Missile	Russian radar and data link	PRC motor, airframe
HQ-9/FT-2000 Surface-to-Air Missile	Russian guidance systems; possible US seeker technology; possible Israeli design assistance	PRC motor, airframe
Luyang 1 DDG	Russian SAM, guidance and search radar; Ukrainian gas turbine engine	PRC hull, antiship missile, defensive systems
Song-A SSK	German engine; possible Russian weapons and design assistance; possible Israeli design assistance	PRC hull, weapons, defensive systems
Project 093 Nuclear Attack Submarine	Russian design assistance; possible Russian weapons	PRC hull, nuclear reactor, defensive systems
Medium Transport/Attack Helicopter	French design assistance for rotor head; Italian design assistance; possible Canadian engine	PRC airframe, engines, avionics, weapons
Type-98 Main Battle Tank	Russian-influenced hull and 125-mm main gun; Russian gun-launched guided missile; British- or German-influenced engine	PRC-designed composite armor, tank design, and integration

from elsewhere. One goal of the Shenyang fifth-generation fighter program appears to be to indigenously develop and sustain all of its component parts. As the PLA assembles weapons with pieces from other countries and improves at this, it is also using its interactions with the West to generally improve its defense industries. But there remains widespread redundancy, overcapacity, and slowness in applying design and manufacturing lessons available from the West. Greater rationalization in the defense sector is often impeded by companies that are able to gather political clout to ensure the survival of firms that should be allowed to fail.

One area where such interaction may be having an impact is in fulfilling one goal of the broad 1998 PLA military-industry sector reforms: to give greater play to market forces. Companies such as Chengdu are apparently succeeding in developing fighters that may be competitive in foreign markets, in part through knowledge gained by interacting with foreign companies. Chengdu is also learning that transparency assists marketing. It is clear that Chengdu has judged that success in foreign markets is critical to company survival. It may need foreign revenues if the PLA decides to rationalize and cut back the number of aircraft manufacturers.

Aircraft Sector

Interaction with Western firms is already having a positive impact in the aircraft sector. In the 1980s this sector reflected older People's War doctrines: multiple redundant design and production facilities dedicated to making large numbers of relatively simple copies of 1950s Soviet fighter and bomber designs. Production methods were crude. Quality control was poor, and as a consequence fighter unit readiness suffered.[111] However, by 2002 Russian sources were reporting that the PLA was making remarkable advances in its aircraft manufacturing. They noted that the production finish of Sukhoi J-11 fighters being co-produced at Shenyang was better than that of the Russian-made fighters from KNAAPO. Such a turnaround did not come fast or easy for the PLA, but its occurrence is in part a consequence of extensive interaction with Western aircraft concerns.[112] By 2006 it became clear that Shenyang was committed to making a fully "indigenized" version, the J-11B, that will have Chinese-developed turbofan engines, a Chinese-made radar, and Chinese-made weapons. In mid-2007 China revealed its intention to make a twin-seat J-11BS, which could perform dedicated attack missions like the Su-30 series.

Russia is having perhaps the greatest impact on improving combat aircraft design and manufacture. Shenyang has the deepest relationship with Sukhoi and KNAAPO, the dominant Russian aircraft concerns. Having purchased the co-production rights to the Su-27SK, Shenyang has learned enough to begin to add more PRC-made content to this fighter. Shenyang and Chengdu have purchased Russian advice to improve indigenous designs such as the J-8II, J-10, and FC-1. The Chengdu Aircraft Corporation received help from the American Grumman Corporation to develop the "Super-7" version of its J-7/MiG-21 fighter, a contract taken up by Russia's Mikoyan after the imposition of Tiananmen sanctions.

Chengdu also received substantial assistance from Israeli Aircraft Industries and Siberian Aeronautical Research Institute (SibNIA) to design the J-10 fighter. The Russian firm Yakovlev has helped the Hongdu Corporation design its new L-15 supersonic trainer, which looks very similar to the Yak-130 trainer. There is very likely significant Russian influence in the Shenyang and Chengdu fifth-generation fighter designs as well.

But other countries are also helping to improve the PLA's own combat aircraft manufacturing capability. In 2002 a Russian source noted with some embarrassment that Shenyang J-11 fighters had a better production finish than did the KNAAPO-made fighters.[113] He noted that much of Shenyang's rapid improvement in J-11 manufacturing finish has been due to the import of modern production machinery from Russia, Japan, Sweden, and even the United States.[114] Sweden's Avure Company had sold the PRC eight of its modern high-power presses to fabricate aluminum aircraft parts; three of the presses were going to the Shaanxi transport aircraft maker and the Changhe and Harbin helicopter makers.[115] And after diverting U.S. five- and three-axis advanced machining tools imported for the McDonnell-Douglas DC-9 jet transport co-production program to Shenyang in the early 1990s,[116] China has emerged in the last several years as a major producer of five-axis machine tools and has even developed state-of-the-art nine-axis machine tools. In addition, it appears that most Chinese aircraft manufacturers use French aircraft-maker Dassault's CATIA software, which enables complex three-dimensional designs. Dassault has been selling its CATIA software in the PRC since about 1983.[117] Computer-aided design software accelerated the building of Chengdu's FC-1 fighter and the twin-seat version of its J-10 fighter. Design drawings for both fighters were delivered in six months, whereas the drawings for just the single-seat J-10 had previously required ten months.[118]

New Large Aircraft Plans

On March 5, 2006, Premier Wen Jiabao presented the government work report to the Chinese National People's Congress, which included an outline of the eleventh Five-Year Plan (2006–2010).[119] While exact details of the Five-Year Plan are not public knowledge, in March 2006 a "senior official" from AVIC 1 called attention to the Five-Year Plan's commitment to develop "large aircraft." This official, Liu Daxiang, also noted that "large aircraft" means aircraft capable of carrying 150 passengers (for airliners) or up to 100 tons (for large cargo aircraft).[120] In 2004 China's State Council ordered the two major Chinese aviation consortia, AVIC-1 and AVIC-2, to study the feasibility of building a 150-seat airliner,[121] so the 2006 decision marks a victory for Liu and other Chinese advocates of large indigenous air transports. In early 2007 Internet images began to emerge of competing concepts for a twin-engine Airbus A-330-size airliner and a four-engine Airbus A-340-size airliner. On December 30, 2007, Wen Jiabao visited the Xian Aircraft Industry Group plant and was photographed next to a model of a Xian airliner concept that matches the size of the 150-seat airliner. Xinhua quoted Wen telling Xian workers, "It is the will of the nation to let (Chinese-made) large aircraft fly up into the sky. It must be done and it must succeed."[122]

China faces steep obstacles to realizing this goal. These obstacles include a current inability to build the jet transport's crucial engines, the question of whether it can avoid subsidizing this program (a violation of World Trade Organization rules), and the question of whether it can achieve product confidence with customers long held by Boeing and Airbus.[123] Despite these obstacles, however, it appears that there may be substantial "nationalist" support for a Chinese large-aircraft program, if only to achieve an important element of national power. In June 2005 Liu Daxiang noted, "If China does not roll out its own trunk liner by 2020, then the country will not succeed in 2030 or 2040. So it is really a rush."[124] From this comment, it can at least be inferred that Liu understands the importance of China's success in becoming a full developer and producer of large transport aircraft to the larger goal of enabling China to become an economic and military superpower later in this century. From his position as a member of the Chinese National People's Congress, Liu has helped to craft resolutions proposing the development of large aircraft during the 2003 and 2004 NPC sessions, and he has apparently reached his goal of focusing government funding toward the development of large aircraft for the eleventh Five-Year Plan. Liu told the press that a 150-seat airliner could be developed by 2015 and be ready for Chinese passenger service by 2020.

China's civil and military aircraft design and manufacturing development has been tremendously aided by China's interactions with Western aircraft companies. It is also possible that PRC companies that do substantial subcontracting assembly work for major aircraft makers such as Boeing and Airbus are taking knowledge gained from this work and applying it to improve their combat aircraft manufacturing. For example, Chengdu makes parts for the Boeing 757 and Airbus 319 airliners, and Shenyang does subcontract assemblies for Airbus. The Xian Aircraft Corporation builds Boeing 737-700 vertical fins and Airbus A320 cargo access doors.[125] Sources who had visited Chengdu's subcontract assembly lines had noted their proximity to the fighter production lines, and that fighter parts they had viewed, in their opinion, benefited from the assembly line for the subcontract parts.[126] There is also a report that China completely dismantled an Airbus A-320,[127] and it would not be surprising if it did the same to a Boeing airliner.

The PRC's AVIC-1 aircraft consortium will likely gain far greater access to Western technologies via its new Advanced Regional Jet ARJ21 program. Revealed in 2002, the ARJ21 grew out of previous attempts to build competitive transport aircraft in the PRC. In the 1980s the PRC co-produced thirty-three McDonnell-Douglas MD-80 airliners, but PRC airlines preferred better built, less expensive foreign-made transports to remain competitive. In the early 1990s there was an attempt to join with Airbus to build a new small airliner, but the program faltered. With the ARJ21, the AVIC-1 consortium has succeeded in enlisting a long line of U.S. and European aircraft subcomponent producers both to co-produce their parts in the PRC and to purchase services.[128] Even if there are safeguards, it can be expected that the PRC will learn a great deal about these components. And once the ARJ21 program is secure, it is likely that AVIC-1 will start producing larger airliners that will compete in markets now dominated by Boeing and Airbus.

China is likely to learn even more from the establishment of an Airbus A-320 production line in Tianjin. Despite a record of failed Western airliner co-production and co-development ventures in China, Airbus decided in 2006 to co-produce this airliner in China, and it expects to start producing A-320 regional airliners in 2011. Airbus expects that production could eventually reach up to fifty airliners per year.[129] An Airbus official has acknowledged that this project could help China master skills needed to advance its own large-transport ambition.[130] Such insights might include mastering "just-in-time" manufacturing techniques, advanced inventory control, and essential quality control. All of these skills, plus the potential price advantage obtained from low-cost labor or possible subsidies, might enable China to challenge Boeing and Airbus in some markets. Russia has also offered to co-develop a large airliner but as of early 2008 it does not appear that China is going to do so.

China is also making organizational and financial moves to better position itself for commercial aircraft competition. In August 2007 AVIC-1 took the commercial elements out of the Chengdu and Shenyang aircraft companies and created the Shenyang Commercial Aircraft Company and the Chengdu Commercial Aircraft company. This was done in hopes of surmounting U.S. and Western technology transfer restrictions that might aid military programs.[131] Then in early 2008 Chinese reports indicated that elements of AVIC-1 and AVIC-2 would be merged to support the development and construction of large aircraft. Following reports in January, in mid-May 2008 China launched the Commercial Aircraft Corporation of China (CACC) to combine resources from AVIC-1 and AVIC-2 to focus on the development and production of world-class transport aircraft.[132] While China immediately downplayed the potential for CACC to compete with Boeing and Airbus,[133] this is the apparent goal of this new company.

In April 2007 AVIC-1 created a consolidated financial group that might someday make strategic foreign investments and seek to raise capital on world markets.[134] In June 2007 Airbus disclosed that AVIC-1 was seeking to invest in six European aircraft parts factories for which Airbus was seeking cost-sharing partners, an offer Airbus rejected.[135] Given China's ambitions to create world-class military and civil aircraft sectors, and the fact that it has no civil-military "firewall" for technology, it is logical to expect that both sectors will be aided by all interactions with Western aircraft industries.

Aircraft Engines

A major obstacle China must overcome to achieve its large aircraft ambition is the development of a commercially competitive large turbofan engine. Research and development of large turbofans for civil and military use is likely being done by the Shenyang Aeroengine Research Group, Shenyang-Liming Aeroengine Group. and the Xian Aeroengine Group. China could opt to use Western engines, but then its airliner sales would be politically vulnerable. China's first large turbofan for a military and commercial transport will likely be derived from its fourth-generation fighter engine program.

China's effort to build an indigenous fourth-generation military turbofan engine probably dates back to the early 1980s. The first indication that China was making substantial progress with its Taihang engine came at the 2002 Zhuhai Show, where a brochure indicated this engine was likely being tested in a J-11 fighter. At subsequent air shows from 2003 to 2007, Russian sources gradually changed their opinion of China's indigenous turbofan from one of doubt to grudging respect. By late 2006 and early 2007 China had made enough progress with the Taihang, or WS-10A, that it was minimally "revealed" at the 2006 Zhuhai Air Show. The Taihang reportedly will have a maximum thrust of 13,200 kg, slightly better than the Saturn AL-31 engine on the Su-27/J-11 fighter. This engine will also eventually have a thrust-vectoring nozzle that will aid aircraft maneuvering and short takeoff capabilities.

There are indications that China has been researching even more advanced engines for its fifth-generation fighter program that will reach thrust-to-weight ratios of 12 to 15 and feature supercruise capability.[136] There was a cryptic mention of a new fifth-generation engine on a display board at the 2006 Zhuhai Air Show, but no data were provided. However, some Chinese sources indicate that this fifth-generation engine will be a development of the *Taihang*, sometimes called the WS-14 or WS-15, that will achieve a greater than 15,000-kg thrust level and a 9.5:1 thrust:weight ratio.[137] This would make it comparable to the Pratt and Whitney PW F119-PW-100 engine that powers the Lockheed-Martin F-22A. But there is also mention of a future engine with a 12:1 thrust-to-weight ratio intended for China's fifth-generation fighters, also called the WS-15, which began development in 2002.

In early 2008 an article on the AVIC-1 Web page made a specific reference to the example of the General Electric F101 engine for the B-1 bomber; this engine later became the basis for successful fighter engines and the best-selling GE/SNECMA CFM56 civil turbofan engine. The article made the point that the Taihang could similarly be the basis for other military aircraft and civil air transport engines.[138] One derivative project that is likely contributing to a new large aircraft engine is the R0110 electricity-generating gas turbine, a project of the 863 Program and completed during the tenth Five Year Plan (2001–2005).[139] Performance characteristics such as low fuel consumption and high reliability over long-term use would be desirable for both electricity generation and civil-transport engines. An early 2008 AVIC-1 report on the progress of the R0110 made clear its relevance to ongoing Chinese aircraft engine programs.[140] At the 2006 Zhuhai show Russia's Saturn and China's Shenyang-Liming engine concerns signed an agreement to build a future joint venture that would include potential civilian engine cooperation.[141] One

European industry source interviewed at the 2008 Singapore Air Show indicated that China likely could produce an efficient turbofan within ten years to power the proposed 150-seat airliner.[142]

China has also made substantial progress in adopting the Russian Klimov RD-33 and the British Rolls Royce Spey turbofans to support "indigenous" turbofan production programs. In 2000 an initial batch of modified RD-93 engines were purchased to support the Chengdu FC-1/JF-17 fighter program, followed by the purchase of 100 more in early 2005, with reports that up to 500 might eventually be acquired.[143] According to Chinese sources, technology for the RD-33/93 was also acquired around 2000 to enable a developed version called the WS-13, or "*Taishan*" turbofan. This engine, developed by the Guizhou Aeroengine Research Institute and produced by the Guizhou-Liyang Aeroengine Company, is reportedly a bit heavier than the RD-33 but also has a slightly higher power rating. In early 2008 this engine was reportedly "certified," or ready to enter production. Some Chinese sources indicate this engine could eventually be developed into a 22,450-pound thrust version called "*Taishan-21*," which could support a range of new manned and unmanned aircraft programs.[144] It is likely that China's success with the Taishan prompted Russia to overrule long-standing Indian objections in late 2007 and approve Chinese re-export of the RD-93 to Pakistan and five other countries.[145]

After having failed to copy initial versions of the Spey turbofan purchased in the 1970s to support the Xian JH-7 fighter-bomber program, in 1998 China swallowed its pride and reached a deal with Rolls Royce to purchase the technology to co-produce this 1960s technology turbofan engine.[146] Repeated approaches to Rolls Royce by the author since 2002 have yielded no insights regarding the extent of Rolls Royce's contribution to China's development of turbofan technology. The Xian Aeroengine Group put this engine, called the *Qinling*, into full production in 2002. This allowed production of the upgraded Xian JH-7A fighter bomber, which equipped about four to five PLAAF and PLANAF regiments in 2008. The Chinese and Western military turbofan engines are summarized in Table 5.5.

Shipbuilding

It is also increasingly apparent that, after some delays, the PLA shipbuilding sector is benefiting from the reforms this sector implemented in the 1980s and 1990s to become globally competitive. But this process was slow. In 1997 the PLA launched a single *Luhai*-class destroyer. Though it featured a modular superstructure and some stealth features, it had only a modest weapons and electronics suite. But by the turn of the millennium, PLA shipbuilding was put into high gear. In 2002–2005 the PLA produced two new classes of stealthy air defense destroyers (the first such Chinese-made ships dedicated to this task), an additional air defense destroyer with long-range Russian weapons, a new class of stealthy frigate, series production of the improved Type 039 *Song* submarine,

Table 5.5 PRC and Western Military Turbofans Compared

Engine	Country	Aircraft	Service Date	Maximum Thrust	Thrust-to-Weight Ratio	Notes
Qinling (WS-9)	PRC, Xian	JH-7A	2003–2004	9,325+ kg (20,500+ lbs)	5+	Co-produced version of Spey Mk 202; initial deal in 1976 founders; revived in 1998; co-production of improved version starts in 2003
Spey RB-168 Mk 202	UK, Rolls Royce	F-4K/M; Buccaneer	1968	9,325 kg (20,500 lbs)	5	Early UK military turbofan development starts in late 1950s
Taishan (WS-13)	PRC, Guizhou	FC-1	2010?	86.37 kN (19,391 lbs)	7.8	Development started in 2000; based largely on RD-33/93 but with substantial new inputs; 2,200 hour life span; reports of 22,450 lbs thrust version in development
RD-33/93	Russia, Klimov	FC-1; MiG-29	1972 (tested)	8,300 kg (18,300 lbs)	7.8	Development of the RD-33 began in 1968; RD-93 is an improved version
Taihang (WS-10A)	PRC, Shenyang	J-11; J-10	2008?	13,200 kg (29,106 lbs)	7.5	Development starts in 1986; initial production reported in 2006; U.S. and Russian tech influences; core serving as basis for new large high-bypass transport turbofan and naval turbine engines
AL-31F	Russia, Saturn	Su-27; Su-30; J-11; J-10	1977 (test flight)	12,258 kg (27,557 lbs)	7.14	Development likely stated in late 1960s; AL-31FM-2 increases to 13,200 kg max thrust

Taihang Mod. (WS-14 or15)	PRC, Shenyang	JXX	2015–2018?	15,500 kg (34,117 lbs)	9.5	Development likely started in early 1990s; component production reported started in 2006
F119-PW-100	U.S, Pratt Whitney	F-22A	2003	15,570 kg (35,000 lbs)	10?	First 5th-generation engine; 43,000 lb class F135 will power the F-35
Item-117S	Russia, Saturn	PAK-FA	2015?	14,500 kg? (32,000 lbs)	10+?	A version is expected to power the Sukhoi 5th generation fighter

Note: Figures for PRC engines estimated. Sources: *Jane's All The World's Aircraft*, AVIC-1, FYJS and CJDBY Web pages.

two new large underway-replenishment ships, and series production of an improved tank-landing craft (LST).

In late 2006 the PLAN launched what may be the first of three or more 20,000-ton landing platform docks (LPDs). This ship also featured heavy use of modular construction and was assembled and launched in about seven to eight months. In early 2007 a source from the China Shipbuilding Company noted they were able to build the Type 081 flat-deck helicopter carrier (landing helicopter dock, or LHD),[147] said to be another 20,000-ton-class amphibious projection ship. In addition, the PLA has produced two 886-class underway-replenishment ships, two new large space-support ships, and in 2007, its first dedicated hospital ship, all of which exceed 20,000 tons displacement. Production of these large warships and the great strides in very large commercial ship construction prove that China is likely well on its way to gathering the technical skills needed to build an indigenous aircraft carrier.

To be sure, the burst of destroyer construction since 2000 and the rapid construction of larger warships was made possible by the modernization of China's shipbuilding industry over the past three decades. China's shipyards are now ranked third in world production, after Japan and South Korea. China's has benefited from technology transfers from both countries, including modular construction methods and use of advanced design software to greatly speed production. In 2007 China completed a 101,000-dwt container ship and a 300,000-dwt floating production, storage, and offloading (FPSO) ship for offshore petroleum production—both among the largest in the world.[148] The PLAN's new air defense destroyers were all built sequentially in the Shanghai Jiangnan shipyard, demonstrating modular construction and very close quality control probably made possible by computers and precision machine tools. The new Type 054 frigate is made in two shipyards. The Guangzhou yard uses a covered assembly line to connect very large modules built in nearby locations, a state of the art technique. The improved Type 039 *Song*-class submarine was built in two shipyards in Wuhan and Shanghai to facilitate a rapid buildup.

Although the PLA took nearly a decade to perfect the Type 039 *Song*-class conventional submarine, it has emerged to be a significant advance over the previous Type 035 *Ming* and is able to pose a significant threat to U.S. and allied navies. In 2004 the United States was apparently surprised by the emergence of the *Yuan*-class non-nuclear submarine, which featured a more advanced Russian style hull similar to the Rubin Bureau's *Lada* class. Russian assistance for the *Yuan* would have been consistent with U.S. assessments that Russia provided technology for the Type 093 SSN and the Type 094 SSBN. Again, Russia's Rubin Bureau was reportedly the source of hull, quieting, and propulsion technologies. Chinese naval technical literature demonstrates a possible substantial Chinese familiarity with modern submarine quieting techniques such as "rafting" (suspending floors on flexible mounts), engine mounting, flexible piping, and sound monitoring, all of which will likely be used to improve the acoustic performance of future Chinese submarines.[149]

The *Yuan* is expected to incorporate advances in sonar, quieting, and combat systems, and it is also expected to incorporate an Air Independent Propulsion (AIP) system. Chinese research into AIP technologies apparently dates back to the 1970s, and China apparently has conducted advanced research in the areas of fuel cells, closed-cycle diesel engines similar to the French MESMA, and Swedish-style Stirling engines. In early 2007 *Jane's Navy International* reported that China had tested a Stirling AIP engine on the *Yuan* in 2004.[150] A Chinese report from early 2008 also noted that China has tested a Stirling engine on a submarine and has undertaken long-standing Stirling engine research at the 711 Institute of the China Shipbuilding Group, which has built a 100-kW output Stirling engine.[151] The Dalian Institute of Chemical Physics, part of the Chinese Academy of Sciences, has apparently developed 100- and 1000-kw fuel cell engines.[152] In addition, academic literature indicates significant Chinese research into closed-diesel engines that use argon gas to absorb exhaust, a technology used by the French-designed MESMA AIP system.[153] China may also be investigating the application of AIP propulsion to unmanned underwater vehicles.[154]

The PLA is experimenting with and producing novel hull forms that produce better speed and sea keeping in rougher seas. Earlier in the decade the PLA imported from the Australian firm AMD a design for a wave-piercing catamaran ferry, which it promptly developed into the Type 022 *Houbei*-class fast-attack craft. The 250-ton Type 022 features extensive use of stealth shaping and coating and is armed with up to eight C-802/803 antiship missiles (ASMs). The PLA may build up to sixty or more of these FACs, which can carry up to eight C-802 ASMs.[155] A VIP ferry version of this design emerged in 2006, as did a larger cargo-offloading ferry version, indicating that the PLA may be considering this hull form for larger transport missions, as are the U.S. Army and Navy. To wit, in late 2007 a Taiwanese military source reported that China was developing a larger 500-ton fast-attack craft based on the Type 022 hull.[156] Such a ship might carry more weapons, or feature a modular design that would allow the conduct of different missions. In the late 1990s the PLA also produced an experimental catamaran Small Waterplane Area Twin Hull (SWATH) hull ship; this design allows smaller hulls to withstand higher sea states. In September 2007 it was revealed that the PLA had launched a new intelligence-gathering ship based on a SWATH design.

"Informationization," or Operationalizing the Information Revolution

One of the key transformations in the PLA since 2000 has been its effort to become an "informationized" force that seeks to exploit advances in computers, communications, computer networks, long-range space and radar sensors, and even information weapons to seek what the United States calls "information dominance." It is in the areas of information warfare that the PLA may be making rapid progress. For the PLA, like the U.S. military, information warfare involves "soft-kill" and "hard-kill" options. Soft-kill options include using computer network attack, electronic warfare such as jamming, or electronic and high-power microwave devices to incapacitate military or civilian computer networks, weapons, or electronic equipment. Hard-kill options involve using antisatellite weapons or antiradiation missiles to destroy radar or communications nodes, or sending Special Forces to attack critical electronic targets.

Exploiting Networks

Ever since the United States first demonstrated the potential for "Network Warfare" during the first Gulf War, the PLA has been seeking to absorb this technology, develop its own, and apply it to the PLA. The goal in Network Warfare is to link sensors, databases, commanders, and their troops to enable ever-faster execution of command decisions that would involve as many different military services or units as required for a mission. A chain of command goes from being "vertical," where information and decisions go up or down, to "flat," where all necessary actors see the same information simultaneously. As this network revolution has been essential to the U.S. ability to undertake ever more "intimate" joint military operations, so has it been for the PLA.

The PLA's Communications Corp is said to represent about 10 percent of the PLA's troops.[157] As the PLA has transitioned from the operational concept of "Joint Operations" to "Integrated Joint Operations" it has also greatly improved its ability to conduct network-based military activities. In early 2000 it was reported that the PLA was building a new integrated command, control, communications, computer, intelligence, surveillance, and reconnaissance (C4ISR) system called Qu Dian.[158] Also called the Regional Integrated Electronic System, or Project 995, this new C4IKSR (China adds "K" for Kill) system builds on several years of PRC investments in building fiber-optic networks. It consists of cellular and satellite communication networks throughout the PRC, integrated with new satellite, aircraft, and electronic sensors. It is thought to consist of a Joint Operations Center that is linked to joint command centers in the Nanjing, Guangzhou, and Jinan Military Regions (MRs), as well as to Navy, Air Force, and Second Artillery commands in these MRs.[159] Since 2004 PLA electronics companies have been marketing their vision of a C4KISR at arms shows by depicting a map of Eastern China covered in ground command centers interlinked to radar, satellites, and AWACS, all giving commands to ground forces, aircraft, naval, and missile forces.

Additional evidence of network integration in the PLA lies in the greater use of large computer display screens in major command centers that allow the simultaneous monitoring of separate operations and data from disparate sensors and intelligence sources. And at the small-unit level, in PLA Army units or in Second Artillery units, there is far greater use of laptops linked to broadband networks. Both trucks and tracked-command vehicles are also increasingly seen with flat-panel displays linked by satellite communication systems. New tanks such as the T-99 and T-96 are believed to have digital communications and displays, and there has been some effort to upgrade older armored divisions with similar digital connectivity.[160]

In early 2008 China's CCTV ran a program on PLA advanced training for amphibious operations. The show featured extensive scenes in which commanders consulted their laptops and issued orders over them, retrieved and disseminated satellite imagery from laptops, and coordinated small Special Force operations as well as larger combined arms landing operations. The show also featured advanced digital model depictions of small unit operations. While much of the footage seemed to be stock scenes from many previous exercises, this should not mask the larger point that digital C4ISR connectivity is transforming the PLA's ability to conduct modern combined-arms military operations.

The PLA, like the U.S. and European countries, is also developing miniature helmet-mounted computer monitors and armband keyboards consistent with the goal of creating a "Digital Soldier" who can personally contribute to the network and take commands. An early version of a soldier's digital rig was revealed to Special Forces troops in 2002, and a more advanced version was tested in the "Northern Sword 2007" exercises in Xinjiang.[161] An article celebrating the eightieth anniversary of the PLA's Communications Corps noted this progress, saying, "'They are out-and-out combatants.' The formation commander explained. Future warfare will bind sensors, computers, communication systems, commanders, and operational platforms together, and the communication support and command and control will be fused to a high degree. The traditional 'messenger' is now changing into an 'information soldier,' directly steering informatized equipment into fierce struggles in complex electromagnetic space."

Exploiting and Restricting Outer Space

A major element of the PLA's drive to exploit information technologies and to be able to fight "information warfare" has been an expensive effort to build military capabilities to both exploit outer space and restrict its use by others (Table 5.6). The PLA is beginning to assemble a new space network of surveillance, communication, and navigation satellites to serve its war fighters and has started testing capabilities to combat enemy space assets; this is explored further in Chapter 4. In early 2008 a Chinese space official commented that China had only thirty-four satellites compared to about 400 for the United States. By the middle of the next decade China's satellite number may be closer to 100.

At the 2006 Zhuhai Air Show, China announced that in 2007 the PLA planned to launch a constellation of three new surveillance satellites: two HuanJing HJ-1A electro-optical satellites and one HJ-1C radar satellite. However, the launch of these satellites has been delayed to 2008. The initial three are to be followed by a series of four more satellites: two HJ-1B multi-spectral electro-optical and two HJ-1C radar satellites.[162] In 2008 the Pentagon

Table 5.6 PLA Emerging Space Satellite Information Architecture

Type	System	Function	Orbit	Launch Date
Radar	JianBing-3/ZiYuan-2	Experimental SAR; S-Band (?)	PEO	9/00; 10/02; 11/04
	JianBing-5/YaoGan-1; YaoGan-2; YaoGan-3	Planar SAR; S-Band (?); 5-m resolution (?); 863 Program project	PEO	4/06; 5/07; 11/07
	JianBing-7	SAR	PEO	2008 (?)
	Second-generation RadarSat	SAR	PEO (?)	2010 (est.)
	HuanJing, HJ-1C	Russian SAR; Russian source: 1-m resolution; PRC source: 5-m; eventual five satellites (?)	PEO	2008–09 (est.)
Electro-optical	HJ-1A	Russian assistance; Russian source: 1-m resolution; PRC source: 30-m	PEO	2008 (est.)
	HJ-1B	Russian hyperspectral >Russian source: 1-m resolution; PRC source: 30-m eventually up to six HJ series satellites (?)	PEO	2008 (est.)
	CBERS-2B	2.5-m resolution; third China-Brazil E/O satellite	PEO	9/07
	JianBing8	High-resolution	PEO	2008 (?)
	ZiYuan-3	>2.5-m resolution (?); also known as CBERS-3	PEO	2009 (est.)
	ZiYuan-4	N/A	PEO	N/A
	FSW-3/4	Multipurpose satellites for imaging and various experiments; short duration	LEO	Twenty-three launches between 1975 and 11/06
ELINT	LeiDian	Purpose-designed ELINT satellite	N/A	N/A
	Shenzhou-1/2	ELINT payload carried on orbital module	LEO	11/99; 1/01

Category	Name	Description	Orbit	Date/Status
Weather	FengYun-1D	Multispectral; can assist missile targeting	PEO	5/05
	FengYun-2C/D	Visible and infrared sensors	GEO	10/04; 12/06
	FengYun-3	L, X band communication, 1-km resolution visual, 250-m resolution MERSI	PEO	5//08
	FengYun-4	Two versions planned: optical and microwave	GEO	N/A
Communication	FengHuo	C band (?); first purpose-built fixed-site PLA milcomsat; theater-level C3I	GEO	1/00;
	Zhongxing-20/ Zhongxing-22A/ ShenTong	Ku band; mobile PLA milcomsat; DFH-3 based	GEO	11/03; 9/06
	DFH-3	Twenty-four C-band transponders; fixed communication; DASA (Germany) technical assistance	GEO	6/07; three previous not in use
	DFH-4	Twenty-two Ku-band transponders; mobile communication capable; Alcatel (France) technical assistance	GEO	10/06 (Failed)
Navigation	BeiDou-1	China regional coverage; four-satellite system relies on ground broadcast; limited text-communication function	GEO	10/00; 12/00; 5/03; 2/07
	BeiDou-2 or Compass	Planned thirty-navsat system; global coverage similar to US, Russian, EU navsat systems	MEO	4/07; complete in 2012?
	Galileo	Partner status in eventual thirty-satellite EU navsat system	MEO	Success not clear in 2007
Data relay	TianLian-1	Based on DFH-3	GEO (?)	4/25/08
	TianLian-2 (?)	New design revealed in 2002, based on DFH-4 (?)	GEO (?)	N/A

Terms: ELINT, Electronic Intelligence; GEO, Geostationary Orbit; LEO, Low Earth Orbit; MEO, Medium Earth Orbit; PEO, Polar Earth Orbit; SAR, Synthetic Aperture Radar

Sources: Author interviews; SinoDefense.com; Europortal.org; *Jane's Defence Weekly*; NASA

reported that there would be an eventual constellation of eleven HuanJing surveillance satellites, but did not specify how many of each.[163] According to the announcement, the satellites would be based on Russian NPO Machinostroyenia electro-optical and radar satellites.[164] One Chinese official stated the electro-optical satellites would have a 1/10-meter resolution.[165] While this would be a small surveillance constellation compared to that of the United States, it would be the largest in Asia, sufficient to give PLA war fighters a twice-daily revisit by both types of satellites.

In addition, the PLA has developed a series of indigenous surveillance satellites. One of the higher-profile 863 Program projects was to develop a space-based synthetic-aperture radar satellite. From 2000 to 2004 China launched a series of three experimental synthetic-aperture radar satellites called the ZiYuan-2 or JianBing-3 series. These satellite may have featured a S-Band radar.[166] Then it launched a more sophisticated JianBing-5/YaoGan-1 in April 2006, and reportedly it will launch JianBing-7 in 2008.[167] Limited data indicate it uses a planar radar array similar to the Canadian RADARSAT. The PLA has also developed a series of high-resolution digital electro-optical satellites, the JianBing-6 and JianBing-8, which will complement the JianBing-5 and -7 radarsats.[168] In early 2007 an Asian source also indicated that China has launched a new series of purpose-built electronic intelligence satellites, the LeiDian series.[169] In addition, Chinese technical literature may suggest that China is also developing its own type of deep-space missile early warning satellite, perhaps similar to the U.S. DSP series.[170]

The PLA currently has designed two purpose-built communication satellites, and it is known to use many Chinese "civilian" communication satellites. The PLA theoretically can utilize most of the communication satellites controlled by Chinese-owned or partially Chinese-owned communication satellite corporations. These would include ChinaSat (three comsats, one more in 2009), Apstar (five communication satellites), and China Orient Telecom Satellite Company (one communication satellite).[171]

China also has plans to loft its own large constellation of navigation satellites to ensure its access to global satellite navigation signals and to rival the U.S. and Russian navigation satellite systems. The PLA now has four BeiDou navigation satellites in orbit; this system is limited by its reliance on ground stations for navigation signal broadcast but does include a limited text-messaging system. This messaging feature was used during rescue operations following the May 12, 2008, earthquake in Sichuan Province. At the 2006 Zhuhai Air Show, China made clear that it would expand the initial BeiDou constellation to five satellites and then loft a second constellation of over thirty true navigation satellites. The first of these new-generation BeiDou-2 or Compass satellites was launched in April 2007. But to guarantee access to navsat signals like those broadcast by the U.S. Global Positioning Satellite (GPS) system, China is now a full partner in Europe's Galileo navsat system, which plans to have thirty satellites in orbit by the early 2010s. China will also use its experience with Galileo[172] to build its own navsat network, and reports indicate it will begin to loft its own network, also in the early 2010s.[173]

The PLA is also moving quickly to develop micro- and nanosatellite technology. This technology can be used to more rapidly repopulate satellite constellations, to create less vulnerable distributed-sensor networks, or to develop interceptor satellites. There are indications that China may consider lofting large numbers of small satellites flying in formation.[174] After its initial 1998 co-development contract with Britain's Surrey Space Systems, in mid-2000 the PLA launched its first 50-kg Tsinghua-1 microsatellite aboard a Russian booster. The launch also featured Surrey's Spot nanosatellite, which photographed Tsinghua; this exercise likely also gave insights to Chinese engineers. China is marketing its MS-1 microsat with a 30-kg payload. In April 2004 it launched its first NS-1 nanosatellite. When China launched its JianBing-6 surveillance satellite on May 25, 2007, it also launched a 1-kg picosatellite developed by Zhejiang University.[175] Surveillance and communication satellites will be able to give new PLA cruise missiles and precision-guided weapons global reach when the PLA completes a constellation of new tracking and data relay satellite system (TDRSS) satellites, the first of which was launched in April 2008. These satellites are used by the United States and Russia to link disparate surveillance and communication satellites to achieve rapid data transmission, rather than wait for satellites to appear over national territories for data transmissions. At the 2002 Zhuhai Air Show the China Aerospace Corporation revealed it had two types of data-relay satellites in development: one based on the DFH-3 satellite bus and one based on the larger DFH-4 but with two large antennae similar to U.S. TDRSS satellites.[176] Also similar to the U.S. system, China's TDRSS likely uses S-band frequencies to relay data through space and Ka-band frequencies to transmit data to ground stations.[177]

The United States, Russia, and Japan use data-relay satellites to reduce the need for its manned space craft and satellites to use ground relay stations that could be vulnerable due to their placement in countries that could cut off access to such stations. In 2005 the PLA received a lesson in this vulnerability when a change in government in the small South Pacific island nation of Kiribati forced China to close a small-satellite communications relay station. China must now rely on a small fleet of seven large-satellite communications relay ships to support its manned space program, a requirement that could be diminished with data-relay satellites. Nevertheless, in 2007 and 2008 China launched two modern "space events" ships, which improve China's ground-based space tracking capabilities.

In addition, the PLA is also expanding its ability to complement satellites with long-range UAVs for surveillance missions. At the 2006 Zhuhai Air Show, Chinese companies revealed two very-long-range surveillance UAV concepts: one from the Chengdu Aircraft Company bearing a close resemblance in shape and size to the U.S. Northrop Grumman Global Hawk, and a slightly smaller surveillance UAV by the Guizhou Company. Company officials did not offer any real information on these concepts, but it can be assumed that they are serious programs. If successful, they will expand the PLA's ability to monitor areas of concern at great distances, or even mount 24- to 48-hour patrols over areas where U.S. naval forces might seek to assist Taiwan.

Soft Kill: Computer Network Operations (CNO)

During a sixteen-day period from late August to early September 2007, the PLA was accused of conducting alarming computer network espionage against government computers in Germany, Britain, France, Australia, New Zealand, and the U.S. Department of Defense.[178] In reply to German accusations and subsequent public outrage, a Chinese Foreign Ministry spokesman issued a statement, saying, "The Chinese government consistently opposes and strictly prohibits all criminal activities that damage computer network performance, including 'hacking' behavior."[179] Quite to the contrary, it is now apparent that China is one of the most (if not the most) aggressive users of computer network operations to conduct surveillance and espionage, and—if they consider it necessary—to attack and shut down the vital military and civilian electronic infrastructures of the United States, Taiwan, Europe, and elsewhere. In fact, a sensational but well-sourced report in the *National Journal* asserted that during 2003 major portions of the United States suffered power outages due to attacks by Chinese hackers.[180] A 2007 assessment ranks China as the world's number one "cyberthreat" in terms of intent and capabilities.[181] In the unrestrained universe of cyberspace it should be considered that the PLA, Chinese intelligence organs, and their allies are waging a war: not a virtual war, but a very real one.

The 2006 Pentagon PLA report offered a useful account of PLA computer network operations:

> China's computer network operations (CNO) include computer network attack, computer network defense, and computer network exploitation. The PLA sees CNO as critical to seize the initiative and achieve "electromagnetic dominance" early in a conflict, and as a force multiplier. Although there is no evidence of a formal Chinese CNO doctrine, PLA theorists have coined the term "Integrated Network Electronic Warfare" to outline the integrated use of electronic warfare, CNO, and limited kinetic strikes against key C4 nodes to disrupt the enemy's battlefield network information systems. The PLA has established information warfare units to develop viruses to attack enemy computer systems and networks, and tactics and measures to protect friendly computer systems and networks. The PLA has increased the role of CNO in its military exercises. For example, exercises in 2005 began to incorporate offensive operations, primarily in first strikes against enemy networks.[182]

In the 1990s the PLA devoted considerable resources to developing the doctrine and then the infrastructure to conduct information warfare, especially via computer network attacks (CNA). In 1995 then–Major General Wang Pufeng, former Director of the Strategy Department of the Academy of Military Sciences, wrote, "In the near future, information warfare will control the form and the future of war. We recognize this developmental trend of information warfare and see it as a driving force in the modernization of China's military and combat readiness."[183] In 1996 PRC analyst Wei Jincheng stated that "the enemy country can receive a paralyzing blow through the Internet, and the party on the receiving end will not be able to tell whether it's a child's prank or an attack from its enemy."[184] In 2001, Timothy Thomas, a top U.S. expert on PLA information operations, listed the following information attack options mentioned by PLA sources:

> Planting information mines; conducting information reconnaissance; changing network data; releasing information bombs; dumping information garbage; applying information deception; releasing clone information; organizing information defense; and establishing network spy stations.[185]

A 2007 assessment noted that China has developed and is capable of using "advanced data weapons." These include self-morphing malicious code applications; electronic circuitry destruction capabilities; self-encrypting/self-decrypting of malicious code; external disruption capacity of wireless networks; and exploitation of unreported vulnerabilities in common commercial software.[186]

A 2003 commentary in the *People's Liberation Army Daily* about the need for China to protect its "information territory" gives an indication of what it may target in foreign countries. According to this definition, information territory "not only refers to the Internet in [the] common sense, but also to key information network systems such as finance, electric power, telecommunications, transportation, energy, military and statistics."[187] As the most highly information-intensive society, the United States is particularly vulnerable to information attacks. In the event of a future war with China the United States should expect that the PLA would use sophisticated computer viruses or "computer bombs" to attack computer systems that control domestic U.S. air traffic, vehicle and rail traffic, emergency control, financial sectors, water, sanitation, and energy. The PLA's goal will be to sow chaos among U.S. civilians while using the same tactics to attack the computer systems necessary to almost every aspect of U.S. military power.[188] It is noted that well-targeted electronic attacks "could be as devastating to a country's economy as damage inflicted by an intercontinental missile."[189]

China's CNO Force

Taiwanese sources contend that the PLA has maintained a formal "Internet Force" since 1999.[190] In 2001 the PLA is reported to have computer-warfare units in the Guangzhou, Nanjing, and Jinan MRs, each with about 500 specialists.[191]

Another 2001 report indicates that PLA Information Warfare reserve units have been formed in the cities of Datong, Xiamen, Shanghai, Echeng, and Xian. It is possible that such reserve units include many specialists who work in the civilian computer development and manufacturing sector.[192] But it now appears that a much larger computer network operations "force" has become elevated within the PLA order of battle. In 2004 and 2005 it became apparent that six of the seven PLA Military Regions would have a "Special Technical Reconnaissance Unit" (STRU) for the purpose of waging both defensive and offensive information warfare (IW). As such, it reasonable to envision that between the STRU and less formal reserve and militia units, the PLA could maintain a force of thousands of "cyberwarriors." Only the Beijing Military Region appears to lack such a unit, but that may be because Beijing serves as the command headquarters for the PLA.

The size of China's potential force of "cyberwarriors" grows even larger when considering China's and the PLA's ongoing cooperation with "cybercriminal" networks. The Chinese government and its intelligence organs have long relationships with traditional Chinese criminal organizations, or Triads, many of which predate the 1949 Communist Revolution. Triads cooperate and compete around the world and are strong in Taiwan and in the United States. It should not be surprising that Chinese criminal organizations have become attracted to the potential profit from "cybercrime" and that the PLA would come to approve of, and even cooperate with, their endeavors. It has been noted that "official" Chinese "cyberwarriors" seek to resemble criminals in their activities.[193] In addition, criminal networks, and apparently the government, use China's labor advantage to find "Zero Day Exploits" (ZDEs), or software flaws that can allow criminals to steal great quantities of valuable information. As ZDEs are often temporary, a large workforce is required to constantly search for more, and China is proving to be an ample source of low-cost hackers and software technicians.[194]

It must also be considered that China could conduct CNO from, or could formally enlist the services of hackers or "cyberwarriors" from allied nations with known interests in computer network operations, such as Cuba, or in the future, Venezuela and Iran. North Korea apparently has substantial computer network operations potential.[195] China and Cuba have had a robust intelligence cooperation relationship since the mid- to late 1990s. China reportedly mans SIGINT facilities in Bejucal and a second facility at Santiago de Cuba to monitor U.S. military satellites.[196] But Cuba has also invested in its own extensive CNO capabilities.[197] It is not beyond reason to consider that cooperative or coordinated CNO may constitute an early form of PLA-Cuba military cooperation. In the future Venezuela may join such activities, especially as Chinese-Venezuelan political and economic cooperation grows. During the August 2006 visit to China by Venezuelan strongman Hugo Chavez, it was reportedly agreed that China would help develop Venezuela's information architecture,[198] which offers opportunities for both China and Chavez to consider future IW cooperation at many levels.

Targeting the United States

As the following list of reports indicates, in less than a decade, China's record of computer network operations against the United States and its allies has grown from political harassment to a serious threat to the security of, and information within, critical U.S. government and business databases and networks. It can be concluded that China is undertaking aggressive and massive computer network operations against American military and civilian computer network targets on a daily basis.

- 2003: China is reported to be the source of most of 294 successful hackings into U.S. Department of Defense computers. China is also accused of entering computers at U.S. Army bases at Aberdeen, where it stole data on the Army's Future Combat System, and intrusions at Fort Bragg and Fort Hood.[199]
- August 2005: Reports emerge about "Titan Rain," code name for a group of Chinese Internet spies of uncanny skill who had been tracked by the FBI since 2003, as they broke into multiple U.S. military and defense contractor computers.[200]
- December 2005: Chinese "hackers" reportedly based in Guangdong send personally tailored e-mails to British Parliamentarians intended to launch "spyware" that seeks and sends information back to China.[201]
- January 2006: The first FBI Computer Crime Survey covering 2005 reveals that China is the origin of 25 percent of computer attacks against U.S. businesses.[202]
- July 2006: China is reported to have broken into the U.S. State Departments computers for the purpose of seizing "information, passwords and other data."[203]
- 2006: China is reported to have attacked and compromised computer systems at the U.S. Naval War College, National Defense University, and the U.S Army's Fort Hood, causing $20 to $30 million in damage to each system.[204]
- June 2007: Chinese military hackers are reported to have broken into computer networks serving the U.S. Secretary of Defense, forcing the network to be shut down.[205]
- January 2008: A leaked FBI briefing given in January 2008 reveals their suspicions that uncontrolled or counterfeit Cisco computer routers made in China and widely used by classified U.S. government and military computers may have created large numbers of undetectable "back doors" that could be exploited by PLA hackers.[206]

Targeting Taiwan

As damaging as they are, it appears that most Chinese CNA operations against U.S. targets are for the purpose of military or industrial espionage—so far. However, to gain insight into how the PLA may use CNA to advance military missions against the United States, it is first critical to examine how the PLA is pursuing CNA and broader IW operations against Taiwan. IW and CNA are viewed by some U.S. officials as part of a wider PLA effort to attack Taiwan's civil infrastructure, to accelerate victory in a direct military campaign. In an October 2004 speech, then–Deputy Assistant Secretary of Defense Richard Lawless stated: "China is actively developing options to create chaos on the island, to compromise components of Taiwan's critical infrastructure—telecommunications, utilities, broadcast media, cellular, Internet and computer networks. . . . These threats range from computer network attacks to compromising Taiwan's public utilities, communications, operational security and transportation."[207] In mid-2008 a Taiwanese source disclosed to the author that in about 2003 Taiwan had to tear down and rebuild entire computer data bases in several ministries, including the Ministry of Foreign Affairs, because of Chinese penetration.

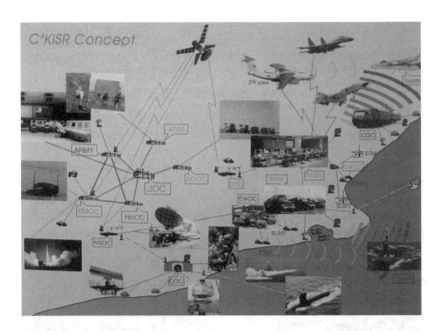

The concept of "Informatization," which has underpinned the transformation of PLA capablities in the last decade, is illustrated by a large poster of a Chinese C4KISR concept (Command, Communication, Control, Computers, Killing, Intelligence, Surveillance, Reconnaisance), linking sensors to commanders to shooters. Informatization applied to a micro level shows the digital monitor and command system for a Chinese unmanned aircraft, seen at the 2004 Zhuhai Airshow. Picture Credit: RD Fisher

Military Space. On January 11, 2007 China fired a modified version of the KT-1 solid fueled and mobile space launch vehicle (top left) and successfully intercepted a target weather satellite in Polar Orbit. The target satellite was very likely tracked by a powerful phased array radar similar to that developed to track China's manned space vehicles (top right). Both of these systems could form the basis for an initial Anti-Ballistic Missile Defense System. Pictures from the 2004 Zhuhai Airshow. China is also making great strides in assembling a satellite network to support regional and extra-regional military operations. Russian technology radar satellites (bottom left), a new constellation of 30 navigation satellites (bottom middle) and tracking and data relay satellites (bottom right) will in the future enable global targeting for weapons. Photo Credit: RD Fisher

山 全部

空间实验室

Manned Space. China's ambitions for manned space include eventual space stations and very likely, a manned presence on the Moon. China's manned space program will serve scientific, economic and military goals. Photos taken at the 2004 Zhuhai Airshow include a model of the Shenzhou manned spaceship (top) with a camera atop the orbital module, a video capture of a future spacelab (middle) and a concept photo for an unmanned Moon rover (bottom). Photo Credit: RD Fisher

Missile Modernization. Since the mid-1990s the PLA has pursued an aggressive modernization for all of its missile forces. The 8,000 km range DF-31 ICBM (top), photographed during the 1999 PLA Parade, is now joined by the 11,000km range DF-31A, which may carry multiple warheads. The DF-21 intermediate range missile (middle) is being succeeded by a new 3,000km version that may also have multiple warheads. The DF-11Mod 1 (bottom left) is the most numerous short-range missile facing Taiwan. These will soon be joined by the 250km range B-611M (bottom right back) and the 150km range P-12 (bottom right front), which along with later models of the DF-11, use satellite navigation guidance systems and feature a variety of warheads. Photo Credit: Defense Technology Monthly and RD Fisher

Precision Strike. China's surveillance and navigation satellites will soon enable modern aerial precision strike capabilities to compliment the PLA's new accurate missiles. The C-602/YJ-62 land attack cruise missile (top) is now available in ship and land-launched versions, and will soon be developed into submarine and air-launched versions. The vernable Xian H-6 bomber, shown in an AVIC-1 video carrying older YJ-63 land attack cruise missiles, is being developed into the more capable H-6K that will carry new LACMs, plus satellite-guided bombs like the FT-1, and laser-guided bombs like the GB1. Photo Credit: RD Fisher

Modern Airpower. Russia has greatly aided the PLA's airpower modernization with the sale of over 250 Russian-made and Chinese co-produced models of the Sukhoi Su-27 and Su-30 fighter bombers. A Su-30MKK model (top left) shows the array of modern Russian air-to-air and ground attack weapons. Chengdu's FC-1 fighter, seen at the 2007 Singapore Airshow, (top right) was aided by U.S. and Russian designers and is now co-produced with Pakistan, using a Russian RD-33 turbofan and a the PL-12 medium-range air-to-air missile using Russian radar technology. Russia has sold China the means to make its version of the RD-33 (middle) called the WS-13 turbofan. Russia may also be aiding China with a new large transport aircraft project, and may still buy the Russian Ilyushin Il-76MF (bottom). Photo Credit: RD Fisher

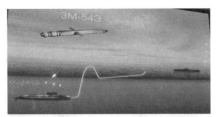

Naval Expansion. The People's Liberation Army Navy (PLAN) is building a force to deter or combat American forces that may seek to thwart a Chinese attack against Taiwan, having purchased 12 Russian-made KILO conventional submarines (top right), 8 of which are armed with the deadly Novator 3M54E long-range anti-ship missile (top right). China has also built about 13 modern Type 039 conventional submarines (middle) plus Type 093 second-generation nuclear attack submarines. Looking to the future, China's Navy will seek to defend China's distant economic and political interests; in May 2007 a Chinese Jiangwei-II frigate visited Singapore and participated in multilateral exercises (bottom left). Over the next two decades China is also expected to build multiple aircraft carrier battle groups. A model of the Russian carrier Kuznetzov (bottom right) is from a display inside the Russian carrier Minsk, now a museum in Guangdong Province visited by the author in November 2004. The Varyag, a sister of the Kuznetzov, has been refitting in Dalian Harbor since 2002. Photo Credit: RD Fisher

Ground Force Modernization. The PLA's ground forces are rapidly increasing their degree of mechanization and their firepower. The MBT-2000 (top left) is the export version of the PLA Army's T-96 medium battle tank, which is now being modernized with a new turret with "arrow" shaped cheek armor (top right). The PLA is also investing in a range of new wheeled fighting vehicles; the 105mm gun armed "Assaulter" (middle left) can fire co-produced Russian gun-launched laser-guided anti-tank missiles. In addition, the PLA has purchased about 200 Russian Mil Mi-17 medium transport helicopters (middle right) and may soon co-produce this effective helicopter. Amphibious Army and Marine units are armed with the 105mm gun armed T-63 amphibious tank (bottom left), which is being succeeded by a larger and faster tank. The PLA has also purchased the Russian "Shelf" parachute system (bottom right) for its new ZLC-2000 airborn tank family. Photo Credit: RD Fisher

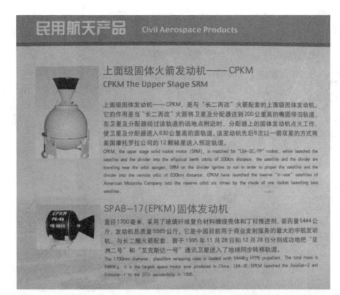

Espionage. China pursues a massive and global campaign of espionage to find military and commercial secrets which can aid its military build-up. In 1999 a former Chinese rocket engineer explained to the author how advice and technology provided by the former Martin Marietta Company in the early 1990s, in connection with the perfecting of the SPAB-17 solid fuel satellite kick motor (top), enabled his colleagues to perfect the rocket motor of the DF-21 intermediate range ballistic missile, and by extension, all succeeding Chinese large solid fuel missiles. Starting in 1999 Noshir Gowadia, who helped develop the infrared masking system for the Northrop Grumman B-2 stealth bomber, started giving occasional lectures in China, for which he was later convicted of espionage. Could China apply his insights to their own future stealth bomber? The Beijing University of Aeronautics and Aerospace, a major subcontractor for PLA aerospace development, displayed a curious radio controlled model (bottom)at the 2004 Zhuhai Airshow, which could represent a potential stealth bomber or UAV design. The scalloping between the vertical stabilizers may indicate an engine signature masking system. Photo Credit: RD Fisher

Proliferation. While China has tried to point to its recent passage of new laws that restrict its sale of dangerous technologies, the fact remains that since the 1970s China has either partially or significantly enabled the nuclear and missile programs of North Korea, Pakistan and Iran. These countries now pose a major threat of secondary proliferation of these technologies to terrorist entities, which might then use them to attack democracies like the United States or Israel. In the case of Pakistan, China has provided the means to enable the production of intermediate range ballistic missiles like the Shaheen-II (top), which poses a major threat to India. China's Hongdu Aircraft Co. has also co-developed tactical anti-ship missiles with Iran (bottom), which could enable Iran to make its own precision guided missiles. Iran could then give these weapons to Hezbollah. Photo Credit: RD Fisher

CHAPTER 6

BUILDING FOR LOCAL WAR DOMINANCE

Chapters 3 and 4 explored the recent doctrinal transformation of the PLA and described the ongoing adoption of new weapons development and information technologies that are propelling that transformation. This chapter will explore how the PLA armed services are fulfilling their doctrinal goal by modernizing and building up their forces to be able to win "Local Wars under High-Tech Conditions." There was a definite PLA shift emphasizing investment in information, missile, air, and naval capabilities during the 1990s and the first decade of the twenty-first century. But by the middle of the decade there was a renewed emphasis on investing in PLA ground forces, making them smaller but more lethal by enabling "Joint Integrated Operations" through a concentration on "Informationization and Mechanization." By 2011–2015 or so all of the PLA services will benefit from current investments in the space and networking infrastructures necessary to enable new "precision" weapons capabilities. In addition, China is seeking the military means to either deter or counter American attempts to militarily counter China's use of force. China will also begin to introduce "Fifth-Generation" military systems that will place it in a much more competitive position versus U.S. forces in East Asia, advancing the goal of undermining the U.S.-led alliance structure.

Local War Contingencies

Potential Local War conflicts that would reflect China's current military modernization preparations include Taiwan, Japan, Korea, the South China Sea and potential Central Asian conflicts. But assumed in these preparations is the requirement to deter or fight a potential "superpower" adversary such as the United States or Russia. Preparations for some specific contingencies are described in the following sections:

Taiwan

It appears that in the early to mid-1990s China's Communist leadership decided that it must have sovereign control over Taiwan for strategic and ideological reasons. Control of Taiwan allows China to break out of the "First Island Chain"[1] and exert greater maritime control over the Western Pacific and the South China Sea. In addition, the continuation of a democratic Taiwan undermines the legitimacy of the Beijing regime by existing as the only fully successful democratic society in Greater China.

China would prefer to "conquer" Taiwan without having to invade and wreck destruction upon its very useful economic partner. It is possible to consider scenarios under which factions within a Kuomintang Party–led Taiwanese government would seek an arrangement whereby Taiwan formally surrenders its claims to "independence" and acknowledges Beijing's ultimate sovereignty over Taiwan; however, even that scenario might not result in "peace" for Taiwan. The Communist regime in Beijing will likely not live in "peace" with a government in Taipei as long as it harbors the potential to realize an "independent" character, either in fact or in law, or continues as a full democracy.

Since the early 1990s, preparations for a Taiwan conflict have been the key motivating factor for China's broad military modernizations. The ultimate goal is to create a military fait accompli on Taiwan in which PLA or pro-China forces rapidly seize control of Taipei, allowing China to combine regional political recognition of its control with the presence of PLA forces on the island to forestall an American military rescue. To do this the PLA requires the means to strike with surprise and overwhelming force sufficient to render Taiwan incapable of repelling PLA amphibious and airborne troop operations. These operations must be sufficient to seize the key ports and airfields needed to rapidly convey follow-on forces. Furthermore, the PLA needs to accomplish most of its goals before the leadership in Washington can make the necessary decisions to dispatch forces from bases in Guam, Okinawa, Japan, and Hawaii.

These requirements have driven the PLA's build-up of nuclear ballistic missiles, antiship ballistic missiles, and antisatellite weapons to deter or combat the United States. To subdue Taiwan, the PLA requires thousands of ballistic and land-attack cruise missiles combined with information attacks at multiple levels. These attacks have two objectives: to produce military and societal chaos and to defeat air and missile defenses early on. The PLA must then sustain waves of follow-on air and naval attacks with precision weapons to demolish Taiwan's air, naval, and ground forces. Almost simultaneously the PLA must successfully accomplish daring Special Forces operations that either kill or capture key political and military leadership figures; conduct information attacks from within

Taiwan; attack key air, naval and army logistics sites; and conduct operations in preparation for amphibious and airborne troop assaults.

If combined PLA missile, air, naval, and Special Forces strikes can cause political paralysis in Taipei and significantly reduce Taiwan's existing defenses, then the PLA can commence amphibious and airborne assaults with far greater confidence and with far less force than would be needed to overwhelm Taiwan's current force size. The PLA will require the means to rapidly capture a key Taiwanese port such as Taijung and a major airfield such as CKS International Airport. This will allow the PLA to use much more extensive civil naval and air transport resources to put the bulk of its invading forces in Taiwan. But these forces must remain for a long period to "pacify" a Taiwanese society that has truly developed an independent and democratic spirit. A rapidly assembled "Quisling" government of compliant Taiwanese would likely require decades of strong support from the United Front Department, the Ministry of State Security, and the People's Armed Police forces to enforce thorough political indoctrination and quickly extinguish all forms of resistance.

Just as important, the PLA is preparing to meet the challenge of defeating U.S. and/or Japanese forces which may try to thwart their attack against Taiwan. Embarrassed by President Bill Clinton's March 1996 deployment of two carriers that trumped their coercive exercises attempting to intimidate Taiwanese voters, the PLA has sought to develop an array of "anti-access" high-tech weapons to exploit "asymmetrical" U.S. weaknesses. By 2010 or so the PLA may be able to employ a range of antisatellite weapons, antiship ballistic missiles, radio frequency weapons, supersonic cruise missiles, and massive naval mine forces—all of which the United States will be hard pressed to overcome. It is very likely that PLA Special Forces will also be used against U.S. forces in Guam, Okinawa, Japan, and Hawaii.

Once China takes control of Taiwan it will have to pacify the island and defend and exploit its new gain. There will likely be an intense campaign of purging known democracy activists and reeducation of all age groups, combined with large-scale population resettlements. A large People's Armed Police presence will bolster large operations by security organs such as the Ministry of Public Security and the United Front Department. At the same time the PLA will exploit the island as a forward missile, air, and naval base. A significant number of intercontinental ballistic missiles (ICBMs) and nuclear-powered ballistic missile submarines (SSBNs) will be based on Taiwan, which for the SSBNs offers immediate access to some of the deepest patrol zones in the Pacific. Future bombers, long-range maritime patrol aircraft, and strategic unmanned aerial vehicles (UAVs) will also be ideally placed to monitor sea-lanes from Japan down to the Straits of Malacca.

Japan

Eventual control over Taiwan is also necessary for China to be able to exercise eventual hegemony over Japan. Japan represents the only East Asian country with the economic, political, and potential military capabilities to challenge China's future dominance of Asia. Even a Japan that decided to pursue a true self-defense capability sufficient to deter China's growing forces would require a military buildup significant enough to be viewed as a vital threat by the Beijing regime. China would likely seek to maintain superiority over Japan by maintaining missile, naval, and air forces sufficient to deter Japan from challenging China's claims to territory and resources in the East China Sea. Furthermore, Beijing will likely expect that as it extends its absolute control over the South China Sea and eventually Taiwan, Tokyo will, over time, adjust to China's new hegemony in order to secure its access to energy and commercial transport routes necessary for its survival. To militarily dominate Japan the PLA will require nuclear and non-nuclear precision medium range ballistic missiles, fifth-generation combat aircraft, and a large number of attack submarines and supporting surface warships. Control over Japan will also be enabled by the future development of long-range power projection forces that allow China to be able to threaten the sources of Japan's energy and commerce.

Korea

China will likely require the means to wage combined-arms mechanized warfare on the Korean Peninsula for as long as Beijing views the survival of the Kim-style authoritarian regime as vital to its national security, and it would want to be able to dictate the new relationship with a unified Korea. While the relationship is often contentious, China has consistently sought to shield North Korea from U.S. and South Korean pressure, has aided North Korea's nuclear and missile capabilities, and has even provided massive economic assistance to ensure that a Communist regime survives in Pyongyang. China's effort to lead the Six-Party Talks since 2004 can be viewed as another attempt to shield Pyongyang from decisive outside pressure. But as of early 2008, Pyongyang's refusal to dismantle its nuclear weapons capability, which is part of a continuing crisis of credibility, may be overwhelmed by the economic and social disintegration of North Korea.[2] China's concerns with such disintegration were expressed in a late 2007 report issued by the U.S. Institute of Peace, in which Chinese experts noted that China was considering "order keeping" or military intervention in North Korea to counter refugee flows, to secure North Korean nuclear weapons facilities near its border, or to deal with the use of nuclear weapons.[3] In 2007 China accounted for 57 percent of North Korea's total trade, and former South Korean presidential candidate Sun Min Jang has asserted, "Economically at least, North Korea has already become a satellite state of China."[4] Even the suggestion of a Chinese military intervention is a chilling prospect that might be opposed by both North and South Koreans and might then involve South Korea's U.S. ally. Accepting such Chinese intervention even on "humanitarian" grounds presents Seoul with the prospect of enduring a divided Korean Peninsula and potentially hostile regime in the North for generations more.

Even though ensuring a divided Korea with a compliant regime in the North may be a crucial Chinese security requirement, a military intervention into Korea could reverse Beijing's patient work to divide Seoul from Washington. Nevertheless, whether it occurred with or without China's help, a united Korea would likely exhibit nationalistic resentments against China; this would require China to seek a level of military superiority sufficient to deter Koreans from seeking greater cooperation with Japan. South Korea has long been interested in its own nuclear weapons capability, and in the late 1990s it committed to developing space launch vehicles that could easily form the basis for nuclear-armed medium-range ballistic missiles. South Korea is also modernizing its air forces and navy with a view toward North Korea and Japan, but these capabilities could easily be directed against China.

South China Sea

China's decision in 1991 to create a law stating its claim to the South China Sea, and to then weather the regional tensions that followed, now seems more than justified from the Chinese leadership's perspective if one assumes China had long planned to base a significant portion of its nuclear-armed missiles on Hainan Island. When PLA Navy (PLAN) SSBNs move to Hainan, there will likely be a more aggressive enforcement of China's territorial claims to the South China if only to ensure its submarines have unfettered access to firing zones. In late November 2007 Chinese press reports noted that China had decided to formalize its claims to the Paracel and Spratly Islands by elevating their government status to municipalities.[5] At about the same time, in mid-November 2007, the PLA held a large exercise in the South China Sea that involved new PLAN warships, aircraft, and missile firings.[6] Internet source imagery suggests that in late 2007 the PLAN sent its first Type 094 second-generation SSBN to its new Hainan base at Sanya.[7] China will likely base aircraft carriers on Hainan Island, but it will also require long-range patrol aircraft, long-range UAVs, and the ships and submarines necessary to control that region's sea-lanes. China has been steadily building up its seven small island bases in the disputed Spratly Island group and some of its larger bases in the Paracel Islands. China will likely build these up further to support limited helicopter, seaplane, or missile military forces.

From this perspective, America's departure from its Philippine military bases in 1991 was a remarkable stroke of fortune for China. China became the most powerful military force in that region, and it will likely seek to sustain this position, working assiduously to block any return of U.S. military forces to the Philippines. Should the United States decide to challenge China's SSBN base, as it did Soviet SSBN bases during the Cold War, it is likely that China will seek to push the United States back through "limited" confrontations and by forcing the region to diminish security cooperation with Washington.

Central Asia

China has sought to secure its twin interests of commercial/resource access and defense of authoritarianism in Central Asia through the formation of the Shanghai Cooperation Organization (SCO) in 2001. The pending membership of Pakistan, Iran, and India, and the conceivable membership of Turkey, will serve to further elevate Beijing's standing within this organization and in the Central Asian region. China has pursued military relationships with all SCO members and observers to varying intensities. The major military requirement for China in the medium term will be to have the ability to intervene with an SCO member on behalf of a favored faction to sustain nondemocratic and pro-Chinese governmental policies. While this is less of a requirement for Russia, the latter may elect to cooperate with Beijing to jointly suppress emerging democratic forces. This will require that the PLA have highly mobile (but not necessarily heavily mechanized) forces, as well as mechanized airborne forces, that can work in cooperation with precision airpower to quickly secure key cities or the capital of a target state.

PLA Preparations for Local War by Branch of Service

Second Artillery and Nuclear Forces

To maintain its use for a broad range of deterrent or coercive missions, the PLA is building up its nuclear forces in ways that will enable it to defeat current and future U.S. National Missile Defenses. The exact numbers of long-range missiles are a closely held secret of the PLA, but the U.S. government and others have offered estimates of the PLA's arsenal. By 2006 China was credited by the Pentagon with having completed deployment of twenty silo-based 8,640+-km-range liquid-fueled DF-5 Mod 2 (CSS-4) ICBMs, which replaced the older Mod 1 version. However, since these are based in a distributed silo-and-cave system, the exact number may not be known.[8] Currently China is either deploying or close to deploying at least three new solid-fuel nuclear-armed intercontinental-range ballistic missiles; two land-based ICBMs, and one new submarine-launched ballistic missile (SLBM). In its 2004 report to the Congress on China's military, the Pentagon stated that ICBM numbers could reach thirty by 2005 and sixty by 2010. This seems to assume the deployment of one unit each of twenty missiles for the 7,250+-km-range solid-fuel and mobile DF-31, which entered service in 2006, and the 11,270+-km-range DF-31A, expected to enter service in 2007.

But this number must soon include new SLBMs, because in July 2004 the PLA launched its first Type 094 SSBN, which carries twelve JL-2 SLBMs.[9] In December 2006 the Office of Naval Intelligence (ONI) estimated the PLA would build up to five 094s, for a total of sixty JL-2s, while a February 2007 Hong Kong report noted the PLA would build six 094s, for a total of seventy-two JL-2s.[10] However, one implication of the Pentagon ICBM estimate and the

ONI SSBN estimate is that the PLA may seek to evenly divide its nuclear missiles between land and sea bases, perhaps meaning that an increase in one could
lead to an increase in the other. This indicates the possibility that China's
"minimal" and "lean" deterrent could expand from twenty missiles to as many
as 140 or more by about the middle of the next decade, if one assumes the PLA
will seek to evenly divide its land- and sea-based deterrents.

Although these missile numbers are still small compared to the United States
(500 ICBM, 336 SLBM in 2007) and Russia (506 ICBM, 252 SLBM in 2007), the
numbers could become closer should the PLA opt to put multiple warheads on
its long-range nuclear missiles. There appears to have been substantial Chiense
research to support the development of multiple warheads for missiles.[11] The
PLA has demonstrated its ability to develop multiple warheads since its successful two-satellite launch of U.S.-made Iridium communication satellites on
Long March space-launch vehicles starting on September 1, 1997. In 1998 the
Cox Report noted that if China were to aggressively develop multiple warheads
for its missiles it could have 1,000 by 2015.[12] A 2002 report notes that China had
test-launched seven to eight multiple warheads (one plus six to seven dummy
warheads) from a DF-21 medium-range ballistic missile,[13] meaning it may be
technically capable of putting multiple warheads on longer-range ICBMs. The
2002 Pentagon PLA report also suggested the DF-5 Mod 2, about twenty of
which would be deployed by 2006, could be armed with multiple warheads.[14] In
mid-2007 an Asian military source disclosed that the DF-5 Mod 2 carries eight
warheads.[15] *Jane's Strategic Weapons Systems* reports that the DF-5A may carry
four to six 150–350 kiloton warheads.[16]

The road-mobile DF-31 is believed to carry only one warhead, but may
employ penetration aids such as decoys to complicate interception. The follow-
on 11,270+-km-range DF-31A may also be designed to carry multiple warheads. Asian sources have suggested to this author that the DF-31A might be
a land-based version of the JL-2.[17] Should the three stages of the JL-2 be of uniform diameter, then there is a good chance it will eventually carry multiple
warheads, perhaps as many as three or four. In February 2007 the PLA-allied
Hong Kong magazine *Wide Angle* reported that a JL-2 SLBM might have up to
eight warheads, for a total of 576 missile warheads on six Type 094 SSBNs.[18]
Jane's Strategic Weapon Systems notes the DF-31A might carry just one or as
many as three to five warheads.[19] But in mid-2007 an Asian military source
indicated the JL-2 most likely would carry four warheads and the DF-31A
could carry three or four.[20] Table 6.1 summarizes the potential numbers of missiles and warheads being developed by the PLA, assuming possible multiple
reentry vehicles (MRVs).

From U.S. and other sources it cannot be concluded definitively that China is
deploying multiple warheads on any of its ICBMs or SLBMs. This author is not
able to confirm the disclosures from an Asian military source in mid-2007 of
multiple warheads on the DF-5 Mod 2, JL-2, and DF-31A; however, this source
has high credibility and it would be logical for the PLA to be equipping its new

Table 6.1 PLA Intercontinental Missiles, 2015–2020

	Range	Low Missile Number Estimate[a]	High Missile Number Estimate[b]	Low MRV & Low Missile Estimate[c]	High MRV & Low Missiled	High MRV & High Missile Estimate
DF-5 Mod 2	8,460–10,000 km	20	20	5 × 20 = 100	8 × 20 = 160	8 × 20 = 160
DF-31	7,250+ km	20	20	1 × 20 = 20	1 × 20 = 20	1 × 20 = 20
DF-31A	11,270+ km	20	40	3 × 20 = 60	4 × 20 = 80	4 × 40 = 160
JL-2	8,000+ km	60 (12 SLBM × 5 SSBN)	72 (12 SLBM × 6 SSBN)	3 × 60 = 180	4 × 60 = 240	4 × 72 = 288
TOTALS		120 missiles and warheads	152 missiles and warheads	360 warheads	500 warheads	628 warheads

[a] Estimates from DoD 2004 and ONI 2006.
[b] High missile number estimate based on author estimate and data from *Kuang Chaio Ching*, February 15, 2007–March 15, 2007, No. 413, p. 80, translated by Open Source Center, February 16, 2007.
[c] Low MRV number based on author estimate.
[d] High MRV estimate based on author interviews.

missiles with multiple warheads. If China were to put multiple warheads on its missiles, the above chart illustrates how China could quickly increase the number of deliverable nuclear warheads over its number of missiles. Should the DF-31A prove to be based on the JL-2, then a high estimate for potential PLA nuclear warheads would exceed 500. While this number is lower than the 2002 U.S.-Russia agreement to limit warhead numbers to 1,700–2,200, it does drastically alter U.S. deterrent calculations given that the United States may soon have to deter a number of rogue nuclear powers, Russia, and a much more powerful China. In late 2007 a Japanese defense official was in agreement with the assessment that China could deploy such a number of warheads, and that this number would affect his assessment of the U.S. ability to provide "secondary deterrence" to protect Japan from Chinese nuclear attack.[21]

Missile Defense

A second option available to China would be to invest in a robust anti-ballistic missile (ABM) defense capability. In the late 1990s China began to declassify information about China's first anti-ballistic missile defense effort, the 640 Program.[22] In 1963 Mao Zedong reportedly ordered his missile engineers to simultaneously develop ABMs and antisatellite interceptors; this order became the 640 Project, which included kinetic kill, laser, antisatellite, and gun-launched weapons plus long-range radar and target discrimination systems.[23] After supporting PLA missile tests the radar system was used to track the fall of the U.S. Skylab in 1979. In spite of the chaos of the Cultural Revolution, China is reported to have tested prototypes of the FJ-1 short-range and FJ-2 long-range ABM and developed two types of long-range radar before the program was ended in March 1980.[24] The very existence of the 640 Program indicates that China's at times harsh rhetoric and vociferous opposition to U.S. missile defense plans in the 1990s and early 2000s was not an attempt to offer a more "moral" strategic posture, but, like its diplomacy to ban space weapons, was another self-serving propaganda campaign intended to limit or delay the defensive programs of others.

It is likely that work on China's ABM system eventually resumed following the termination of the 640 Program. China's January 2007 satellite interception demonstrating direct-ascent or "direct-kill" capability indicates China has mastered most of the technologies needed to assemble a modern ABM defense. The SC-19 ASAT is also a "mobile" missile system, indicating that a potential ABM based on the SC-19 may also be mobile, in contrast to the U.S. use of "fixed" ABMs in Alaska. Russia would be a potential source for advanced long-range radar and perhaps space-based surveillance systems that would constitute a future targeting architecture for an ABM system. Furthermore, there may be ample Chinese technical literature relating to technologies that would be useful for ASATs and ABMs, on the topics of Kinetic Kill Vehicles (KKVs), pulse reaction jet missile controls for rapid maneuverability at high speed, plus space- and ground-based early warning systems.[25] One Chinese Internet source monitored in 2007 indicates that a new Chinese ABM program carrying the designator "863-8" may emerge in the next decade.[26]

In early 2008 an Asian military source disclosed to the author that China's next ABM system may be operational before 2025.[27] Asian sources have also noted that in 2006 China tested a Russian S-300PMU-2 in an antitactical ballistic mode against DF-15 and DF-11 SRBMs, indicating their interest in this capability.[28] At the 1998 Zhuhai Air Show Chinese officials disclosed to this author their intention to build an antitactical ballistic missile (ATBM) capable version of the then-new FT-2000 surface-to-air missile (SAM). In 2004 a Pakistani source disclosed his expectation to the author that China would sell Pakistan its new ATBM should India develop or acquire missile defense systems.

During the late 1990s China mounted a very loud political campaign to oppose U.S. antimissile cooperation initiatives with Japan, South Korea, and Australia. But while maintaining its opposition to Asian missile defenses, China had reduced its rhetoric significantly by the middle of the first decade of the twenty-first century. However, in 2007 and 2008 China took care to join Russia in its protests of U.S.-led plans to put missile defenses in Eastern Europe to help defend Europe from looming Iranian nuclear missile threats. But a generally reduced propaganda campaign may have been an indication that China accepted it could not stop Washington, but it may also have been a tacit signal that China was making progress with a similar ABM capability.

At this point it is only possible to speculate about the size and capabilities of China's future nuclear missile force. Missile production rates, for example, would suggest that China has many more DF-5 ICBMs, but such estimates have not been suggested by the public data released by U.S. intelligence agencies. One possible motivation for China to keeping its nuclear arsenal "small" might be to avoid commitment to nuclear missile arms control agreements with Russia or the United States. But such logic also suggests that China could build a force of hundreds of missiles and still have far fewer than the United States or Russia, which would serve to justify future refusals to join verifiable missile limitation agreements. But given U.S. commitments to missile and nuclear warhead reductions, a larger number of PLA offensive missiles combined with multiple warheads and an active ABM capability would go far to erode the deterrent effect of U.S. nuclear forces on China's leadership.

Theater Missiles and Precision Weapons

For terror-political missions as well as military missions, the PLA targets Taiwan with hundreds of ballistic missiles and has started to deploy less expensive and more accurate land-attack cruise missiles (LACMs) against Taiwan. But its missile forces may soon be eclipsed by the advent of thousands of precision-guided munitions (PGMs) that would arm hundreds of tactical fighter and bomber aircraft. The PLA's growing number of medium-range ballistic missiles are targeted against Japan, Okinawa, and Guam. These include about twenty to thirty older, liquid-fueled 2,800-km-range DF-3As and about 50 to 100 newer solid-fueled DF-21A missiles.[29] In 2006 Asian sources indicate that the PLA has tested a version of the DF-21 with multiple warheads, an indication that the PLA is working to counter U.S. and Japanese missile defense systems.[30] In 2006 and 2007 the Chinese released Internet imagery of a new mobile solid-fuel missile referred to as the DF-25.[31] A Chinese source claimed the DF-25 has a range of 3,200 km,[32] while Western estimates place the range between 2,500 and 3,000 km, but it may have a very large 1,500-kg warhead capacity.[33] However, in early 2008 an Asian military source disclosed this missile was in fact a new version of the DF-21, but that it did have the ability to carry multiple warheads and its range was about 3,000 km. Such a large warhead means this missile would be able to deliver larger and more effective non-nuclear warheads based on cluster munitions, fuel-air explosives, and non-nuclear radio-frequency devices. It could also carry much larger antiship or precision-guided warheads.

Back in early 1999, leaked U.S. intelligence figures indicated that by 2005 the PLA might have 650 short-range ballistic missiles (SRBMs) pointed at Taiwan—what seemed to be an outrageous figure at that time. But in its 2005 PLA Report the Pentagon estimated that numbers had reached 650 to 730, with a growth potential of 75 to 120 a year. In November 2006 Mainland Affairs Council Director Joseph Wu stated that PLA was targeting 900 missiles against Taiwan.[34] The 2008 edition of the Pentagon's *China Military Power* report offers a high estimate of 1,070 SRBMs in the PLA inventory.[35] As a force-in-being, Beijing hopes that its accumulating missile force will serve as a main military-political tool to intimidate Taiwanese political leaders. In early 2006 Taiwanese military officials estimated that 20,000 to 30,000 military personnel alone would be killed or wounded in an initial PLA missile attack.[36] But when China strikes, these missiles will be used in large-wave attacks coordinated with cruise missile, electronic warfare, air strikes, and Special Forces strikes.

Currently there are two types of SRBMs that form the bulk of the PLA's inventory. The Second Artillery uses 600-km-range DF-15s, 1,000-km-range DF-15 Mod 1 or DF-15A missiles, and the 300–600-km-range DF-11. The DF-11 arms some PLA Army SRBM units. Later versions of the DF-15 and the newer DF-11 Mod 2 are believed to have been made more accurate by guidance systems that use navigation satellite inputs. Both DF-15 and DF-11 missiles carry a variety of warheads including high-explosive, cluster, fuel-air-explosive, and non-nuclear radio frequency warheads. Some DF-15s may have tactical nuclear warheads.[37] Early this decade the PLA began developing cheaper SRBMs like the 150-km-range B-611, which could be improved to a 250-km range, and the more recent P-12. Both are lighter than the DF-15 and can be carried two to a truck-based transporter erector launcher (TEL). Both employ satellite navigation guidance, are maneuverable to avoid defenses, and can carry high explosive or cluster munitions warheads. At the 2007

IDEX show Chinese sources noted both types of missiles would be acquired by the PLA. Table 6.2 summarizes the expanding range of SRBMs of interest to the PLA.

There is new information that the PLA may be considering a more rapid expansion of the numbers of SRBMs it can deploy against a target by using new technologies to improve the range and accuracy of artillery rockets, which are far less expensive than SRBMs. In early 2007 Chinese sources revealed that the WS-1 and WS-2 artillery rocket families were being developed into extended-range SRBMs. The 200-km-range WS-2, revealed in 2004, is apparently being developed into the WS-2C, which uses a passive homing guidance system; the 300-km-range WS-2C; and the 400-km-range WS-2D. There is also a WS-3, with a 300-km range, that comes from a competing factory. Due to their lower cost, these new SRBMs offer the PLA the option to rapidly double or even triple the number of missiles it can deploy against Taiwan or another target.

LACMs

In early 2007 Taiwanese sources noted that the PLA had deployed about 100 of a new class of land-attack cruise missile (LACM) near Taiwan.[38] The 2008 Pentagon PLA report notes offers a high estimate of 250 LACMs.[39] Asian sources have noted that new LACMs would first be deployed by the Second Artillery, with a brigade forming in 2006.[40] Beginning in the 1970s the PLA has placed a high priority on developing an indigenous LACMs comparable to the U.S. Tomahawk strategic cruise missile. This effort has been aided by the PLA's success in obtaining advanced cruise missile technology from Russia, Israel, Ukraine, and the Untied States.[41] Though late in coming, Ukraine's contribution was reportedly substantial, including six copies of the Raduga Kh-55 LACM; engineering information on the Ukrainian Korshun, based on the Kh-55; and optical seeker technology to give LACMs and bombs a terminal-guidance capability.[42] In Russian service the Kh-55 would have a 2,500-km range; this indicates the potential range for the new PLA LACM. In early July 2005 an Internet-source photo appeared of a new Chinese cruise missile with unmistakable LACM characteristics; the missile was later identified as the 280-km-range YJ-62 antiship missile, which arms the new *Luyang* II/Type 052C destroyer.[43] However, Asian sources indicate this missile will serve as the basis for a family of Navy and Air Force LACMs.

In early 2007, the PLA Air Force (PLAAF) version of an LACM was revealed being carried by the new H-6K version of the venerable Xian H-6 bomber. A second company is developing a LACM for the Second Artillery.[44] An Asian military source estimated that the PLA might also produce up to fifty H-6Ks able to carry at least six LACMs each, indicating a potential attack salvo of 300 air-launched LACMs. With their very high accuracy, such cruise missiles allow strategic targets to be destroyed with non-nuclear warheads. An earlier LACM, the 200-km-range optically guided YJ-63, arms some H-6H bombers.

Table 6.2 Expanding Range of PLA SRBMs Capable of Reaching Taiwan

Missile Range (km)	150	200	300	400	600	800
	WS-1B: 4x MLRS; truck TEL, 180-km range; 150-kg warhead	**WS-2B:** 6x MLRS; truck TEL; inertial, satnav, or passive antiradiation guidance; 200-kg HE, cluster, or FAE warhead	**WS-2C:** possible truck TEL; passive anti-radiation guidance	**WS-2D:** possible truck TEL; possible satnav guidance; little else known	**DF-15:** 1x special TEL; satnav guidance in later versions; 500–700-kg HE, RF, or tacnuke warhead	**DF-15X:** 1x special TEL; satnav guidance; HE, RF, or tacnuke warhead
	WS-2: 6x MLRS, truck TEL; 200-kg warhead	**B-611M:** 2x truck TEL; satnav guidance; 260-km range; 480-kg HE, Cluster, or FAE warhead	**WS-3:** From a competing factory; little else known	**WS-1F:** possible truck TEL; 500-km range; little else known	**DF-15B:** apparent maneuvering warhead, may be for antiship missions	
					DF-15C: 1x special TEL; satnav guidance; new deep-penetrating warhead	
	P-12: 2x special TEL; possible air-mobile; inertial and satnav guidance; 450-kg HE or cluster warhead				**DF-11 Mod 1:** 1x special TEL; satnav guidance; 500–600 km range; 500-kg HE, cluster, FAE, or RF warhead	
	B611: 2x truck TEL; inertial and possible satnav guidance; 480-kg warhead					

Abbreviations: FAE, fuel air explosive; HE, high explosive; kg, kilogram; km, kilometer; MLRS, multiple launch rocket system; RF, radio frequency; satnav, satellite navigation; TEL, transporter erector launcher; tacnuke, tactical nuclear.

PGMs

While primarily carried by PLA Air Force and Naval Air Force aircraft, it is appropriate to mention here the PLA's development of precision-guided munitions (PGMs), as they may come to eclipse missiles in terms of cost efficiency and accuracy.[45] The PLA's investment in space surveillance and navigation satellites makes possible its new investment in PGMs. At the 2006 Zhuhai Air Show the PLA revealed that two companies, the China Aerospace Industries Corporation (CASIC) and Luoyang (under the AVIC-1 consortium), had developed aircraft-carried navigation-satellite-guided bombs. Luoyang's LS-6 (LS, Lei Shi) has apparently been in testing since 2003,[46] while CASIC's FT-2 (FT, Fei Teng) was shown being carried by a JH-7 fighter-bomber. In mid-2007 it was disclosed that CASIC is building the smaller 100-kg FT-4 precision-guided bomb.[47] Similar to the U.S. GBU-39 Small Diameter Bomb, more can be carried per strike aircraft than larger PGMs. Navsat-guided PGMs have an advantage over laser-guided PGMs—which Luoyang is also building—in that they can be used during bad weather. They are also much cheaper to produce than ballistic and cruise missiles and can be sized to reduce collateral damage, an important political consideration. It is likely that China will develop dual-guidance systems to enable destruction of moving targets by its navsat-guided PGMs.

These PGMs may also arm the new Xian H-6K bomber: the latest version of this elderly bomber was revealed in early 2007[48] Chinese Internet imagery revealed during 2007 indicates the H-6K will have a large powerful nose-mounted radar and an electro-optical targeting pod, both useful for all-weather ground targeting of PGMs.[49] The H-6K might be able to carry up to sixty of the new FT-4 "Small Diameter Bombs."[50] A new variant of the Y-8 revealed in 2005 utilizes two large radar arrays mounted on the fuselage side; these are thought to be phased-array radar for all-weather detection of small ground targets such as tanks, vehicles, and emplacements. This Y-8 might conceivably team with a PGM-armed H-6K and perform highly accurate aerial artillery missions, as the United States envisions for its E-8 JSTARS radar aircraft teamed with a PGM-armed B-52 bomber. Assuming a Second Artillery SRBM Brigade controls 100 to 200 missiles, then only two to four FT-4 armed H-6K bombers could potentially cover the same number of targets, representing a major increase in efficiency.

PLA Air Force Modernization

By 2010 the PLA's air forces may be able to deploy integrated strike packages of multirole fighters with modern support elements such as airborne radar, electronic warfare, and aerial refueling platforms that are able to undertake autonomous or joint-force offensive missions. These fighters will be able to undertake all-weather air-superiority missions and could shoulder the majority of the PLA's long-range precision-strike missions. By the end of this decade this force could reach a point of qualitative and quantitative air superiority on the

Taiwan Strait and pose a real threat to one or more U.S. carrier battle groups or to U.S. and Japanese air forces on Okinawa. Table 6.3 shows a comparison of munitions-capable fighters and attackers held by the PLA and Taiwan. In 2007 the Pentagon estimated that 700 PLA aircraft could conduct operations against Taiwan without refueling,[51] a number that has not increased since its 2005 assessment. By 2010 this number could include 300 or more Su-30, J-11, J-10, and JH-7A multirole fighters capable of precision strikes against Taiwan or long-range strikes against U.S. naval forces. These could be backed by about 200 or more single-role Russian and Chinese-made fourth-generation fighters plus hundreds more third- and second-generation Chinese-made fighters. Taiwan's modern fighter inventory is not expected to increase beyond 330.

By 2007 the PLA had about 280 Russian Sukhoi Su-27 fighters, Su-30MKK/MKK2 fighter-bombers, and co-produced Shenyang J-11 fighters. The Su-27s are being upgraded to be able to fire modern medium-range self-guided R-77 air-to-air missiles (AAMs). In addition, the PLA is now pressing ahead with plans to build a new version, the Shenyang J-11/Su-27, which features increasing domestic content including radar, weapons, and new WS-10A turbofan engines. The PLA revealed more of this indigenized "J-11B" at the 2006 Zhuhai show, and Internet images of this J-11 armed with PL-12 AAMs had been revealed by early 2007. In mid-2007 the twin-seat J-11BS was revealed: this plane could form the basis for training and attack versions. As of 2006, about seventy-six Su-30MKK fighter-bombers were in the PLAAF and twenty-four Su-30MKK2s were in the PLA Naval Air Force (PLANAF). Additional PLANAF Su-30MKK2 orders were expected[52] but did not materialize. Instead, the PLANAF may order up to 50–100 Su-33s for future aircraft carriers.

The PLAAF may be interested in pursuing either the purchase of new Sukhoi fighters or the purchase/co-development of key components to upgrade its current Suhkoi and J-11 forces. In late 2006 the PLA was reportedly considering a Russian offer to sell the Su-35,[53] which features an advanced passive phased-array radar, more powerful AL-31M2 engines, and advanced combat systems to combine inputs from radar or passive imaging sensors to attack air, land, and sea-based targets. The new Phazotron Zhuk MFSE (Multi Functional Export) active electronically scanned array (AESA) radar has an advertised range of about 300 km; it can track twenty-four aerial targets and attack eight of them.[54] It can also be mechanically slewed to an amazing 160-degree field of view, which may allow long-range missile strikes while flying away from a target, something modern U.S. fighters cannot do.[55] The competing Tikomirov bureau is developing an AESA radar for the Sukhoi-designed Russian fifth-generation fighter.[56] These radars can be expected to eventually have the same advanced electronic-attack capabilities intended for new U.S. AESA radar.[57]

Long derided by Western analysts, China's first domestic fourth-generation fighter, the Chengdu J-10, is now in production, with 150–350 to be powered by the Russian AL-31FN turbofan before it is supplanted by the indigenous WS-10A turbofan engine.[58] Though long in development, the J-10 represents a

Table 6.3 PLA and Taiwan: Smart Munitions-Capable Fighters and Attackers in 2008

	Number/Status	Self-Guided BVR AAM	NavSat PGMs	Laser/Optical PGM
PLAAF/NAF				
Xian H-6H/K (Bomber)	H-6H: @20; H-6K: 50 (est. Development)	None	H-6K: LS-6, FT-1/3/4, 6x LACM-H-6K	H-6H: 2x YJ-63
Hongdu Q-5X	Development	None	FT-1/3/4	LT-2, GB1
Shenyang J-8F/H	F: 120/5 Reg.	4x PL-12	LS-6, FT-1/3/4	?
Xian JH-7A (2-seat attack)	120/5 Reg.	4x PL-12	LS-6, FT-1/3/4	LT-2, GB1; KD-88
Chengdu J-10	150/5 Reg.	4x PL-12/PL-13[a]	LS-6, FT-1/3/4	LT-2, GB1; KD-88
Chengdu J-10S (2-seat attack)	Development	4x PL-12/PL-13	LS-6, FT-1/3/4	LT-2, GB1; KD-88
Shenyang J-11B	Development	8x PL-12/PL-13[a]	LS-6, FT-1/3/4	LT-2, GB1; KD-88
Shenyang J-11BS (2-seat attack)	Development	8x PL-12/PL-13[a]	LS-6, FT-1/3/4	LT-2, GB1; KD-88
Shenyang J-11/A	100+ /5 Reg.	8x R-77 ?	None	None
Sukhoi Su-30MKK/K2 (2-seat attack)	97/4 Reg.	8x R-77	KAB-500S	KAB-500, KAB-1500; Kh-59
Sukhoi Su-27SK	36	8x R-77 Upgrade ?	None	None
Sukhoi Su-27UBK	40	8x R-77 Upgrade ?	None	None

Taiwan AF

Lockheed F-16A	146	6x AIM-120	None	None
Lockheed F-16C Block 50	(66) Request not approved by U.S. as of early 2008	6x AIM-120	?	?
Dassault Mirage-2000-5EI	57	6x MICA	None	None
AIDC IDF	128	2x TC-2	None	None

Terms: BVR AAM, Beyond Visual Range Air-to-Air Missile; LACM, Land Attack Cruise Missile; NavSat, Navigation Satellite; PGM, Precision Guided Munition; PLAAF, People's Liberation Army Air Force; Reg, Regiment.

Notes: [a] J-10 and J-11 use of the future PL-13/14 ramjet powered AAM would be dependent initially on the availability of data links and off-board targeting data, and later on the availability of long-range AESA radar.

Source: Jane's Air Launched Weapons 2006; Jane's All The World's Aircraft 2007; IISS Military Balance 2006–2007; press reports; author interviews.

Table 6.4 Russian Estimation of J-10 Versus Other Major Combat Aircraft[a]

	J-10A	Lavi B-2	MiG-29SMT	F-16C Block 50	Mirage-2000-5
Length (M)	16.5	14.57	17.32	15.03	14.34
Wingspan	9.36	8.78	11.36	9.45	9.13
Wing area (m²)	34.6	33.05	38.1	27.9	41.0
Weight (kg)	8,300	7,030	11,200	8,600	7,500
Empty Max. weight	18,000		21,000	19,200	17,000
Max. Engine Thrust (kg)	1 × AL-31FN	1 × PW 1120	2 × RD-33	1 × GE F110-129	1 × M53
Max. Thrust (kg)	12,550	9,340	8,300	13,160	9,700
Speed (Mach)	2.2	1.85	2.3	2.0	2.2
Range (km)	2,300	3,700	2,100	2,000	1,650
Internal Fuel With Tanks	2,900	N/A	3,500	2,485	3,300
Altitude (m)	18,000	15,240	17,500	15,240	16,460

[a] Figures for the J-10 are estimates; as of early 2008 China had not released formal performance figures.

Sources: *Aviatsya i Vremya*, March 2007; *Jane's All the World's Aircraft*; Gerard Frawley, *The International Directory of Military Aircraft, 2002–2003.*

substantial achievement for China's aerospace industries (Table 6.4). The first J-10 starts its career with a performance and weapons potential similar to a Lockheed-Martin F-16 Block 30. In contrast to the F-16, the J-10 will start its career armed with self-guided Luoyang PL-12 medium-range AAM and new Chinese laser and navsat-guided PGMs. The J-10's air-to-air combat performance is about the same as the F-16, but according to one analyst, the J-10 may have a remarkable 2,540-km combat radius with external fuel tanks, compared to 1,430-km for the F-16.[59] By the end of 2007 at least five PLAAF regiments were expected to be equipped with the J-10. Reports indicate that Chengdu is also developing an advanced version of the J-10 with stealth features and a thrust-vectored engine for enhanced maneuverability.[60] In November 2007 a Russian source confirmed that the Saturn engine company and the PLA were negotiating for the sale of the thrust-vectored AL-31FN engine.[61] This is to support a future naval version of the J-10, plus a version better able to carry full payloads from high-altitude bases in Tibet. In addition, the twin seat J-10S, which is now a trainer, is being developed into a dedicated strike fighter. There are also persistent rumors from Chinese sources of a twin-engine version of the J-10, sometimes called the J-10C, which will feature advanced radar, infrared optics, and new weapons.

Both the PLAAF and PLAN are buying the Xian JH-7A fighter-bomber, which features modern radar, precision weapons, and supersonic antiship missiles and is powered by a modified version of the British Rolls Royce Spey turbofan engine.[62] Recent reports note China's desire to double engine output, which may enable up to thirty JH-7As to be built per year.[63] The JH-7A is expected to use the range of new Chinese-developed navsat and laser-guided munitions. At the 2006 Zhuhai Air Show an AVIC-1 calendar revealed what may be a previously unknown twin-engine stealthy fighter-bomber, similar in size to the U.S. Northrop F-117. Little is known about this fighter-bomber, which was probably developed during the 1990s.

A noticeable deficiency in the PLA's combat aircraft lineup has been the lack of a modern close air support (CAS) fighter to provide accurate heavy support for ground forces. While the PLA has in the past considered the Sukhoi Su-25 *Frogfoot*, the Russian counterpart to the U.S. Fairchild A-10 *Thunderbolt-II*, it has not purchased this capable CAS aircraft. Instead, since the 2004 Zhuhai show it appears that Hongdu has been marketing a radically upgraded Q-5 attack fighter, which suffers from a short range and low payload. The latest version, called the Q-5E/F, appears to feature a nose-mounted targeting system, a larger fuselage fuel tank, and four wing mounts for weapons (double the previous number).[64] Other versions have been seen with targeting pods. Armed with up to eight new small FT-4 navsat-guided bombs, or four larger PGMs, the Q-5E/F would provide an inexpensive CAS solution that could be built quickly. A new armored version of Hongdu's L-15 trainer might provide another more capable CAS solution.

Modern Weapons

While the PLA has recently developed many new precision-guided ground attack weapons, China has traditionally been dependent on foreign technology to both purchase and craft modern AAMs (Table 6.5). Its Luoyang Electro-Optical Corporation, which makes all of its air-to-air missiles, has relied on U.S. and Russian technology to make its early short-range infrared (IR) guided air-to-air missiles and Israeli technology from its Python-3 to make the Luoyang PL-8 and PL-9 short-range AAMs. Since the 1990s China has purchased thousands of Russian Vympel R-27 semiactive radar-guided and IR-guided medium-range AAMs, and then the more modern Vympel active-radar-guided R-77. These AAMs are used on Russian-made Su-27SK, Su-30MKK, and early co-produced J-11 fighters. Vympel is reportedly working on the R-77 Izdeliya 180, which uses a dual-pulse motor that could give it a possible range of 160–240 km.[65]

China has imported modern Russian and South African technology to produce fifth-generation AAMs. In the late 1990s China purchased design data from Russia's AGAT firm to help it develop an active-guided radar for the Luoyang PL-12 active-guided 70-km-range AAM, which now equips J-10 and J-11B fighters. In early 2008 Chinese Internet sources revealed the existence of the

Table 6.5 Comparison of Advanced Active Radar-Guided AAMs

Missile	Country	Range/Weight	Notes
Rocket Powered			
AIM-120C-7	US/Raytheon	50-80 km/160+ kg (est.)	Processor/guidance improvements; 218 sold to Taiwan in 2007
AIM-120D	US/Raytheon	75-110 km /160+ kg (est.)	Conformal seeker antennae; two-way data link; GPS guidance
R-77	Russia/Vympel	80 km/175 kg	R-77 in PLA service; improved version with possible active/passive seeker in development
R-27AE	Russia/Vympel	110 km/350 kg	Active guided variant of R-27 family; not produced.
AAM-4	Japan/Mitsubishi	100 km (est.)/220 kg	In limited service with Japanese F-2 fighters
Sky Sword 2	Taiwan/CSIST	60 km/183 kg	In service with Taiwan IDF force
MICA EM	France/Matra	60 km/112 kg	960 ordered by Taiwan
PL-12	China/Luoyang	70 km/180 kg	Russian aided seeker and Chinese motor; data link; in service with J-10 and J-8II fighters
New Small Radar-Guided AAM	China/Luoyang (?)	20+ km/100+ kg (est.)	First seen in December 2007; appears to be influenced by R-Darter, but appears to be much smaller; radar seeker type unknown; may include Russian or Ukrainian technology
Ramjet Powered			
Meteor	EU/MBDA	100+ km/185 kg	Claimed no-escape zone 3x that of AIM-120B
R-77M-PD	Russia/Vympel	160 km/225 kg	Never completed, not purchased by Russia
PL-13/PL-14	China/Luoyang	160+ km/225+ kg (est.)	Existence not yet confirmed; data link likely; Russian and/or South African help likely

Very Long Range

K-100/K-172	Russia/Novator	200–400 km/700 kg	First offered w/Su-35; future version may be anti-missile capable
R-77 Izdeliye 180	Russia/Vympel	160–240 km	Unconfirmed upgraded variant
AIM-54C	US/Raytheon	150 km/463 kg	Armed F-14 fighter; retired in from USN in 2004; AIM-54A still in service with Iran
AIM-120 NCADE	US/Raytheon	200 km/160+ kg (est.)	Future 2-stage development of AIM-120; antimissile mission with possible AAM application

Note: AAM range figures are estimates but can be greater at higher aircraft speed.
Sources: Jane's Air Launched Weapons, 2006–2007; MBDA Web site; Flight International; Aviation Week and Space Technology.

PL-10 or PL-13, a new AAM that look like a copy of the 20-km-range South African A-Darter AAM. Also revealed was the PL-13 or PL-14, a ramjet-powered missile with features very similar to a Russian Vympel program to produce a 160-km-range ramjet-powered version of the R-77.[66] Chinese sources say development on the PL-10 began in 2004,[67] when it was reported that Denel and the PLA were discussing the sale of the A-Darter.[68]

In December 2007 a Web page for China's Northwestern University revealed a new radar-guided AAM similar to the Denel 63-km-range active radar-guided R-Darter. However, the new Chinese AAM is smaller than the R-Darter but appears to use its unique roll-stabilization fins. While this new AAM had not been identified as of early 2008, there was speculation that the seeker was derived from a new 150-mm seeker being developed by Russia's AGAT firm, which would better enable this missile to conduct 360-degree attacks.[69] South Africa very likely also sold China technology for the critical Helmet-Mounted Display (HMD) needed to fully exploit these missiles and to give its pilots an aerial combat potential that matches or exceeds that of the United States and Japan. The PL-10 may have a 20-km range, twice that of the U.S. HMD-targeted AIM-9X AAM.[70] China has also purchased Russian infrared search and tracking (IRST) systems such as the OLS-30, which can passively search for targets out to 70 km without having to use radar, which would give away the location of the PLA fighter.

China may also be interested in purchasing or developing its own ultra-long-range AAM to gain a clear asymmetrical advantage over U.S. and Japanese sensor aircraft. Russia has long offered to China its 300-km-range Russian Novator KS-172 AAM, now called K-100-1, which is intended to counter airborne warning and control systems (AWACS) and other critical support aircraft.[71] At the 1993 Moscow Air Show a mockup of the KS-172 was hastily put on display for a PLA delegation. The Russian Air Force version of the KS-172 may be capable of a 400-km-range, and a version is being offered for sale with the new Su-35.[72] Some sources indicate this missile may be developed into an antisatellite (ASAT) weapon,[73] an application that may also interest the PLA. The PLA may also be interested in a future 100-km-range version of the R-77 medium-range AAM, or the 230-km-range R-37, both being developed by the Vympel Company for the Russian Air Force.[74] A mid-2007 disclosure by an Asian military source that China is developing a 400-km-range SAM[75] also raises the possibility that it is developing a similar range air-to-air version of this missile, perhaps to be followed by an ASAT version.

Russian-made Su-30MKK fighter-bombers are armed with a range of Russian PGMs such as the 3,300-lb KAB-1500. When it is available in about 2007–2008, China is also expected to buy the 288-km-range Kh-59MK antiship missile for the Su-30MKK2.[76] The PLAAF and PLAN may also purchase the new 3M-54AE air-launched version of the deadly two-stage member of Novator's Club family of antiship missiles, revealed at the 2007 Moscow Air Show.[77] The air-launched version of this missile likely approaches a 300-km range, and its supersonic second stage is designed to defeat gun-based ship defensive systems.

Multiple Fifth-Generation Programs

Both Shenyang and Chengdu are working on advanced fifth-generation fighter designs (called fourth-generation in China) that could enter service from 2015 to 2020. The Shenyang design was once estimated by the U.S. Office of Naval Intelligence to resemble the Boeing F-15 fighter.[78] But at the 2006 Zhuhai Air Show Shenyang's 601 Design Institute displayed a model of a single-engine stealthy wide flat fuselage with a forward-swept wing. This design likely assumes heavy usage of composite materials, AESA, and internal weapons carriage. Chengdu's large twin-engine concept, as seen in a 2002 brochure of the affiliated 611 Design Institute, is less stealthy but optimized for high maneuverability. While China has declined Russian offers to co-develop a fifth-generation fighter, in contrast to India's decision to go ahead with Russia, it can be presumed that at least Chengdu will employ the consulting and testing services of the SibNIA design institute in Novosibirsk. China appears committed to using its fifth-generation effort to broadly advance its military aerospace industries, and a brief review of possible Chinese technical literature shows considerable effort in the areas of stealthy materials and aircraft structures, avionics, fifth-generation high-thrust-to-weight engines, engine thrust vectoring, and engine stealth. There is also appears to be a deep interest in plasma stealth technology, which may be applied to a new combat aircraft.[79]

There may also be a "lightweight" fifth-generation program. In early 2005 a Chinese source told this author that the Chengdu Aircraft Corporation was studying whether to build a competitor to the Lockheed-Martin F-35 Joint Strike Fighter, which would indicate a stealthy but low-cost and capable fighter design or even a V/STOL design.[80] The probable Russian design help for Chengdu's large fifth-Generation design augurs well for Russian participation in its smaller "F-35" design.[81] It may also be the case that Shenyang's new forward-swept design revealed in 2006 will be pitched to meet this possible new requirement.

Another area of potential PLAAF growth is unmanned combat aerial vehicles (UCAVs). There are indications of Chinese research in the areas of developing the platforms, software, command control, and operational control methods for UCAVs.[82] At the 2006 Zhuhai Air Show the Shenyang Aircraft company unveiled a concept model of its "Dark Sword" stealthy supersonic UCAV, for which it offered no details except to note it was designed for air-to-air missions. This UCAV reportedly benefited from South African technology.[83] While the United States has invested heavily in UCAVs over the last decade, it has decided against near-term development of air-combat UCAVs; computer, control, and radar technologies may not be mature enough to support counter-air missions. In August 2007 the U.S. Navy decided to proceed with the Northrop Grumman X-47B as the basis for its UCAS-D unmanned combat aircraft to perform strike and surveillance missions. Although it is not known whether China is meeting success where the United States has encountered difficulties, China's commitment to this new next-generation technology indicates that the United States and Europe will not dominate this technology. In the meantime, Taiwanese and U.S. sources remain concerned about the PLA's conversion of about 200 older J-6 fighters into unmanned aircraft. These could serve as missiles, relatively simple UCAVs, or decoys to force Taiwan to waste valuable antiaircraft missiles.

Bombers and Support Aircraft

Bombers are also experiencing a revival in the PLA. Following the failure in the early 1990s to obtain Russian Tupolev Tu-22M3 supersonic Backfire bombers, the Xian Aircraft Company resumed development of the Soviet-era H-6 (Tupolev Tu-16).[84] By the late 1990s the H-6H emerged, armed with the 200-km-range optically guided YJ-63 land attack cruise missile. Then in 2002 it was revealed that Xian had resumed full production of a revised H-6, one equipped with four wing pylons,[85] called the H-6M. In early 2007 the "H-6K" emerged, upgraded with Russian D-30 turbofan engines to give it a potential 3,000-km combat radius, and modifications to carry at least six new long-range Tomahawk-like LACMs. Asian military sources estimate the PLA may acquire up to fifty H-6K aircraft,[86] while recent PLA purchases of the D-30 engine indicate it may build about thirty.

However, China may be designing a new advanced long-range bomber, as it considers Russian offers since 2003–2004 to sell Tupolev Tu-22M3 Backfire supersonic bombers and Tupolev Tu-95/142 Bear long-range subsonic bombers.[87] The Tu-142's 15,000-km range will allow it to roam the Pacific and Indian oceans providing targeting data, while the Tu-22M3 has a 2,400-km strike radius. Both Russian bombers were high-profile participants in the Peace Mission 2005 exercises, and the Tu-22M3 was being marketed at the 2004 Zhuhai Air show. An August 2007 report indicated a sale of advanced versions of the Tu-95 and the Tu-22M3 remained possible.[88]

China's apparent reluctance (as of mid-2008) to purchase Russian bombers may indicate that China has a next-generation bomber program underway. Chinese Internet rumors have often cited the probability of an "H-8" or "H-9" heavy or even supersonic bomber program, but there have not been credible Chinese or Western indications of such a new large-bomber program. But there are indications that China is interested in such a program, including a deep interest in stealth and counterstealth technologies: former B-2 bomber stealth expert Noshir Gowadia was hired to give lectures on stealth technology. An AVIC-1 calendar released at the 2006 Zhuhai Air Show depicts a possible twin-engine F-177 size delta-wing stealth bomber. This could represent an ongoing tactical combat aircraft program or just a platform to test new stealth technologies. In 2007 Russia was reported to have revived a stealth bomber program abandoned following the Cold War,[89] and if the report is true, this program could provide a source of technology or cooperation to advance China's bomber ambitions.

The PLA is also developing new families of critical support aircraft. China reacted to the U.S. affront in June 2000 of stopping Israel's sale of its advanced Beriev A-50 equipped with a Phalcon active phased-array airborne radar by starting a crash program to build its own active phased-array airborne radar.[90] Asian sources indicate the PLAAF may build up to four A-50-like AWACS and also note that its radar signals are consistent with the Israeli Phalcon, meaning the PLAAF has perfected a large AESA radar.[91] These have been joined by a new version of China's Shaanxi Y-8 transport outfitted with linear-shape active-phased array radar, a prototype of which has been in testing since 2001. Large AESA arrays are important, as they can be developed into weapons capable of damaging enemy electronics with powerful microwave spikes. In addition, Shaanxi has developed two other Y-8 support aircraft. One features large "cheek" arrays, very likely AESA, on the fuselage; their mission is not known but speculation ranges from electronic jamming to ground-mapping radar. A second Y-8 variant may be a new airborne command and control aircraft, giving campaign commanders a secure airborne location.

The PLA is also developing a range of long-range unmanned aircraft that could serve a number of critical support missions. At the 2006 Zhuhai show the Chengdu Aircraft Company revealed a concept for a large UAV that bore an uncanny resemblance to the U.S. Northrop Grumman Global Hawk, which can fly at altitudes higher than 50,000 feet and stay aloft for one or two days. At the same show the Guizhou Corporation revealed its concept Soar Dragon UAV with a modern diamond-wing configuration: this UAV can carry a 650-kg payload to a distance of 7,000 km. It appears that both the Chengdu and Guizhou UAVs could conduct surveillance, communication, or data link missions out to Guam or down to the Straits of Malacca. Should they enter service, it appears they could assist the missions of antiship ballistic missiles and LACMs launched from aircraft, submarines, or surface ships.

The PLA has already converted a small number of H-6 bombers to serve as aerial refueling tankers for J-8D fighters used by the PLAAF and PLA Navy Air Force (PLANAF). This H-6 tanker has also refueled at least one J-10 fighter modified for refueling. When the PLAAF takes delivery of its six Russian Ilyushin Il-78 aerial tankers ordered in 2004, it will be able to allow greater persistence for Su-30s over Taiwan and the South China Sea, or allow a small number to strike as far as Guam. In the next decade, should China's ambitions to produce a wide-body Airbus A-330/340 size airliner prove successful, it will likely be developed into tanker, command, and electronic warfare/surveillance versions.

Modern SAMs

In addition, the PLA is also purchasing large numbers of advanced Russian S-300 SAMs.[92] These advanced SAMs present a formidable obstacle to Taiwanese and U.S. air forces that may seek to interdict PLA forces attacking Taiwan. In August 2004 the PLA was reportedly close to buying eight new batteries of S-300PMU-2 (SA-20) missiles, on top of twelve batteries of S-300PMU and

S-300PMU-1 missiles.[93] Russian reports from October 2006 indicate that China purchased eight more batteries.[94] A battery may contain thirty-eight to forty-eight missiles, meaning the PLA is on its way to acquiring over 1,000 of this deadly SAM family by the end of the decade. The 200-km range of the S-300PMU-2's 48N6/2 missile enables coverage of most of the Taiwan Strait, and, if they are based on Peng Hu Island, most of Taiwan as well. This missile may also be able to intercept ballistic missiles with a range of 1,000 km.[95]

Asian military sources reported in mid-2007 that the PLA was developing a new 400-km-range SAM, but no further information was provided.[96] The PLA is a reported investor in Russia latest 400-km-range S-400 SAM, and it can be expected to be an early customer for this highly advanced SAM capable of targeting both cruise and ballistic missiles.[97] In addition the PLA is deploying a new advanced SAM derived from its FT-2000 family, which apparently uses Russian, U.S., Israeli, and Chinese technology. In 2007 the Pentagon reported this missile might have a 150-km range. But in mid-2006 Russian sources familiar with this missile said it is not as capable as the latest versions of the S-300,[98] but it does use a cold-launch system and has been developed for use on large warships. Nevertheless, Russian intentions to build a "fifth-generation" air defense missile capable of hitting targets in space may also indicate the next step in air defense missile for the PLA.

Naval Force Buildup

China is also rapidly building up its naval forces for Asian contingencies. By 2010 the People's Liberation Army Navy (PLAN) may purchase and produce up to thirty-five new conventional and nuclear submarines. These will not only stress Taiwan's four new air defense destroyers and twenty-two frigates; they will also be able to pose a steadily greater threat to U.S. and Japanese naval forces that may have to support Taiwan. A PLAN submarine-led blockade force will also have increasing support from new Russian and indigenous destroyers with modern medium- to long-range air defense systems, ten of which could be in service by 2006–2007. In addition, the PLAN and PLAAF will be able to mass new Su-30MKK, Su-30MKK2, and JH-7A fighter-bombers, plus new H-6 bombers to attack ship and shore-naval targets. Naval engagements could also be supported in the future by new antiship ballistic missiles as well as ballistic missiles and new land-attack cruise missiles that can attack Taiwan's naval facilities. In addition, the PLAN's long-standing emphasis on mine warfare presents a serious threat to military and civilian shipping around Taiwan. Finally, the increasing likelihood that China will soon build an indigenous aircraft carrier raises the prospect of the PLA being able to reinforce omnidirectional attacks against Taiwan and being able to counter U.S. and Japanese forces at greater distances.

Growing Submarine Force

While the Bush administration's 2001 offer to sell Taiwan eight new conventional submarines had been stalled by Plan Blue legislative opposition until late

Table 6.6 PLAN Submarine Growth Estimates

	2000	2005	2010 (est.)
Type 094 *Jin* SSBN	0	1	2–4
Type 092 *Xia* SSBN	1	1	1
Golf SSB	1	1	1
Type 09X SSN	0	0	2
Type 093 *Shang* SSN	0	2	3
Type 091 *Han* SSN	5	4	3
(Type 041 ?) *Yuan* SSK	0	2	6
Type 039/039A *Song* SSK	2	12–14	@14
Type 035 *Ming* SSK	19	19	@19
Type 033 *Romeo* SSK	@35	@20	0
Project 887 *Kilo* SSK	2	2	2
Project 636 *Kilo* SSK	2	2	2
Project 636M *Kilo* SSK	0	@5	8
TOTALS	@68	@76	@64

Source: Jane's Fighting Ships; International Institute for Strategic Studies; www.sinodefense.com; press reports; author interview data. Numbers count launched, not commissioned, submarines. Kilo numbers for ships in China. *Song* projection assumes annual production of 2–3.

2007, the PLAN is well on its way toward buying and building about thirty-five new conventional and nuclear-powered submarines by 2010 (Table 6.6). In early 2008 most PLAN submarines are of the obsolete and noisy Type 033 (ten to twenty) and Type 035 SSKs (non-nuclear-powered submarines) (about twenty), which are being supplanted. The PLAN built about twelve to fourteen modern Type 039 *Song* attack submarines before halting production in 2006. The Type 039 has benefited from some foreign assistance, including Israeli electronic and design assistance, German diesel engines and, very likely, German design assistance to correct the Israeli assistance.[99] It incorporates modern quieting technology such as a seven-blade skewed propeller and anechoic tiling, it is equipped with extensive digital command and sonar processing equipment, and it is armed with the 40-km-range YJ-81Q and perhaps the 120-km-range YJ-82Q antiship missile.

Having purchased four Russian *Kilo*-class submarines in the late 1990s, by mid-2006 the PLAN had taken delivery of all eight Project 636M *Kilo* submarines ordered in 2002. Known for their quiet and combat-survivable design, the 636M will be armed with the formidable Novator Club-S antiship, land-attack, and antisubmarine warfare (ASW) missile systems. There could be follow-on orders for the *Kilo* after the eight are delivered in 2006. But in 2004 the PLAN launched the first of its new *Yuan* class, which bears a suspicious resemblance to

Russia's new Project 677 *Lada*-class SSK. However, a model of the *Yuan* viewed from Internet sources in 2006 indicate that dimensionally, it may be more comparable to the stouter *Kilo*. In early 2008 Internet images could be viewed of the second and third *Yuan*-class submarines having emerged from their Wuhan shipyard. Asian military sources indicate that the *Yuan* may also be built in Shanghai, indicating that two yards may be building this class.[100] The second two *Yuans* were launched by the Wuhan yard in late 2007.

Inasmuch as the 677 incorporates improved crew-reducing automation, better sonar, and in the future, Air Independent Propulsion (AIP) systems, it is likely that the *Yuan* may benefit from all these technologies. The PLAN has been developing German-style fuel cells for AIP systems, but in early 2007 the *Yuan* was reported to be powered by a Swedish-style Stirling AIP developed during the 1990s. Such systems will allow the *Yuan* to spend one to two weeks under water. Only South Korea's new German Type 212 SSKs and Japan's future Oyoshio SSKs will have AIPs and similar tactical flexibility. China may also use AIP for unmanned undersea vehicles (UUVs).[101]

This analyst estimates that by 2010 the PLAN could be armed with at least thirty new and far more capable SSKs. The PLAN may also retain more than ten of the older Type 035 *Ming* class, many of which were just built in the 1990s. These submarines are still very quiet when running on batteries and can be used for a number of critical secondary missions such as surveillance to assist targeting, delivery of mines or Special Forces, or acting as decoys to help ambush U.S. and Japanese submarines.

Far less is known about the PLAN's second-generation fast-attack nuclear-powered submarine (SSN), known as the Type 093, or *Shang* class by its U.S. Navy code name. According to Asian sources, three new PLA SSNs had been launched from 2002 to 2006. However, vague images and models revealed at the Beijing Military Museum's PLA eightieth anniversary display in the summer of 2007 indicate that there may be two SSN versions. The initial variant of the Type 093 features a sail with dive planes, but the new version may instead have the dive planes on the hull. The initial version also features a fully rounded hull beam profile, whereas the new version has a minor flat deck, perhaps indicating a future intention to insert vertical missile tubes. One interpretation is that the initial Type 093, which has been in development since the 1970s, was not able to keep up with quickly advancing technology, necessitating a redesign in the 1990s.

Inasmuch as the PLAN is believed to be building a second nuclear submarine base on Hainan Island, it stands to reason that more SSNs will be built. An Asian military source noted that at least two SSNs may be built per SSBN, which the U.S. projects may eventually number five. U.S. sources have noted that the Type 093 will benefit from extensive Russian assistance, especially in its nuclear power plant.[102] And while U.S. sources note that the Type 093 will approximate the capability of the Soviet/Russian *Victor III* SSN,[103] there is the potential for future PLAN SSNs to benefit from better SSN technologies Russia is developing for its new fourth-generation Project 885 *Severdovinsk*-class SSN. This is suggested by Russia's increasing propensity to sell China its most advanced military technologies, and the fact that Project 885 production has seen a recent revival, raising the possibility that this was made possible by Chinese funding. Should the 093's performance exceed that of the *Victor III*, that would present a new and serious challenge to the ability of new U.S. SSNs to contain the PLAN.

Naval Air Defense

At the beginning of the twenty-first century, Chinese destroyers and frigates had only limited short-range air defense, in the form of naval SAMs such as the 10-km-range HQ-61 or the 13-km-range HHQ-7 derived from the French Crotale SAM. By 2008 the PLAN will have purchased or launched ten new destroyers and up to five new frigates that could bring about 640 medium- to long-range SAMs into battle. For the first time, these missiles could provide credible air defenses for naval blockade forces deployed against Taiwan—a substantial milestone for the PLAN, which until the end of the 1990s had no effective medium-range SAMs (Table 6.7). In 1997 China purchased two Project 956 *Sovremenniy* DDGs armed with the formidable supersonic Moskit ramjet-powered supersonic antiship missile, forty-eight Shtil (25–32-km-range SA-N-7 or 60-km-range SA-N-12) SAMs, and Kamov Ka-28 ASW and targeting helicopters. By

Table 6.7 Estimated Naval Air Defense Balance on Taiwan Strait in 2010

	Number/ Displacement	Number of SAMs	Range of SAMs
PLAN DDG + FFG			
Sovremenniy	4/7,940 tons	48x; SA-N-7/12	25 km/35 km
Type 052C *Luyang 2*	2/7,000 tons	48x; HHQ-9	150 km
Type 052B *Luyang 1*	2/7,000 tons	48x; SA-N-12	35 km
Type 051C	2/7,000 tons	48x; RIF-M	150 km
Type 054A	12/4,000 tons[a]	32x; Shtil-1	60 km
Total PLAN ships and SAMs	22	864	
ROC DDG + FFG			
Kidd	4/9,574 tons	54x; SM-2MR	167 km
Perry	8/4,105 tons	40x; SM-1MR	46 km
Knox	8/4,260 tons	10x; SM-1MR	46 km
Total ROC Navy ships and SAMs	20	616	

Source: Jane's Fighting Ships; Sinodefense.com; interview data.
Note: [a] Estimated production run.

mid-2006 Russia delivered two additional Project 956EM with improved 240+km-range Moskit missiles and new Kashtan combined gun/missile close-in defenses.

Since 2003 the PLAN has produced three new types of DDGs and a new FFG armed with modern Russian or other foreign-influenced weapons. Two Type 052B/*Luyang I* DDG are armed with the forty-eight SA-N-12 Shtil SAMs per shipand Russian/Ukrainian-designed radar systems. Its helicopter hanger can also accommodate the Ka-28. Two Type 052C/*Luyang II* are equipped with a new vertical-launched SAM and "Aegis" configuration phased-array radar that is likely derived from systems developed by the Ukrainian Kvant company.[104] The SAMs on this ship are a new type that has not yet been revealed but could be based on the SA-N-7 or the FT-2000/HQ-9 family. In addition, the Dalian shipyard has completed two new Type 051C DDGs that are slightly larger versions of the *Luhai* design, but outfitted with forty-eight of the Russian 120-km long-range RIF SAM, which is based on the S-300 SAM, per ship. These ten DDGs, when they enter service, will significantly expand antiair coverage for PLAN submarines. Their ability to deploy Ka-28s adds a new ASW dimension to PLA naval capabilities. It can be expected that the PLAN will decide that at least one of its three new indigenous DDGs is deserving of follow-on production.

After a two-year hiatus, in 2006 the PLAN resumed construction of the new stealthy Type 054 *Jiankai* frigate in two shipyards, this time armed with thirty-two SAMs per ship of a new vertical-launched version of the 9M317ME Shtil SAM, which has a Mach 4 speed and a range of about 60 km. By May 2007 a fourth Type 054A was launched. At the May 2007 IMDEX show a European source noted that China would build at least twelve Type 054A frigates.[105] The Type 054A is also outfitted with the Ukrainian Mineral E active/passive targeting radar and the Russian Fregat E search radar, which may now be co-produced in China, and it is expected to carry the Ka-28 ASW helicopter. At the IMDEX show European sources also confirmed that China was planning to develop a second new class of frigate that would use combined diesel/gas turbine engines, rather than the diesels of the Type 054. These are expected to replace older frigates but will offer a great increase in capability.

Antiship Missiles

The PLAN is now fielding new antiship missiles (ASMs) with greater range and sophistication than its 40-km-range YJ-81 (C-801) ASMs. China is now marketing its 280-km-range YJ-62 (C-602) antiship missile,[106] which may also form the basis for a longer-range LACM family for the PLAN and PLAAF. In PLAN service this missile's range is likely greater than 300 km. This missile most likely arms the *Luyang 2*/Type 052C DDG and may arm new versions of the Xian H-6 and JH-7A bombers. And while the 40-km-range YJ-81Q sub-launched antiship missile is known to be available, there may also be a sub-launched version of the 120-km-range YJ-82. The PLAN may also be fielding a longer-range 180-km-range version of the YJ-82 called the YJ-82A.[107] An air-launched version would have slightly longer range. This missile may also be the reported (but not confirmed) YJ-83 (C-803). Of particular concern are the PLAN's new 240-km-range Russian Raduga 3M-80MBE Moskits on its *Sovremenniy* 956EM destroyers and the 220-km-range Novator 3M-54 Club-S supersonic antiship missiles that will arm the eight Project 636M *Kilo* submarines now being delivered to China. Both missiles are capable of high-speed "jinking" maneuvers, which greatly complicate ship defenses.

The PLA Navy has also long maintained shore-based antiship missile units. These units started with fixed emplacements for the HY-201 antiship missile, a development of the Soviet Styx missile. China has in the last decade developed a mobile shore-based version of the 120-km-range YJ-82 (C-802) and sold this to Iran; there is little data to suggest this verison is in service with the PLAN shore defense units. However, in early 2008 an Asian military source disclosed that these units are being upgraded with the YJ-62C, a land-based version of the new 400- to 500-km-range YJ-62 (C-602) antiship cruise missile. This source noted that by early 2008 about 120 of these new antiship missiles had been deployed to coastal sites near Taiwan. As such they also pose a danger to U.S. Navy ships that may seek to come to Taiwan's aid in the event of a PLA attack.

In addition, the PLAN is improving its littoral surface and mine combat capabilities. In 2004 it started producing the Type 022 *Houbei*-class fast-attack craft (FAC), based on an Australian wave-piercing catamaran fast-ferry design. In early 2008 an Asian military source estimated that the PLAN would eventually acquire up to eighty Type 022 fast-attack craft. The Type 022 features stealth shaping and coatings, water pump–jet propulsion for high speed, and the capacity to carry up to eight C-802-size ASMs, guided antisubmarine missiles or perhaps varying numbers of artillery rockets. In mid-2008 a Chinese source suggested that a larger, helicopter-carrying version of the Type 022 may be developed, which would allow the manned or unmanned helicopter to perform long-range targeting for the missiles on other ships.[108] In 2004 the PLAN began building two new classes of open-ocean-capable minesweepers that will carry new autonomous mine-searching unmanned underwater vehicles. Both vessels can serve to clear the way for follow-on combat or invasion naval forces. The Type 022 can also combat new Taiwanese FACs such as the KH-6 class. The minesweepers can then deal with the dangerous mines the Taiwanese Navy may sow.

Growing Ground Expeditionary Forces

The PLA has taken to heart the hard-learned U.S. lesson of the Persian Gulf and the Balkans: airpower can win wars or compel adversaries only if backed by the use, or credible threat, of ground invasion. To make military suasion credible against Taiwan, Korea, India, or potential Central Asian targets, the PLA has been strengthening its airborne, amphibious, and Special Forces strike capabilities. These forces alone could comprise over 80,000 troops. All of these specialized troops have become increasingly mechanized during the last decade. But in addition, the PLA is making regular Army units more mobile and lethal by developing new families of wheeled armor, armored personnel carrier (APC), air support, and logistic support vehicles to enable the creation of light mechanized units. These are more easily transported by new PLAN transport ships, and in the future, will be made even more mobile by new large transport aircraft.

In 2006 the Pentagon noted that the PLA maintains 400,000 troops in the three Military Regions (MRs) opposite Taiwan, an increase of 25,000 over 2005.[109] This available force would consist of eight group armies, two Marine brigades, three airborne troop divisions, up to 2,700 tanks, and 3,200 artillery pieces.[110] By about 2010–2014, this analyst concludes, the PLA may be able to lift over 1,000 tanks to Taiwan with just the formal amphibious lift available to the PLA, not counting the hundreds of other "civilian" ships that would be pressed into service (Table 6.8). Taiwan only has 1,800 tanks to defend its whole island, a number that could be significantly degraded by air and missile strikes (Table 6.9). Once derided by some Western experts as the "million-man swim," by early in the next decade PLA "invasion" forces may be able to capture ports and airfields on Taiwan, leading to the capture of a large city such as Taipei and forcing a rapid surrender.

Table 6.8 Estimated PLA Formal Amphibious Lift Against Taiwan in 2015–2020

Ship Type	Displacement	Number	Main Battle Tanks	Troops
Type 081 LHD	20,000+ tons	6 possible	40	500
Type 071 LPD	20,000 tons	3 possible	50	800
Type 072 Yukan LST	4,170 tons	7	10	250
Type 072 IV Yuting 1 LST	4,800 tons	10	10	250
Yuting 2 LST	4,800 tons	10	10	250
Yunshu LSM	1,800 tons	10	6	250
Type 073 Yudeng LSM	2,000 tons	11	6	150
Yubei LCU	800+ tons	150	3	150
Type 079 Yuliang LSM	1,100 tons	32	3	150
Type 074 Yuhai LSM	799 tons	13	2	250
Type 271 LCU	800 tons	25	3	200
Type 068/069 Yuchin LCM	85 tons	20	NA	150
Zubr Hovercraft	550 tons	6-8 planned	3	10 APC + 230 troop
Estimated Totals		300+	1,600	57,250

Notes: Data for Type 081 and 071 estimated; totals represent estimated maximum for either main battle tanks or troops, not a combined estimate. Tank numbers much higher if light tanks or wheeled infantry fighting vehicles (IFVs) are used.
Sources: Jane's Fighting Ships 2007; IISS; www.sinodefense.com.

Table 6.9 PLA, Taiwanese, and U.S. Tanks Compared

Type	Weight/ Crew	Gun-launched missile	Main Gun	Gun lethality		Armor protection		Engine	Remarks
				KE Round	CE Round	KE Round	CE Round		
PLA									
Type 99 (ZTZ-99)	52 tons/ 3 crew	Russian 9M119 Reflex, 6-km range; 700-mm RHA penetration	125 mm; 41 rounds	800 mm; 960 mm reported w/ new DU rounds	680 mm est.	830 mm	1,060 mm	1,500 hp diesel	New arrow turret armor; Russian influence; autoload gun; composite armor; thermal/laser sight; fire-while-move; new laser counter-measure/counter-fire device; 100+ in service
Type 96 (T-88C)	48 tons/ 3 crew	Same as above	125 mm; 41 rounds	Same as above	680 mm est.	700 mm est.	800 mm est.	730–1,000 hp diesel	Cheaper & simpler than T-98; same gun; thermal/laser sight; composite armor; 1,400 built by 2006
Type 59D	37 tons/ 4 crew	Copy of Russian 9M117 Bastion 5.2-km range 700-mm RHA penetration	105 mm; 40 rounds	540 mm; 600 mm w/DU round	390 mm est.; 750 mm w/SPEAR round	520 mm of armor in front turret	Not available	580-hp diesel	Cast iron turret upgraded with ERA; new gun; thermal/laser sight; fire-while-move; large numbers to be upgraded
Type 63A	18+ tons/ 4 crew	Same as above	105 mm; 40 rounds est.	Same as above	Same as above	n/a	n/a	520-hp diesel	Amphibious tank; upgraded with new gun, turret; 500-600x being modified

Table 6.9 (continued)

Type	Weight/ Crew	Gun-launched missile	Main Gun	Gun lethality		Armor protection		Engine	Remarks
				KE Round	CE Round	KE Round	CE Round		
ZBD-2000 (EFV)	@25 tons	Very likely for IFV version	100 mm for IFV; 30 mm for APC	n/a	n/a	n/a	n/a	n/a	20–25 kt speed in water; retractable treads; IFV, APC (10 Marines) and logistic versions
Taiwan									
M-60A3	58 tons/ 4 crew	No	105 mm; 63 rounds	420 mm	340 mm est.	300 mm	380 mm	750-hp diesel	Thermal sight; fire-while-move; Cast iron turret a weakness; 460 in service
CM-11	55 tons/ 4 crew	No	105 mm; 54 rounds	420 mm	340 mm est.	290 mm	360 mm	750-hp diesel	M-60 chassis and M-48 cast iron turret; thermal/laser sight; fire-while-move; 450 in service
CM-12	55 tons/ 4 crew	No	105 mm; 50 rounds	420 mm	340 mm est.	290 mm	360 mm	750 hp diesel	Upgraded M-48; thermal/laser sight; fire-while-move; 100 in service
U.S.									
M1A2	69.5 tons	MRM-KE/ CE, 12+ km range; in development	120 mm/ 40 rounds	765-mm (M829A3 DU rnd est.)	n/a	940 mm– 960 mm	1,320 mm– 1,620 mm	1,500 hp gas turbine	Current U.S. model; Taiwan considered but so far has not purchased this tank.
EFV	37 tons (combat)	No	30 mm/ 150 rounds	n/a	n/a	n/a	n/a	850 hp (land)	20-kt speed in water; 17 Marines

Notes: RHA, rolled homogeneous armor; KE, kinetic energy round; CE, chemical energy round; ERA, explosive reactive armor; DU, depleted uranium. Gun lethality is measured as penetration at 2,000 m vs. RHA. Armor protection is measured at frontal arc of turret in RHA.

Sources: Morris Che and Chris Cardine, "Threat Analysis Report: T-98MBT & T-63AT"; ZTZ-98, *Armory Magazine; Battlefield Magazine; Russia's Arms, 2001–2002; Military Balance, 2006–2007; Jane's Armour and Artillery;* interview information.

There are now new shipbuilding and aircraft acquisition programs to address PLA sealift and airlift deficiencies. In December 2006 the PLA launched its first 20,000-ton LPD-class (Landing Platform Dock) amphibious ship, the Type 071, which will use new hovercraft tank and troop conveyers similar to the U.S. LCAC (Landing Craft Air Cushion), and large helicopters, enabling assaults from greater distances and against more difficult shore terrain. This ship could potentially carry about fifty armored vehicles and up to 800 troops. Asian sources suggest that the PLA may build up to six Type 071 ships.[111] In addition the PLA may be planning to build up to three 20,000-ton Type 081 LHD (Landing Helicopter Deck) helicopter-carrying assault ships that may carry about 500 troops and up to fifty combat vehicles.[112] As of early 2008 Russian sources indicated that China remained interested in purchasing the purchase Russian Zubr large hovercraft, which can carry three main battle tanks or up to ten APCs and 230 troops.[113] Previous reports had noted China's interest in six to eight Zubr.[114] The PLAN is now building two new types of LSM medium tank and troop landing ships, a total of about twelve since 2002, added to twenty or so ships of the same class. These ships can carry an average of about ten tanks and 250 troops. In addition, the PLA has access to 200–300 smaller specialized landing ships and a much larger number of civilian fast ferries and large RO-RO (roll on-roll off) cargo ships that can use captured ports. For example, China could mobilize over 150 "civilian" fast ferries that can carry 100–500 troops each.[115] In 2006 Taiwan's Ministry of Defense estimated that the PLA may be able to mobilize 800 civilian merchant ships, enough to transport five to seven infantry divisions.[116]

In addition to new ships, the PLA is also investing in essential specialized equipment for amphibious landings. In recent years Internet images have appeared of trucks emerging from LSTs carrying large rolls of ground matting which then allows subsequent vehicles to reach the shore more easily. Such equipment is required to traverse Taiwan's many mud flats, which would pose an obstacle to wheeled vehicles essential for early logistic support for amphibious forces. The may also be correcting a deficiency in amphibious artillery support. In recent years the PLA has experimented with placing Army artillery guns and artillery rockets on merchant ships to provide emergency support, but such fire would be very inaccurate. However, with the development of navigation satellite–guided artillery rockets and laser-guided artillery shells, this option becomes more attractive. In addition, if the PLA were to arm its Type 022 fast-attack craft, which may reach eighty in number, with guided artillery rockets, that may allow the PLA to support its landing troops with up to thousands of new precision guided munitions.[117]

Upgrading Amphibious Troops

To fully exploit their growing lift capacity, the PLA is also introducing more specialized combat equipment into its Marine and Army amphibious units. The goal is to make these forces more powerful and mechanized in order to secure objectives and contribute to follow-on attacks. Army and Marine forces may soon receive a family of fast-moving amphibious assault vehicles apparently based on the new ZBD-97 infantry fighting vehicles; these have been identified by some sources as the ZBD-2000. So far Internet imagery has shown three versions of this vehicle armed with a 100-mm cannon, a 30-mm cannon, and a machine-gun armed troop-carrying version. This vehicle uses powerful pump jets and planing surfaces to achieve high speeds similar to the new U.S. Marine's Expeditionary Fighting Vehicle (EFV) fast amphibious APC. This family of vehicles is apparently designed for the new Type 071 class LPD and future Type 081 LHD. Like the U.S. EFV, they enable assault operations to begin far out of the range of shore-based artillery, but unlike the EFV, the ZBD-2000 tank version arrives on the beach with about the same combat power as the T-63A tank.

Since the late 1990s, Marine and Army amphibious units have received about 600 of the new Type 63A amphibious tank, armed with a 105-mm gun that fires new 5-km- range laser-guided missiles based on the Russian Bastion, which outranges the 105-mm guns on Taiwan's tanks. Both have also received the new Type 63C armored personnel carrier (APC), and Army units are receiving a new family derived from the larger Type 89 family. Though only capable of slower speeds, these new tanks and APCs can be launched from miles offshore to reduce ship vulnerability. Armor units will have better logistic support now that the PLA has devised new rolled-mesh surfaces to lay on sand or coral beaches to better enable LSTs to land trucks. The development of such highly specialized amphibious assault equipment demonstrates how seriously the PLA takes this mission.

In addition, the PLA Army is investing in new wheeled combat vehicles that would allow it to create medium-weight mechanized units similar to the U.S. Stryker Brigade Combat Team. The PLA has long made some use of wheeled armored personnel carriers for infantry and antitank missile carriage. In 2004 the PLA revealed a new wheeled light tank based on the WZ551 APC. Its export name is the Assaulter, and it is armed with a 105-mm gun that fires a co-produced version of the gun-launched Bastion missile.[118] In 2006 the PLA began unveiling a new family of 18–22 ton 8x8 wheeled combat vehicles similar to those now featured in many militaries, including the U.S. Stryker wheeled combat vehicle family. Its reported designation is PF2006.[119] So far, this new PLA 8x8 family features a 105-mm gun tank, infantry fighting vehicles, 122-mm gun artillery, and command versions. A version armed with a twin 120-mm mortar may also be planned. In 2004 the PLA revealed its Yitian, a combination 25-mm cannon- and missile-armed wheeled APC able to provide mobile air defense for light mechanized units. During the Peace Mission 2005 exercise, the PLA amphibious beach assault featured a second wave of "Army" units that used wheeled APCs, an indication that new light mechanized units may become an import new contribution to an amphibious assault on Taiwan. However, they could also be transported by Il-76 cargo aircraft. Such light units are ideally suited to exploit Taiwan's extensive network of roads.

In addition, it should be expected that the PLA would put its new heavy tanks on Taiwan as soon as it was able. The new Type 99 (also called the T-98G or ZTZ-99) is an upgrade of the T-98 first seen in 1999. The upgrade is primarily in the form of new wedge-shaped modular turret armor and probably improved electronic systems. But its 125-mm gun fires high-explosive and armor-piecing rounds in addition to a co-produced version of a 6-km-range Russian Reflex gun-launched missile. The Type 99 may in production in at least two factories. PLA armored units have already taken delivery of over 1,400 of the less expensive T-96, which also uses the same 125-mm gun. In 2006 two new versions of the T-96 were revealed, one with turret armor upgrades similar to those of the T-99 and another with a unique turret armor upgrade. All versions of the Type 99 and Type 96 are expected to outclass the U.S.-built 105-mm-gun-armed M-60 and modified M-48 tanks used by the Taiwanese Army. The Type-99 can also be expected to compare well with Japan's T-90 and South Korea's KTX-1. Currently, the Type 99's 125-mm gun is larger than the 120-mm gun on the U.S. M1A2 Abrams, and the Chinese tank uses removable and upgradable turret armor "cheeks" to respond to new threats. One report in 2003 noted that China was developing a new tank with a 153-mm autoloading gun and an active protection system.[120]

The PLA is committed to developing superior armor systems. To counter the threat of guided antitank weapons, the PLA's Norinco Company was proposing to purchase the Russian Engineering Design Bureau's (KBM) Arena-E active tank defense system, which uses a radar to direct a shotgun-like device to destroy incoming antitank missiles.[121] In 2006 and 2007 Internet imagery emerged of PLA T-99 and T-96 tanks equipped with a passive protection system similar to the Russian Shtora, which uses infrared and laser emitters along with smoke to confuse the semiactive and laser-guidance systems of guided antitank shells and missiles. The PLA was also reported to be interested in KBM's unique Khrisantema Mach-2-speed, 6-km-range antitank missile, which can penetrate an astounding 1,200 mm of rolled homogeneous armor (RHA).[122] This missile could be fitted to a range of current PLA tracked and wheeled armored vehicles. Should the PLA purchase or co-produce the Khrisantema in large numbers, it would have a weapon that could come close to defeating the U.S. M1A2 with a frontal attack. Its speed may also enable it to defeat many kinetic-based active tank defense systems. The U.S. Army is now developing a gun-launched missile for the M1A2 tank and for the much lighter Future Combat System tank, decades after the Russians have done so.

PLA Airborne Capabilities

By early 2007 PLA airlift consisted of about twenty Russian Il-76 heavy jet transports capable of carrying 120 paratroops, three KLC-2000 light tanks, or a 47-ton payload. The PLA also had about fifty Y-8 transports which can carry ninety paratroops or about twenty tons of cargo. Though it was in doubt in mid-2008, a September 2005 agreement to buy thirty to thirty-four more Il-76 transports, should it be realized, would represent about a 150-percent increase in capacity. Ukraine's Antonov Corporation is also helping Shaanxi perfect its new Y-9 transport, a radical upgrade of the Y-8 copied from the Antonov An-12. The Y-9 is due to fly in 2007, but Shaanxi has already started producing modified Y-8s with Y-9 technology to create new electronic support aircraft. There have also been discussions with Ukraine about acquiring or even co-producing its very large Antonov An-124, which can carry over 150 tons. Ukrainian sources have noted that AVIC-1 and AVIC-2 are competing to build a new 60-ton capacity airlifter,[123] which could fly between 2015 and 2020. This is close to the capacity of the Boeing C-17 transport. The latest 2006–2010 Five-Year Plan devotes special funds to developing large transport aircraft. However, once airfields are captured and secured, the PLA can mobilize over 500 "civilian" Boeing and Airbus airliners to ferry troops and material. There is increasing coverage on Chinese television of PLA exercises that test the reserve transport mobilization of civilian airliners.

The 2006 Chinese Defense White Paper notes that modernizing Army aviation is a top priority for the PLA Army. One Russian company estimates China's military could be using 10,000 helicopters by 2020. While perhaps an exaggeration, the PLA is devoting considerable resources to foreign and domestic helicopter capabilities. The PLA Army now operates about 240 helicopters of the Russian Mil Mi-17 family and is expected to purchase about 160 more.[124] In mid-2008 a Russian report noted that China and Russia had reached an agreement to being Mi-17 co-production in China, starting at twenty in 2008 and eventually growing to eighty per year.[125] The Mi-17 can easily carry twenty fully equipped troops across the Taiwan Strait. Russia's Rostevertol is actively marketing to the PLA its unique Mi-26, currently the world's largest transport helicopter, which can carry twenty tons of cargo or eighty fully equipped troops. In late 2006 Rostevertol reached an agreement to lease one helicopter to a private Chinese company, but Rostevertol officials have noted eagerness by the PLA to purchase more.[126] At the September 2007 Beijing Air Show Rostevertol invited the PLA to participate in a new 12-ton capacity version of the Mi-26, which would be ideally suited to transporting a single airborne tank such as the ZLC-2000 or the Russian BMD. While China had not yet responded positively by late 2007 according to a Russian source,[127] such a lift capability would allow the PLA to conduct precision assaults with light mechanized airborne forces or Special Forces.

China is also working with Eurocopter to develop a new 6–8-ton-class transport helicopter, the EC-175, which is due to be produced in China and France.[128] This helicopter is slated to carry sixteen civilian passengers, which might translate to about twelve fully equipped troops. While Eurocopter officials insist there will not be a PLA version of this helicopter,[129] all previous Chinese copied or co-produced Eurocopter designs have been used by the PLA. Internet source imagery indicates that the long-awaited WZ-10 attack helicopter shows a resemblance to the Italian Agusta A-129 attack helicopter.[130] The WZ-10 is expected to be armed with modern low-light and automatic targeting systems, new HJ-10 guided antitank missiles, and a range of unguided munitions and a 23-mm or 30-mm gun, making it a world-class helicopter gunship. Since about 2004 China has been producing the latest verision of the HAIG WZ-9 gunship, the WZ-9G, which features a new chin-mounted electro-optical targeting turret.. An attack/scout version of the Z-11 helicopter has also been tested and is likely in production in 2008.[131]

The PLA's 15th Airborne Army has about three divisions of 35,000 troops,[132] and there is some concern that the PLA is building a second airborne army. There is now a major effort underway to build up airborne units into mechanized formations similar to those of the Russian airborne forces.[133] Since 2004 PLA airborne units have started to receive a new family of 10-ton air-mobile armor vehicles after the failure of attempts to manufacture the Russian BMD vehicle. With the initial designation ZLC-2000, this vehicle will come in a 30-mm cannon-armed infantry fighting vehicle, an HJ-8 antitank-missile vehicle, and command vehicle versions.[134] Airborne units are also receiving new Italian-designed IVECO light trucks, some of which are armed with HJ-9 antitank missiles and give airborne troops added mobility.

Special Forces

PLA Special Forces can also be expected to play a key role in a Taiwan invasion, from the assassination of key civilians, military figures, and personnel such as pilots to general sabotage and preparatory attacks for airborne and amphibious assaults. The Pentagon notes that the PLA has "devoted considerable resources to the development of Special Operations Forces (SOF)," and they are "an integral element of ground force modernization."[135] Each of the seven MRs has a Special Operations Dadui (unit).[136] Another source notes that each PLA Group Army has a Special Operations battalion, for a total of 25,000 men.[137] According to a Chinese source, SOF units range in size from 100 to 1,000 men,[138] although one source notes that SOF make up division-size units in the Chengdu, Lanzhou, and Shenyang MRs.[139]

By 2003, the PLA is also reported to have built up to six Western-style Long-Range Operations Groups. The first such unit was built up in the Guangzhou MR, made operational in 1989, and composed of 4,000 troops that received army parachute, air force, and navy training. The unit is also equipped with satellite communications, GPS navigation equipment, and a wide range of PLA and Western weapons. Most of its officers are university educated and its soldiers are cross-trained in a variety of tasks.[140] During the 2002–2003 U.S. war against the Taliban regime in Afghanistan, it is reported that the PLA sent small units of Special Forces into Afghanistan to monitor U.S. operations. Five new and more intensely trained units were to be deployed by 2003. It was expected that these units would provide the initial clandestine assault units for future Taiwan operations, but they could also perform counterterrorist operations.[141] In a Taiwan campaign, it is even possible that SOF units will operate against U.S. forces, especially those in Japanese bases.

PLA SOF missions are likely to include conducting battle surveillance and battle damage assessment, locating and/or destroying C4I (command, control, communications, computer, intelligence) nodes, destroying logistic depots, capturing and/or destroying airfields and ports, supporting invasion forces, destroying air defense assets, conducting denial and deception operations, conducting psychological operations, and conducting information operations.[142] PLA SOF units will also provide target illumination to assist in guiding precision weapons.[143] It is also possible that PLA SOF teams will also try to capture opposing military and political leaders. SOF personnel are chosen for their physical stamina and are expected to be able to operate light and heavy weapons, foreign weapons, and multiple transports such as tanks, trucks, helicopters, and assault boats.[144] Another source notes that PLA SOF units also make use of female combatants.[145]

Seeking to follow the U.S. example set during the Gulf War and more recently in Afghanistan, the PLA Army has spent the last decade investing heavily in equipment and training for Special Forces.[146] There is substantial open-source information from the PRC indicating that Special Forces train hard for their intended tasks. Special Forces troops train with powered paragliders that can transport lightly armed troops up to 100 km. The PLA has also purchased small, fast commando transport ships from Sweden. SOF units are often portrayed emerging from Mi-17 helicopters. Special Operations units also have the best weapons and equipment the PLA can offer. They employ a variety of PLA small arms and Western small arms, all modified when necessary.

The PLA has invested heavily in expanding the size, training, and specialized equipment for Special Forces. For example, the PLA is experimenting with a "Mechanized" Special Forces unit in the Chengdu Military Region. This unit features new jeeps armed with automatic 120-mm mortars or twin 25-mm anti-aircraft guns, new lightweight all-terrain vehicles (ATVs) to carry troops, and a one-man five-wheel ATV armed with a bank of 130-mm rocket launchers: all of these vehicles are designed to be transported by helicopters. Such a unit might be used to secure critical areas of an airfield or a port that would open the way for heavier airborne or amphibious forces.

Preventing American Military Support for Taiwan

Since the Clinton administration's move to deploy two U.S. Navy carrier battle groups near Taiwan during the March 1996 PLA exercises intended to intimidate Taiwanese from voting for then–presidential candidate Lee Teng Hui, the PLA has worked to steadily acquire the means to prevent future U.S. military support for Taiwan. It is the certainty of the U.S. commitment to defend Taiwan that girds the island's leaders to behave as the leaders of a de facto independent country and inspires Taiwanese citizens to believe that they can have a future free from Chinese political control. Taiwan estimates it would take the United States ten to fourteen days to respond to a surprise Chinese attack, which is why Washington presses Taiwan to improve its defenses.[147] For

China, victory over Taiwan entails not just defeat of its military, but also success at delaying, preventing, or defeating U.S. military forces that may come to Taiwan's rescue.

Part of China's strategy to deter U.S. intervention has been to occasionally threaten to use nuclear weapons against the United States if it aids Taiwan; at the same time, the PLA is modernizing its nuclear missile forces to make such threats credible. Another element of PLA strategy has been to gather information on submarine, aircraft, and missile forces to enable it to attack U.S. aircraft carrier groups that come within threatening range of Taiwan. A third element has been to begin to develop power-projection forces that could potentially challenge other U.S. interests, which may make Washington more willing to allow China a sphere of influence in East Asia.

Electronic/Information Attack

It would be consistent with the PLA's doctrinal stress on offensive and asymmetrical operations for it to undertake a range of electronic and Special Forces strikes against a range of U.S. and Japanese targets as part of the opening phase of general hostilities against Taiwan. Both modes of attack have the advantage of causing low numbers of casualties while creating maximum chaos, both of which the PLA deems essential in order to delay an American or Japanese response during the crucial early phases of PLA operations against Taiwan.

Electronic attacks would seek to disrupt or destroy the networks of sensors, communications links, and command systems at the center of the current U.S. war-fighting capabilities. Computer network attacks would originate from China and many other locations, including inside the U.S. military or key civilian electronic infrastructure centers. Cutting off key command figures in Washington from the Pacific Command in Hawaii, and in turn, from key deployed elements of U.S. forces in the Pacific, would be a top priority. Electronic attacks can also be expected against key U.S. civilian electronic infrastructure with the aim of crippling new media, communication, transportation, and financial sectors. The United States has no experience in defending against a massive and dedicated attack against its military and civilian electronic infrastructure.

In addition, the PLA can be expected to use antisatellite and radio-frequency weapons to attack U.S. military electronic infrastructure. The PLA's successful January 2007 destruction of a weather satellite with a direct-ascent antisatellite weapon demonstrated its ability to destroy U.S. surveillance, weather, and communications satellites that use polar and low-earth orbits. This addresses a particular U.S. weakness: high reliance on all types of space satellites. Inasmuch as China is known to arm some SRBMs with radio-frequency weapons, it is possible China has also developed a range of radio-frequency weapons including bombs or even grenades, perhaps even purchasing these from Russia. These weapons can damage critical electronic systems without killing large numbers of people.

Special-Forces Attack

The United States should also expect PLA Special Forces to stage attacks against all critical U.S. military bases in the Pacific, Hawaii, and the U.S. West Coast, and even against key officials in Washington, DC. Such attacks could range from sabotage against power plants, communications facilities, water facilities, or key ship or aircraft weapons systems, to attacks (nonlethal or lethal) against key personnel such as top commanders, ship crews, pilots, or key political officials in Washington responsible for making military decisions. Covert transport of Special Forces could be accomplished by submarines or commercial ships and airlines. China's extensive use of Chinese Americans for espionage in the United States and its organization of Chinese students in the United States for political harassment activities should raise questions about China's willingness to use these communities for military missions.

Targeting Aircraft Carriers

Since the mid-1990s the PLA has been seeking to assemble the necessary space, missile, air, and naval forces to deter or attack U.S. carrier battle groups that may come to Taiwan's aid (Table 6.10). There may even be sentiment in the PLA that by sinking a U.S. carrier, the PLA could succeed in deflating the U.S. will to contest Taiwan. In May 2002 Major General Huang Bin of the Chinese National Defense University told a Hong Kong newspaper:

> Missiles, aircraft, and submarines all are means that can be used to attack an aircraft carrier. We have the ability to deal with an aircraft carrier that dares to get into our range of fire. Once we decide to use force against Taiwan, we definitely will consider an intervention by the United States. The United States likes vain glory [*sic*]; if one of its aircraft carrier[s] should be attacked and destroyed, people in the United States would begin to complain and quarrel loudly, and the U.S. president would find the going harder and harder.[148]

Although the General's expectation that such a loss will deter the United States may be gravely mistaken, the PLA has made great progress in gathering the very forces he mentions. By 2007 the PLAN had taken delivery of the last of twelve Russian *Kilo* submarines, eight of which are armed with the Club antiship missile system. In addition the PLAN now has twelve to thirteen Type 039 *Song*-class submarines that are also armed with a version of the YJ-82 antiship missile. In addition, the PLAN's nineteen or so older Type 035 *Ming*-class submarines are quiet diesel-electric submarines that can conduct surveillance against U.S. ships, lay mines, or act as decoys against defending U.S. nuclear attack submarines. A *Song* was reported to have approached within five miles of the USS *Kitty Hawk* in October 2006, undetected until it surfaced.[149] The ability of the *Song* to remain undetected suggests the PLAN was able to anticipate the location of the U.S. carrier, which

Table 6.10 Estimated PLA Anticarrier Weapons by 2015

Space/ISR	Attack Aircraft
Direct-ascent antisatellite missiles	New attack aircraft
Laser antisatellite weapons	15 Su-33KK
Radar satellites	70 Su-30MKK
Electro-optical satellites	24 Su-30MKK2
ELINT/SIGINT satellites	220 J-11A/B
OTH radar	170 JH-7A
Long-range high-altitude UAV	250 J-10
Underwater sonar networks	40 H-6M/K
Missiles	**Surface Warships**
Antiship ballistic missiles	1 Aircraft carrier, limited usage
YJ-62-derived long-range antiship cruise missiles	4 *Sovremenniy* DDG
YJ-82-derived antiship missiles	4 New antiair DDG
Novator Club antiship missiles	2 *Luyang*-2 Aegis DDG
Moskit supersonic antiship missiles	2 *Luyang*-1 DDG
Kh-31-derived antiship/antiradar missiles	2 051C DDG
New indigenous supersonic antiship/antiradar missile	12 Type 054A FFG
Non-nuclear radio frequency warheads	12 New Type FFG
Submarines	
3 09X SSN	
3 093 SSN	
3 091 SSN	
12 *Yuan* AIP SSK	
12 *Kilo* SSK	
13 *Song* SSK	
15 *Ming* SSK	

also suggests the PLAN may be investing in a new ocean surveillance system.[150] During the Cold War a U.S. surveillance system based in large part on seabed-moored sonar gave the United States a tremendous advantage in locating Soviet submarines. For the PLA such a system, netted with new ocean-monitoring radar satellites and long-range over-the-horizon radar, would give their forces an equal advantage to enable rapid targeting of U.S. surface and subsurface forces.

Once targets are located, the PLAN's twenty-four Su-30MKK2 fighter-bombers, the PLAAF's seventy-six Su-30MKK, the growing numbers of Xian JH-7As in the PLAAF and PLANAF, the Shenyang J-11B and Chengdu J-10 fighters, and new Xian H-6M bombers could potentially coordinate with submarines to launch volleys of long-range antiship missiles. Later in the next decade the PLAN may also be able to fly some air-interdiction missions from its first aircraft carrier. New PLAN air-defense destroyers can also provide some degree of air cover to allow submarines to get closer to U.S. ships. Should the PLAN purchase Su-30K fighters with upgraded active electronic scanned-array (AESA) radar, more powerful AL-41 engines and anticipated very-long-range Russian air-to-air missiles, they would be superior to the U.S. F/A-18E/F, the dominant U.S. carrier combat aircraft for many years to come.

Mine Warfare

An often less considered but serious challenge to U.S. "access" would be the extensive PLAN use of advanced naval mines. The PLAN has always taken seriously the requirement to wage extensive naval mine warfare, has devoted considerable resources to this capability, and has kept abreast of the latest mine warfare technologies. Mines would be a critical part of a PLA attempt to blockade Taiwan, used against Taiwanese naval bases, ports, and major sea-lanes. The PLA can also be expected to deploy mines to try to "ambush" U.S. naval forces either near Japanese bases or in likely operating areas near Taiwan. China may also regard naval mines as a "poor man's ASW" to compensate for the PLAN's weak antisubmarine warfare capabilities compared to the U.S. SSNs.[151] By some estimates, the PLAN maintains a stock of naval mines that reaches into the tens of thousands.

While many of the mines are obsolete moored mines, the PLA has more recently invested in modern, deadly deep-moored fast-rising mines, self-propelled mines, bottom-dwelling mines, and remote-control mines. In the 1980s China developed its novel EM-52, a moored mine that contains a fast-rising rocket with a large warhead; this mine may be capable of breaking the keel of an aircraft carrier. China is also marketing the EM-55, a submarine-delivered moored fast-rising mine. Both mines could be used to cover deep-water areas near Taiwan where U.S. submarines may lurk. China is also marketing the EM-66, a long torpedo-shaped self-propelled mine useful for standoff mining of ports and naval bases. China has also very likely purchased a range of advanced Russian mines such as those produced by the Gidropropridor Company.[152]

Most Chinese-built warships are designed to carry mines, and the PLAN has a few dedicated mine-laying ships. The Russian-built *Sovremenniy* destroyers are also outfitted with mine rails on their decks. In addition it can be expected that the PLAN will use aircraft to deliver mines. The PLAN has recently started building new classes of minesweeping ships, like the Wozchi class and new smaller minesweepers.

Antiship Ballistic Missiles

Another key antiaccess weapon for the PLA may be terminally guided maneuvering antiship ballistic missiles (ASBM), a revolutionary weapon for which the United States and its allies lack any defenses. Chinese military technical literature viewed on Chinese Internet data bases indicates that the Second Artillery has taken a considerable role in the development of antiship ballistic missiles.[153] The PLA will likely attempt to coordinate ASBM attacks with attacks by air and submarine-launched cruise missiles in order to saturate a carrier group's air defenses. A public indication that China was working toward an ASBM first came at the Zhuhai Air Show in November 1996, when a Chinese engineer disclosed to this author that China was developing a terminal guidance system for the DF-21 medium-range ballistic missile.[154] Chinese sources indicate that research toward this advanced guided missile began before the 1996 U.S. deployment of aircraft carriers to confront threatening PLA exercises, but that the U.S. action increased the urgency of this program. Chinese technical literature indicates that the new PLA ASBM may have been greatly influenced by the now-defunct U.S. Pershing II MRBM of the 1980s, which used radar to correlate digital imagery and achieve phenomenal accuracy. Internet imagery from 2007 of models of the DF-21 and the new DF-15B shows that their nose/warhead sections correspond with Chinese technical literature describing bi-conical finned reentry vehicles similar to those of the Pershing II.[155]

In a 2004 report the U.S. Office of Naval Intelligence (ONI) warned, "Chinese writing state[s] China intends to develop the capability to attack ships, including carrier strike groups, in the waters around Taiwan using conventional theater ballistic missiles (TBMs) as part of a combined-arms campaign."[156] ONI assessed that the PLA was developing a maneuverable ballistic missile warhead containing a terminal guidance system that apparently may use both active and passive radar.[157] According to U.S and Asian sources the PLA has tested antiship ballistic missiles in 2005 and 2006.[158] Asian sources note the main missile being developed for this mission is the 2,000+-km-range DF-21C solid-fuel mobile ballistic missile.[159] In early 2007 a Chinese technology official noted that "antisatellite technology" could be used to enable missiles to intercept aircraft carriers, as "these technologies are interrelated."[160] In early 2008 an Asian military source disclosed that a new 3,000-km-range version of the DF-21, first seen in 2006 and then 2007, which is also equipped with multiple warheads, will also have an anti-ship capability.

The success of PLA ASBMs is directly linked to the PLA's ability to develop and deploy new surveillance and navigation satellites, new long-range surveillance UAVs, and over-the-horizon (OTH) radar, in addition to a range of ships and submarines that can monitor target locations. The PLA's imminent deployment of a larger electro-optical and radar satellite network was covered in Chapter 5. In addition, Chinese technical literature may indicate significant research toward the development of very long-range "Sky Wave" OTH radar.[161] In early 2008 an Asian military source disclosed to the author that indeed, China had about five operational OTH sites, which for the first time allowed the PLA to secure constant coverage of U.S. naval movements in the Western Pacific.

CHAPTER 7

BUILDING FOR FUTURE POWER PROJECTION

Chapters 2 through 6 described China's developing global interests, the transformation of its military forces, and the ways those forces are shifting the balance of power in Asia. Chapter 3 examined how China's economic and resource requirements are pushing it into new international activism. Chapter 3 also explored how China is building new institutions, such as the Shanghai Cooperation Organization, to better enable continental "power projection" and is also beginning to exercise more distant military "soft power" by participating in United Nations peacekeeping exercises. Chapter 6 examined how China is transforming its military forces and building for regional dominance. This chapter explores the inevitable next question: is China building the capacity to exercise military-political influence beyond East Asia? The accumulating evidence is in the affirmative. China is developing capabilities to project power in space and on the sea as well as developing advanced heavy-lift jet transports and potentially new long-range bombers, and it is expanding the range and sophistication of its military exports.

Post 2005—New Concerns

By 2005 the U.S. Intelligence Community began expressing concerns that China could develop military capabilities powerful enough to challenge the United States in the Greater Asian region or beyond. In the 2005 issue of its annual review of Chinese military modernization, the Department of Defense (DoD), after noting the that PLA's first priority is to prepare for a conflict over Taiwan, went on to note:

[S]ome of China's military planners are surveying the strategic landscape beyond Taiwan. . . . Over the long term, improvements in China's command, control, communications, computers, intelligence, surveillance and reconnaissance (C4ISR) capability, including space-based and over-the-horizon platforms, could enable Beijing to identify, target, and track foreign military activities deep into the Western Pacific and provide, potentially, hemispheric coverage. . . . Current trends in China's military modernization could provide China with a force capable of prosecuting a range of military operations in Asia—well beyond Taiwan—potentially posing a credible threat to modern militaries operating in the region.[1]

In its 2006 *Quadrennial Defense Review* the DoD warned matter-of-factly, "China has the greatest potential to compete militarily with the United States and field disruptive military technologies that could over time offset traditional U.S. military advantages." During February 28, 2006, hearings of the Senate Armed Services Committee, Chairman John Warner (R-VA) noted that China is seeking to "project influence and perhaps even force elsewhere in the region." At that same hearing Deputy Intelligence Director Michael Hayden observed of China, "[T]here's almost a momentum in Chinese thinking that . . . great powers need certain things, and they aren't necessarily tied to a specific military event, either proposed or expected, but simply become the trappings of their global legitimacy."

A determination that China is developing or building long-range "power-projection" forces amounts to a new view of Chinese intentions and capabilities that flies in the face of recent conventional assessments. It has been more usual in Western academic circles to describe China's military modernization ambitions as largely "defensive" or "limited" for the purpose of solving the Taiwan issue or exercising influence in its immediate East Asian region.[2] In addition, some analysts correctly noted that in 2006 China exhibited few of the needed elements of a robust power-projection capability in terms of doctrine, deployable Army forces, or robust deployable naval forces.

However, as discussed previously, China's ambition in the current era is to resume its "traditional" role as the leading power in Asia. In 2005 the Chinese government promoted domestic and international celebrations of the 600th anniversary of the first voyage of the famous Ming Dynasty Muslim eunuch Admiral Zheng He, suggesting that its current economic outreach should be considered as helpful and peaceful as that of the Ming Dynasty.[3] But as historian Edward Dreyer has written, the purpose of Zheng He's voyages was "to enforce outward compliance with the forms of the Chinese tributary system by the show of an overwhelming armed force."[4] Far from being peaceful, Zheng He's troops overthrew a government in Sri Lanka and attacked another in Sumatra. Despite China's oft-repeated assurances of "non-interference," as China's power projection capabilities grow, it will be tempted to use them to advance its increasingly distant interests.

Justifying a Greater Military Role

In recent years Chinese military officials have issued statements that indicate China may be considering a larger military force able to play a role in global strategic affairs commensurate with China's growing leadership role in global political and economic affairs. In late 2004 Hu Jintao began to develop the concept of "the historical mission of the army," with a component that the PLA "must provide a security guarantee for national interests."[5] This apparently goes beyond participation in U.N. peacekeeping operations and foreign military exercises, which the PLA is also doing. The Chinese leadership appears to be considering missions to protect sea-lanes of communication, missions that would protect access to resources, and projection of Chinese power into space.

In early 2005 PLA Air Force (PLAAF) Lt. General Liu Yazhou, previously noted for his maverick though nationalist views, told a reporter, "When a nation grows strong enough, it practices hegemony. The sole purpose of power is to pursue even greater power. . . . The frontiers of our national interests are expanding. Our military strategy should embody characteristics of the time."[6] Then in mid-May 2006, Rear Admiral Yang Yi, director of the Institute for Strategic Studies of the National Defense University of the PLA, told an interviewer, "What is particularly noteworthy is that compared with the political, diplomatic, and cultural means of safeguarding China's interests, China's military force lags far behind. As a responsible big power, China needs to build a military force worthy of its international status. . . . This makes it necessary to combine "soft force" and "hard force."[7]

As Michael Pillsbury has explored in his 2000 analysis, there is a community of Chinese government analysts who assess that China will become the dominant power in the *world*, with some debating whether this may happen as soon as 2020 or as late as 2050.[8] Assumed in such projections is that China will have to build military forces able to project power in both maritime and continental arenas on a far greater scale than current capabilities allow.

China's quest for greater military reach is viewed by some promoters of "Greater China" nationalism, such as the Singapore *Straits Times*, as a natural and acceptable development. In a March 23, 2006, editorial it advised: "As China's economic networks multiply across the globe, it would be compelled to ensure its trade and oil-supply routes are never impeded. Force projection, even if only implicit, is the method of choice." Ominously, the *Straits Times* advised Americans to stop "hectoring" China about its military buildup, and "make space" for China's new power.

Developing a Power-Projection Doctrine?

Official government statements and statements by PLA officials in 2007 indicate that the PLA may be developing a "doctrine" of power projection. Although the content of this doctrine may never be explained publicly, the first indication that the PLA is considering "distant" missions for its armed services came in the December 2006 National Defense White Paper, which noted (italics added):

> The Army aims at moving from regional defense to trans-regional mobility, and improving its capabilities in air-ground integrated operations, *long-distance maneuvers*, rapid assaults and special operations. The Navy aims at *gradual extension of the strategic depth for offshore defensive operations* and enhancing its capabilities in integrated maritime operations and nuclear counterattacks. The Air Force aims at speeding up its transition from territorial air defense to both offensive and defensive operations, and increasing its capabilities in the areas of air strike, air and missile defense, early warning and reconnaissance, and *strategic projection.*

As is characteristic of these documents, the White Paper offers no definition for these new highlighted terms. For the Army, "long-distance maneuvers" and "trans-regional mobility" could mean across the expanse of just China itself, or it could mean between China and the Persian Gulf. For the Navy, "gradual extension of strategic depth" may have a limit, perhaps an East Asian regional limit, or it may not. For the Air Force, however, "strategic projection" would have a clearer meaning: the ability to project force a long distance. When considering the long-range-capable air and naval forces that the PLA is developing, these terms begin to suggest China's intention to develop operational concepts of "power projection" in the sense of sending significant military force well beyond China's borders.

Sea Power Debate

Recent Chinese statements also indicate that the Chinese leadership may be considering a new military operational theory of "sea power." On December 26, 2006, before the Tenth Congress of Commissars of the PLA Navy (PLAN), CCP Secretary General and Central Military Commission (CMC) Chairman Hu Jintao stated, "We should strive to build a powerful navy that adapts to the needs of our military's historical mission in this new century and at this new stage. . . . We should make sound preparations for military struggles and ensure that the forces can effectively carry out missions at any time."[9] "Mission," he explained, meant to "uphold our maritime rights and interests."[10] In the July 2007 issue of the CCP journal *Qiushi*, PLAN commander Admiral Wu Shengli stated that expanded navy missions would "protect fishing, oceanic resource development, and oceanic investigation and tests; maintain the safety of oceanic transportation and the strategic passageway for energy and resources; ensure the jurisdiction of our nation."[11]

There are also some who echo the notion of Otto Von Bismarck that the "flag should follow trade." One military scholar has noted that China's "maritime rights and interests are scattered all over the world and continue to expand as the size of the Chinese economy grows."[12] An author writing in August 2007 issue of *Modern Navy* magazine noted, "At the current stage, China's use of the land will come to an end, but its use of the ocean is just getting started. Whether today or in the future, the ocean will be a source of power and a lifeline for the survival and growth of the Chinese nation, and it will enable China to travel down a significant path in the world. . . . [China] should be maintaining a stable peripheral environment, sparing no effort to manage the ocean, and safeguarding a sea-oriented security."[13]

However, there are other indications that the PLA does not have a "sea power theory" or doctrine as of yet, only a "sea defense theory." One writer laments, "In the nearly 100 years since Mahan from the US suggested the idea of 'sea power,' the Chinese have not fully understood and digested sea power and its study."[14] In 2007 other Chinese academics also wrote that a blue-water navy with aircraft carriers may be obsolete, that building such a fleet risks confrontation with the United States, and that China can retain access to resources though equal and mutually beneficial trade.[15] But it does not appear they are winning the arguments.

Peace Mission 2007

Although it may not be possible to offer precise descriptions of a developing PLA "doctrine" of power projection, a preview of the PLA's ambitions in power projection was provided by the Peace Mission 2007 exercises held August 9–17, 2007, in the Chelyabinsk region of Russia, under the auspices of the Shanghai Cooperation Organization (SCO). The first Peace Mission 2005 was held on Chinese territory in August 2005 and involved only Russia sending airborne troops, Marines, Su-27 fighters, and Tu-22M Backfire bombers to China's Shandong Peninsula. China had reportedly originally wanted the exercises in Fujian Province opposite Taiwan. Furthermore, during Peace Mission 2005, PLAN and Russian Navy destroyers and submarines conducted exercises. These exercises marked a turning point for the PLA in that after fifteen years of investments in modernized forces, they were able to conduct modern military exercises with a "peer" military force that could boast recent combat experience in Chechnya. They conducted joint airborne troop drops, an amphibious beach assault, air defense, and naval blockade missions, all skills that the PLA would require to attack Taiwan.

In contrast, Peace Mission 2007 did not involve naval forces or long-range bombers. Both Russia and China practiced long-distance deployments for airborne, light mechanized armor, and air support elements, which included many first-time foreign deployments for the PLA. Although the exercise only involved about 6,000 troops total, it did allow both Russia and China to extend the exercise to include small numbers of troops from Kazakhstan, Kyrgyzstan, Tajikistan, and Uzbekistan. Although the exercise was advertised by Russian and Chinese spokesmen as directed primarily against "terrorism," Russian statements in particular indicated the goal of defending "stability," presumably against forces of democracy. In that sense, Peace Mission 2007 could be viewed to be similar to former Soviet incursions into Hungary in 1956 and Czechoslovakia in 1968, to defend the existence of compliant regimes. As such, Peace Mission 2007 provided a platform for Russia and China not only to assert their leadership over this strategic region, but also to indicate they are willing to deploy forces to prevent democratic revolutions.

Peace Mission 2007 did advance key PLA operational ambitions related to the development of future power-projection capabilities. Senior Colonel Lu Chuangang, chief of the command group for the exercises, noted that the Peace Mission 2007 force included "one Army task force, one air force task force, and one integrated support task force," indicating that future projection exercises would involve service-based units and perhaps a new joint logistics support unit.[16] Lu also noted the exercise would allow the PLA to test four key capabilities: "capability in long distance mobility . . . capability in joint operations . . . capability in carrying out precision engagement . . . [and] capability in long distance integrated support."[17] It is important to examine these further.

Capability in Long-Distance Mobility

Lu noted, "This is the first time that the PLA conducts a large scale and long-distance transnational force delivery involving different branches of the armed forces in a systematic way." The PLA deployed a force of 1,600–1,700 troops from the 31st Group Army from the Nanjing Military Region opposite Taiwan, the 36th Group Army near Beijing, the 15th Airborne Army, and Air Force units. The mechanized units were equipped with two new versions of the six-wheel WZ-551 armored personnel carrier. One version is armed with a 25-mm automatic cannon, and the other, armed with a 105-mm gun, is marketed as the "Assaulter." These were transported by train over a distance of 10,300 km. Their air support was provided by 16 HAIG WZ-9 and WZ-9G attack helicopters, plus sixteen Mil Mi-8/17 transport helicopters, which deployed over 2,700 km by air over two days. Airborne forces consisted of about 120 troops and ten combat vehicles,[18] including the new ZLC-2000 airborne tank. These were transported on six Ilyushin Il-76MD transport aircraft. Finally, a PLAAF regiment dispatched eight new Xian JH-7A fighter-bombers, each using three drop tanks to extend their range.

Capability in Joint Operations

In sharp contrast to 2005, the PLA took a small but decisive step toward greater joint operations in the 2007 exercises by appointing as commander of the deployed force a PLAAF general, Xu Qiliang, who is also a Deputy Chief of the General Staff Department. This may be the first time a PLAAF general was given such a high-profile command opportunity and augurs well for greater

PLA comfort with "joint" commands. Xu assumed command of the PLAAF soon after the exercise.

Also as in 2005, Chinese, Russian, and other forces were able to exercise "joint operations," at the level of planning and sequencing. It does not appear that truly intimate "joint operations" between countries, or even between respective PLA forces, was accomplished. *Xinhua's* report noted this more limited objective, quoting Lu Chuangang as saying that "the Chinese troops participating in the maneuver not only have to conduct *coordination* [italics added] with the armed forces of other five countries but also have to do a good job in conducting *coordination* among the troops of different services and arms and different units." Chinese and Russian armor units, attack helicopters, and attack aircraft all appeared in sequence, rather than in joint formations. It appears that the only operation of the exercise in which Chinese and Russian units operated in close proximity was the airborne airdrop. Reports noted language difficulties but that Russian and Chinese pilots could communicate in English and that they managed to reduce their takeoff sequencing from three minutes to one and a half.[19]

Capability in Carrying Out Precision Engagement

Peace Mission 2007 did not include the use of precision-guided weapons, such as laser or navigation satellite guided bombs, which China and Russia both possess. "Precision Engagement" appears to refer to the simple ability of large and diverse forces to organize and accomplish their missions accurately. Senior Colonel Lu noted that the Peace Mission forces contained "a very high technological content of informationization" and that the "participating troops are required to have a higher accuracy in assembling, dispersing, commanding, and attacking operations." However, there should be little doubt that when the PLA deploys for future distant exercises or actual operations, they will use a range of ground, naval, and aerial precision weapons.

Capability in Long-Distance Integrated Support

Logistic support is one of the most important aspects of power projection. For example, the PLA forces in Peace Mission 2007 used about 100,000 rounds of ammunition, compared to 700,000 rounds used by the Russian forces.[20] For a real operation, the PLA would have to transport much more ammo as well as many other critical supplies. For Peace Mission 2007 Senior Colonel Lu indicated that "long distance integrated support" included "support in communications, equipment, meteorology, logistics, and translation [that] is indispensable in any kind of joint maneuver." The depth and manner of such logistic support will determine the success or failure of a distant deployed operation. The creation of an "integrated support task force" indicates the PLA does take seriously the need to provide logistic support for deployed forces. The fact that this integrated support task force had to meet the needs of multiple PLA Army and

PLAAF units is also an indication of the PLA's progress in performing joint-force logistic support.

Airmobile Power Projection

When considering how China is now building its power projection capabilities, Peace Mission 2007 focused attention on the PLA's gathering of new airmobile army forces and its commitment to developing new indigenous large transport aircraft. Until recently, the major-platform air transport capabilities of the PLAAF were limited to about twenty-five to forty Shaanxi Y-8 medium transports, copies of the Ukrainian Antonov An-12 *Cub*, and about twenty Russian Ilyushin Il-76MD heavy transports purchased during the 1990s. In the last two years, however, Shaanxi has started producing a series of new transports and electronic warfare aircraft based on substantially modified Y-8 designs. A new 20-metric-ton-capacity ("ton") transport called the Y-9 may prove to be both economical and capable. In addition China is working to realize its ambition to develop and build much larger or "strategic" 50- to 60-ton air-transport aircraft, albeit with substantial help from Russia or Ukraine. China may also be interested in either purchasing or co-producing the Antonov's 150-ton An-124 *Ruslan*. What cannot be determined is how many large air transports the PLA intends to acquire, which would indicate what size force the PLA would like to be able to project by air.

But an initial airmobile projection capability could gather early in the next decade. Soon after Peace Mission 2005, it was reported that China had agreed to a $1.5 billion deal to purchase an additional thirty to thirty-four Il-76MD transports and four to eight Il-78M[21] dedicated aerial-refueling aircraft.[22] But in 2006 and 2007 this contract became mired in Russian production relocations out of Uzbekistan—China's preferred production location—and price hikes, and at one point Russia reportedly offered thirty to thirty-four upgraded Ilyushin Il-76MD or Il-76MF transports.[23] Russia was also requesting an additional $80 to $100 million to help pay for assembly line relocation[24] while also offering partial production in Uzbekistan,[25] at which China apparently has balked, leaving the deal's status uncertain in mid-2008. However, a late 2007 report noted that Russia had approved $400 million to fund production transfer to Ul'yanovsk, which was expected to begin delivering Il-76s in 2009, indicating that a sales deal remains possible.

The Il-76MF can carry a slightly larger payload than the Il-76MD, but more importantly, it is longer, meaning it can airdrop four of the PLA's new ZLC-2000 lightweight airborne tanks, versus three for the IL-76MD. A potential force of twenty Il-76MDs and thirty-four Il-76MFs could conceivably airdrop two notional mechanized battalions of 2,400 troops and up to 136 ZLC-2000 light tanks up to 4,000 km. In an actual operation the number of tanks would be smaller because of supplies and other logistic necessities. In addition, PLA airborne units have developed air-droppable trucks, and new Humvee chassis–based lightweight air-defense systems such as the FB-6 could give airborne troops air cover.

But this amounts to an initial large rapid deployment shock force that the PLA could use either for peaceful exercises or to accomplish rapid, deep forcible-entry strikes or assault operations with its allies. These forces could operate alone, perhaps to support a favored military faction in a potential North Korean military coup against the Kim dynasty. They could also deploy in "exercises" with allied regimes designed to intimidate their political opposition. Peace Mission 2007 coincided with elections in Kazakhstan that saw the removal of all opposition party candidates. With larger transports and refueling aircraft the PLA could similarly assist client regimes in the Persian Gulf, Africa, or Latin America.

As noted in chapter 6, the PLA is developing new medium-weight wheeled armored vehicles that could form future mechanized units as airmobile as the U.S. Stryker Brigade Combat Team (Table 7.1). Such airmobile armor capability expands the CCP leadership's options to take on increasingly capable, hostile, and distant challenges. These might include leadership in future U.N.-sponsored peacekeeping operations as far away as Africa, or they might include friendly support for a "partner" regime in Southeast Asia or the Persian Gulf. It is likely that such development of medium-weight Army units is in large part driving the PLA's development of new heavy-lift transport aircraft.

The PLA has likely paid close attention to the American development of distant airmobile projection. Beginning with the 1948 Berlin Airlift, followed by scores of military actions, small and large, and humanitarian exercises, far more numerous though unheralded, large U.S. Air Force (USAF) transport aircraft have become the ubiquitous symbol of American "hard" and "soft" power. The justification for the first U.S. fleet of large jet-powered transports can be traced to the early 1960s doctrines of "Flexible Response," which held that the United States must be able to project large-scale conventional forces for contingencies that did not warrant the use of nuclear weapons.[26]

By 1968 the USAF had acquired 284 of the 41-ton-capacity Lockheed-Martin C-141 *Starlifter*, of which 270 were modified into longer-fuselage C-141Bs; all were retired by 2005. Advances in engine and construction technology allowed the USAF to acquire eighty-one of the 118-ton capacity Lockheed-Martin C-5 *Galaxy* transports between 1968 and 1973, plus fifty more C-5Bs between 1968 and 1969. About 111 of these are slated to be upgraded to C-5Ms, with more powerful engines and upgraded electronics; the first was completed in May 2006.[27] These along with 180 to 190 of the smaller 77-ton capable Boeing C-17 *Globemaster III* will constitute the new core of USAF heavy-lift power projection.

Shaanxi Advances

By the middle of the first decade of the twenty-first century, China started demonstrating the capacity to develop new transport aircraft first by producing

Table 7.1 PLA and U.S. Airmobile Armor Compared

System	Weight/Type	Crew/Troops	Weapons/Comments
PLA Air-Dropped			
ZLC-2000	8–12 tons/ IFV-tracked	3/@ 5 troops each	Dedicated Airborne light tank first seen in 2004; Infantry Fighting Vehicle (IFV) version has a 30-mm cannon and HJ-73 antitank guided missile (ATGM); HJ-8 ATGM armed and command version expected; 3x carried by Il-76MD; 4x by Il-76MF
"VN-3"	6+ tons/4x wheeled light fighting vehicle	3	Larger version of VN-3 revealed in 2007, armed with the 30-mm cannon turret seen on the ZLC-2000; available for PLA Airborne but not known to have been purchased by early 2008
82-mm mortar "Humvee"	4 tons/4x wheeled light vehicle	3–5	Copy of U.S. Humvee armed with 82-mm automatic mortar, 6,200-meter range; vulnerable to medium fire
U.S. Air-Dropped			
M1114 Uparmored Humvee	5.8 tons/4x wheeled light vehicle	3–6	General-purpose carrier for U.S. Airborne units; can be equipped with mortar, ATGM; vulnerable to concerted fire
PLA Medium-Weight			
WZ551/ZLS92	15+ tons/6x wheeled vehicle family	2/11 troops	1980s design; serves in Armored Personnel Carrier (APC); 25-mm cannon armed IFV; 100-mm tank gun armed "Assaulter;" 30-mm cannon IFV; 120-mm mortar version; command; recon; artillery recon; ambulance; recovery versions; 2–3x per Il-76MD

PF2006/WZ0001	18–25 tons/8x wheeled vehicle family	3/10 troops	Variants: Infantry Fighting Vehicle; 105-mm tank cannon armed; 122-mm artillery gun armed; command; recovery versions; twin 120 mm mortar system possible; 2–3x per IL–76MF
U.S. *Medium Weight*			
LAV-III Stryker	16+ tons/8x wheeled vehicle family	2/9 troops	Variants: Infantry Carrier Vehicle (ICV); 120-mm mortar armed; 105-mm cannon armed Mobile Gun System; command; ambulance; recovery versions; 2,740 planned for 8 Stryker Combat Brigades
Future Combat System	@25 tons/tracked vehicle family	3/@9 troops	New medium-weight armor family in development for 2010s. Variants: 120-mm tank gun; IFV; 120-mm mortar armed; 155-mm cannon armed; recon; command; ambulance; recovery; new gun-launched missiles; active protection systems; 3x per C-17

Source: Jane's Armour Systems; Jane's Defence Weekly; Chinese brochures; author interviews.

a series of new versions of the old Shaanxi Y-8 in 2004 and 2005. Even though the Y-8 is based on a Ukrainian/Russian design that first flew in 1957, it is possible that with a complete redesign, new versions could meet with the domestic and foreign sales success that has so far eluded China's only large transport design. Shaanxi's quick success, however, is again largely dependent on foreign assistance. But what is different is that China is already taking design knowledge gained from the new Y-8 variant and creating new special-mission versions before a dedicated cargo version is put into production. A June 3, 2006, crash thought to involve one of these new models indicates that such success comes with a price, especially if demand for rapid results led to design or production shortcuts that may prove fatal.

The Shaanxi Y-8 is a copy of the Antonov An-12 *Cub* that China started building in 1969, with a first flight in 1974. But it saw a low production rate due to limitations such as lack of pressurization that would allow for useful high-altitude flying. Critical to the Y-8's revival has been the May 2001 establishment of a new consulting arrangement with Ukraine's Antonov Bureau.[28] Antonov signed an additional agreement with Shaanxi and China Aviation Industries Corporation Two (AVIC 2) in November 2002. This relationship began apparently with no consideration or compensation for China's previous copies of the An-12. As explained by one source, Antonov engineers have produced design work for China's First Aircraft Design Institute, responsible for design work on large aircraft. Antonov engineers have redesigned the Y-8's wing and fuselage and have performed design work that has been applied by Chinese engineers at Shaanxi to several new variants of the Y-8. Antonov's work on the wing, for example, has increased the Y-8's fuel capacity by 50 percent.[29]

Another important contribution to Shaanxi's new aircraft production capabilities has been the absorption new composite material fabrication technology. Shaanxi's Web site and other promotional materials indicate it has imported a great deal of machinery needed to master composite technology. Composite materials combine polymer fibers and resins in precise configurations to produce materials with far greater strength and endurance than metals of equivalent weight. Success with this technology will allow Shaanxi to master the development of larger aircraft than the Y-8. However, the production, curing, and molding of composites requires exacting precision as the stresses of flight would cause to slightest flaw to contribute to airframe failure.

Y-8X to Y-9

An early product of Antonov's collaboration with the First Aircraft Design Institute was the Y-8X, an ambitious effort to compete with the popular Lockheed-Martin C-130J, revealed at the 2002 Zhuhai Air Show. Since 2002 there have been no reports of progress regarding the Y-8X design; however, in 2005 Shaanxi began a process of gradually revealing its Y-9 transport aircraft program. This began in January 2005 when Chinese television revealed a brand-new

Shaanxi aircraft that was clearly a highly modified Y-8, including a redesigned fuselage nose area and empennage, or rear-fuselage area. It was powered by what appeared to be Chinese-made engines equipped with a new type of modern six-bladed propeller. Over the summer of 2005 additional reporting from the Chinese press began to reveal more, with the designation "Y-9" confirmed by the time of the September 2005 Beijing Air Show.

A Shaanxi brochure released before the Beijing show explained that the Y-9 was indeed a significant upgrade of the Y-8, including many of the design features apparently intended for the Y-8F600. In fact, the dimensions of the Y-8F600 and the Y-9 are identical.[30] One major difference is that the Y-9 will be powered by Chinese WJ-6C turboprop engines, not the Pratt and Whitney PW150B. The engines will also use Chinese-made JL-4 composite-material propellers that look very much like the Dowty R406. Although a Dowty role in the JL-4 cannot be confirmed, a loophole in British dual-use military technology export policy that allows for "co-production" but not "sale" might account for the new Chinese propeller. The Y-9 will have a modern "glass" cockpit with digital multifunction displays (MFDs) to allow reductions in crew size and a fully pressurized fuselage capable of lifting its maximum payload of 20 tons out to 1,000 km. Shaanxi has produced illustrations which show the Y-9 can carry alternate payloads including: ninety-six troops; one light tank; two attack helicopters; or a short-range ballistic missile, in addition to loose or palletized cargo. If the Y-9 performs as advertised, then it may constitute a very long-awaited success for China's aircraft sector: an economical as well as capable medium-size military transport.

However, it is curious that Shaanxi and AVIC 2 have apparently chosen to supersede the Y-8F600 with the Y-9. It may be that the PLA fears U.S. opposition should the Canadian subsidiary of U.S.-owned Pratt and Whitney supply large numbers of PW150B engines to power PLAAF transports. This will certainly ease China's ability to export the Y-9 to allied regimes such as Iran, as well as to a wider range of countries that cannot afford the C-130 or A-400M. Over the next decade the West may become increasingly familiar with the Y-9 and its various derivatives.

Large Cargo Ambitions

With the announcement that China will be funding the development of new large transport aircraft in the 2006–2010 Five-Year Plan, it is not surprising that there are proposals to build new large cargo aircraft as well (Table 7.2). According to Ukrainian sources there will be a competition between AVIC-1 and AVIC-2 to develop China's first turbofan-powered large military transport. The AVIC-1 design was revealed in Internet-disclosed images in January 2007. Showing a high-wing four-turbofan-powered airlifter similar in dimension to the U.S. C-17, Ukrainian sources confirmed this was AVIC-1's proposal.[31] Later, Chinese sources indicated the AVIC-1 proposed air transport would be able to

Table 7.2 Asian Large Air Transports Compared

	AVIC-1 Proposal (China)[a]	AVIC-2 Proposal (China)[b]	Ilyushin Il-76MD (Russia)	Ilyushin Il-76MF (Russia)	Boeing C-17 (U.S.)	Airbus A-400M (EU)	C-X (Japan)
Service Date/Number	2015–2020/ number n/a	2015–2020/ number n/a	20 + 34 for PLA (may change to Il-76MF)	Possible 30+ for PLA	190 ordered by U.S. mid-2007; used by Australia (4); Canada (4)	192 on order in mid-2007	Up to 44 may be built for Japan
Maximum Payload	60 tons	50–60 tons	50 tons; 128 paratroops	60 tons;154 paratroops	78 tons; 102 paratroops	37 tons	38 tons
Un-refueled Range	4,000 km	n/a	4,700 km (max. payload)	5,800 km (50-ton payload)	4,444 km (w/72-ton payload)	4,537 km (w/30-ton payload)	5,600 km (max. payload)
Cruise Speed	Mach 0.75	n/a	432 kt	460 kt	Mach 0.74–077	300 kt	Mach 0.8

[a]Estimated figures from Chinese Internet sources.
[b]Estimated figures from interview sources.
Sources: Jane's All the World's Aircraft, 2007; Yefim Gordon; interview sources.

carry a 60-ton payload up to 4,000 km. In early 2007 Ukrainian sources also indicated that AVIC-1 was in the process of canvassing Russia's Tupolev and Ilyushin, and Europe's Airbus, for possible technical cooperation.[32] As of March 2007 Airbus officials could not confirm any approach by the Chinese.[33]

Ukrainian sources had noted in early 2006 that Antonov had proposed a $1 billion project to develop a new version of its An-70. It was proposed to be powered by turbofan engines and featured a lengthened fuselage to allow a total cargo payload of between fifty and sixty tons.[34] Both the AVIC-1 and AVIC-2 proposals would approach the 78-ton capacity of the U.S. C-17 and exceed the 50-ton payload of the Russian Il-76. It is possible both the AVIC-1 and AVIC-2 proposals are being designed to drop up to four ZLC-2000 airborne tanks, versus three for the Il-76MD. If realized, this new aircraft will give China an "indigenous" strategic transport that will enable its leadership to more rapidly project "hard force" and "soft force" far beyond East Asia.

A key variable for program success will be China's development of new high-bypass turbofan engines. These could be purchased from Ukraine, but that would make the aircraft program and potential exports vulnerable to political pressures. However, should the new "Chinese" transport prove successful, it will surely compete with future Antonov products, as well as with the 35-ton Airbus A-400M and the U.S. C-17.

There has been long-term PLA interest in either purchasing or co-producing the even larger 120- to 150-ton payload Antonov An-124 *Ruslan*, based on repeated reports to this effect.[35] Co-production has been a reported option though a future Chinese purchase of An-124s may be more realistic, budgets willing. Antonov has been seeking investors to support a revival of An-124 production and estimates future demand for fifty to eighty of these large airlifters.[36] Ukrainian sources say China is considering how best to participate in this company, an indication that it will purchase this mega-lifter.[37] Antonov has developed the A-124-100M version that would raise its payload capacity to 150 tons, with a range of 2,820 km, and it has plans for the A-124-300 that would lift 150 tons out to 8,100 km.[38] At the November 2007 Dubai Air Show a Russian source told this author of potential Chinese interest in the 1,000-ton-capacity Beriev Be-2500 concept amphibian airlifter.[39] Beriev's acknowledgement that this aircraft will require a multinational investment and production effort the size to build the Airbus A-380 decreases the chance that China will ever acquire this aircraft, but it is noteworthy that China is interested in such megacapacity aircraft.

Maritime Projection: Carriers, Amphibious, and Cruise Missiles

China's efforts to expand its ability to project maritime military power are of great interest to the littoral Asian states and other maritime powers such as the United States. For China, building maritime projection capabilities is not just an issue of defense, it is also perceived through the lens of nationalism. It constitutes an affirmation of Chinese determination to reverse the "humiliation" of the era of Western and Japanese dominance while asserting China's claim to regional leadership. Although it is not possible today to clarify the dimension of China's maritime power ambitions, it is possible to explore China's progress in three areas: aircraft carriers; amphibious projection, and non-nuclear cruise missiles to be delivered by nuclear submarines. All three provide the Chinese leadership with the means to intervene in distant countries with military force to protect Chinese interests. Carriers and amphibious forces also allow for the projection of "soft power," be it shows of force, high profile exercises with allies, or participation in peacekeeping and humanitarian missions.

Aircraft Carriers

Since the early 1980s, when Western military officials began gaining tentative access to the PLA after decades of isolation, analysts have debated the question of whether China would build aircraft carriers. The events of 2005 and 2006 have now given us the answer: yes, China will build aircraft carriers. The debate now shifts to new questions: what type, what size, how many, and how soon?

After a lengthy period of denials and obfuscation, Chinese officials are beginning to admit their near-term plans to develop and build aircraft carriers. In a provocative article published in late 2006, Andrew S. Erickson and Andrew R. Wilson of the U.S. Naval War College quote an unnamed Chinese official in Beijing who told them in 2006 that "China will have its own aircraft carrier" in "twelve to fifteen years." But during an earlier interview in 2004, "he had declared to a group of Western academics that there was an internal political and military consensus that China had no intention of developing an aircraft carrier."[40] In March 2006 Hong Kong's *Wen Wei Po* quoted General Wang Zhiyuan, a Deputy Director of the Science and Technology Committee of the General Armaments Department, as saying that in "three to five years," "The Chinese army will conduct research and build an aircraft carrier and develop our own aircraft carrier fleet." He went on to add that the escort and support ships for this carrier group are either being built or have already been built.[41] These would likely include the new *Luyang 1*, *Luyang 2*, and *Luzhou*-class air defense destroyers launched from 2003 to 2005, new Type 093 nuclear-powered attack submarines, and new *Fuchi*-class underway replenishment ships.

In 2007 Chinese spokesmen and officials made more revealing comments. In early January 2007, Huang Qiang, a spokesman for the Committee on Science, Technology, Industry and National Defenses (COSTIND) noted "China has the ability to build an aircraft carrier, but has not determined a specific time to do so."[42] In late April 2007, *People's Daily* reported that in March 2007 COSTIND Chairman Zhang Yunchuan had said that China "was doing researches for the building of aircraft carriers through its self reliant efforts."[43] Then, during a mid-May visit to China, U.S. Pacific Command commander Admiral Timothy Keating discussed China's intentions to build aircraft carriers with PLAN commander Admiral Wu Shengli. Apparently not encountering denials, but learning Chinese leaders were "intrigued" with the idea of acquiring aircraft carriers, Keating stated, "I do not have any better idea as to China's intentions to develop, or not, a carrier program, but we had a very pleasant and candid exchange about the larger issues attendant to a carrier program."[44] By July 2007 the KANWA organization was reporting that China had started lining up subcontractors for carrier components and had purchased at least two carrier aircraft landing systems from Russia, speculating that one may be intended for the *Varyag*.[45] Then in November 2007 a U.S. official relayed to this author a recent exchange with PLAN officers during which a PLA Vice Admiral remarked that China would build eventually build four to six carriers.

Critical to China's recent quest for aircraft carriers has been the leadership and persistent advocacy of General/Admiral Liu Huaqing, a career Army officer who served as PLAN commander from 1982 to 1988, then rose to Executive Vice Chairman of the CMC until his retirement in 1997. Liu was Deng Xiaoping's choice to promote a high-tech revolution in the PLA, which allowed Liu to advance his long-standing dream to build aircraft carriers. In his 2004 memoirs, he notes the military and political value of aircraft carriers, saying:

> Aircraft carriers symbolize a country's overall strength. . . . Building carriers has all along been a matter of concern for the Chinese people. . . . Our purpose of developing carriers was not to race with the United States or the Soviet Union. The primary goal was to meet the need of struggle against Taiwan, to solve the Nansha Island disputes, and to safeguard our sea rights and interests. Apart from that, in peacetime the carriers could be used to maintain world peace, thereby expanding our international influence. . . . To modernize our national defense and build a perfect weaponry and equipment system, we cannot but consider the development of aircraft carriers.[46]

Liu Huaqing's 2004 memoir also outlines his role in pushing for feasibility studies starting in 1970, continuing during his time as PLAN Commander, and extending to his tenure on the CMC and even afterward. Liu notes that during the mid- to late 1980s he led intense studies regarding aircraft carriers versus land-based aircraft. During the first half of the 1990s, he made studies of different types of aircraft carriers, with the goal of enabling a decision regard the type of aircraft carrier to be made by 2000.[47] Liu also made special note of his effort to gather foreign information and technology about aircraft carriers, noting:

> I gave approval for experts of the Navy and related industries to visit France, the United States, Russia, and Ukraine to inspect carrier development. Meanwhile, departments related to the national defense industry invited Russian carrier design

experts to China to give lectures. Technical materials on carrier designs were intro-
duced into our country, and progress was made in the pre-studies of key accessories
aboard carriers.[48]

Table 7.3 provides information on specifications of aircraft carriers from Russia,
France, and the United States.

China's gathering of "technical materials" was quite extensive. In 1985 China
purchased the former Australian carrier HMAS *Melbourne* (built in 1943 as
Britain's HMS *Majestic*). In 1998, China purchased the former Soviet Pacific Fleet
ASW carrier *Minsk*, then the *Kiev*, and then was reported to have purchased the
former Soviet/Ukrainian large-deck carrier *Varyag* for $20–$45 million.[49] In the
meantime China was reported to have purchased Russian plans for the *Kiev* class
and in 1996 reportedly tried to purchase the French carrier *Clemenceau*, which
had just been retired.[50]

Liu himself remarks that he was "deeply impressed" by his personal visit to
the carrier USS *Kitty Hawk* in May 1980.[51] France and its mid-size carriers may
also have a heavy influence on the PLAN. One Chinese article notes, "Since the
1970s, China has dispatched a large number of military personnel to each of the
French Navy's research institutes for exchange. [They] have conducted
thorough analysis on aircraft-carrier-related technology. Many people follow
France's aircraft carriers carefully, even learning from personal experience how
to pilot carrier-based aircraft for deck landings."[52] Apparently in 2004 or 2005 a
PLA delegation sailed on the new French nuclear-powered aircraft carrier
Charles DeGaulle for a five-day exercise.[53] In mid-2007 current PLAN commander Admiral Wu Shengli visited the USS *Nimitz* nuclear-powered aircraft
carrier. Russia's apparent decision to build up to six 40,000+ ton nuclear-
powered aircraft carriers starting in 2011–2020, should that materialize, may
provide a more extensive technology acquisition or co-development opportunity
for the PLAN.[54]

Despite this activity there was never unanimity among Western observers
that China would indeed build its own large conventional takeoff/landing
(CTOL) carriers.[55] And as to be expected, Chinese sources sought to sow confu-
sion by planting disinformation. An oft-cited Chinese excuse for not building
carriers was their cost, certainly a substantial reason.[56] A second set of obstacles
revolved around considerations of doctrine and strategy. Chinese naval doctrine
was largely defensive through the 1990s, and China's naval strategic periphery
did not extend far enough to justify aircraft carriers over submarines.

Chinese disinformation, though often farfetched, was regularly effective. In
1999, when reports began to emerge that China was seeking to purchase the
Varyag, a cover story emerged that it was actually being sought by a company in
Macau for the purpose of building a large casino. This cover quickly fell apart
when it was later learned that the Macau company was composed of former
Chinese naval officers, and the company faded as soon as the hulk ended up at
the Dalian shipyards.[57] In mid-June 2005 a Chinese Vice Minister responsible for

Table 7.3 Influencing China: Aircraft Carriers Compared

	Type 1143 *Kuznetsov*: Russia	Type 1153 *Ulyanovsk*: Russia	Type ?? Russia	*Charles DeGaulle*: France	*Nimitz*-Class: United States
Displacement	58,500 tons	80,000 tons	50,000+ tons	42,000 tons	91,500 tons
Power/Speed	Steam/30 kts	Nuclear/30+ kts	Nuclear	Nuclear/27 kts	Nuclear/30+ kts
Aircraft	24 fighters (Su-33); 17 helicopters (Ka-28/31)	70 total: Su-33; MiG-29K; Yak-44 AWACS; Ka-28/31	30 combat aircraft and helicopters	32 combat aircraft (Rafale-M; Super Entendard; E-2C); 4 helicopters	58 combat aircraft (F/A-18C/E/F; E-2C; EA-6B) 15 helicopters; 90-aircraft capacity
Aircraft Launch method	Ski jump	Catapult	Catapult	Catapult	Catapult
Number in service	1 (Same class as *Varyag*, obtained by China in 2002)	None: partial build, scrapped in 1992	6 carriers planned in the next decade	1	9

Source: Jane's Fighting Ships; GlobalSecurity.org; press reports.

their shipbuilding sector responded to a press conference question by flatly denying that China was at that time building an aircraft carrier in Shanghai, but did not rule out future plans.[58] The U.S. government may also have been a victim of Chinese disinformation activities. The 2003 issue of the Pentagon's annual report to the U.S. Congress on PLA modernization makes a rather definitive conclusion: "While continuing to research and discuss possibilities, China appears to have set aside indefinitely plans to acquire an aircraft carrier."[59] It is now clear that this conclusion was at best premature, given the timelines necessary for China, or any country, to build large-size CTOL carriers. Although China did not begin to reveal its true intentions until mid-2005, it must have made substantial investments during the 2001–2005 Five-Year Plan cycle to begin to realize its goals.

One early indication was a large model of a *Varyag*-like carrier with Chinese weapons built by the students of the Harbin Institute of Technology, to celebrate the school's fiftieth anniversary in 2003.[60] Then in mid-2005 patriotic Chinese enthusiasts posted Internet photos of the *Varyag* undergoing major work at about that time. In late May 2005 the *Varyag* moved into a dry dock for the first time,[61] and it emerged in early August with a fresh coat of paint—this time in standard PLAN gray. While a seemingly minor development, the adoption of this color clearly indicates the *Varyag* is to be adopted by the PLAN for some yet-to-be-determined missions. Subsequent photos seen in December 2005 appear to show activity on the deck to apply new coatings consistent with aircraft operations. By early 2007 satellite photos were showing that the *Varyag's* aircraft-arresting gear was receiving some work. There is some question regarding the carrier's steam turbine engines, with some sources indicating they were either not installed in the hull or were damaged by Ukraine before being sold to China in response to U.S. or other requests.[62] The hull did not have rudders when it arrived in Dalian. If true, it would then follow that China might have to pay a high price to purchase and install new engines, or pay for repairs at an unknown but possibly lower cost.

China's future aircraft carrier will likely benefit from the purchase of foreign technology as well as from many years of indigenous research. One 2007 report noted that China has purchased four sets of Russian-made carrier aircraft arresting gear, with the intention of using one for study/emulation, one to refit the *Varyag*, and two for future Chinese-built carriers.[63] In addition, there are indications that Chinese military and academic-technical organizations have studied a range of carrier-related technologies, to include automatic carrier landing systems, carrier aircraft arresting systems, deck motion problems, carrier landing pattern issues, special features of carrier aircraft, and carrier deck coatings.[64]

Gathering Carrier Air Wing

In addition to the work on the *Varyag*, the other major "visible" Chinese preparations for future aircraft carriers has been its efforts to gather its carrier air wing. At the 2005 Moscow Air Show, Russian sources had initially disclosed that

China was interested in the Su-33, a much-modified carrier compatible version of the basic Su-27 heavy fighter.[65] They also demonstrated the larger twin-seat Su-33UB training and attack fighter for a PLA delegation.[66] But in late October 2006 Russian reports in *Kommersant* and elsewhere revealed that China has made an initial purchase of two Su-33 fighters for evaluation, likely to be followed by an order for twelve, and the possibility of additional sales that could lead to a total of forty-eight to fifty of these fighters, for about $2.5 billion.[67] At the subsequent Zhuhai Air Show in November 2006 and afterward, Russian sources disclosed that the ultimate number of Su-33s to be purchased by China might reach 100.[68] An August 2007 Russian report noted that a contract to purchase sixteen Su-33s was in "coordination."[69] However, by mid-2008 it was not possible to confirm that China and Russia had made progress toward this deal. Nevertheless, a regiment of twenty-four to twenty-five would be enough to outfit a Russian style carrier like the *Varyag*. At the 2005 Moscow show, one Russian source noted that purchased fighters would not equip the *Varyag*, but a carrier to be built in the future, so the purchase of two regiments might be an indication that China intends to build two more carriers about the same size as the *Varyag*.

However, this is only speculation: Russia is now developing a new class of aircraft carrier that it hopes to launch later in the next decade. In 1992 Russia was forced to scrap its partially completed 80,000-ton Project 1153 *Ulyanovsk*, which was to be its first nuclear-powered, aircraft catapult–equipped carrier. In June 2007 Russian Navy Commander Vladimir Masorin told reporters that a future Russian aircraft carrier would displace 50,000 tons, be nuclear-powered, and carry thirty combat aircraft.[70] The would place the future Russian carrier in the same league as the French *Charles DeGaulle* class. It cannot be predicted whether Russian economic fortunes will continue sufficiently to fully fund this future carrier fleet. But it should be expected that a future Russian commitment to new nuclear-powered aircraft carriers will lead to interest from China and India.

One indication that the PLAN is considering a catapult-equipped design is its interest in small airborne warning and control system (AWACS) aircraft for its carrier. Such a small naval AWACS model was revealed in mid-2005 in a Chinese magazine showing the visit of Politburo Member Wu Bangguo to a design institute. The aircraft model seemed to indicate an aircraft about the size of the old U.S. Grumman E-1 *Tracer*.

As for the *Varyag* itself, some in the U.S. intelligence community and others view it as a possible "transitional" ship to develop PLA carrier aviation, but with potential military applications as well.[71] The purchase of two to twelve Su-33s as a start would be consistent with the more limited goal of assessing the aircraft and obtaining initial experience with carrier aircraft operations. Also, a *Varyag* with twelve Su-33s, a small number of Su-33UBs, and supporting helicopters would pose a formidable political symbol of Chinese strategic ascendance to Asian allies of the United States already wary of declining U.S. influence vis-à-vis China. A *Varyag* so equipped would also allow the PLA to more quickly develop difficult combined-arms operations between PLAN, PLAAF, Second Artillery, and space forces to better combat U.S. aircraft carrier groups.

But the purchase of just a small number of Su-33s may convey other intentions when considering the revelation from the Russian press that China had managed to acquire from Ukraine one of the T-10K prototypes for the Su-33.[72] This may indicate that, although the PLA is purchasing some Su-33s, its real intention is to obtain the ability to produce its own version of the Su-33; this version would be based on the J-11B, the "indigenized" version of the J-11 in advanced development at the Shenyang Aircraft Company in mid 2008. Shenyang and KnAAPO, the maker of the PLA's Su-27 and Su-30 fighters, have been at loggerheads since 2004 over Shenyang's desire to build a much-modified J-11 that would vastly reduce Russian content and potentially allow China to market its own version of yet another Russian fighter. KnAAPO and its parent company Sukhoi would like to maximize their profits from future upgrades or modifications Shenyang may make to its J-11s. KnAAPO has also produced all of the Russian Navy's Su-33s and would likely want to retain this business.

At Moscow in 2005 a Russian source was rather confident that China could not master all of the necessary modifications to turn its J-11s into carrier-capable fighters such as the Su-33.[73] Compared to the basic Su-27, the Su-33 has a much modified and strengthened airframe designed to properly channel the great stresses of carrier takeoff and landing. It is also covered with corrosion-resistant materials and has much-strengthened landing gear, "canard" lift devices and larger wing flaps to lower landing speed, folding wings, an aerial refueling probe, and a landing system that automatically controls the aircraft to land on the carrier deck.[74] The Su-33UB contains further aerodynamic refinements, uses more stealthy composite materials, and can carry a larger radar for attack missions. The Su-33UB has also been proposed for airborne warning and control system (AWACS) missions with the addition of a phased-array radar atop the dorsal spine or under the fuselage. The Su-33UB demonstrated for the PLA in 2005 had also been modified with thrust-vectoring engines that greatly improve maneuverability, and it has also been used to test the new Phazotron Zhuk MFSE active phased-array radar.

But a year later, it is possible to conclude that perhaps as far back as the late 1990s the PLA has been trying to develop an indigenous carrier-capable J-11. Such a fighter may also benefit from Shenyang's indigenized land-based J-11 program, which will likely incorporate new 13,200- to 13,600-kg-thrust WS-10A "Taihang" turbofan engines, new advanced PLA-developed radar, PL-12 and future longer range PL-14 advanced air-to-air missiles, and new precision-guided ground-attack weapons. A navalized J-11 based on this program would be decidedly superior to the Su-33 now in service with the Russian Navy. Should such a J-11 later acquire phased-array radar and long-range antiaircraft missiles (AAMs), it might then be competitive to superior to the Boeing F/A-18E/F.

To head off this program, and to appeal for future Russian Navy orders, Sukhoi is promoting upgrades for the Su-33. These will likely benefit from an upgraded version of the Su-35 that was marketed at the recent 2006 Zhuhai Air Show.[75] One major upgrade will be replacing the 12,500-kg-thrust AL-31F engines with 13,500-kg-thrust AL-31-F-M1 engines, which will allow for more rapid takeoffs and larger weapons carriage.[76] And although funding constraints have prevented radar and weapon upgrades, it is now possible to envision new Su-33s being equipped with new active electronic scanning array (AESA) radar such as the Phazotron Zhuk-MFSE revealed in 2005. This radar can simultaneously track thirty aerial targets or two ground targets simultaneously, guide AAMs to eight aerial targets, and locate naval targets out to 300 km. Russian radar maker NIIP is also working on AESA radar. With additional development such phased-array radar can themselves become weapons for delivering a range of electromagnetic attacks into enemy electronics. The Su-33UB's ability to carry a much larger active array makes more attractive for such electronic weapons. The Su-33 can also be expected to carry the full range of Russian weapons such as the Vympel R-77 active-guided BVR AAM, the 300-km-range Novator KS-172, the Kh-31 supersonic anti-radar/antiship, the Raduga 300-km Kh-59MK antiship missile, and, soon, the air-launched 300-km-range Novator 3M-54AE antiship missile and the 300-km-range 3M-14AE land-attack cruise missile.

But China may also have the option later in the next decade to purchase a possible carrier version of Russia's Sukhoi-developed fifth-generation fighter. In November 2007 a Russian industry source disclosed that if Russia builds new carriers, it will also require a "new fighter."[77] This fighter can be expected to combine stealth, supercruise, AESA radar, and advanced weapons.

Should China instead opt for a quick solution and fund a maximum Russian upgrade for the Su-33 instead of developing its own version, the PLAN could begin limited carrier operations by the middle of the next decade with a fighter competitive to, if not in some respects superior to, the U.S. Navy's Boeing F/A-18E/F fighter-bomber (Table 7.4). In terms of range and maneuverability, it appears that the larger Su-33, with lower wing loading and higher-thrust engines, will dominate the F/A-18E/F.[78] This advantage will multiply should the new Su-33 use thrust-vectoring engines. Such "platform" advantages may be regarded as obsolete considering the U.S. use of long-range off-board sensors such as AWACS, unmanned aerial vehicles (UAVs), and even satellites, plus the ability of new helmet-mounted displays for reducing the advantages of platform maneuverability. However, the Russian and Chinese investment in counter-AWACS and antisatellite systems could revive requirements for Western aircraft platform superiority, especially when there is rough equality in radar and helmet-display systems.

In terms of electronic systems, the U.S. Navy is leading by fitting current and future F/A-18E/Fs with the Raytheon AN/APG-79 AESA radar, but Russian AESA radar may soon be available for the Su-33. There may be rough parity regarding weapons, with the Su-33 having access to more and longer-range antiship missiles than the F/A-18E/F. Although it is due to be supplemented by

Table 7.4 China's Potential Carrier Fighters vs. Boeing F/A-18E/F

	Boeing F/A-18E/F Block 2	Sukhoi Su-33	Sukhoi Su-33+ (data estimated)	Shenyang J-11B+ (data estimated)
Multirole: Antiair and Ground/Naval Attack-Capable	Yes	No	Yes	Yes
G Limit	+7.6	8+	8+	8+
Wing Area	500 sq. ft.	666 sq. ft.	666 sq. ft.	666 sq. ft.
Max. Wing Loading (less is better)	132 lbs/sq. ft.	99.63 lbs/sq. ft.	@100 lbs/sq. ft.	@100 lbs/sq. ft.
Engine	2x GE-414-400 (2x 22,000 lbs thrust)	2x AL-31F (2x 27,557 lbs thrust)	2x AL-31F-M1 (2x 29,760 lbs thrust)	2x WS-10A
Supercruise potential	None	None	Possible if fitted with AL-41 engine	None
Thrust Vectoring	No	No	Available option	Available option
Helmet Display	Joint helmet-mounted Cuing system	Helmet sight only	Very likely	Yes
AESA Radar	AN/APG-79 Range: 150+ km²(air target) Tracking: ?; Targeting: ?	No	Phazotron Zhuk MFSE Range: 300 km (ship) Tracking: 30; Targeting: 8	China believed to be developing long-range AESA radar

High Off-Boresight Air to Air Missile	AIM-9X 10–20-km range	R-73	R-73 and successor	PL-13, 20-km range
Self-Guided BVR AAM	AIM-120D, @100-km range	Only semi-active R-27 family	R-77, 80-km range; R-77+, 160+ km range	PL-12 70-km range
Very Long Range BVR Missile	No	No	400-km range KS-100-1 or other designs	PL-13/14 160-km range estimate
Antiship Missile	AGM-84H SLAM-ER, 270-km range	No	3M-54AE, 220-km range	"C-602" 500+ km range

Source: Jane's All the World's Aircraft; Jane's Air Launched Weapons; Yefim Gordon and Peter Davidson; press reports; interview data; and author estimates.

the stealthy attack mission–oriented Lockheed-Martin F-35C in the next decade, the F/A-18E/F will remain the numerically dominant U.S. Navy combat aircraft for the foreseeable future. Although the United States would retain a commendable advantage accrued from generations of professional carrier operations and development, it would be an unwelcome development for the PLA to begin its carrier aviation era with a combat aircraft competitive to or superior to the F/A-18E/F.

After a long debate, it can be concluded that China is now actively preparing for the day when it acquires large CTOL aircraft carriers. There is no solid information regarding the ultimate purpose for the *Varyag*, though speculation ranges from use for pilot training to performing the role of moving target to help the PLA perfect its emerging anticarrier doctrine and operations. Furthermore, it is not yet possible to conclude that China is going to build a Russian-style carrier, though that would appear to be the fastest solution. Nor it is possible yet to conclude how China will employ its carriers. If it opts for Russian-style carriers, that may indicate an intention to follow Russian doctrine and integrate its operations with land- and sea-based assets for the larger purpose of defending nuclear ballistic missile submarines. But if China instead opts for larger, U.S.-style carriers, that may indicate even greater strategic ambitions to be able to project political-military power beyond East Asia. Either way, the number and types of new destroyers and nuclear attack submarines entering the PLAN would also allow China to build sufficient task groups around its future carriers.

New Amphibious Projection Forces

In addition to aircraft carriers, the PLA is also now building new large ships applicable for distant amphibious force projection. On December 20, 2006, Shanghai's Hudong Zhonghua Shipyard launched the PLAN's largest indigenously designed combat ship to date, known as the Type 071 landing platform dock (LPD) amphibious assault ship (Table 7.5). Like the aircraft carrier, the new large LPD marks an important step toward building a navy that can project both "hard" and "soft" power far from China's East Asian littoral. Large amphibious assault ships such as these carry Marine or Army troops and their associated armored, mechanized, and transport vehicles; artillery; and a small number of transport or attack helicopters. Equipped with new hovercraft, the LPD enables naval landing operations to commence far from the coastline and even bypass initial coastal defenses, whereas smaller tank landing ships (LSTs), which need to unload at the shoreline, would be very vulnerable to opposing Army forces. For the PLAN these ships would be most useful for deploying leading units for an amphibious invasion of Taiwan. However, due to their size and range, these LPDs can also project influence by carrying troops to distant exercises with allies, or to participate in peacekeeping or humanitarian rescue missions.

Sources made available to this author state the Type 071 displaces about 20,000 tons. That would place the Type 071 in the same range as the 16,000-ton

Table 7.5 LPD-Class Ships in Asia Compared

	China: Type 071[a]	U.S.: *Whidbey Island*	U.S.: *San Antonio*	Japan: *Oosumi*	Taiwan: *Anchorage* (U.S.-built)	Australia: *Newport* (modified)
Displacement	20,000 tons	16,000 tons	25,800 tons	14,000 tons	13,500 tons	8,400 tons
Speed	20+ kts	22 kts	22 kts	22 kts	22 kts	20 kts
Number in Service	1 launched 12/20/06; up to 6 estimated	12	9 planned	3	1	2
Troops	500–800	500	800	330	360	450
Cargo	25 to 50 combat vehicles	64 LVT or 40 tanks	14 AAAV	10 main battle tanks	50 LVT	500 tons
Helicopters	2–4+ (Z-8; Ka-29; Z-9; Z-10)	2–4+ (CH-46; CH-53; UH-1; AH-1Z)	2–4+ (CH-46; CH-53; UH-1; AH-1Z; V-22)	2 (CH-47J)	Platform for up to 2–4 (UH-1)	1–4 (UH-60; SH-8; CH-47)
Hovercraft	1–4 LCAC-type	1 LCAC	1–2 LCAC	1–2 LCAC	none	none

[a] All figures estimated.
Source: Jane's Fighting Ships; press reports; author estimates.

Whidbey Island class, which can carry up to 500 troops and up to forty tanks. The *Austin* class is now being replaced by the 25,000 ton *San Antonio*–class LPDM, which can carry up to 800 troops, up to fourteen of the new Expeditionary Fighting Vehicles (EFV) fast troop landing/fighting vehicles, two to four helicopters, and two LCAC-style transport hovercraft. On January 1, 2008, several Chinese Web sites featured photos of the first Chinese "LCAC," which is likely powered by Ukrainian turbine engines and shows a configuration almost the same as the U.S. LCAC.

At this point it is not possible to determine the actual cargo capacity or the eventual number of Type 071 LPDs the PLA will build. If it were to carry two LCAC-size hovercraft, it would appear that the Type 071 could accommodate 500–800 troops plus about twenty-five to fifty combat vehicles. It is possible that two Type 071s could carry as much as fifteen Chinese-size LSTs. An Asian source indicates that China will initially build six Type 071 LPDs. An authoritative Asian source has told the author that initially the PLA may only build three Type 071 LPDs. What is clear, however, is that the PLA is able to build these ships relatively rapidly. While the program was likely designed during the 2001–2005 Five-Year Plan, the first Type 071 hull was built rather rapidly from late summer to December 2006. Although this ship has yet to be outfitted and tested, it reasonable to estimate that under conditions of series production output could reach one ship a year per yard.

For both military and humanitarian power projection missions, the Type 071's ability to carry and use helicopters and hovercraft is critical. The 071 has the deck space to accommodate two Changhe Z-8 size helicopters, which can carry thirty armed troops as well as 4,000 kg of cargo internally or 5,000 kg on a sling. Z-8s have long served in the PLAN and have in recent years been photographed exercising with PLA Marines. The May 2008 issue of the Chinese magazine *Shipborne Weapons* featured a concept Z-8 modified for airborne warning and control missions with a distributed fixed phase array radar system. In July 2007 Internet imagery revealed a full-scale mockup of a new "navalized" Z-8 with a folded main rotor, indicating China intention to develop the Z-8 for its assault ships. The PLA is also reportedly negotiating to purchase up to forty Russian Kamov Ka-29 naval assault helicopters,[79] which can either carry sixteen armed troops and 2,000 kg of internal cargo or be armed with a variety of unguided or guided missiles. In addition the 071 can support operations by future PLA attack helicopters, such as the five-ton WZ-10 now in advanced testing or armed versions of the lighter WZ-9 and WZ-11 helicopters. The 071's ability to use large hovercraft also ensures its ability to transport large payloads ashore without need for ports or even smooth beaches. This is an especially important consideration during some disaster relief missions, such as responding to a massive tsunami like the one in late 2004. In this regard, in 2007 the PLA Navy launched its first large hospital ship, which could add to China's "soft" power projection by contributing to future disaster relief exercises.

Type 081 LHD

Chinese sources at the IMDEX naval technology show in May 2007 confirmed that China is developing a new amphibious assault ship, a Landing

Helicopter Dock (LHD). However, it is not known when such ships might be built. This ship had previously been identified as the Type 081, described by Asian sources as displacing about 20,000 tons (Table 7.6). Although Chinese officials as IMDEX would not disclose details about the Type 081, they did note, "[W]e have the capability right now to build that ship."[80] As of mid-2008 there were no indications that China had commenced construction of the Type 081 LHD, although one report notes that China may build up to six of these ships.[81] In mid-2008 Chinese sources did reveal initial artists projections of the Type 081, which revealed it to be a 20,000+ ton ship that may be heavily armed with a phased array radar/SAM suite similar to that on the Luyang-II class destroyer.[82] This ship could also carry about 500 troops. The PLA is known to have been seeking foreign LHD and small carrier design data since the late 1990s.[83]

The U.S. Navy/Marine combined has remained the world's premier amphibious power-projection force since World War II, with a current amphibious projection fleet of thirteen LHA/LHD (flat deck helicopter-carrying assault ships) and twenty-four LPD/LSD ships (landing ship dock assault ships). However, the emergence of the "Type 071" LPD and perhaps an LHD indicates that China too is building up its capacity for future amphibious force projection. If the PLA actually builds the projected nine-ship amphibious assault force, it might be to lift 7,200 troops with just these ships for short-range missions against Taiwan or other neighbors. But for longer-range missions, and if the PLA builds more underway support ships, it is conceivable that the projected force of nine ships might be able to lift a force of 4,000 troops plus armor and supplies. Such a force could be used to advance China's military diplomacy in the greater Asian region or beyond. It is also likely that China will build larger second-generation LHD and LPD ships. Future LHDs may even carry a V/STOL aircraft. In 2005 a Chinese source told this author that the Chengdu Aircraft Company was considering a F-35 class fighter program,[84] which may indicate an intention also to build a V/STOL version. PLA interest in such fighters is long-standing. In the early 1990s the PLA apparently considered co-producing the Russian Yak-141 supersonic V/STOL fighter for a future carrier,[85] and in 1979 Britain came close to selling Harrier V/STOL fighters to the PLA.[86] One nonflying British Harrier GR3 resides in the museum of the Beijing University of Aeronautics and Astronautics.[87]

China's interest in larger helicopter carriers could indicate possible plans to follow the Type 071 with an LHA/LHD-class amphibious projection ship. But were China to build LHD/LPD ships in isolation, such a force would be useful only for potential military operations against Taiwan or elsewhere near China's periphery. However, China development of carrier aviation for its navy indicates that China may also have the ambition to be able to escort Marine or Army amphibious action units to distant regions. By the end of the next decade it is not inconceivable that China's single Type 071 LPD could be part of a larger carrier/amphibious action group, asserting China's interests far from its shores.

Table 7.6 Asian LHD/LHA Ships Compared

	China: Type 081 LHD[a]	U.S.: Wasp, LHA-1	South Korea: Dokdo LHD	Japan: Oosumi LHD	Australia: Canberra LHD
Maximum Displacement	20,000 tons	40,650 tons	18,900 tons	14,000 tons	27,000 tons
Speed	20+ kts	22 kts	22 kts	22 kts	21 kts
Number in Service	In development; 3 estimated	8	1, +2 or 3	3	2 planned
Troops	500	1,800	700	330	1,000
Cargo	25–50 combat vehicles	5 M1 tank; 25 LAV; 68 truck	10 tanks	10 main battle tanks	46 tanks
Helicopters	20 (Ka-29; Z-8; Z-9; Z-10)	30+ (AV-8B; F-35B; AH-1Z; CH-53E; MV-22; MH-60S; UH-1Y)	10 (CH-46; UH-60; Ka-32; AH-1)	2 (CH-47J; UH-60; AH-1)	Up to 30 (MRH-90; CH-46; UH-60; Tiger)
Hovercraft	1–2 LCAC	None	1–2 LCAC	1–2 LCAC	1–2 LCAC

[a] All figures estimated.
Source: Jane's Fighting Ships; press reports; author estimates.

Cruise Missile Power Projection

The first form of power projection that may be available to the Chinese leadership, as early as 2010, could be the ability to target non-nuclear cruise missiles from all littoral regions of the earth. By that time the PLA will have three or more new Type 093 nuclear-attack submarines and will likely have developed a sub-launched version of one of the two land-attack cruise missiles it is developing. It may also take the option of equipping its Type 093s with Russian Novator 3M-14E 300-km-range land-attack cruise missiles, inasmuch as these have been purchased for the PLAN's *Kilo* 636M non-nuclear powered submarines. Both Chinese- and Russian-made cruise missiles will be targetable by the PLA's constellation of radar and electro-optical surveillance satellites and guided by access to Russian, European, and PLA-controlled navigation satellites, with links through PLA-controlled communication satellites.

Although the ability to project a few hundred kilograms of explosives may seem insignificant, it has the potential to allow the Chinese leadership to play a decisive role in conflicts around the world in which it perceives that military action would serve its interests. The ability of cruise missiles to undertake strikes with high precision means that China will have the option to target individuals as well as critical leadership, military, and infrastructure centers of groups it decided to oppose. In a developing country where China has resource interests, the ability to target individuals may ensure the survival of a regime serving China's interests. As the United States has done many times, the Chinese leadership will have the option of targeting threats it determines to be "terrorist" in nature.

Power Projection into Space

Although China's oft-stated policy is to "not enter into an arms race" and to "ban weapons" in space, the fact is that the PLA has invested considerably in both the strategic thought[88] and the specific technologies need to wrest eventual control of outer space. The successful January 2007 antisatellite missile demonstration may constitute but the first of many future Chinese military-space developments. China is projecting its power into space not only to challenge the American "monopoly" on space power but to seek superiority in space to dictate the outcome of future conflicts on Earth and in outer space. This effort will involve the development of specific space combat systems as well as an extensive manned space program to serve political, scientific, and military goals. The Communist Party apparently understands that exercising greater leadership in space is a prerequisite to wielding greater power on Earth.

This is one of the most ambitious and most risky ventures for the Communist Party leadership, as the price of failure may be very steep. In late 1971 financial constraints forced Mao Zedong to end China's first manned space program, Project 714, which had recruited and trained China's first astronauts and was in the process of developing a two-man spacecraft based on China's first Fanhuishi

Shiyan Weixing (FSW, recoverable experimental satellite) recoverable space capsule.[89] In August 2007 a report emerged that China's first manned space flight in October 2003 came close to suffering a communication failure that might have delayed reentry parachute deployment, leading to a catastrophe.[90] There are occasional indications that some in the Chinese political and military hierarchy may not support such an effort. In April 2007 an editorial writer in the *People's Liberation Army Daily* sought to promote support for an ambitious space program by highlighting a threat: the need to resist American "attempts to control space through plans to return to the moon and land on Mars."[91]

As long as the Communist Party remains in power, China's journey to the Moon or beyond will be a joint Party-PLA enterprise. The Party is using the space program, especially the manned space program, to bolster the legitimacy of its claim to sole power within China.. It also seeks to use the space program to strengthen China's economy and to help shape the rules of conduct in outer space. And although China has long touted its advocacy for the demilitarization of space, the PLA has long sought to exploit space for military gain whenever possible. China has integrated military features into its manned space program from the beginning, and this military character will likely continue to the Moon or elsewhere.

As noted in Chapter 4, it is the PLA that controls China's main activities in outer space. Specifically, the General Armaments Department (GAD) under the Central Military Commission develops requirements that are then fulfilled by military industries, controls and maintains all space launch and space control facilities, and controls the manned space program. PLA control over the manned space program was signaled in 2003, when after the unmanned Shenzhou 3 mission, then–Party Chairman Jiang Zemin congratulated then–GAD Director Cao Gangchuan and acknowledged he was the "chief" of the manned space program. As noted earlier, China is considering the formation of a new service, a "Space Force" that would gather all space activities, perhaps to include missile defense, under the direct command of the CMC. Although the PLAAF and Second Artillery are known to have pushed to gain control of this new service, it appears that the GAD will be its dominant force.

Politics and Leadership

The Communist Party has sought to identify China's success in space with its continued leadership. The first unmanned test mission of the Shenzhou space capsule took place shortly after the huge October 1999 fiftieth-anniversary celebration of the Communist Party. All six Shenzhou missions, including two manned missions in October 2003 and October 2006, have dominated China's state media. The seventh Shenzhou mission was originally intended for 2007 but was delayed to 2008, presumably to enhance China's prestige as it hosts the 2008 Olympics. Space success is used to generate nationalist pride as well as to give justification to a large aerospace sector that supports the multiple needs of this complex undertaking. An October 2006 White Paper on space activities issued by the State Council states, "China considers the development of its space industry as a strategic way to enhance its economic, scientific, technological and national defense strength, as well as a cohesive force for the unity of the Chinese people, in order to rejuvenate China."[92]

China also hopes to bolster its claims to greater global leadership by exercising leadership in outer space to the point of influencing the rules. China is the third country to master the technology needed to send humans into space. It is able to offer a range of space launch services at rates competitive with Russia, Europe, and the United States, and it is building a greater array of satellites, from large DFH-4 Ku-band communication satellites to new small micro- and nanosatellites, which lack controlled Western technology and are thus attractive to states that wish to avoid Western controls. China also plans to loft is own constellation of thirty or more navigation satellites, competing with existing U.S. and Russian constellations (and soon, a European constellation). China clearly hopes that its demonstration of military space power by its destruction of a weather satellite in January 2007 will cause other space-faring nations, especially the United States, to take more seriously its long advocacy of vague agreements that could ban weapons in outer space. Washington has long refused to consider such agreements because the United States has a far greater military dependence on space, and it views such agreements as fraught with definitional and verification obstacles.

Among the leading space powers, China's cooperation is most advanced with Russia: this cooperation includes significant Russian sales of manned space technology and training. European space companies and governments have been eager to initiate broader space cooperation with China. In 2004 China joined the European Space Agency's (ESA) Galileo navigation-satellite system as an investing partner, but China's determination by 2006 that it would not exercise sufficient control over the constellation is said to have contributed to its decision that year to go ahead with its own navsat constellation. Nevertheless, ESA is also eager to initiate manned space cooperation with China. European cooperation, however, is delayed by the U.S. refusal to initiate cooperation with China. Despite some enthusiasm in the Bush administration to initiate a dialogue that might lead to substantive cooperation, many in the U.S. Congress and the Defense Department have not forgotten the experience of the 1990s, when China took advantage of lax U.S. technology controls. In addition, China's January 2007 demonstration of an antisatellite weapon (ASAT) has increased U.S. wariness of China's ability to use for military purposes any technology that would flow from even minimal cooperation. This test caused the Bush administration to suspend a tentative dialogue between the U.S. National Aeronautical and Space Administration (NASA) and China's National Space Agency.

While waiting for the established space powers to pay it more heed, China is also leading the creation of new space cooperation organizations that for now exclude the United States. In October 2005 China hosted an organizing convention for its Asia Pacific Space Cooperation Organization (APSCO). The founding conventioneers included China, Bangladesh, Indonesia, Iran, Mongolia, Pakistan, Peru, and Thailand, with Turkey joining in June 2006. In addition China leads its Small Multi-Mission Satellites Project which joins Bangladesh, China, Iran, the Republic of Korea, Mongolia, Pakistan, and Thailand. The danger that space vehicle cooperation might enable Iran or Pakistan to build intercontinental ballistic missiles does not appear to trouble China. China hopes that these and other countries will become customers for low-cost Chinese satellites and space launch services. It is also likely that as China builds larger manned space structures, it will offer "friendly" countries astronaut rides in order to bolster bilateral relations and strengthen China's image as a space leader.

But China's pursuit of regional space leadership will not go unchallenged. China's efforts have spurred a reaction by Japan and India, both of which have established space programs and are expanding space exploration activities, initially aimed at the Moon. In September 2007 Japan launched its SELENE multisatellite Moon surveillance mission, and India intends to launch its Chandrayaan-1 Moon surveillance satellite in early 2008. India may launch a manned space capsule by 2014 and may send an unmanned probe to Mars.[93] Japan has funded its "Kibo" module on the International Space Station (ISS), may have a man-rated space launcher by 2015, and has long-range plans for a space plane.[94] In response to perceived threats from China, both Japan and India could use their manned space technology as the basis for active military-space programs.

Warfare in Space

It is also increasingly apparent that China is preparing to wage war in outer space. In his book *Space Warfare*, Colonel Li Daguang describes potential PLA operational goals as, "Destroy or temporarily incapacitate all enemy satellites above our territory, [deploy] land based and space based ASAT weapons, counter US missile defense systems, maintain our good international image [by covert deployment], space strike weapons concealed and launched only in time of crisis."[95]

Should China establish a new "Space Force" service, then the SC-19 ASAT demonstrated in January 2007 may be just the first of many types of space weapons that China may develop in the coming decade (Table 7.7). These could include more powerful direct-ascent ASATs, perhaps based on the KT-2 and KT-2A, inasmuch as the KT-1 space launch vehicle provided the basis for the SC-19. The larger KT-2 and KT-2A would allow the PLA to target very-high-orbit U.S. early-warning and electronic-surveillance satellites. The Air-Launched Space Launch Vehicle (ALSLV) revealed at the 2006 Zhuhai Air Show, designed to loft microsatellites into low Earth orbit (LEO), would give much greater launch flexibility for small ASATs. The H-6 bomber launch vehicle might be able to reach launch points with greater surprise and be able to attack satellites that do not fly over Chinese territory. The addition of boosters to ALSLV, along with a

Table 7.7 Current and Potential Future PLA Space-Warfare Systems

	Operational Time Frame	Weight of Space System	Orbital Usage/Comments
Antisatellite—Ground Launched			
KT-1/SC-19	2007–2010	50–100 kg	LEO/PEO; tested three times between 2005 and 2007; based on KT-1/DF-21 MRBM; mobile; uses radar and/or IR-guided interceptor.
KT-2/SC-20 (?)	2010	50–100 kg	LEO/PEO/GEO; tests not yet reported; based on KT-2/DF-31 SLV; mobile; may use interceptor similar to that on SC-19.
Air Launch 1	2010+	20–50kg	LEO/PEO?; test not yet reported; based on ALSLV; lofted by H-6 bomber or large airliner; will require larger engine or boosters to reach PEO; more mobile and flexible than ground-launched missiles.
Air Launch 2	2010+	20+ kg	LEO; based on fighter-launched emerging long-range AAM; more mobile than ground launched missiles; more responsive than larger bomber-launched system.
Laser Systems	2000+	n/a	LEO; PLA likely had a limited fixed-site laser ASAT dazzling capability for most of this decade; lasers could be placed on large transport aircraft to reduce atmosphere interference with laser and provide more attack options.
Orbital Combat Systems			
Unmanned Weapon Platform	2010–2015+	7–8 tons	LEO/PEO/GEO; Shenzhou experience enables development of space weapon platforms for Earth combat with projectiles and interspace combat with missile or energy weapons.
Manned Space Station	2015+	8–10 tons	LEO; 921-2 space lab concept can be modified for passive surveillance and active combat missions, by adding mission tailored modules.
Manned Space Plane	2020+	20–50 tons	LEO/GEO; space plane mission bay can carry multiple military modules, from missile and energy weapons to launchers for micro- or nanosatellite–based weapons for launch into higher orbits.

Abbreviations: ALSLV, Air-Launched Space Launch Vehicle; GEO, Geostationary Orbit; LEO, Low Earth Orbit; MRBM, Medium-Range Ballistic Missile; PEO, Polar Earth Orbit.

smaller interceptor satellite, might allow it to reach some Polar Orbits used by many surveillance satellites.

Unmanned Space Weapons

China may be researching the feasibility of using unmanned space platforms for both space and Earth-attack combat missions. Chinese aerospace literature indicates that the PLA may be developing a "space-based ground attack weapon system," meaning a satellite that can dispense weapons for attacking targets on Earth. This literature describes the use of a "war capsule" which delivers the weapon through the atmosphere to its target. One Chinese aerospace article notes, "The greatest advantage of a space-based ground attack weapon system is its high speed and short reentry time. It is extremely difficult for the enemy to intercept such a weapon."[96] Indeed, U.S. missile defense systems very much depend on the warning time and interception cues given by a missile launched from great distances, whereas a stealthy space platform might strike with no warning from nearly atop its target. Although China has disclosed no information about possible plans for such a space weapon platform, there should be little doubt that it is capable of producing such a weapon if it so chooses. The ability to develop and launch manned space vehicles the size of the Shenzhou or a similarly sized space lab point to China's space weapons platform potential. In addition, China may be developing an unmanned "space plane." Such space weapon platforms could potentially carry a range of nuclear, non-nuclear, kinetic, energy, and chemical/biological weapons.

Two other potential unmanned space combat platforms were revealed in December 2007 from Chinese Internet sources. First, the "Shenlong" or "Divine Dragon" space plane was seen suspended from a Xian H-6 launch aircraft.[97] Other Internet sources suggest the Shenlong is also known as the "863-706," indicating that its funding comes from the 863 Program of high-technology research to support military modernization. The Shenlong's design and testing is apparently being led by the 611 Institute associated with the Chengdu Aircraft Company. Its development has also been assisted by the Nanjing University of Aeronautics and Astronautics, Northwest University, and the Harbin Institute of Technology. Shenlong is apparently a test article designed to validate new reusable transatmospheric vehicle technology. China's work toward a trans-atmospheric vehicle is indicated by possible Chinese military technical research.[98]

A second unmanned space aircraft is similar to the aborted French Hermes space plane design of the early 1980s. In 1996 a Chinese brochure revealed a wind tunnel model similar in configuration to the Hermes,[99] and then in December 2007 another Chinese Internet source image of this same spacecraft appeared, indicating the program may still be active.[100] Mark Wade has noted that the 611 Institute may have gained insights regarding space planes from cooperative programs during the 1980s with France, which was developing the Hermes space plane.[101] The Shenlong or Hermes design could fulfill a number of civil and commercial missions, but it could also be configured to launch military microsatellites and satellite interceptors, and to deliver "war capsules" to attack ground targets.

In addition, the PLA may be considering the use of nuclear-powered ballistic missile submarines (SSBNs) to launch ASATs, which would allow surprise attacks on many LEO and geostationary satellites critical to the U.S. electronics infrastructure. In early 2004 one Chinese author with the Dalian Naval Academy noted, "By deploying just a few anti-satellite nuclear submarines in the ocean, one can seriously threaten the entire military space system of the enemy. In addition to anti-satellite operations, these nuclear submarines can also be used for launching low orbit tactical micro-satellites to serve as powerful real time battlefield intelligence support."[102]

Manned Military Space

China's second manned space program reached its first point of success on October 1999, when the first unmanned flights of its manned Shenzhou space capsule were conducted. China's manned space program has involved military missions from the beginning, and it is reasonable to expect all Chinese manned space activities to serve military as well as civilian needs. On October 13, 2003, *People's Daily* stated, "Manned spacecraft can carry out missions of reconnaissance and surveillance better and enable the military to deploy, repair and assemble military satellites that could monitor and direct and control military forces on Earth."[103] Here China may have reached conclusions opposite to that of the United States and the former Soviet Union, both of which planned for manned military space missions but ultimately abandoned them, with the Soviets only undertaking three military Almaz/Salut military space-station missions in the 1970s.

Originally proposed by the Shanghai Astronautics Bureau, the 921-1 project was revamped in 1994 following former President Jiang Zemin's visit to Russia, which led to a 1995 agreement to transfer Russian manned space technology. China purchased a Russian Soyuz space capsule, life support and docking technology, space suits, and astronaut training.[104] Although the PRC has boasted that it was responsible for the design and production of its subsequent spacecraft, it is clear that Russian technology has made possible the PRC's first manned space program. For its November 20, 1999, test flight, Jiang renamed the Project 921-1 space capsule the "Shenzhou," or "Divine Vessel." To wit, the 921-1 craft revealed in 1999 was a scaled-up Soyuz featuring the same three-part design: orbital module, descent module, and propulsion module. However, the 921-1, at a weight of 7800 kg and a length of 7.79 m, is about 550 kg heavier and over a meter longer than the Soyuz. Unlike Soyuz, the 921-1 has a cylindrical orbital module that has its own solar panels and thrusters, making it capable of independent operation. All Shenzhou flights have entailed extended orbital module missions following the return of the manned reentry capsule.

To date all of the unmanned and manned Shenzhou flights (Table 7.8) have performed military missions. Shenzhou 1 and Shenzhou 2 very likely performed

Table 7.8 Shenzhou: Civil and Military Mission Expansion

Mission	Launch Date	Crew Module Duration	Scientific Mission Highlights	Orbital Module Duration	Military Mission Highlights
Shenzhou 1	11/19/1999	88 day	First mission to test craft flight and recovery of command module; carried seeds	6 days	ELINT module external to OM
Shenzhou 2	1/9/2001	6.7 days	64 scientific payloads including monkey, rabbit; reported hard landing	6 months	ELINT module external to OM
Shenzhou 3	2/25/2002	6.7 days	First near full man-rated version; use of sweating manikin to test space suit	260 days	Medium-resolution imaging radar external to OM
Shenzhou 4	12/29/2002	6.7 days	52 science payloads; orbital track simulated rendezvous with second spacecraft	6 months	E/O Earth observation cameras; monitored U.S. buildup to Iraq War
Shenzhou 5	10/15/2003	.89 day	First manned mission, one crew member	152 days operations	Two apparently larger E/O Earth observation cameras internal and external to OM
Shenzhou 6	10/12/2005	4.8 days	Two-member crew; first manned use of orbital module; lengthy OM mission supported future docking missions	@ 2 years; boosted to higher orbit	Apparent one E/O camera internal to OM
Shenzhou 7	10/2008 ?	n/a	Three-member crew; depressurization of OM; first use of manned EVA suit; external video of EVA mission	n/a	Apparent space for internal OM camera

Abbreviations: E/O: electro-optical; ELINT: electronic intelligence; EVA: extra-vehicular activity; OM: orbital module.
Sources: Mark Wade, *Encyclopedia Astronautica;* Chinese press reports.

ELINT missions. This observation was made by Swedish scientist Sven Grahn.[105] The orbital module for these first two practice missions had external Yagi-type antennae mounted on three extendable poles, construction that is consistent with ELINT missions. A Chinese space flight official indicated in early 2003 that Shenzhou 4 conducted ELINT missions, perhaps indicating that Shenzhou 2 and Shenzhou 3 did so too. This same official also noted that Shenzhou 4 carried a "microwave" sensing device, very likely a prototype satellite radar.[106] In addition, the orbital modules for Shenzhous 3–5 all have box structures that resemble cameras. In fact, close-up photos of the orbital module for Shenzhou 5, launched in October 2003, reveal an external box that very likely contains a camera, plus an aperture in the orbital module itself, very likely for a second camera. This could mean that both a hyperspectral camera and a close-up camera were included.[107] According to a report from Hong Kong, a PRC scientist claimed the Shenzhou 5 camera had a resolution of 1.6 meters.[108] The two-person manned October 2006 Shenzhou 6 mission only carried one high-resolution camera in its orbital module, which, like all the previous missions, continued its mission after the return of the crew module.

Space Lab

Early in the next decade China intends to launch a larger space laboratory that might accommodate a crew of two to three for one or more weeks. This has been referred to as Project 921-2, which was not approved for development until 1999. In 2000 the Russians made an attempt to interest the PRC in purchasing their faltering Mir space station. Beijing declined, apparently in favor of seeking Russian technology to assist its own space station program.[109] A small but detailed mock-up of the Project 921-2 was revealed at the 2006 Zhuhai Air Show, confirming video depictions from the 2004 Zhuhai show of a larger crew compartment attached to a smaller power and booster module. This configuration is strikingly similar to the early Russian Almaz/Salyut small space station from the 1970s and 1980s. Although 2004 depictions show the 921-2 lab as having only one docking point, the 2006 mock-up showed two docking points at both ends of the lab cylinder. Such a configuration would allow specialized modules to be used, such as for cargo or military missions, while allowing the other capsule to be the primary crew transport. There are also indications from Chinese sources that the space lab will be followed by a larger space station, but its dimensions or endurance have not been made public knowledge.

The Zhuhai 2006 depiction of the 921-2 space lab could serve a number of potential military missions. The main compartment will likely have one Earth-monitoring camera port. Additional attachments of Shenzhou-size orbital modules could be configured to carry additional optical or ELINT surveillance equipment. Such modules might also eventually carry weapons to include a gun, missiles, or picosatellites configured as antisatellite weapons. Other modules might also be configured to deploy ASAT interceptor missiles or nanosatellites with boosters of sufficient power to reach targets in other low Earth orbits.

Other modules might also be equipped with high-power microwave or laser weapons to prosecute targets in other Earth orbits.

Space Plane

A space shuttle or smaller space-plane that could serve military as well as civil purposes has been a long-standing Chinese ambition. Chinese missile and space program founder Dr. Qian Xueshen designed a space plane for the United States in 1949 before he was deported to China in 1955.[110] But China's more recent knowledge of space planes may have received a great boost from former Rockwell and Boeing engineer Dongfan "Greg" Chung, who, starting in the mid-1980s, gave Chinese intelligence operatives many documents related to the U.S. Space Shuttle and gave lectures in China relating to the Shuttle.[111] In 1988 Chinese concerns proposed three "shuttle" concepts. The Chang Cheng 1, from what is now the Shanghai Academy of Spaceflight Technology, involved a space plane, two-thirds the size of the U.S. Shuttle, atop three large boosters. What is now the China Academy of Launch Technology proposed a much smaller space place atop Long-March–size boosters, and the 601 Institute, connected to the Shenyang Aircraft Corporation, proposed a small space plane atop an air-breathing hypersonic launcher. Only the latter would have involved a truly reusable space-access system, but all were deemed beyond China's capabilities. But had they been implemented, these proposals would have resulted in space planes flying in this decade.[112]

This ambition has apparently been revived. In October 2006 the China Academy of Launch Vehicle Technology (CALT) revealed that China is developing a winged space shuttle for use in the 2020 time frame.[113] Concept images indicate the planned space plane may be about two-thirds the size of the U.S. and Russian space shuttles. Before then, China may develop a "recoverable" space plane that will be reusable only after substantial rebuilding.[114] Both concepts would allow for a range of surveillance and even space combat missions. A shuttle or space plane could be equipped with missiles or nanosatellites that could serve as "space mines," or they could be equipped with high-power microwave or laser weapons to destroy a range of targets in Earth orbit. Such spacecraft might also be equipped to deploy hypersonic projectiles to targets on Earth.

Military Moon Bases

Should China follow the United States to the Moon, or even to Mars, it is likely to use its Moon or Mars presence for military missions. In February 2007 a *People's Daily* editorial noted, "[T]he moon can be the top height for environment monitoring with vital military importance."[115] In a June 2007 speech, Academician Ouyang Ziyuan, director of the Chinese Lunar Exploration Program, noted that a Chinese presence on the Moon was necessary to monitor "Earth's large-scale climate change, environmental change, major disasters, including our major projects, and even military activities, the moon is a very important scientific research base, is a new military platform."[116] Both Ouyang and the *People's Daily* have noted the Moon contained potential energy reserves for the Earth for "10,000 years," including vast amounts of helium-3 that "can satisfy China's energy consumption output for a whole year."[117]

In 2007 China plans to launch its first of several Moon probes as part of the Chang'e program. This will eventually include the use of a robot to gather Moon samples for return to Earth. In 2006 Chinese officials reviewed Russian space technology to control its Moon missions,[118] and this could potentially lead to cooperation in manned Moon exploration technology. Although China has not revealed in official form its manned Moon programs, China appears to have many programs to create the vehicles necessary to carry out this mission. One report notes that China may undertake circumlunar Shenzhou missions in the 2015 time frame and then send people to the Moon around 2020 or after.[119] In late 2007 one Chinese military journal contained illustrations of expansive Chinese Moon bases, indicating at least some element of Chinese aspiration.[120]

Barring negotiations that settle boundaries and insist on demilitarization on the Moon, much as there have been similar agreements regarding Antarctica, it is probable that China will develop the means to claim and defend Moon territory, especially if the Moon becomes an economically viable source of mineral or energy wealth. Furthermore, if intelligence, surveillance, or combat-oriented outposts on the Moon become strategically advantageous, it is likely that the PLA will pursue such advantages for China. The Moon could serve as a base for high-power radar, and in the vacuum of space, large laser weapons could accomplish more damage at greater distances than in the atmosphere of Earth. In early 2008 a popular Chinese military issues Web site suggested that basing lasers on the Moon could help overcome the challenges of atmospheric distortion faced by Earth-bound lasers when attacking satellites.[121] That such is not far-fetched is illustrated by a 2005 Chinese academic journal article that explored the feasibility of a laser linkage between the Earth and the Moon for communication purposes.[122]

Projecting Power via Sales of Advanced Arms

China is already well practiced at the art of projecting its power via arms and military technology sales. In the past it has tried to link sales to U.S. concessions on Taiwan-related issues, but in the future these sales will be used more generally to expand China's political influence. This marks a critical change: until very recently, China has not produced sophisticated weapons that could effectively compete with Russian, European, or U.S. weapon systems. In the 1980s and 1990s it helped Pakistan become a nuclear-missile power and at discreet moments in the 1970s and 1990s, it is believed to have helped North Korea toward the same goal.[123] Having so enabled these countries, China retains substantial leverage over them and over other actors who in turn fear its newly powerful clients. In the 1990s China sometimes suggested to Washington that its sale of missile technology to Pakistan was linked to U.S. arms sales to

Taiwan.[124] More recently, the Bush administration has had to deny fears that China's willingness to push North Korea toward nuclear concessions might lead to U.S. concessions over Taiwan.[125]

The dangers of China's unconsidered weapons exports were demonstrated to Israel during the summer of 2006. On July 14, 2006, as an Israeli Navy corvette cruised unsuspecting off the coast of Lebanon soon after the commencement of Israeli attacks on the Iranian-supported group Hezbollah, an Iranian-supplied Chinese C-802 antiship missile exploded in a very near miss. Two crew members were killed, but a direct hit might have sunk the ship. The missile was a 1980s vintage design, but when used with such surprise by Hezbollah, it produced a stunning effect against Israel. The larger lesson is that Iran's willingness to share such a dangerous weapon of Chinese origin portends that China would care little to nothing should Iran give Hezbollah or other groups that employ terrorism even larger Chinese-assisted weapons, such as long-range ballistic missiles. Should China sell potential future terminally guided long-range artillery rockets or short-range ballistic missile to Iran or others who may pass them to rogue groups, they could potentially target U.S. naval forces well out at sea.

Furthermore, the Chinese leadership can now dispense a greater array of modern, capable, price-competitive weapons, to enable other rogue regimes or countries that would not qualify for top-line U.S. weapons, to rapidly acquire the means to inhibit U.S. military power (Table 7.9). China is now able to offer a complete and modern air-defense complex, from surveillance satellites to phased-array radar AWACS, multiple fourth-generation fighter options, advanced antiair and ground attack weapons, ground-based surveillance radar, and advanced SAMs. China can also offer missile complexes to include highly accurate navigation satellite–guided medium-range, short-range, and artillery rockets, plus antiship and land-attack cruise missiles. When paired with satellite or passive sensors, Chinese antiship ballistic missiles could hold the U.S. Navy at bay. These could also be combined with modern Chinese guided and fast-rising rocket-propelled naval mines to effectively deny access to U.S. naval forces. Furthermore, China's army systems such as its T-99 and T-96 main battle tanks, its new ZBD-97 IFV, and its new eight-wheel armored personnel carrier (APC) family, are quite competitive with late-model U.S., European, and Russian tanks and APCs. They are much better armed and armored than the older, simple T-63 APCs in Iraqi service that were demolished by U.S. forces in 1991.

Furthermore, China is willing to sell substantial amounts of military technology to gain and defend market share and to cement strategic military-technical relationships. Pakistan is China's most important military-technical client, having received Chinese technologies necessary to enable Islamabad to manufacture Chinese-designed nuclear weapons, missiles, frigates, fighter aircraft, tanks, antitank missiles, and small SAMs. The cooperative program to develop and manufacture the Chengdu FC-1/JF-17 Thunder gave Pakistan's aerospace industry a significant boost by allowing it to market an advanced price-competitive fighter that could be greatly upgraded with stealth features

Table 7.9 Cost of New PRC Weapon Systems Compared

Weapon System	Performance	Per-System Price Estimate
Type 039G Conventional Submarine (PRC)	Perfected by PLA in late 1990s; about as good as 1980s-level Agosta; armed with cruise missiles; 13 in PLAN service.	$230 Million
Agosta Conventional Submarine (France)	Capable 1970s-era French design, continually upgraded, now available with AIP, cruise missiles; 13 to be built.	$350 Million
Type 071 LPD (PRC)	A 20,000-ton amphibious assault ship capable of carrying up to 800 troops plus armor and supplies; 20-kt speed; PLAN may build up to 6.	$500 Million
LPD 17 (U.S.)	A 25,000-ton amphibious assault ship capable of carrying up to 800 troops plus armor and supplies; 20-kt speed.	$1.76 Billion
J-10 Fighter (PRC)	Modern single engine fourth-generation fighter capable of BVR antiair and PGM ground attack; just entering PLA service; about 100+ built.	$25–40 Million
F-16 Block 50+ Fighter (U.S.)	Late version of modern single engine fourth-generation fighter capable of BVR antiair and PGM ground attack; over 4,000 built.	$70+ Million
Y-9 Medium Transport Aircraft (PRC)	Much modified version of Y-8/An-12 with new turboprop engines, composite material 6-blade propellers, digital cockpit, and 20-ton cargo capacity.	$30–40 Million
C-130 Medium Transport Aircraft (U.S.)	Over 2,300 built, latest C-130J features better engines, 6-blade propellers, digital cockpit and 20-ton cargo capacity. Stretched C-130J-30 is more expensive.	$66–100 Million
KongJing-200 AWACS (PRC)	Y-9 airframe with new linear phased-array radar, greater endurance, and more radar operators than E-2.	$180 Million
E-2D AWACS (U.S.)	Latest version of U.S. Navy AWACS with better radar for over-land operations.	$200+ Million

Abbreviations: BVR, beyond visual range; PGM, precision-guided munitions.
Source: Prices for PLA systems are for 2007 and based on author interview data; prices for U.S. systems are from press reports.

and European engines, weapons, and electronics.[126] France is apparently emerging as an early partner to provide radar and missiles for a Pakistani modernization of the JF-17, providing potential opportunities for French technology to leak to China.[127] Such a large-scale transfer of fighter production technology may be attractive to other countries such as Egypt or even Indonesia. Chinese officials report that up to twenty Asian and African countries have expressed interest in the FC-1 fighter.[128] China has transferred artillery rocket and short-range ballistic missile development and production technology to Turkey, and may do so as well for Indonesia and Thailand.

China can use its new modern arms to strengthen its ties with a tier of small but strategically placed countries that are hostile to the United States, such as Cuba, Venezuela, Syria, and Zimbabwe. For example, in 2005 Venezuela's neo-Marxist strongman Hugo Chavez considered buying Chinese fighters to replace his U.S.-made F-16s, after already buying Chinese long-range radar and a communication satellite in 2005.[129] Some reports indicated that Chavez might seek up to fifty Chengdu J-10 multirole fighters while other sources indicate he may be interested in Chengdu's new lightweight FC-1 multirole fighter.[130] It turned out that Chavez purchased Russian Sukhoi Su-30s in mid-2006. But this does not preclude his buying Chinese fighters in the future, complementing them with Y-9-based AWACS to support his fighters and new effective Chinese-made air-to-air and precision-guided weapons to arm them. For that matter, Chavez could also buy 200+-km-range B611 ballistic missiles, which in the future may feature antiship-capable warheads. He might also look to equip his Army with new armor such as the Assaulter light tank armed with gun-launched missiles, or even consider new *Yuan*-class SSKs (diesel-electric attack submarines) with air-independent propulsion. China has transferred to Sudan the means to manufacture main battle tanks and armored personnel carriers.

But these weapons could also be purchased by countries that China is courting for the purpose of increasing its political and economic influence in a particular region, sometimes at the expense of established military and arms relationships with the United States, Europe, and Russia. This tier of countries would include Argentina, Brazil, Chile, Nigeria, Angola, Indonesia, and Malaysia. Malaysia, for example, which has purchased Russian Sukhoi Su-30 and U.S. Boeing F/A-18D multirole fighter-bombers, is being targeted at the first potential customer for a new multirole twin-seat version of the Chengdu J-10. The J-10 is likely to offer comparable performance at a lower price. Malaysia has also been approached as the first potential customer for a version of the Type 071 LPD; the PLAN's first launch of the Type 071 was in December 2006. By selling sophisticated weapons to Malaysia, China can substantially strengthen its military relationship with a country that controls the Straits of Malacca, a waterway critical to China's economic health. Furthermore, sales success in Malaysia will go far to prove to other countries that purchasing weapons from China is "acceptable" and financially attractive.

CHAPTER 8

HOW THE CCP-PLA CHALLENGES
AMERICA AND ITS ALLIES

The first two chapters of this book describe a Chinese Communist Party–People's Liberation Army (CCP-PLA) alliance, which, in spite of China's glaring weaknesses, is demonstrating an increasing commitment to challenging American power in Asia while building a network of global relationships hostile to democracy and conducive to the future exercise of even greater Chinese power. The following three chapters suggest three troubling conclusions. First, China has not yet achieved a condition of decisive force on the Taiwan Strait, but it is building to that position quickly. Second, China is not yet able to deploy forces globally, but it is demonstrating a clear commitment to building the naval and air projection capabilities that could allow it to do so increasingly by 2020 or soon thereafter. And third, China has devoted great effort to building a military industrial complex that is increasingly capable of indigenous innovation and China is not hesitant to use its new capabilities to achieve decisive levels of superiority, even in outer space.

All of this points to a central fact: China is building a military capability that far exceeds its regional defensive needs and is on a trajectory to compete with the United States to achieve Asian military dominance and then, at its choosing, to extend similar dominance into additional strategic priority areas. This competition already extends into near outer space and could extend to the Moon and beyond. Furthermore, this trend will continue as long as the essential CCP-PLA alliance remains in power. It is this alliance which has made possible China's transformation from a military backwater to a potential superpower in two short decades, as it has transformed China's economy into a global powerhouse able to fund such a military buildup. A democratic evolution in China has the potential to reduce the current leadership's deep commitment to building such a level of military force, as it may also change the current regime's deep hostility to democracy. However, as of late 2007 there is no apparent collection of forces that could effect a democratic evolution in China that the CCP could not detect and destroy beforehand.

It is thus necessary for America's leaders and those of its allies to balance their desire for a peaceful and cooperative relationship with China and the oft-spoken assurances of Chinese leaders with the reality of China actions. Although Chinese spokesmen use the phrase less and less, they would still prefer that foreigners view their overall trajectory to be that of a "peaceful rise." Chinese leaders repeatedly say China's defense buildup is for "defensive" purposes, that China policy is one of "no first use" of nuclear weapons, and that its strategy of "active defense" means "not striking first." They say that China will not engage in "arms races" nor will it enter into "military alliances." Furthermore, China says that it opposes the "militarization of outer space" and that it does not seek "hegemony." The information presented in previous chapters of this book, at a minimum, gives considerable cause to doubt all of these stock Chinese assurances.

Such an outlook, however, does mean that U.S. policy makers must proceed as if war with China is a certainty. The Chinese-American economic interrelationship is one of critical importance to both parties, and the prosperity of much of the world would be threatened by a state of real mutual hostility. As much as it remains necessary to "engage" or seek to convince Chinese leaders of the proper content of a "peaceful" relationship, it remains even more important for U.S. leaders to regard Chinese actions for what they are. Such an honest perspective was reflected in the February 2006 U.S. Department of Defense Quadrennial Defense Review, which described China's challenge by noting:

> Chinese military modernization has accelerated since the mid-to-late 1990s in response to central leadership demands to develop military options against Taiwan scenarios. The pace and scope of China's military build-up already puts regional military balances at risk. China is likely to continue making large investments in high-end, asymmetric military capabilities, emphasizing electronic and cyberwarfare; counter-space operations; ballistic and cruise missiles; advanced integrated air defense systems; next generation torpedoes; advanced submarines; strategic nuclear strike from modern, sophisticated land- and sea-based systems; and theater unmanned aerial vehicles for employment by the Chinese military and for global export. These capabilities, the vast distances of the Asian theater, China's continental depth, and the challenge of en route and in-theater U.S. basing place a premium on forces capable of sustained operations at great distances into denied areas.[1]

As this passage from the 2006 Quadrennial Defense Review (QDR) notes, China's military challenge to the United States is most obvious on the Taiwan

Strait, where China is assembling the means to take over Taiwan and force a new democracy to end its existence as a free society. China cannot convince Taiwanese to voluntarily surrender the free society they have come to embrace, but the very existence of which serves to undermine the legitimacy of the Communist Party–led regime in China. So China is building toward an ultimate resort to brutal force, regardless of cost in lives or the ultimate political and economic impact on the Chinese themselves. But while the PLA's ongoing buildup stresses the capabilities needed to conquer Taiwan, it is also beginning to assemble the means to project military power on a level that follows the increasingly global scale of China's economic and political interests. Here China is focusing on developing a broader array of military capabilities that more specifically challenge those of the United States in space, in the air, in the sea, and on the ground.

Threat No. 1: Proliferation

Perhaps the most critical military threat that the CCP-PLA alliance poses to the United States and to other democracies is its unwillingness to embrace and follow global conventions on the proliferation of nuclear and missile weapons. Furthermore, China poses an additional threat by its willingness to sell increasingly advanced non-nuclear weapons to regimes that threaten the regional order, support terrorism, or otherwise threaten the United States and its allies. This is a threat that will likely continue to exist for as long as the CCP regime believes that its interests can be advanced by nuclear, missile, or major non-nuclear weapons technologies regardless of the consequences. There is reason to believe that top members of China's political and military leadership benefit personally from nuclear and missiles sales. What makes this threat more pernicious is that China's conscious nuclear and missile proliferation has enabled critical secondary proliferation, which will only hasten the day that Chinese nuclear and/or missile technology is passed along to terrorists who may use the resulting weapons against the United States and its allies.

In particular, China has given extensive nuclear weapon and missile technology to Pakistan and provided critical nuclear and missile technologies to Iran. China made Pakistan a nuclear missile power as part of its strategy to contain India and to ensure that India's obsession with the threat from Pakistan would divert even a small amount of attention away from the increasing threat posed by China. A likely secondary goal was to create a source of nuclear missiles for Saudi Arabia, and perhaps other Islamic states, that would prevent China from having to take immediate responsibility for a potentially destabilizing act. But starting in the 1990s, Pakistan, through the actions of its leading nuclear engineer, Abdul Qadeer Khan, sold a set of Chinese nuclear weapon documents to Libya, and has sold some nuclear technology to Iran. It is not known whether Libya passed the documents along to other radical states or terrorist groups, but the possibility must be considered.

Iran received open Chinese assistance with its nuclear power program in the 1990s, and though it ostensibly stopped following U.S. protests, there are reports of occasional Chinese sales of materials critical to its nuclear sector. China, however, has been a constant source of long-range and tactical missile technology to Iran. Should A. Q. Khan's nuclear technology sales to Iran eventually help it to build a nuclear weapon, China might be responsible from two directions. When Iran obtains nuclear weapons it will surely be tempted to give them to Hezbollah or other radical/terrorist groups who might then use them against Israel, the United States, England, or other European states.

A third recipient of China's nuclear and missile assistance has been North Korea. While China has received great credit for leading the Six-Party Talks process since 2004, its role in helping North Korea to reach the stage of a nuclear missile state seems almost forgotten. At key points China provided North Korea with assistance that, while not comprehensive, did help Pyongyang to develop nuclear weapons and long-range ballistic missiles. North Korea has since most visibly been a key source of liquid-fuel missile technology to Pakistan and Iran. Should the Six-Party process fail to gain total North Korean compliance with the goal of eliminating nuclear weapon stocks and their development and production capability, then the danger of North Korean nuclear proliferation will remain.

It does not appear that China is willing to take any responsibility for its past proliferation or the dangers created by the secondary proliferation it has made possible. In fact, during the 1990s and for all of this decade, China has repeatedly used its power in the United Nations to shield Pyongyang and Tehran from punitive sanctions seeking to end their nuclear weapons quests. That China would do so given their potential to unleash an age of nuclear terrorism demonstrates either a profound irresponsibility borne of unfathomable myopia or, perhaps, it represents an insidious policy of promoting an indirect attack against the United States and other democracies from which Chinese leaders believe they can escape responsibility. At a minimum it can be expected that China will take advantage of a future terrorist nuclear attack. China was able to use the 9/11 tragedy to help avert the initial hostility of the administration of President George W. Bush. Might it use a future nuclear terrorist attack against the United States to advance its goal to control the future of Taiwan?

Threat No. 2: Taiwan Temptation

China's continuing military buildup will propel several challenges to the United States and its allies. The first could be an attempt in the next decade by China to achieve "reunification" with Taiwan by military force. In 2008 China will emerge from its hosting of the 2008 Olympics with a surge of nationalist pride. CCP leader Hu Jintao may also be facing a scheduled end to his career when his second five-year term as Secretary General ends in 2012. During this period the PLA will be able to generate increasing levels of superiority over

Taiwan's military forces, which could reach decisive levels should the PLA succeed in conducting a massive surprise attack that severely reduces Taiwan's air and naval defenses. Might Hu be tempted to secure his place in Chinese history by attempting a military campaign to finally achieve the "historic task" of bringing Taiwan under full Chinese control?

A Chinese decision to pursue a "military solution" against Taiwan absent a clear casus belli would depend on many factors. One of the most important would be consideration of the PLA's level of superiority over Taiwan's forces, including its calculation of how much a first strike would further increase that level of superiority. By 2012 is possible to consider that the PLA would have close to 2,000 short-range ballistic missiles (SRBMs) of many varieties, land-attack cruise missiles (LACMs), and 600–700 strike aircraft capable of delivering precision-strike weapons. By this same time Taiwan may not be able to shoot down more than a few hundred missiles, and its air forces will not be much larger than the 325 or so fighters it has in 2007. Enhanced by cyberwarfare and Special Forces strikes, it is possible that a surprise first strike might succeed in taking out most of Taiwan's air and naval forces in their bases and collapsing its military and civilian command and control. Following such an attack a Democratic Progressive Party–controlled government in Taipei might decide to resist, whereas a Kuomintang Party–controlled government might contain many more Beijing sympathizers who might push for a "peace" that would ultimately surrender Taiwan to CCP control.

But if Taiwan did resist and manage to maintain government integrity after a devastating first missile and air strike, by 2012 to 2015 it is also possible that China would have the option of undertaking an invasion. Should the PLA succeed in building six Type 071 amphibious landing dock (LPD) transports in this time frame, a number that some Asian sources indicate is the PLA's goal, combining these with existing transports the size of tank-landing ships (LSTs) and medium landing ships (LSMs) may give the PLA the ability to lift over 1,000 tanks in a first wave. A formal PLAN sealift would be joined by hundreds more civilian ships organized for such an operation, which may be able to use captured ports. Furthermore, PLA Airborne forces may have enough Il-76 transports to drop enough airborne tanks and troops to capture a large airport or two, facilitating further air transport by hundreds of mobilized civilian airliners. All of this points to the increasing potential for the PLA to at least establish a bridgehead from which it will be increasingly difficult to reverse, creating greater pressure on the government in Taipei to surrender and vastly increasing the potential cost to U.S. forces seeking to repel a PLA invasion, thus forcing Washington to sue for "peace."

For China a decision to initiate a war against Taiwan would in most cases also entail a decision to go to war with the United States. Were the United States able to prevent the fall of Taiwan, China's pattern is not to accept defeat but to prepare for another try. There are some who estimate that a failure to take Taiwan in a military operation would lead to level of popular revolt necessary to cause the fall of the CCP regime. While there would be public anger, its longevity would

218   China's Military Modernization

be determined in large part by the ability of the United States and others to "punish" Chinese aggression by imposing embargoes that cause a severe economic downturn. Although the United States and Japan might seek to impose an economic embargo against China, the public support for embargo in each country may depend on the level of its casualties. There is much less prospect for European and Middle East support for such an embargo. Were the PLA to win "control" in a battle that did not necessary require a massive and bloody invasion, for example, if a compliant government in Taipei "surrendered" before the United States could mobilize its forces, then it might be questionable whether the United States could sustain support for an embargo.

A collapse of Chinese public support for the CCP might also depend upon whether the PLA's performance led to a rapid Chinese defeat, a large loss of life, and a high level of public understanding of the cause and extent of the defeat. But these factors must be balanced by the likelihood of a high level of CCP control and manipulation of public information. Furthermore, the CCP is likely to have considered the possibility of such a defeat and made plans for channeling public anger against the United States, Japan, and Taiwan, in order to prepare for another attempt.

The fall of Taiwan to Chinese domination would immediately alter the Asian strategic environment. Not content with controlling Taiwan alone, it is likely that China would proceed into a new arms race to emerge as the dominant military power in Asia. A victorious China would also likely mobilize its economic and diplomatic leverage to split Japan, South Korea, and Australia from their military alliances with Washington. Existing PLA weapon trends indicate the PLA would develop further capabilities to be able to isolate U.S. forces on Guam, and it would further its dominance of the South China Sea and seek to enhance naval cooperation and access with Burma, Pakistan, and even Iran. Should China succeed against Taiwan, would American allies like Japan and Australia redouble their defensive efforts or seek subservient accommodation with Beijing? Might a continuing defense relationship with the United States require Washington's agreement to assist its allies'acquisition of a nuclear deterrent?

Threat No. 3: Growing Asymmetric Capabilities

America's ability to deter war on the Taiwan Strait and elsewhere will depend on many factors, but most important will be the calculations of PLA leaders as to whether the United States can bring sufficient force to bear soon enough to affect the outcome of PLA military operations. This will in turn depend on three key factors: the number of U.S. forces close to the potential combat zone in East Asia; the speed with which more distant forces in Guam, Alaska, Hawaii, and the U.S. West Coast can be transported to the theater of operations; and the ability of emerging PLA "asymmetric" capabilities to successfully impede or prevent American deployments.

Geography

The first "asymmetric" advantage possessed by China, especially on the Taiwan Strait, is geography. China is centrally located in the Greater Asian region whereas the United States suffers from the "tyranny of distance." As shown in Table 8.1, when China decides to concentrate decisive force on the Taiwan Strait it will be much closer to its target than the U.S. forces are. China will have the same advantage on the Korean Peninsula and in Central Asia. The United States and its allies must traverse great distances in order to bring sufficient forces to bear, and U.S. ability to project power by air and sea will remain a critical component of its ability to deter potential conflicts. As China builds larger numbers of large air and naval transports it will be able to mass more force more rapidly. This will further stress the U.S. ability to mobilize and to move air and naval forces at great distance, and increasingly, into potential Chinese naval, air, and missile forces configured to stop them.

Counter Network/Resolve Systems

A key U.S. advantage regarding China is its ability to network allies and bases, and to deploy networks weapon collections that go far to compensate for numerical inferiority versus China. However, China is gathering weapons which can, on a strategic level, target U.S. base and electronic networks globally. China may also be planning to use nuclear weapons in ways designed to challenge U.S. resolve to use force in Asia, especially over Taiwan. The collection of PLA asymmetric capabilities—antisatellite weapons, cyberwarfare, mines, and ballistic and cruise missiles—all serve to place obstacles between U.S. force concentrations and their objectives (Table 8.2). Even if the PLA is only able to delay a U.S. military response, that may be sufficient to enable the successful conduct of initial strikes and the initial deployment of ground forces, which then serve to accentuate political pressures for a negotiated settlement to end hostilities in China's favor.

Antisatellite weapons can target U.S. and Japanese satellites from ground, sea, air, and future space-based launchers. These and growing Chinese cyberwarfare capabilities can threaten both military C4ISR (Command, Control, Communications, Computers, Intelligence, Surveillance, and Reconnaissance) networks and can cause chaos among civilian electronic networks. American military reliance on satellites is already heavy and is bound to grow, especially as all the U.S. military services put new unmanned platforms into service. The simple prospect of taking down or degrading U.S. satellite communication links not only reduces essential communication between Washington and deployed forces, it also reduces mission potential by disabling the United States' ability to fully exploit air defense and air strike packages, disables the full utilization of naval fleets, and even affects the ability of soldiers to fully exploit new ground weapon systems that require satellite linkages to process targeting data and fire commands.

Table 8.1 Tyranny of Distance: Proximity of PLA and U.S. Forces to Taiwan (2007–2014)[a]

	PLA:	Japan/Okinawa	Guam[c]	Alaska	Hawaii	U.S. West Coast
Distance to Taiwan	160 km[b]	2,000 km (Yokosuka)/640 km (Okinawa)	2,750 km[c]	7,523 km (from Anchorage)	8,269 km (from Honolulu)	11,100 km (from San Diego)
Military Resources	Troops: 400,000; Tanks: 2,700; LPD/LHD: 1 (4); Carrier: (1); SSK: 53 (59); SSN: 6 (8–10); DDG: 25; FFG: 47 (57); Fighters: 450 fourth-generation (600); Bombers: 275; SRBM: 900 (2,000); MRBM: 50–100	**Japan:** Carrier: 1; CG: 2; DDG: 5–7; FFG: 1; MCM: 2 (+2); LHD: 1; LPD: 2–3; Fighters: 100+; ASW: 24; **Okinawa:** Marines: 17,850 (9,550 by 2014); Fighters: 66	Marines: III MEF (10,000 by 2014); Carrier: berthing; SSN: 2 (+3?); SSGN: (2?); Fighters: USAF temp. rotations; 12+ Marine Fighter-Bombers: temp. rotations; Transports: 8; Air Tanker: N/A U.S. Army Air Defense Unit	Army: 25th Div: 1st BCT (Stryker), 4th BCT (Airborne); ABM: 20+; Fighters: 40x F-22 (2008); Transports: 8	Army: 25th Div: 2nd BCT (Stryker), 3rd BCT (Infantry) (17,000 troops); Marines: 3rd Marine Regiment; SSN: 18 (2010); CG: 3; DDG: 5; FFG: 2; Fighter: 24 (18x F-22 in future); ASW: 48; Transport: 8; Tankers: n/a	Army: 2nd ID: 3rd BCT (Stryker); Marines: I MEU (19,000 troops); Carriers: 5; SSN: 5; SSGN: 2; CG: 6; DDG: 15; LHD: 4–5; LPD: 5; Fighters: 300; (USN/MC) ASW: 48 Transports: 60+

[a] Force numbers are estimates as deployments constantly change.

[b] PLA forces in Taiwan area of operations in 2007 identified by Department of Defense; author estimates for 2014 are in brackets. Many more forces can be moved to the theater from adjacent Military Regions.

[c] The United States is now in the process of relocating new forces to Guam, with active duty personnel to triple to 19,000 by 2014–15, but Japan will lose U.S. Marines, most Marine Air, and some Navy Air forces.

Definitions: ABM, antiballistic missile; ASW, antisubmarine warfare; BCT, Brigade Combat Team; CG, carrier group; DDG, guided missile destroyer; FFG, guided missile frigate; LHD, landing helicopter dock; LPD, amphibious landing dock; MC, Marine Corps; MCM, mine countermeasures ship; MEF, Marine Expeditionary Force; MEU, Marine Expeditionary Unit; MRBM, medium-range ballistic missile; SRBM, short-range ballistic missile; SSN, fast-attack nuclear-powered submarine; SSGN, guided missile nuclear-powered submarine; SSK, diesel-electric submarine; USAF, U.S. Air Force; USN, U.S. Navy.

Sources: Department of Defense, *China's Military Power*; International Institute of Strategic Studies, *The Military Balance*; COMSUBPAC Web page; *Combat Aircraft* magazine, May 2004, March 2005, and May 2007; Federation of American Scientists; *U.S. Navy Fact File*, www.navy.mil; U.S. Army 25th Division History, http://www.25thida.com/divroots.html

Table 8.2 U.S. Strategic Military Strengths vs. Chinese Asymmetric Measures in 2015

U.S. Asian Alliance and Basing Network:

Allows the United States to maintain forces in Okinawa, Japan, and Guam, to facilitate later reinforcing deployments from Hawaii and continental United States.

Chinese Network Assault:

Antisatellite weapons, cyberwarfare operations, and Special Operation Forces can all combine to threaten U.S. military and civilian information and electronic infrastructure essential to U.S. military operations in Asia. Growing economic reliance on the Chinese market can also reduce the willingness of U.S. allies to join it in opposing Chinese designs.

U.S. Aircraft Carrier Battle Groups:

Can deploy air-strike forces from multiple directions to destroy forces and secure air and sea space for ground-force deployments.

Chinese Counter Carrier Forces:

China is seeking to be able to orchestrate, out to 1,000 km or more, combined ballistic-missile, cruise-missile, and submarine strikes that would saturate aircraft carrier defenses.

U.S. Nuclear Attack Submarines:

Perhaps the world's quietest and best-armed submarines, they could attack PLA ships almost at will and launch cruise missile and Special Forces strikes.

China's Larger Numbers of Non-nuclear Subs and Mines:

Of about twenty-five to twenty-seven U.S. SSNs in Asia, perhaps eighteen can deploy quickly, and would face up to thirty-five third-generation and fifteen second-generation SSKs, operating cooperatively and with large numbers of deep-sea "Captor" mines, all of which will produce U.S. submarine attrition.

U.S. Networked Air Strike Forces:

The U.S. will increasingly combine long-range sensor aircraft like JSTARS and AWACS to find land, sea, and air targets at long range to be attacked by stealthy fifth-generation F-22A, F-35, and F-15E strike fighters armed with precision AAMs and PGMs.

China's Long Range SAMs and AAMs:

China may have a 400-km-range SAM and a 300-km-range AAM by 2012 to target JSTARS and AWACS, taking away the U.S. information advantage and giving the advantage to superior numbers of PLAAF fighters.

Future U.S. Unmanned Weapon Systems:

The United States is nearing a revolution in being able to produce unmanned bombers and air surveillance, underwater combat, and ground combat vehicles. Key to U.S. success will be ultrasensitive sensors to find targets and powerful computers for autonomous operations.

Chinese Cyberwarfare Operations:

China can be expected to devote great resources to attacking the electronic "tether" which allows the United States to control its unmanned systems, by either taking control of the U.S. system or forcing a mission termination.

Definitions: AAM, antiaircraft missile; AWACS, airborne warning and control system; JSTARS, Joint Surveillance Targeting and Attack Radar System; PGM, precision-guided munitions; PLAAF, PLA Air Force; SAM, surface-to-air missile; SSN, fast-attack nuclear-powered submarine.

Special Forces units may provide the PLA with another option for causing disruptions in strategic networks. Special units can be used in coordination with cyberstrikes to take down communication or power networks that sustain key U.S. military bases in Japan, Guam, Hawaii, Alaska, and the continental United States. They can also be employed to attack U.S. ships and aircraft in Japan and Okinawa, and to attack key U.S. military personnel needed to make urgent command decisions. A determined military assault on Taiwan might also include a campaign of attacks against infrastructure and personnel in the greater Washington DC area.

Antiship ballistic missiles (ASBMs) are another emerging PLA asymmetric weapon. In 2007 the navies of Taiwan, Japan, and the United States all lacked the means to defend against maneuvering ASBMs. This weapon not only poses a direct threat to the freedom of U.S. naval maneuver, it also serves to generally decrease deterrence in Asia. Absent the means to defeat the ASBM, U.S. naval commanders must endeavor to keep their ships out of this missile's range. The range of a medium-range ballistic missile (MRBM)-based ASBM would exceed the unrefueled range of the F/A-18E/F Super Hornet, the main U.S. Navy strike fighter. This means fewer fighters can be devoted to strike missions because more will have to perform refueling missions. And with the U.S. Navy further away, the PLA will have more freedom to employ its assets offensively against Taiwan, increasing the chances for victory.

China may also be contemplating the use of nuclear weapons in ways that would strike at U.S. resolve to defend Taiwan or actually attack deployed U.S. forces. China's oft-repeated assurance that it adheres to a "no first use" policy regarding the use of nuclear weapons falls into grave doubt when compared to PLA doctrinal literature and some Chinese government statements. Chinese Ambassador Sha Zukang's 1996 statement that Taiwan was not covered by the "no first use" pledge should be warning enough, especially when considering that some DF-15 SRBM may be armed with tactical nuclear warheads. These could be fired in front of a U.S. naval formation as a warning, or over it to create a powerful electromagnetic pulse strike. Such a use of nuclear weapons would be intended to force the U.S. leadership to withdraw its forces. For that matter, China could also fire a multiple-warhead intercontinental ballistic missile (ICBM) between Hawaii and the U.S. West Coast to serve as a similar warning. The potential for China's direct use of tactical nuclear weapons against a U.S. amphibious landing zone on Taiwan cannot be dismissed.

Counter Air, Naval, and Ground Weapon Systems

Although Chinese antisatellite weapons (ASATs) and cyberwarfare efforts can also degrade deployed U.S. air, naval, and ground forces, the PLA is gathering weapons which target specific U.S.-networked weapons. In the air, the U.S. E-3 AWACS long-range airborne radar aircraft has long been the centerpiece for air-dominance operations by F-15 and F-16 fighters. The E-8 Joint Surveillance Target and Attack Radar System (JSTARS) ground-mapping radar aircraft is being paired with the older B-52 bomber so it can find targets for its new satellite and laser-guided precision weapons. To counter these aerial networks, the PLA is deploying long-range antiradiation missiles such as the Russian Kh-31 and its new FT-2000 surface-to-air missile (SAM), which can target radar aircraft such as AWACS and JSTARS as well as key naval radar such as AEGIS that allow the U.S. to coordinate defensive and offensive operations by air and naval forces.[2]

Reports from Asian military sources that the PLA is developing a new 400-km-range SAM raise the possibility this could form the basis for a similar-ranged antiaircraft missile (AAM). The PLA could also decide to purchase Russia's 300+ km-range Novator K-100-1 AAM. In addition, early 2008 revelations that a ramjet powered "PL-13" with a potential 150+ km range may be in development presents another threat. At such ranges PLA Air Force (PLAAF) fighters can pose enough of a threat to critical U.S. electronic and tanker aircraft to force their withdrawal. When these critical aircraft leave the fight, U.S. fighters then lose the critical advantage of situational awareness and combat persistence. So even if they have superior technology and weapons, U.S. fighters such as F-22A and F-15 aircraft face the danger of being overwhelmed by larger numbers of PLA combat aircraft. This danger become even more acute considering that late-model PLA Sukhoi, Shenyang, and Chengdu fourth-generation fighters are increasingly competitive with U.S. fourth-generation fighters such as the F-15, F-16, and F/A-18.

Networked U.S. naval forces are also increasingly vulnerable to PLA radio frequency (RF) weapons, which destroy computer microcircuitry, and missile weapons. New PLA antiship ballistic missiles are likely to be armed with RF warheads, combining a missile that cannot be shot down with existing U.S. defenses with a warhead that can disable ships without large numbers of casualties. The PLA will likely seek to coordinate strikes by ASBMs with attacks by air- and submarine-launched antiship cruise missiles and submarine torpedo attacks. If successful, such a strike could disable or sink large U.S. ships such as aircraft carriers and cruisers. RF weapons can also degrade or disable a ship's communication and data link systems, making it far more vulnerable to missile or submarine attack. Key carrier air wing aircraft such as the E-2 Hawkeye airborne warning and control system (AWACS) are also vulnerable to PLA antiradar missiles and potential long-range AAMs.

Two other asymmetric capabilities the PLA is gathering include increasing numbers of advanced submarines and sophisticated naval mines, both of which pose growing threats to U.S. Navy surface and submarine forces. The ability of a PLA Navy *Song*-class submarine to approach the USS *Kitty Hawk* in October 2006 was but the latest illustration of a sobering fact: professionally crewed non-nuclear submarines have often demonstrated their ability to approach large U.S. combat ships close enough to deliver a fatal strike. In the past, Australian, Canadian, Chilean, and Dutch conventional submarines have "sunk" U.S. aircraft carriers during friendly exercises.[3] Although the *Kitty*

Hawk was apparently "not looking" for submarines,[4] that would be of little comfort were the PLA looking to deliver a surprise first strike. What is more disturbing is that the PLAN's new *Kilo* 636M and *Yuan*-class non-nuclear submarines are likely to be even more quiet than the *Song*, and there are reports that the *Yuan* may use an Air Independent Propulsion (AIP) system, meaning it can stalk U.S. ships for much longer. The *Kilo* is also armed with the 220-km range Russian Club antiship missile, further increasing its threat to U.S. ships.

These new PLAN submarines also pose a threat to U.S. nuclear submarines. In the past U.S. SSNs have also been "sunk" during exercises with Australian, Canadian, Japanese, and Swedish conventional submarines.[5] Russia's Rubin design bureau advertises its new *Kilo* 636M as slightly quieter than the U.S. improved *Los Angeles*-class nuclear attack submarine,[6] and says its new *Lada* class is much quieter than the improved *Los Angeles*. China may also be planning to use its less-quiet Type 035 *Ming*-class conventional submarines as "bait" to lure U.S. submarines into ambushes by more advanced PLAN subs. The U.S. Navy must also overcome PLAN submarine numbers. In an emergency, maybe twelve of the twenty-six or more Pacific-based U.S. SSNs could deploy quickly, and their rapid transit speeds would create noises that would broadcast their approach. These dozen or more U.S. submarines might reasonably be facing thirty to forty waiting PLAN submarines. A two-to-one loss ratio would still favor the PLAN in the early stages of a campaign, perhaps giving the PLA time to muster an amphibious assault.

PLA RF weapons also pose a great threat to the U.S. Army's Future Combat System (FCS). Built around fourteen manned and unmanned vehicles and systems, these emphasize 24-ton lightweight combat vehicles, but they compensate by relying on a network of ground and air sensors that allow the United States to see and attack first. But this network, relying on broadband wireless and satellite communication systems, will likely be targeted heavily by PLA RF weapons, antisatellite weapons, and cyberattacks. If the FCS communication and sensor network is degraded or taken down, then FCS "fails," according to a U.S. Army General.[7] The lightweight armored vehicles then have to rely on their individual sensors, which condemns them to individual combat with PLA armor, which may be heavy and just as able to attack first. One U.S. Army officer has commented, "Virtually every tank in the Chinese inventory packs a cannon system that can penetrate the hull of every vehicle contemplated under FCS."[8]

Challenging Unmanned Systems

It is clear that both the United States and China intend to make far greater use of unmanned air, naval, and ground weapons systems in the future. For the U.S. military, ever greater use of unmanned systems is viewed increasingly as one of the most critical ways to maintain or increase capabilities while containing spiraling costs. The U.S. experience in Iraq with airborne unmanned aerial vehicles (UAVs) like the Global Hawk, Predator, and hand-launched surveillance

UAVs, along with small robots for urban combat, has encouraged all the U.S. services to devote great resources to the development of larger and more sophisticated unmanned systems. U.S. Army unmanned vehicle use has grown from 163 in 2004 to over 5,000 in 2007, while unmanned air vehicle time has grown from 100 hours per day to 500 hours per day over the same period.[9] Unmanned systems are especially attractive because in many cases they allow controllers to remain in stateside bases, avoiding the expense of forward deployment. In August 2007 the U.S. Navy selected Northrop-Grumman to develop a prototype for the first unmanned carrier strike and surveillance aircraft. The U.S. Army plans to buy 3,000 more small combat robots by 2012.[10] FCSs eventually will include the unmanned "Mule" logistic support vehicle and larger unmanned combat vehicles. The U.S. Navy looks to unmanned underwater vehicles to conduct countermine and antisubmarine missions. For its part the PLA is also developing large surveillance and air combat UAVs, as well as unmanned naval platforms for countermine missions and urban combat robots for the PLA Army.

In response to the American unmanned weapon system plans, the PLA can be expected to attack the unmanned vehicles' weakest component—the electronic "tether" which allows controllers near and far to command the vehicle. The U.S. Army is developing a UAV that can find and attack the controller by tracing back the data link, a method that the PLA could emulate.[11] In mid-2007 a U.S. source indicated that hostile parties may have actually tried to take control of U.S. unmanned systems in Iraq by electronic means.[12] While no details of such incidents were offered, this kind of operation illustrates one danger of how an increasing reliance on unmanned systems may quickly turn from panacea to threat. Similar attempts to control U.S. unmanned systems should be expected from the PLA's extensive cyberwarfare forces. The PLA can be expected to attack unmanned systems from the outside by compromising electronic linkages, as well as by using assets on the inside to alter programs or actually take control.[13] Should the United States come to use large unmanned aircraft to conduct surveillance near China, it can be expected that China will attack them or perhaps even try to capture them, in the expectation that U.S. leaders will not respond strongly when no loss of life is involved. The PLA can also attack and degrade U.S. unmanned systems by attacking their satellite linkages, which would be critical for long-range airborne strike and surveillance UAVs.

Threat No. 4: Looming Conventional Challenges

China's ability to pose asymmetric military challenges will soon be joined by a growing ability to pose a number of conventional military challenges. It seems clear that China intends to invest not only in the most modern military technologies but also in ever-better means to project its new military power to far greater distances. Even as a country which continually bemoans the predations of colonial occupiers of the nineteenth century and the "Imperial" forces of the

United States or the former Soviet Union, China is now on a trajectory to gather the military-technical trappings of an imperial power—one able to impose its will wherever its interests or caprices dictate. China's ability to do this on a level comparable to the United States may not come to pass until 2020–2030, but in Asia its military growth will soon pressure Japan, South Korea, and Australia to consider new defensive options. This too will challenge the United States to sustain a level of military capability in cooperation with its allies to sustain deterrence, as the United States must also consider what balance of force levels and technology can meet its alliance commitments.

Competing Military Networks

China will increasingly seek to organize strategic networks for the purposes of advancing the pursuit of economic and political interests, increasing military interaction, assuring military access, and outmaneuvering rival powers. In 2005 and 2006 China and Russia offered repeated assurances that their "Peace Mission" military exercises were not "directed against any one party," as they did not mean the Shanghai Cooperation Organization (SCO) was forming a military alliance. However, the 2005 exercise advanced the PLA's ability to conduct operations against Taiwan and the 2006 exercise aided its ability to conduct power projection into Central Asia. The SCO is emerging as the principle example of a Chinese-dominated semi-alliance structure which does not require formal obligations, but which China can use to organize ad-hoc military coalitions to secure military-political objectives. When China is able to project significant forces with new large air and sea transports it will also have the option to "empower" new networks with military exercises or lead "coalition" military operations designed to "stabilize" a favored regime or destroy another. Continued greater Russia-China military cooperation could lead to a complementary assemblage of power projection forces, especially if Russia proceeds with intentions to build up to six new nuclear-powered aircraft carriers.

In the case of the SCO China seeks to exploit Russia's post-Soviet revived aspiration to greater international influence following a decade of perceived losses to NATO and the United States. But as it moves toward greater coordination of economic, political, and military policies, the SCO faces considerable challenges to its future cohesion. Russia and China, for all their cooperation, are vying for leadership in Central Asia. It is perhaps an impossible challenge for the SCO to satisfy the divergent security needs of membership aspirants. These include nuclear rivals India, a democracy; Pakistan, which is dissembling under Islamist pressures; and the soon-to-be-nuclear-armed rogue state Iran, intent on leading a proxy war against nuclear-armed Israel. Iran's joining would help assert its desire for influence in Central Asia, but it will also expose its military forces to cooperation with Russia and China, further increasing its ability to threaten Israel and its Sunni neighbors. It is also possible for China and Russia to ignore these fissures, and to deepen their military-technical cooperation to include some degree of operational military cooperation in the event of a Chinese attack on Taiwan. China would likely reward Russian "passive" assistance, including intelligence gathering, cyberstrikes, and coordination with Cuba and Venezuela to undertake cyber- and Special Forces activities.

In East Asia, China is using its "soft power" to leverage a reduction in East Asian military cooperation with the United States, as it gradually builds new competing political-economic networks that could be pushed in a military direction. Victories include South Korea's public refusal to allow U.S. military forces on Korean territory to be used to help defend Taiwan. Manila also refuses to revive military cooperation with the U.S., including cooperation in a possible Taiwan emergency, in large part due to subtle Chinese pressure. China's pressure on Australia to limit missile defense cooperation with the United States and to refuse to help the United States in the event China attacks Taiwan is another example of the kind of pressure that could be more widespread.

China's military relationships with North Korea, Burma, and Thailand are deep, based on unique circumstances such as ideological-historic shared sacrifice in the case of North Korea, unique political-strategic reasons in the case of Burma, or ethnic-strategic reasons in the case of Thailand. But China is now more willing to use its economic-political influence to seek to advance new military relationships among its historically suspicious neighbors. First using its influence in Malaysia, Chinese promoted the creation of the ASEAN +3 Forum and the East Asian Forum, both of which specifically exclude the United States. But in 2006 and 2007 China began to quietly advance the idea of selling modern arms to Malaysia, and by early 2007 China was suggesting multilateral military exercises. While there is yet no overt sign that China is using new military entrée to push out American influence, such is to be expected.

In Africa and Latin America, China is also increasing its military interaction, to complement its aggressive pursuit of economic and political goals. Formal military diplomatic ties are growing, and naval visits to Africa started in 2000. It can be expected that military-technical ties are greatest with Brazil and South Africa, the most advanced military-technical powers on their respective continents. China has the option to increase the strategic power and independence of both, through the sale of advanced missile or nuclear technologies, should its economic-political or strategic interests vis-à-vis the United States make this attractive. But more troubling military cooperation is reserved for the most antidemocratic states on both continents. China could emerge as the economic or even military guarantor of the Castro dynasty on Cuba, as both China and Cuba have deepened their intelligence cooperation directed at the United States. Strongman Hugo Chavez looks to China to eventually replace the United States as Venezuela's main economic partner, as limited Chinese arms sales started in 2005. Sudan's harsh genocidal regime is now dependent on China's economic and military support, as China is now a major source of advanced weapons for Zimbabwe's autocratic ruler Robert Mugabe.

It is also possible to envision circumstances in which China may emerge as a near rival for influence with the United States in NATO. Like the U.S. military, many European militaries engage the PLA in multiservice diplomatic interactions, to include naval pass-ex or search-and-rescue exercises. In August and September 2007 a PLAN *Luyang-1*-class destroyer and an 866-class underway-replenishment ship sailed to Europe and conducted simple exercises with the British, Spanish, and French navies. This was the first time the PLAN conducted exercises in the Atlantic and Mediterranean Oceans. Should there be a lifting of the 1989 post-Tiananmen European Union arms embargo, it can be expected that many European arms companies will rush to find collaborative relationships with Chinese counterparts, as many European governments will seek deeper interactions with the PLA. The Europeans will be seeking profits to fund new development while the Chinese will be seeking cutting-edge technology they hope will surpass that of Russia. This will require increasing military-technical personnel interaction, raising a host of security questions for the United States, which may be forced to limit arms sales or military-technical access should China seek to compromise U.S. military technology, as is to be expected. This, of course, will also be one of China's goals.

Space-Nuclear Competition

A second pressing "conventional" challenge will be China's rise as a military-space power and the potential for a rapid increase in its strategic nuclear offensive and defensive capabilities. If space or nuclear weapons become areas of China-U.S. competition, it could quickly heighten U.S. fears of potential Chinese hostility. For the United States, access to space and space assets are critical components of its ability to deter nuclear strikes. Space early-warning satellites will provide the first data regarding a hostile missile strike while surveillance and navigation satellites will ensure the accuracy of any retaliation. An attack against U.S. space assets could be interpreted as the opening round of a nuclear strike, which would at least trigger U.S. preparations for nuclear counterstrikes.

Despite their potential to increase nuclear instability, Chinese military literature, the PLA's demonstration of laser and missile-based antisatellite weapons, and China's growing military satellite networks indicate that China does not intend to allow outer space to remain an American domain. Having had at least two space weapons in development for over a decade, it is possible that before the end of this decade that China will have operational ground-based and air-launched ASAT capability that could be deployed well beyond Chinese territory. China's January 11, 2007, antisatellite interception demonstration, plus at least two previous attempts, indicate that China can now pose a credible threat to satellites that fly over Chinese territory. The inherit mobility of the SC-19 direct-ascent ASAT, the potential for China to turn a new air-launched satellite launcher concept into an even more mobile ASAT, and the fact that Chinese naval officers have written about the possibility of using nuclear-powered ballistic missile submarines (SSBNs) as ASAT launchers, indicate that China can move space warfare assets far from the Chinese mainland.

The SC-19 ASAT system may also indicate China's intent to develop an antiballistic missile (ABM) defense system. With mobile high-power radar and satellite early-warning capability, the mobile SC-19 could be configured as a mid-course missile interceptor. The relationship between China's first ABM program, started in 1963, and a subordinate ASAT program serves as warning that the current ASAT program could be related to an equal or larger ABM program. The possibility of a Chinese ABM system should then focus greater attention of the growth of China's ICBM and submarine-launched ballistic missile (SLBM) force. As indicated earlier, Asian sources have spoken to the likelihood that the DF-5 Mod 2, DF-31A, and JL-2 missiles could all carry multiple warheads; in the worst case, could potentially indicate a Chinese intent to build a force of 500 warheads. It should be stressed that no U.S. public source has indicated that either possibility is being realized, but the evidence examined in chapter 6 does provide cause for concern and close attention.

Chinese military literature also indicates that China has at least considered what may be a range of unmanned space combat platforms, while China's Shenzhou manned space capsules prove China's interest in manned military space platforms. From micro- or nanosatellites that are launched covertly acting as Space Mines, to larger platforms armed with a variety of weapons for striking space or Earth targets, China has the capability and apparent interest to pose a varied threat in and from space. The fact that the first six Shenzhou missions (the sixth was in 2005) carried military surveillance equipment indicates that, like the Soviets, China may also intend to have its larger space stations perform military missions as well. At this point the United States must also consider seriously that China's eventual progress to the Moon and beyond will also include a military character. Moon bases could serve as ideal locations to monitor the very strategic region between the Moon and the Earth, the location of important deep-space surveillance satellites. The Moon might also serve as a better location for nuclear or other future energy sources to enable high power lasers. The United States considered military Moon bases in the 1960s and developed plans for manned military space platforms in the early 1960s, but neither was implemented.

China's quickly growing space-information architecture will also become an increasingly important component of PLA power and Chinese political-military power projection. A robust satellite surveillance network will allow the Chinese leadership to share near-real-time information on U.S. or other forces hostile to a Chinese client regime. Sharing such data with a regime like Iran would also mean it would be shared with terrorist groups such as Hezbollah, aiding their operations against Israel or U.S. forces. If China will permit Iran to be a conduit for Chinese weapons to Iraqi and Afghan Islamist insurgents, then allowing the conduit of intimate imagery or electronic intelligence to assist insurgent operations is but an added benefit. Pakistan's and Iran's cruise missiles can be assured highly accurate guidance data from China's future Compass navigation satellite network.

Energy Weapons

The next decade could also see the introduction of PLA energy weapons on a larger scale. The PLA already employs non-nuclear RF warheads in SRBMs, and presumably, aerial bombs to attack electronic targets. Inasmuch as military laser research has been a high priority, especially under the 863 Program, it is to be expected that the PLA will introduce military lasers for a range of missions. In 2004 an Asian military source disclosed a serious concern that the PLA at that time may have been testing a tactical antiaircraft laser device. In 2005 Chinese Internet imagery revealed that the PLA Army had a laser-based chemical/biological weapon detection vehicle. It is likely that the PLA is working toward the goal of fielding an array of tactical laser weapons for ground, naval, air force, and eventual military-space applications. It is likely that PLA, like the United States, is investigating chemical, free-electron lasers, which use direct electrical energy feeds. The PLA is also likely very interested in rail gun technology, which the U.S. Navy is developing to give a projectile a 350-km range. As such guns can propel rounds up to Mach 5 speed, they also can be used for missile defense.

Air-Sea Power Projection

As reviewed in Chapter 7, the PLA is now developing the ground, air, and naval assets to accomplish distant power projection. This is being driven by the Chinese leadership's desire to protect access to resources and trade routes and to further develop its aerospace and maritime industries to better compete with the West. Furthermore, China desires this capability to reflect its aspirations for global leadership and to bolster the CCP's political prestige among Chinese. As China is able to organize further economic-political networks similar to the SCO in more distant regions, the ability to project air and naval power will be a critical factor in promoting their cohesion and affirming Chinese leadership. Although China could also use this power for humanitarian missions, responding to natural disasters or to support U.N.-sanctioned peacekeeping missions, it must also be considered that China may also decided to support governments or movements that threaten vital U.S. interests. So at a time when the United States will be further challenged to maintain the capabilities needed to deter Chinese aggression in Asia, it will also be stressed to sustain and improve capabilities needed to be able to rapidly deploy forces to distant locations.

The PLA's first serious power projection capability may be realized should it revive its 2005 intention to purchase thirty to thirty-four more Russian Ilyushin Il-76 transport aircraft, a 2005 contract complicated in 2007 by Russia's move to change factories and raise prices. A potential force of thirty-four Il-76MFs and twenty or so Il-76MDs could transport up to 106 light tanks and 3,200 troops over 3,000 km. While such a force could be used to take airfields on Taiwan, it could also be used to support a favored military faction in Pyongyang in a coup against the regime of Kim Chong Il. Or for that matter, it could be deployed quickly to help a Central Asian dictator stamp down pro-democracy demonstrators who might otherwise topple a China-compliant regime. The ability to strike with speed and surprise before the United States can act, especially if the target is low U.S. political priority, could assure that Chinese forces and their allies win the battle. In addition, such a force could be used for a one-way assault on Guam.

China is now funding the development of new military and civil transports that could be realized in the 2015 time frame; this would further increase the PLA's airborne projection capabilities by 2020 or thereafter. The current 2006–2010 Five-Year Plan is funding a program for a new 60-ton, 4,000-km-range-capable transport, most likely with new Chinese turbofan engines. This transport, with a wider and taller fuselage than the Il-76, could be used to transport heavier wheeled combat vehicles the PLA is now developing. It also appears that perhaps a new aerospace concern will develop two families of civil transports: a single-aisle narrow-body and a twin-aisle wide-body. While intended primarily to compete with Boeings and Airbuses, as these companies have done, the new Chinese civil airliners can be expected to support a number of military versions. But the more important consideration is whether the wide-body will be developed into an aerial tanker that would give greater range to the new larger military transports and allow for air combat fighter escorts.

But even before the new indigenous air power projection systems enter the PLA, it could have an initial naval amphibious projection fleet. China has the shipbuilding capacity to build, in the next decade, an initial fleet of three Landing Platform Dock (LPD)- and six Landing Helicopter Dock (LHD)-size amphibious assault ships, a number projected by one Asian source. These ships, plus several more underway-replenishment ships, would enable the PLA to transport about 4,000 troops and associated armor and supplies to conduct assaults as far as the Persian Gulf. A smaller contingent could be dispatched for either humanitarian missions or military exercises around the world. Quite often, the mere appearance of such ships in the harbor of a target country is enough to produce a desired positive or negative political effect. Again, these forces could be used for missions benign or hostile. But what they also enable is the possibility of PLA naval amphibious groups being the centerpiece of SCO-sponsored air-land exercises in Iran, or the dispatch of a combined Marine force to chase "terrorists" in Africa.

The ability of a future PLA amphibious group to conduct operations in a potentially hostile environment, however, will depend on the PLA's success in building aircraft carriers and in using China's ability to convince new political-economic networks to provide access for PLA air and naval forces. As described earlier in this chapter and in previous chapters, both are being sought. It is increasingly apparent that China will begin building its first indigenous aircraft carrier as early as the 2011 Five-Year Plan, as the *Varyag* becomes a platform for carrier training and doctrine/operations development. Should the PLA elect to purchase highly modified Sukhoi Su-33s for its first-generation carrier wing, the PLA Navy would begin its carrier era with an air wing equal to or more capable than the U.S. Navy carrier air wing. The Su-33, with a modern active phased array radar and new Novator K-100-1 300+ km range AAMs, might handily take out U.S. Navy AWACS and electronic warfare aircraft and then exploit its greater maneuverability and modern weapons array to pose a real threat to slightly less capable U.S. Boeing F/A-18E/F fighters.

Fifth- and Sixth-Generation Airpower

As the latter half of this decade sees an acceleration in the PLA's acquisition of fourth-generation combat aircraft, it must also be considered that China has had two or maybe more fifth-generation combat aircraft programs underway for more than a decade. Furthermore, it is increasingly apparent that China will not rest as the U.S. forges ahead with sixth generation high-supersonic or even hypersonic unmanned air combat systems. What little evidence China has revealed indicates that it too will follow the United States with its own sixth-generation systems.

To be sure, China has yet to fully exploit the multirole air-combat and attack potential of its fourth-generation fleet, which will see a second round of growth as the new versions of the Chengdu J-10 and Shenyang J-11 enter production. With the expected incorporation of Russian or early indigenous active phased-array radar designs, plus new longer range active-guided AAMs and new precision-guided munitions (PGMs), these multirole combat aircraft will be comparable to current late-model Lockheed Martin F-16 and Boeing F-15 fighters. The imminent introduction of fifth-generation AAMs such as the PL-10 and PL-13 will give the PLA's fourth-generation fighters (and even some third-generation fighters) clear advantages over current U.S., Japanese, and Taiwanese fighters. The fourth-generation fighter cohort will also give the PLA the ability to develop better joint-forces operations and tactics and give a greater proportion of its force more experience with long-distance strike operations.

But this is not all. By the middle of the next decade it is possible that China may finish its first fifth-generation design, most likely a Shenyang model, which could be closely followed by a Chengdu model. Both can be expected to stress stealth, supercruise speeds, active phased-array radar, and new long-range active guided munitions. There is also a possibility of a third or even more programs, inasmuch as in 2005 a Chinese source disclosed to the author that Chengdu was considering an "F-35" class design. Might it also include a vertical/short takeoff/landing (V/STOL) version to put on future larger LHD amphibious assault ships? It is not certain though it is at least implied. But Chengdu's interest in a lighter-weight, perhaps more affordable fifth-generation design may also mean that Shengyang is offering a model as well. True, the United States may by that time have a decade of experience with the Lockheed Martin F-22A fifth-generation fighter, plus a few years' initial experience with the Lockheed Martin F-35, but it is most unsettling that China could be that close on the heels of these two fighters.

Several hundreds of newer J-10 and J-11s, combined with earlier purchases of Russian-build Su-27s and Su-30s, will place much greater pressure on the air forces of Taiwan, Japan, and South Korea. But the relatively rapid emergence of Chinese fifth-generation fighters will be additionally unsettling. In mid-2008 the U.S. was still leaning toward established policies of not allowing foreign sale of the F-22A, preferring instead to protect a U.S. advantage by not allowing technology migration. Such a policy, however, is not going to prevent China from pressing ahead with its fifth-generation fleet. This makes even more problematic the current U.S. decision to limit F-22A production to 183 aircraft. This means that only 138 are available for combat operations, and of these, only fifty-eight are to be based between Alaska and Hawaii. There should be no expectation that the PLA will so limit its production of fifth- generation combat aircraft.

Beyond the fifth generation, it is clear that China is considering what it requires for a sixth-generation air force. For the United States, the sixth generation, though undefined, will apparently include largely unmanned combat platforms performing most combat missions envisioned today. Shenyang's revelation in 2006 of its supersonic unmanned Dark Sword unmanned combat aircraft concept, plus the revelation of new long-range unmanned strategic reconnaissance platforms, certainly indicate that China is investing in an unmanned airborne future. The PLA can be expected to develop a large number of subsonic and helicopter-based UAVs and unmanned combat aerial vehicles (UCAVs), some with some capable of supersonic speeds or higher. Eventual hypersonic UCAVs may involve the ability to perform in Low Earth Orbit.

Heavy and Light Army

While the U.S. Army has vacillated over the last decade between whether to retain heavy "Cold War"–style armor units or to move toward a new generation of lightweight armor that stresses deployability and superior electronic networks, it is apparent that the PLA is going to pursue both. The PLA will be capable of dominating heavy armor–dominated battles that could occur in the Greater Asian region as it will also develop innovative lightweight armor systems for long range air and sea deployment. Should the U.S. opt to use more rapidly deployable "light" units like Stryker Brigade Combat Teams or future units build around new FCS technologies, they may be facing heavy PLA units with dangerous advantages if they are able to close combat.

The latest versions of the 125-mm-gun-armed ZTZ-99 and ZTZ-96 (Improved) main battle tanks revealed in 2005 and 2006 stress the PLA's commitment to ever more modern heavy tanks. With a numerical advantage these tanks could likely serve a deadly blow to the fabled U.S. M1A2 Abrams. These tanks will also be accompanied into battle with the new ZBD-97 infantry-fighting vehicle armed with the Russian Bachka combined 100-mm gun and 30-mm gun turret. The PLA has used Russian models to develop

5–6-km-range gun-launched missiles that outrange regular tank gun rounds. At the same time the PLA has developed a family of air-droppable airborne armor vehicles inspired by the Russian BMD series. And by 2006 it was apparent that the PLA was putting into service a new family of 8-wheeled light-medium armor systems comparable to 8-wheel families developed by European and U.S. companies. Furthermore, the PLA is already fielding experimental mechanized Special Forces units with new helicopter-deployable automatic mortars and all-terrain vehicles. The PLA already uses advanced depleted-uranium penetrator rounds which can penetrate most armor. In the future the PLA can be expected to seek new technology armor for heavy and lightweight applications as it will also develop new longer-range missile and shell-based armor weapons.

PLA artillery is also going heavy and light. In 2005 it revealed its new PLZ-05 self-propelled 155-mm artillery system based on the autoloading Russian MSTA. Though first seen in 2006 the PLA chose the 2007 IDEX show to reveal two lightweight truck-based 155-mm and 122-mm artillery systems. China already manufactures a laser-guided 155-mm shell and can be expected to be working on satellite-guided artillery shells similar to the U.S. Excalibur. As discussed in Chapter 6, PLA rocket artillery is quickly modernizing to the range, accuracy, and cargo capabilities of modern SRBMs. The PLA can be expected to launch smart self-guided antitank munitions as well as UAVs from artillery rockets.

Both heavy and light units will also have increasingly capable missile- and gun-based air defenses as well as better air support. There is a major push by the PLA to add new medium-weight attack and transport helicopters to Army units, and Marine units may follow suit. The new Z-10 attack helicopter influenced by French and Italian technology is about as good as or better than the U.S. AH-1 Cobra. A heavier attack helicopter similar to the AH-64 Apache may follow. By the end of this decade the PLA may also be reaching a new level of transport helicopter absorption with the help of Eurocopter, and start producing a competent 6-ton transport helicopter. A new tracked combined missile–35-mm-gun air defense system may soon enter service, with the gun employing Swiss Advanced Hit Efficiency and Destruction (AHEAD) technology. The Swiss-German Skyshield can, in a two-second burst, spew nearly 5,000 subprojectiles to stop cruise missiles and a wide range of precision-guided munitions. The PLA is also producing new wheeled missile-gun combinations that will give effective short-range air defense to lightweight units.

Challenges to Deterrence: Trend of U.S. Reductions

China's looming military challenges that could begin to materialize by the first half of the next decade are gathering at a time of American military reduction, overextension, and problems affording the level of forces required to deter China. In the late 1990s a common wry joke was that the collected

Table 8.3 American Military Reductions: 1987–2007[a]

System	1987	1997	2007
ICBM	1,000	550	500
SLBM	640	432	336
Nuclear Missile/ Bomber Warheads[b]	13,685	6,720	3,820
Aircraft Carriers	14	12	11
Amphibious LHD/ LPD/LST	13/34/20	13/28/91	2/20/0
SSBN	36	18	14
SSN/SSGN	100	72	55
Cruisers	37	30	22
Destroyers	70	59	55
Bombers	399	207	173
Tac Fighter—Air Force + Navy + Marine	6,329	3,854	3,434
Total Troops—Army/ Marine[c]	1,733,525	1,276,406	1,113,957
Active Force Troops—Army/Marine	771,000/198,025	481,323/171,035	488,944/175,350
Tanks—Army/Marine	13,474	18,771	8,023

[a] Best estimate based on composite sources.
[b] Active warheads.
[c] Active + Reserve + National Guard.
Sources: International Institute for Strategic Studies, *Military Balance, 2006–2007, 1996–1997, 1987–1988*; Natural Resources Defense Council; Congressional Research Service; U.S. Navy.

U.S. military reductions of the previous decade would constitute the third or fourth largest military force on Earth. Table 8.3 offers an estimate of the amount of U.S. reductions from 1987 to 2007.

Since the end of the first Gulf War, the basic U.S. planning measure has been to maintain the capacity to fight in two major wars nearly simultaneously. In the absence of an overarching Soviet threat, this planning requirement generally assumed the need to fight an Iraq-size war and then be able to confront a North Korean attack on South Korea. This requirement had been expected to be dropped by the 2006 QDR as it has been viewed unfavorably by former Secretary of Defense Donald Rumsfeld. The 2006 QDR did not drop the basic two-war requirement, but did not make it the centerpiece of U.S. planning, which was to include preparations for a broader range of less than full-scale war scenarios, prompted by the wars in Iraq and Afghanistan.

In addition, since 2001 the United States has been heavily engaged in the anti-Islamist insurgencies in Iraq and Afghanistan, which has accelerated the service-lives of many weapons, in addition to putting great strain on U.S. military personnel resources. In early 2008 it appears that these Islamist forces will continue to wage war against the United States and its interests, raising the prospect of any U.S. leader having to continue the Iraq and Afghan campaigns or even to begin new ones, such as against a nuclear-armed Iran. The next decade may present an equal requirement for the United States to sustain counterinsurgency-intensive capabilities needed to fight Islamist terror-insurgencies as well as the high-technology capabilities needed to deter or combat the PLA.

While the U.S. Navy has been called upon continuously to respond to crises and U.S. security requirements, its ability to meet future demands is not certain. The decade of the 1990s saw the cancellation of many important weapon system programs on grounds of cost and complexity and the U.S. military services are going to be hard-pressed to afford both adequate numbers and new more capable military technologies. The U.S. Navy saw the cancellation of the Naval Advanced Tactical Fighter (NATF/F-22C) program in 1990 and its fifth-generation multirole fighter.[14] In 1991 its 1,800-km radius A-12 *Avenger II* was cancelled, taking long-range strategic stealth strike missions away from the Navy.[15] By 2007 the number of carriers had fallen from fifteen to eleven, with reports of considerations of further reductions to help pay for war on terror.[16] In 2005 the Navy leadership set a goal of maintaining a 313-ship fleet,[17] which the Congressional Budget office estimated in mid-2006 may exceed Navy annual cost projections by about 42 percent ($15.4 billion vs. $22 billion).[18] As a consequence the Navy has reduced planned aircraft purchases to pay for ships.[19] One analyst suggests that budgets and capabilities can be met with a fleet of ten carriers that make greater use of long-range unmanned strike aircraft and a forty-eight-SSN fleet that invests sooner in next-generation submarines, and by making the planned DDG 1000 cruise a technology demonstrator, instead building more upgraded *Burke* class destroyers.[20]

The U.S. Air Force has been similarly stressed to respond to wars in the Persian Gulf and in the Balkans while facing increasing resource constraints.[21] One analyst asserts that U.S. Air Force leaders "see a decrepit air fleet in which the average aircraft is older than the average Navy warship and which is rapidly approaching a breaking point as a result of continuous use in the wars in Iraq and Afghanistan."[22] The disintegration of a Boeing F-15 fighter during hard maneuvering exercises in late November 2007 led to repeated groundings of this fighter fleet, and it may result in the permanent grounding of 180 out of 440 fighters.[23] In 1994 the Clinton administration limited production of revolutionary Northrop Grumman B-2 stealth bomber to twenty-one, down from 132 envisioned by the Reagan administration. Then in 2005 the Bush administration decided to limit F-22A production to 183 fighters despite U.S. Air Force requirements for 361, down from over 700 before 1990. This only allows fifty-eight to be deployed in Pacific theater. And then the following year the Bush administration canceled the E-10 advanced radar aircraft that was intended to eventually combine phased-array air search and ground-mapping radar, also useful for cruise-missile defense. In 2007 Air Force leaders were considering a $100 billion budget shortfall from 2008 to 2013, forcing a premature shutdown of production lines for key aircraft including the F-22A and the C-17 transport.[24] In addition the Air Force faces the expensive prospect of replacing its 525 Boeing KC-135E aerial tankers, with an average age of forty-eight years, and its 514 Lockheed-Martin C-130 medium transports.[25]

Tension between the need to address new low-intensity wars while also preparing for high-tech wars has been acute for the U.S. Army and the Marine Corps. The wars in Iraq and Afghanistan have stressed Army and Marine personnel; in mid-2007 up to twenty-three of the Army's forty-two active duty brigades were deployed, raising fears that those stateside did not have the material to respond to an unexpected crisis.[26] Sophisticated insurgent attacks have also created needs for a new class of Mine Resistant Ambush Protected (MRAP) vehicles—$1.1 billion budgeted for them in 2007. Both the Army and Marines have had to lose or cut back on favored high technology programs. The Army lost its *Crusader* 155-mm automated cannon program in 2002 and its stealthy compact *Comanche* attack helicopter in 2004. In 2007 the Marines had reduced from 1,013 to 573 the number of U.S. Marine high-speed Expeditionary Fighting Vehicles to support distant amphibious assault.[27] The Marines have had to prevail over developmental challenges and harsh political resistance to keep their 360 Bell-Boeing MV-22 *Osprey* tilt-rotor assault transports and the Lockheed-Martin F-35B fifth-generation V/STOL combat jet.

Starting in 2004 the Army began a massive reorganization, taking division-based units and reforming them into smaller Brigade Combat Teams (BCTs) that are more deployable. The goal is to form forty-two BCTs though the cost of the FCS program of medium-weight networked combat systems may see a reduction to thirty-nine BCTs.[28] Earlier this decade it was expected that the Army would be rid of its heavy-armor M1A2 *Abrams* tanks and armored personnel carriers, in favor moving toward lighter and more easily deployable "modular" units like the Stryker Brigade Combat Team (SBCT). Built around more "networked" Stryker wheeled combat vehicles, these are precursors to the FCS, which envisions eighteen new medium-weight combat vehicles, missile artillery, UAVs and more intensive sensor networking to ensure information dominance. However, the FCS has seen cutbacks and controversy surrounds in ability to successfully create and meld new technologies.

Nevertheless, delivering new lighter Army units by air will still stress airlift assets. Delivering the U.S. Army's 3,000+ troop Strategic Brigade Airborne (SBA) takes an initial forty-eight C-17s to conduct a thirty-minute airdrop, which is then followed by 53 C-17 sorties to land follow-up equipment and supplies at a secured airstrip over a twenty-hour period.[29] The larger 3,500-man-equipped and 1,145-vehicle-equipped (about 327 armored infantry combat vehicles and 818 other vehicles) SBCT was intended to be airlifted in ninety-six hours with up to 288 C-17 loads. But a 2002 RAND study concluded that it would take about thirteen days to lift a SCBT from Hawaii to the Taiwan area, and this lift would use 76 percent of the U.S. C-17 and C-5 fleet.[30] Alternatively the SCBT could be transported by two U.S. Navy Fast Sealift Ships the same distance in about thirteen days.[31] In wartime, of course, airlift and sealift assets would be in very high demand by all the services. There is also concern that this size deployment limits the size of the Brigade Support Battalion so that overall combat operations are limited by lack of significant resupply.[32] The heavier Future Combat Team Brigade will require more airlift or sealift to accomplish the same deployment timeframes.

Pacific Theater Attention

Early in its term under the leadership of former Defense Secretary Donald Rumsfeld, the Bush administration considered the need to shift U.S. military priorities and deployments to be better able to deter Chinese aggression, especially against Taiwan. It offered Taiwan a large package of weapons to purchase to make up for the dearth of such sales under the Clinton administration. In addition, the Bush administration began to consider redeployments of U.S. forces, in part to respond to political pressures for U.S. force reductions in South Korea and Japan, and to respond to China. By 2001 the Bush administration had signaled its interest in building up forces in Guam to make sure U.S. forces could respond faster to crises, and by 2005–2006 it made a series of decisions of long-term importance. Furthermore the U.S. Pacific Command has sponsored a series of large near-annual exercises, such as the "Valiant Shield" series in 2006 and 2007, which tests the U.S. ability to rapidly combine U.S. Navy, Marine, and Air Force units for possible threats in the Western Pacific such as a PLA attack against Taiwan. The August 2007 exercise involved 22,000 troops, 30 warships, and 275 combat aircraft at a time of intense activity in Iraq and Afghanistan.[33]

Japan

Japan remains the cornerstone of the U.S. alliance network in Asia. Its importance vis-à-vis Taiwan is enhanced by the willingness of the Japanese government to publically recognize its interests in maintaining peace on the Taiwan Strait, as well as by statements by South Korea's government indicating that it will not allow ROK-based U.S. forces, which include 72 F-16C Block 30/40 fighter-bombers, to be deployed for a Taiwan conflict. While Japan may not yet contribute combat elements in a potential Taiwan scenario, it may willingly provide basing and logistic support for such. Nevertheless, as part of Japan's evolution toward a "normal" defense posture, the United States and Japan are creating the basis for a "joint" command structure that far better facilitates combined defense operations. The command elements of the Japanese Air Force and of U.S. air forces in Japan will share the same building on Yokota Air Base. Japanese jet fighters now deploy to Guam and Alaska for joint training and in 2006 Japanese Marines traveled to California for exercises for the first time. Japanese and U.S. joint development of missile defense technology has accelerated since North Korea's provocative August 1998 missile test, and this cooperation is extending into laser systems. A Japanese decision in 2007 to share missile intercept data gained from their radar and other sensors marked a clear upgrade in this relationship: Japan for the first time is assisting the defense of the U.S. homeland.

But in 2007 the front line U.S. response option for any potential surprise PLA attack on Taiwan would be the fifty or so Boeing F-15C fighters of the 18th Wing on Kadena Air Base. These have suffered from fatigue issues due to their age,[34] but in 2007 they began to be replaced with newer active electronic scanned-array (AESA) radar and helmet display sighted 10-km-range AIM-9X AAM equipped F-15Cs formerly based in Alaska.[35] These modifications increase competitiveness against PLA Sukhois that have been using helmet-sighted AAMs since the early 1990s. AESA radar greatly increases their ability to intercept cruise missiles. However, the future introduction of the new 20-km range PL-10 AAM and potentially 150+ km-range PL-13 on PLA fighters may shift the air balance back in China's favor. About fifty more Lockheed Martin F-16C Block 50 fighters are further North in Misawa Air Base. An additional line of defense would be the forty-eight Boeing F/A-18C/E/F fighters with Carrier Air Wing Five aboard the USS *George Washington*, which will be based in Japan's Yokosuka Naval Base starting in 2008. This will be the first nuclear-powered carrier to be deployed to the U.S. 7th Fleet.

Guam

Although the United States lost access to Philippine bases in 1991, it has moved to build up its forces on Guam, a U.S. territory taken from Spain in 1898. Guam is three hours away from Taiwan by jet plane and three days by submarine. In its last years the Clinton administration looked to an increased use of Guam to position U.S. forces to better respond to North Korean and Chinese challenges, a view reconfirmed by the 2001 QDR. In October 2002 the first of and intended three *Los Angeles*-class SSNs were stationed in Guam. This number was later reduced to two, but there has been consideration of increasing this to six SSNs.[36] In early 2008 the SSGN *Ohio*, capable of carrying 154 *Tomahawk* cruise missiles, visited Guam. The U.S. Air Force has considered stationing on Guam a fighter wing, about forty aircraft and has built new facilities to support a regular flow of "temporary" deployments of F-15E fighter-bombers and B-52, B-1, and B-2 bombers.[37] Starting in 2009 the USAF may start stationing Northrop-Grumman *Global Hawk* strategic-surveillance UAVs in Guam. In October 2005 the United States and Japan decided to relocate about 10,000 U.S. Marines from Okinawa to Guam, along with a supporting fighter squadron and maritime prepositioning ships.[38] While Guam apparently will not be the base for a forward-deployed carrier group, it will gain the berthing facilities for a carrier. The U.S. Army will also station a Patriot air defense unit in Guam. When complete in about 2014 these additions will triple Guam's active duty troop population to almost 19,000.[39]

Hawaii and Alaska

Both Hawaii and Alaska remain vital rear basing areas for assisting any potential U.S. projection into the Western Pacific, and the United States has taken steps to improve their posture. Hawaii is the largest forward Pacific base for U.S. Navy SSNs, with the sixteen or so *Los Angeles*-class ships of Submarine Squadrons One, Three, and Seven to start receiving the latest *Virginia*-class SSNs. From about 2011 to 2015, the Hawaii Air National Guard F-15A fighter unit will receive eighteen Lockheed-Martin F-22As and an air transport unit started receiving eight new Boeing C-17 transports in 2007. The 25th Light Infantry Division is transitioning to a force based on a one Stryker, one Infantry, and one Aviation Brigade Combat Team.

In August 2007 the 3rd Wing at Elmendorf Air Force Base near Anchorage, Alaska, began receiving two squadrons of forty F-22A fighters to replace its two squadrons of forty-eight F-15C fighters and one squadron of twenty-four F-15E fighter-bombers. This base will also gain eight C-17 transports. Eielson AFB lost its A-10 close air support fighters in 2007 but consolidated its position as host for the most sophisticated air combat training range in the Asian theater, as the location of the regular "Cope Thunder" air force exercise series, which now sees participants from Australia, India, and Japan.[40] The First SBCT of the 1st Brigade, 25th Infantry Division is located at Fort Wainwright. Fort Greely is the critical first location for the Ground Based Missile Defense (GMD), with a planned twenty-five to thirty missile interceptors intended to provide a limited missile defense for Alaska and the continental United States.

Requirements for Deterrence

It is necessary for the United States to continue to invest in its own defensive capabilities and to promote and strengthen its alliances and military networks. This is the surest hope that China's Communist leaders will remain unconvinced of the desirability of warfare with the United States and its allies and thus be deterred from starting conflicts. But inasmuch as deterrence is ultimately the result of a state of mind held by the top leaders of the CCP and the PLA, and they are anything but transparent, there will be a growing requirement for U.S. military and intelligence services to devote ever-greater attention to the study of China's capabilities and intentions, and then to assuring that U.S. military forces have what is necessary to defeat China should it decide to attack a U.S. friend or a vital U.S. interest. A list of measures needed to sustain deterrence of the PLA are discussed in the following sections.

Defend Democratic Principles

Defense of American friends and interest against a China that is more powerful militarily and potentially more aggressive starts with leadership willing to defend American values and accepted principles of behavior. This starts with the recognition that aggressive military buildup and potentially aggressive foreign policies reflect the nature and realities of a Communist Party with thin legitimacy that must continually impose its will on an empire that might collapse without it. To put it in terms of Leninist logic, Chinese must resolve the fundamental contradiction of a Communist Party that will not permit the political freedoms and institutions of real justice that are necessary to fully empower Chinese to achieve the real potential of economic freedom. Chinese themselves will not have the ability to alter the governmental behavior which threatens neighboring countries, and ultimately, themselves, until their government can reflect a collective will expressed by democratic institutions rather than by a single dictatorial faction. But until that day arrives, explaining these contradictions is a key requirement for American leadership. The U.S. must explain how CCP-PLA proliferation, its military designs against Taiwan, and its quest for hegemony over Asia all ultimately threaten Chinese themselves, as these will surely cause concerned countries to unite to oppose China's aggression.

Defend Democratic Taiwan

American support for Taiwan, as grounded in the 1979 Taiwan Relations Act, and consistent American policies to insist that Taiwan and China settle their differences peacefully, are strategically as well as morally correct. As Americans have learned from painful historical experience, democracy cannot be imposed on a nation but must be embraced and developed by its citizens. This has been the experience of Taiwan and will hold true especially for China. Americans can best hasten the day that Chinese embark on a democratic future by defending and preserving their own democratic example and that of their democratic allies threatened by China. This requirement becomes most acute for Taiwan, which has yet to sift though many issues of identity and is still developing the content of its unique democratic culture. It is thus important for the United States to make clear what Taiwan must do to advance its own chances of survival in the face of China's preparations for war. Then the United States must be prepared to sell Taiwan new and better weapon systems to allow its armed forces to present a level of strength that deters a Chinese attack, as the United States itself prepares for a decisive intervention should China attack Taiwan. In the face of the PLA's threatening buildup, it will be valuable for Taiwan to develop a limited ability to strike key PLA nodes, which in turn can help preserve deterrence on the Taiwan Strait.

Furthermore, the United States must provide regular recognition of Taiwan's democratic accomplishments and of its democratic leadership. The 1970s diplomatic framework created by President Nixon and former Secretary of State Henry Kissinger no longer allows the United States to effectively advance its interest in strengthening Taiwan's democracy.[41] It is time for the United States to take the lead to devise a new framework that recognizes Taiwan's laudable transition to democracy. Washington must also take an active role in countering China's long campaign to "extinguish" Taiwan's de-facto existence by destroying its legal rights. Taiwan's existence serves to undermine the legitimacy of the CCP regime by proving that political and economic freedoms actually work better together. A free Taiwan will provide a better example to instruct Chinese should the CCP collapse or become unable to rule, and it will perhaps speed China's transition to a new and better stability which would serve many larger interests.

Strengthen Alliances

In the face of Chinese attempts to push the United States out of East Asia, it is necessary for Washington to make clear that the United States will instead strengthen its alliances. This is necessary for U.S. security so as to prevent an aggressive China from causing new nuclear and conventional arms races which could end up in catastrophe. A key to resisting Chinese pressure is for the Washington to press for greater quadrilateral coordination and eventual regularized cooperation between Australia, India, Japan, and the United States.[42] Washington should redouble efforts to increase missile defense cooperation with Japan, Australia, Taiwan, and India. The United States should also sell advanced F-22A fighters to Japan and increase weapons co-development to include a range of energy weapons and space systems. The United States should also encourage Japan to become a regular participant in peacekeeping operations or in future major campaigns for the War on Terror. As the PLA builds aircraft carriers the United States, this should also help Japan, India, and Australia to rebuild or improve their naval air capabilities, which may require manned or unmanned aircraft. In addition the United States should press to expand space exploration cooperation with India and Japan to include joint Moon exploration.

Declare War on PRC Espionage

It is time to view China's conduct of cyberwarfare and espionage against the United States as the equivalent of an undeclared war. China's cyberwarfare activities have caused tens of millions of dollars of damage to U.S. military computer networks alone. China is also likely working to "prepare the battlespace" for future attacks to cripple U.S. military and civilian electronic infrastructure to support potential military operations against U.S. targets. China's espionage, especially its use of Chinese Americans and ethnic Chinese in the United States, constitutes a grave challenge that requires a firm response. There is a greater need for public education about the dangers posed by China's cyberwarfare and espionage efforts. There is also a need for a bipartisan political effort to reach out to Chinese Americans to request their assistance to find and stop members of their community who are engaged in espionage. This effort must also be extended to U.S. universities inasmuch as the Chinese government seeks to organize and control PRC citizens on U.S. campuses. Furthermore, the Department of Homeland Security and the Federal Bureau of Investigation require additional personnel and language resources to better defend against this threat.

Identify Nuclear Proliferators

Once Hezbollah or a heretofore-unknown mutation of Al Qaeda obtains a nuclear weapon and uses it against an Israeli or American target, it can be assured that others will seek to do the same, ushering in an age of unprecedented horrors. But before this happens, it is critical that Washington exercise the leadership necessary to make clear who tried to stop this new scourge on humanity and who was its handmaiden. Washington should take steps now to make clear that all contributors to a future nuclear terror attack will be tried for war crimes. To allow China to escape its responsibility for its contribution to such a calamity would in effect empower the CCP leadership to believe that it can utilize proliferation as a legitimate weapon with which to acquire even greater global power. While some in Washington may pale at the prospect of having to identify specific members of China's leadership who have sanctioned or even profited from the proliferation of nuclear and missile technology, there should be much less controversy about demanding that China acknowledge its role and take concrete steps to reverse its acts of proliferation in order to help prevent an age of nuclear terrorism.

Prepare for War in Space

Sometime in late 2005, when China made its first attempt to use a SC-19 ASAT to shoot down a weather satellite, it also made the decision to make outer space a realm of future combat. China's move to build a robust ASAT capability and indications it is developing weapon platforms are in part a response to fears of U.S. moves and capabilities, but they also represent a conscious assessment of China's military requirements. It is not likely that China's development of unmanned and manned space weapons will be a temporary threat, as was the threat of the former Soviet Union. Loss of access to space surveillance and communications assets would cripple the C4ISR networks at the heart of America's current and future manner of warfare. China's move to militarize space now requires the United States to develop the capabilities needed to defend its critical space assets, counter potential unmanned and manned Chinese space weapons, and develop the ability to use space to deliver retaliation. Since the beginning of the Strategic Defense Initiative in 1983, there have been advocates inside and outside the U.S. government advocating space-based missile defense systems as offering the best chance to intercept enemy missiles soon after their launch. Although the United States has funded small experimental ASATs and satellites with potential offensive capabilities, it has not decided to put defensive or offensive weapons into space. It is also necessary to do both and to press ahead with the goal to build an Operational Responsive Space (ORS) capability that allows the United States to replace attacked satellites.[43] The United States must also preserve its leadership in space by leading the way back to the Moon. This is required to advance science, explore potential economic benefits, and preserve U.S. strategic-military options.

Strengthen Missile Defenses and Offenses

Since 2001 the Bush administration has sought to convince China that the limited U.S. missile defenses planned for Alaska and perhaps California are not sufficient to degrade China's ability to strike the United States. This will be increasingly true as the PLA builds more DF-31, DF-31A ICBMs, and JL-2 SLBMs, and even more so should it deploy multiple-warhead missiles. But this fact has not stopped the Chinese leadership from opposing U.S. missile defense cooperation with its Asian allies, or from making common cause with Russia and Iran to stop U.S. missile defense initiatives directed against future Iranian missiles made possible by Chinese and Russian technology. The dream of Ronald Reagan to defend Americans from nuclear blackmail and death remains valid, especially given the recent history of China's repeated nuclear threats. The United States should increase its land- and sea-based strategic missile defenses for the purpose of defeating the majority of Chinese and Russian nuclear missiles aimed at Americans. This will also serve to deter China from undertaking conventional attacks against U.S. friends including Taiwan. Furthermore, the United States must work to make its missile defenses survivable by making missiles and radar mobile and by ensuring the rapid replacement of surveillance satellites attacked by the PLA.

On a tactical level, U.S land- and sea-based missile defense capabilities must evolve to include defense against accurate medium-range missiles, space-launched weapons, and cruise missiles. The PLA is now deploying a "Tomahawk"-class cruise missile on ground launchers with the Second Artillery; it will soon deploy new versions of this cruise missile on long-range aircraft and nuclear attack submarines. Russian Club and other PLA-developed cruise missiles pose an increasing threat to U.S. ships. There is a need to develop laser-based point defenses to defeat new supersonic missiles like the Club, as well as a need to develop better radar for fighters and radar aircraft[44] to find stealthy cruise missiles, and long-range antiair missiles for interception.

The United States should also be prepared to resume production of long-range nuclear missiles should the PLA "break out" of its current "minimal" deterrent posture by increasing its missile numbers and arming them with multiple warheads to a degree that threatens the U.S. ability to deter China, Russia, and potential new nuclear rogue states. As both China and Russia utilize mobile ICBMs, this may present the most economical and quick way for the United States to increase missile numbers and increase their survivability.

Remain a Military Technology Leader

The broad lead that the United States enjoys in many to most areas of military technology could erode significantly in the next decade as China's military industrial complex gains further momentum and comes to benefit from a freer market in military investments. The next decade could see a Chinese breakout in space weapons, long-range highly accurate ballistic missile, energy weapons, fifth-generation combat aircraft, unmanned weapons platforms, and nanosystems and nanomaterials harnessed to spur a range of military advancements. These are areas in which the United States must also excel, but in addition, the United States must also be working toward the next generation whenever possible. But as such effort will entail greater expense, it is important that the United States increase collaborative military technology development with key allies such as Britain and Japan.

Maintain Electronic Dominance

In the face of China's growing capabilities in cyberwarfare, its development of RF weapons, and its growing ability to target key nodes in the U.S. military electronic architecture such as satellites and key electronic warfare aircraft, it is necessary for the United States to continually invest in better electronic systems while securing them from external and internal threats. Success in protecting electronic dominance will in large part determine whether disbursed U.S. forces can respond to Chinese aggression. China's cyberwarfare efforts must be countered by both active and passive means, including greater public education and the building of secondary emergency-network or network-repair capacities. This should include the ability to rapidly replace key military and civilian satellites as well as key elements of the U.S. national communications infrastructure. The wireless broadband networks on which the U.S. armed forces increasingly rely must be made to withstand RF weapons and intrusions. Measures to protect the electronic "tether" to unmanned vehicles must be expanded. It will also be necessary to devote greater military and civil counterintelligence resources to defend against internal sabotage against these networks. At the same time, the United States must also continually develop the doctrines and systems needed to exploit or take down China's key electronic infrastructure.

Quick Strike, Quick Reach

The United States should develop quick strike and quick transport systems that can overcome all of the asymmetric weapon barriers that the PLA is developing against the deployment of U.S. forces. While the Air Force should proceed with the development of hypersonic platforms to wage very quick response missions, both the Air Force and the Navy should develop missile-based quick-strike systems in the near-term.[45] The U.S. goal should be to equip ICBMs with enough non-nuclear precision-guided munitions to take out enough of a PLA invasion fleet to guarantee an invasion will fail. These systems are needed to supplement the U.S. Navy's four new cruise-missile-equipped *Ohio*-class SSGN submarines, which may not be available in the event of a surprise PLA attack. But as the Navy considered new "modular" SSNs, it might also consider large detachable modular units that could carry 100 or more cruise missiles, to increase the potential number of missiles that can be massed to repel a PLA invasion force.

In addition, the United States should consider that an Army-centric PLA might be psychologically more deterred if it knew that the U.S. Marine and Army units could deploy to Taiwan rapidly. The United States should continue to develop new air and sea large transport systems that can deploy U.S. forces much faster than current ships and transport aircraft. To be sure, the U.S. Air Force needs adequate numbers of Boeing C-17 (78-tons capable) and modernized C-5 (110-tons capable) transports. One group of retired U.S. officers has suggested the U.S. needs 350 strategic air transports,[46] rather than the 299 authorized by the Congress in 2006.[47] It is necessary to consider the Boeing C-17B, a proposed upgrade with added engine power and better landing gear[48] that can better transport FCS systems closer to the battle. In addition, the U.S. should develop new larger air transports which leverage new 100,000-lb-thrust turbofan engines. The eight-engine Russian Myasishchev M-52 concept, which carries a 500-ton-capacity detachable pod, is an example of a near-term possibility. The U.S. Navy and Army should also continue to invest in new technology ships based on larger fast-ferry technologies which can move mechanized units at speeds of 40–50 kts. Such ferries should be pre-positioned at Guam to assist Marine deployments.

Secure Dominance at Sea

China's investment in asymmetrical naval capabilities will in the next decade put the United States in danger of losing naval battles which may turn out to be as historically pivotal as the Battle of Midway. The U.S. Navy will be stressed to develop the capabilities needed to defend against antiship ballistic missiles, preserve electronic network connectivity in the face of PLA ASAT and RF weapons, and at the same time defend against PLA submarines, deep-sea mines, and future aircraft carrier/amphibious groups. The U.S. Navy should simultaneously invest in laser and rail-gun weapons for ballistic/cruise missile defense and strike missions, and in UAV or airship technologies that can supplement satellites. At the same time, the Navy must sustain a carrier and submarine fleet with growing offensive capabilities. The U.S. Navy should also develop a new type of intermediate range ballistic missile which can simultaneously perform missile interception, space defense, land attack, and ship attack missions.

Under the sea it is critical that the United States sustain submarine superiority as it increases its antisubmarine and countermine defenses. The Navy's interest in modular nuclear submarine design offers the potential of greater weapon or unmanned system carriage while reducing crew size, complexity, and cost.[49] Although the U.S. Navy may be looking to these technologies to sustain combat capability amid declining overall submarine numbers, there may come a point when expanding PLA submarine numbers demand a U.S. response. Furthermore, the growing PLAN submarine threat dictates that the U.S. Navy must return a long-range dedicated antisubmarine capability to the carrier air wing (Table 8.4). This was lost in 1998 when the long-serving Lockheed Martin S-3 Viking stopped performing this mission. The S-3 will leave the carrier air wing by 2008. This mission might be performed by fighter aircraft with special sonobuoy/torpedo pods or by a similarly modified future unmanned aircraft based on the X-47B.

In the future a U.S. Navy carrier air wing may only have forty-four to forty-six combat aircraft (24–36x F/A-18E/F and 10–20x F-35). F/A-18s must perform tanking missions to extend the range of these fighters, meaning they cannot perform defense or attack missions. It is critical that the Navy consider seriously investing in a new post-fifth-generation air-superiority fighter. Upgraded PLAAF and PLANAF Sukhoi fighters could be equal to better than the Boeing F/A-18E/F—and future PLAAF fifth-generation fighters could present an even greater threat—during the next decade. The 600 F-35B/C fighters the Navy intends to purchase will add a stealth advantage, but their aerodynamic performance will similar to that of the F/A-18E/F.[50] A near-term solution might be a new version F-35 able to supercruise with greater range and carry more internal AAMs. The Navy must also go ahead with a new unmanned or manned long-range strike platform so that PLA attack systems do not outrange carrier strike groups.[51]

Secure Dominance in the Air

In the face of an accumulating number of capable PLA fourth-generation fighters, the near-term introduction of fifth-generation air-to-air missiles, and the potential for the PLA gaining fifth-generation combat aircraft as early as the next decade, the U.S. must strive to maintain both the sophistication and the numerical strength of its air forces. In addition, potential PLA 300- to 400-km SAMs and AAMs pose a real threat to the radar and tanker aircraft essential for the United States to secure air dominance. To counter both, the United States requires not just adequate numbers of fifth-generation air dominance fighters, but also needs to improve them with better radar, stealth, longer-range missiles, energy weapons, and higher performing lighter-weight engines. For example, the United States needs to proceed with a reported new 400-km-range AESA[52] radar to counter new Russian and Chinese ASEA radar. To counter the growing number of advanced PLAAF SAMs, it is also necessary to purchase adequate

Table 8.4 U.S. Navy Air: Outranged by PLA Systems

System	DF-21 ASBM (PLA)	Su-30MK K2 (PLA)	H-6K (PLA)	Tu-22M3 (PLA, Possible)	F-35C (USN)	F/A-18E/F (USN)	X-47 UCAS-D (USN, Projected)	A-12 (USN, Canceled 1991)	USAF regional bomber (2018)
Range/ Radius	2,500 km[a]	1,500 km[b]	3,000 km[a]	2,410 km	1,188 km[c]	1,230 km[d]	>2,300 km	1,800 km	3,700 km[a]

[a] Estimated range for missile or radius for aircraft.

[b] Internal fuel; 2,600-km radius with one refueling.

[c] Internal fuel, 2x 2,000-lb internal bombs; about 1,740 km with external tanks, internal bomb load.

[d] With 4x 1,000-lb weapons, three external tanks.

Source: Jane's Strategic Weapon Systems 2007; Jane's All the World's Aircraft 2007; The International Directory of Military Aircraft, 2002/2003.

numbers of F-22s, the only fighter which can evade them, and to develop integral laser weapons for combat aircraft as a better defense against AAMs and SAMs. Inasmuch as the United States may be considering an aerial Anti-Tactical Ballistic Missile (ATBM) based on the Raytheon Patriot PAC-3 or a new two-stage version of the AIM-120, the U.S. should also consider using this as a very long-range antiair weapon as well. It is necessary to question whether the Air Force's requirement for 361 F-22A fighters is enough should the PLA start flying indigenous fifth-generation fighters.

The United States is now perfecting the cooperative employment of JSTARS ground-mapping radar aircraft and legacy B-52 and B-1 bombers armed with very accurate satellite-guided bombs. But both radar and bomber aircraft are threatened by potential long-range PLA SAMs and AAMs. It is necessary to consider whether the mission capabilities of the former E-10 should be placed on a much faster platform so that it can get close enough to the fight and have a better chance of survival. The United States has led the use of "offboard" sensors as a "force multiplier" to support air combat missions and this advantage must be preserved. Such airborne radar is especially needed to better enable legacy and newer fighters/bombers to be able to counter new PLA cruise missiles.

It is also necessary to accelerate plans to develop a new long-range subsonic "regional" bomber that exploits modern stealth technology before the end of the next decade.[53] The current force of B-52 and B-1 bombers will be threatened by increasingly long-range PLA SAMs, and will only be useful for launching a few long-range standoff weapons. A new bomber with a better chance of close penetration is needed to be able to carry large numbers of PGMs.

Maintain Heavy and Medium Army

The U.S. Army will require both heavy- and medium-weight forces to meet the future PLA challenges. America's experience in Iraq has reconfirmed that the U.S. Army requires heavy armor for the foreseeable future, and it is now planning on maintaining a version of the M1A2 Abrams tank until 2050.[54] However, the PLA's commitment to developing heavy armor is sure to erode the viability of the M1A2 and so the Army should also consider developing a successor heavy-armor fighting vehicle. This could take advantage of potential breakthroughs in far stronger nanomaterial-based armor,[55] energy weapons, and more efficient hybrid engines. Absent superior tactical information, the Army's SBCT would also face severe threats from PLA tank units and even newer medium-weight combat vehicles, especially if they are faced in greater numbers. While the Army's FCS represents a daring attempt to meld barely proven technologies to create a powerful but medium-weight and rapidly deployable force, its singular reliance on secure broadband networks is troubling. A variety of PLA radio frequency weapons and cyberwarfare weapons can be expected to target this network. The Army should work to prevent the network from becoming the

"Achilles heel" of this future force. In addition, Army and Marine units require a new gun or energy-based mobile air defense system that can defend against new PLA precision-guided weapons.

Concluding Comment

In a brief but provocative book, journalist James Mann identifies and takes down one of the commanding myths in the American debate over policy toward China: "if we treat them like an enemy then they become one."[56] It is a fear that has been oft repeated and one that Mann regards as part of a "Lexicon of Dismissal" in which China and its supporters conspire to deflect criticism and isolate critics.[57] It is a fear that has riven U.S. policy debates on China, from economic policy, to strategic military engagement, to the more recent Bush administration policies to limit its support for Taiwan's potential desire for "independence," even though it may emerge from a legitimately democratic process. But by giving in to this fear in the mistaken "hope" that China would behave responsibly or even as a "friend," the United States has consistently lost leverage over China and has helped facilitate outcomes that may in the future threaten Americans, Chinese, Taiwanese and many others.

After debates over "Most Favored Nation" status of the early 1990s that led to American approval for China's membership in the World Trade Organization on very favorable terms, Beijing shows little inclination to reverse highly pro-tectionist trade and financial policies which produce massive trade surpluses. After nearly two decades of U.S. "engagement" with China regarding nuclear and missile weapon proliferation, Beijing shows little inclination to halt this traffic to rogue states such as Iran. It also shows no willingness to reverse its previous enabling of secondary nuclear proliferation from Pakistan and North Korea, which could lead to nuclear-armed terrorists. And after nearly three decades of U.S. "military engagement," the PLA shows little inclination to become as "transparent" militarily as its democratic neighbors and shows the potential of becoming more hostile to the United States as its military power increases.

It is hard for this analyst to conclude that, since the opening to China in the early 1970s, the United States has even approached treating China "like an enemy." To the contrary, America's welcome has facilitated China's post-Mao integration into the world economy and has thus enabled China to gather the indicators of power that may soon match or exceed those of the United States. This volume has sought to document how China has used this period, especially since the early 1990s, to gather a level of military power that may soon place it in the predominant position among Asian powers and then, within the next two decades, give China a greater ability to exercise military power on a global scale. This transformation has occurred along with consistent criticisms from Americans as well as many others about the CCP's opposition to democratic reform, its suppression of most dissent, and its support for dictatorial regimes around the world. China is not likely to change these attributes as long as the Communist Party remains in power. There is thus a clear danger that China's gathering of a globally capable military will be wedded to an antidemocratic and even anti-American foreign policy agenda. In 2008 the United States may have a clear superiority in most measures of military power, but American power is also stretched dangerously thin. U.S. policy makers have little choice but to sustain a large investment in ever more modern military capabilities lest the United States lose even more potential to deter China, first on the Taiwan Strait, and then perhaps well beyond.

Notes

Chapter 1

1. Thomas E. Ricks, "Rumsfeld Outlines Defense Overhaul: Reorganization May Alter, Kill Weapon Systems," *The Washington Post*, March 23, 2001; Michael R. Gordon, "Pentagon Review Puts Emphasis on Long Range Arms in the Pacific," *The New York Times*, May 17, 2001.

2. Michael R. Gordon and David S. Cloud, "U.S. Knew of China's Missile Test, but Kept Silent," *International Herald Tribune*, April 23, 2007, http://www.iht.com/articles/2007/04/23/asia/23missile.php.

3. *Xinhua*, September 6, 1985, recounted in Bonnie S. Glaser and Banning N. Garrett, "Chinese Perspectives on the Strategic Defense Initiative," *Problems of Communism*, March-April 1986, p. 28.

4. "Number of CPC Members Increases by 6.4 Million over 2002," *Xinhua*, October 8, 2002.

5. Mark Davis, "A Blueprint for Crises Near and Far," *Sydney Morning Herald*, July 6, 2007, http://www.smh.com.au/news/national/a-blueprint-for-crises-near-and-far/2007/07/05/1183351373152.html.

6. For more detailed examination of China's historic and current desire to control Asia, see, Steven Mosher, *Hegemon: China's Plan to Dominate Asia and the World* (San Francisco: Encounter Books, 2000), Chapter 3; Ross Terrill, *The New Chinese Empire* (New York: Basic Books, 2004), Chapter 10; Constantine C. Menges, *China, The Gathering Threat* (Nashville, TN: Nelson Current, 2005), pp. 8–10.

7. As cited in General Tao Hanzhang, *The Modern Chinese Interpretation of Sun Tzu's Art of War* (New York: Sterling Publishing, 1987), p. 13.

8. Qiao Liang and Wang Xiangsu, *Unrestricted Warfare, Assumptions on War and Tactics in the Age of Globalization* (Beijing: PLA Literature Arts Publishing House, 1999), Chapter 2, pp. 34–59 (FBIS Translation, October 29, 1999); Richard D. Fisher, Jr., "China

Not Yet An Ally," *Jamestown Foundation China Brief,* September 27, 2001, http://jamestown.org/china_brief/article.php?articleid=2372988.

9. Alistair Iain Johnston, "Beijing's Security Behavior in the Asia Pacific: Is China a Dissatisfied Power?" in Allen Carlson, Peter Katzenstein, and J. J. Suh, *Rethinking Security in East Asia: Identity, Power and Efficiency* (Stanford, CA: Stanford University Press, 2004), p. 49, viewed at http://www.people.fas.harvard.edu/~johnston/cornellpaper.pdf.

10. Ralph D. Sawyer, *The Tao of Spycraft* (Boulder, CO: Westview Press, 1998), Chapters 2 and 3.

11. Chi Haotian, "War Is Not Far from Us and Is the Midwife of the Chinese Century," *Epoch Times,* August 8, 2005, http://en.epochtimes.com/news/5-8-8/31055.html. This speech is a highly provocative justification for biological war against the United States, and though it appeared on Chinese Web sites, its veracity cannot be confirmed. However, its similarity to General Zhu Chenghu's very real 2005 threats to cause and suffer large casualties in a nuclear war with the United States over Taiwan warrant consideration of the potential legitimacy of this document.

12. Significant recent scholarship seeking to analyze China's unique strategic culture include Alistair Iain Johnston, *Cultural Realism: Chinese Grand Strategy in the Chinese History* (Princeton, NJ: Princeton University Press, 1995); Andrew Scobell, *China's Use of Military Force: Beyond the Great Wall and the Long March* (New York: Cambridge University Press, 2003).

13. John Tkacik Jr., Joseph Fewsmith, and Maryanne Kivlehan, "Hu's Hu?: Assessing China's Heir Apparent," *Heritage Foundation Lecture No. 739,* April 19, 2002.

14. Data provided in an interview of Mr. Xin Haonian, Director of the Chinese Contemporary History Research Institute in Lin Dan, Xie Longyan, and Chen Xiuwen, "Hu Jintao's New Idea: An Inevitable Sino-U.S. Battle, Part 1," *Epoch Times,* April 19, 2006, http://en.epochtimes.com/news/6-4-19/40567.html. The British Embassy was burned by Red Guards on August 22, 1967, and hundreds of Red Guards attacked and beat then-British Ambassador David Hobson.

15. "Hu Jintao's Speech on NATO Attack," *People's Daily Online,* May 10, 1999, http://english.peopledaily.com.cn/english/199905/10/enc_990510001002_TopNews.html.

16. Jacqueline Newmyer, "Domestic Instability and Chinese Foreign Policy," *Yale Law School Opening Argument,* April 4, 2007.

17. For an insider's assessment of the Clinton Administration's efforts, see Kurt Campbell and Richard Weitz, "The Limits of U.S.-China Military Cooperation: Lesson from 1995–1999," *The Washington Quarterly,* Winter 2005–2006.

18. Former Secretary of Defense Donald Rumsfeld is reported to have complained directly to Hu Jintao about China's lack of reciprocity during Hu's May 2002 visit to the Pentagon; see Kenneth Timmerman, "Rumsfeld Demands China Reciprocity: As Beijing Builds Forces for Attacks against Taiwan, the Pentagon Sends Peter Rodman to Talk Sense to the Hardline Maoist People's Liberation Army," *Insight on the News,* July 15, 2002.

19. U.S. Department of Defense, Office of the Assistant Secretary of Defense (Public Affairs), News Transcript, Presenter: Secretary of Defense Donald H. Rumsfeld, Saturday, June 4, 2005, "Secretary Rumsfeld's Remarks to the International Institute for Strategic Studies." http://usinfo.state.gov/xarchives/display.html?p=washfile-english&y=2005&m=June&x=20050604154832emohkcabhplar0.3478052.

20. "China: Recent Security Developments," Prepared Statement of The Honorable Richard P. Lawless, Deputy Under Secretary of Defense for Asian and Pacific Security Affairs, before the House Armed Services Committee, Wednesday, June 13, 2007.

21. For a review of the history of U.S.-PLA exchanges see Kevin Pollpeter, *U.S.-China Security Management: Assessing the Military-to-Military Relationship* (Washington, DC: RAND, 2004).

22. H. Josef Hebert, "Top Chinese Diplomat Tells US To 'Shut Up' On Arms Spending," *Agence France Presse*, August 17, 2006.

23. David Lague, "A Mystery in Beijing: Who Runs the Military?" *International Herald Tribune*, June 22, 2007, http://www.iht.com/articles/2007/06/22/asia/china.php.

24. "Keating: China Proposed Splitting the Pacific with the US," *East-Asia Intel.com*, August 1, 2007.

25. "China Tells Bush Barred Ship 'Misunderstanding,'" Reuters, November 28, 2007.

26. "China Says U.S. Ship Snub Was No Error," *Taipei Times*, November 30, 2007, p. 1. http://www.taipeitimes.com/News/front/archives/2007/11/30/2003390442.

27. Transcript, Admiral Timothy Keating, Commander, Pacific Command, Press Roundtable, Beijing, January 15, 2008.

28. Ralph D. Sawyer, "Chinese Strategic Power: Myths, Intent and Projections," *Journal of Military and Strategic Studies*, Winter 2006/2007, pp. 4, 5.

Chapter 2

1. "Beijing Displays 'Peace' Troops on 80th Anniversary," *Taipei Times*, August 2, 2007, p. 1.

2. "President Hu: PLA Budget to Rise with Economy," *China Daily*, August 2, 2007.

3. *Xinhua*, August 1, 2007.

4. *Xinhua*, August 2, 2007.

5. Office of the Secretary of Defense, *Annual Report to Congress, Military Power of the People's Republic of China 2007*, p. 25; hereafter referred to as DoD PLA Report 2007.

6. Office of the Secretary of Defense, *Annual Report to Congress, Military Power of the People's Republic of China 2006*, p. 20.

7. Interview with David Shambaugh conducted by Michael Camarda, "Dissecting the Embargo," *ThePolitic.org*, August 28, 2007, http://thepolitic.org/index.php?option=com_content&task=view&id=39&Itemid=39; for a view suggesting that China's announced military spending figures are realistic, see Richard A. Bitzinger, "Is What You See Really What You Get? A Different Take On China's Defense Budget," *RSIS Commentaries*, February 27, 2007, http://www.idss.edu.sg/publications/Perspective/RSIS0142007.pdf.

8. "Pentagon Report 'Interference' In Internal Affairs," *China Daily*, May 29, 2007, http://english.people.com.cn/200705/29/eng20070529_378873.html; "U.S. Report on China's Military Forces 'Ill Motivated,'" *Xinhuanet*, June 1, 2006, http://news.xinhuanet.com/english/2004-06/01/content_1502724.htm; "Pentagon's China Military Report Reflects Cold War Mentality," *Xinhua*, July 21, 2005, http://news.xinhuanet.com/english/2005-07/21/content_3362052.htm; "Chinese FM Refutes Pentagon Report on China's Military Forces," *Xinhua*, June 1, 2004; "China Refutes Pentagon, Insists No Hidden Spending," *Kyodo*, July 25, 2002.

9. DoD PLA Report 2007, p. 26. This Pentagon chart lists estimates from RAND, Stockholm International Peace Research Institute, and the International Institute for Strategic Studies.

10. Estimates for July 2007, Central Intelligence Agency, *World Factbook*, https://www.cia.gov/library/publications/the-world-factbook/geos/ch.html#People.

11. Craig K. Elwell, Marc LaBonte, and Wayne M. Morrison, "Is China a Threat to the U.S. Economy?" *CRS Report for Congress*, updated January 23, 2007, p. 5; China's GDP statistics, like many other Chinese statistics, are viewed skeptically by some. For an estimate that China's economic growth may actually be 4 percent annually, see Lester Thurow, "A Chinese Century? Maybe the Next One," *New York Times*, August 19, 2007.

12. Estimates derived from the analysis and consulting firm Global Insight, cited in Elwell et al., op. cit. This report noted that the Economist Intelligence Unit predicts that China's GDP will not surpass that of the United States until 2018.

13. Mark Clayton, "Does The U.S. Face An Engineering Gap?" *Christian Science Monitor*, December 20, 2005.

14. "China to Become 3rd Largest U.S. Export Market by End of the Year," *Xinhua*, August 23, 2007, http://www.chinadaily.com.cn/china/2007-08/23/content_6037675.htm.

15. U.S. Census Bureau, *Foreign Trade Statistics*, http://www.census.gov/foreign-trade/balance/c5700.html#2006.

16. "Major Foreign Holders of Treasury Securities," http://www.ustreas.gov/tic/mfh.txt.

17. "China Creating Company to Invest $1 Trillion in Reserves," *Associated Press*, March 7, 2007; William Hawkins, "Wake Up Call: Threat from the Chinese Hoard," *U.S. Industry Today, The World of Manufacturing*, August 20, 2007, http://www.usitoday.com.

18. "China Becomes Iran's Largest Trading Partner, Surpassing Japan," *Kyodo*, September 9, 2006.

19. Peter Ford, "China's Middle Classes Entice Businesses," *Christian Science Monitor*, January 2, 2007.

20. William Foreman, "China's Influence Spreads Around the World," *Associated Press*, September 1, 2007.

21. Alice Miller, "Hu Jintao and the PLA Brass," *Hoover Institution PLA Monitor*, Summer 2007, http://media.hoover.org/documents/CLM21AM.pdf.

22. Leah Kimmerly and Johanna Cox, "Evaluating Trends In Central Military Commission Membership," *Jamestown Foundation China Brief*, January 10, 2007.

23. Mao Tse Tung, "Problems of War and Strategy," *Selected Works of Mao Tse Tung*, November 6, 1938, http://www.marxists.org/reference/archive/mao/selected-works/volume-2/mswv2_12.htm.

24. "Article Sees Continuing Hu Jintao-Jiang Zemin Struggle for Power," *Ping Kuo Jih Pao*, July 30, 2007, OSC translation.

25. Mao's use of deception and treachery to achieve his early control over the Party is well described in Jung Chang and Jon Halliday, *Mao: The Unknown Story* (New York: Anchor Books, 2006), Chapters 5 and 6.

26. Dennis J. Blasko, "Always Faithful: The PLA from 1949 to 1989," in David A. Graff and Robin Higham, eds., *A Military History of China* (Boulder, CO: Westview Press, 2002), p. 256.

27. Xiaobing Li, *A History of the Modern Chinese Army* (Lexington: University Press of Kentucky, 2007), p. 243.

28. Wei Jingsheng, "The Fifth Modernization," http://www.echonyc.com/~wei/Fifth.html. Former Red Guard Wei posted his wall poster essay on December 5, 1978.

For this, he was imprisoned until 1997, after which he was allowed to emigrate to the United States.

29. Li, p. 268.

30. In March 2000 President Bill Clinton quipped, "We know how much the Internet has changed America, and we are already an open society. Imagine how much it could change China." See The White House, Office of the Press Secretary, Address by Bill Clinton at Johns Hopkins University, Re: Permanent Normal Trade Relations Status for China, March 8, 2000; for a contrary view see Ethan Gutmann, "Who Lost China's Internet," *The Weekly Standard*, February 25, 2002, http://www.weeklystandard.com/Utilities/printer_preview.asp?idArticle=922.

31. Edward Timperlake and William C. Triplett II, *Red Dragon Rising: Communist China's Military Threat to America* (Washington, DC: Regnery, 2002), p. 45.

32. David Shambaugh, "China's Commander-In-Chief: Jiang Zemin and the PLA," in C. Denison Lane, Mark Weisenbloom, and Diamon Liu, eds., *Chinese Military Modernization* (Washington DC: AEI Press, 1996), p. 234.

33. *Apple Daily* has reported that Jiang's handing the CMC Chair to Hu followed Defense Minister Cao Gangchuan's switch of allegiance to Hu; *Ping Kuo Jih Pao*, op. cit.

34. "Yazhou Zhoukan Views Hu Jintao's Full Control of PLA Following Reshuffling," *Yazhou Zhoukan*, July 15, 2007, OSC translation.

35. This account was drawn from Jung and Halliday, Chapter 52.

36. For more on the impact of the "Lin Biao Incident" on the PLAAF's political reputation, see Jacqueline Newmyer, "China's Airpower Puzzle," *Policy Review*, No. 119, June–July 2003.

37. "Lin Biao Regains His Place in Army History," *Shanghai Daily*, July 17, 2007, http://english.cri.cn/2946/2007/07/17/53@250302.htm.

37. James Mulvenon, "They Protest Too Much (Or Too Little), Methinks: Soldier Protests, Party Control of the Military, and the 'National Army' Debate," *Hoover Institution China Leadership Monitor No. 15*, http://media.hoover.org/documents/clm15_jm.pdf.

38. "DM Affirms PLA Loyalty to Party," *Xinhua*, July 17, 2007.

39. Mulvenon, op. cit.

40. Alfred Chan, "A Young Turk in China's Establishment: The Military Writings of Liu Yazhou," *Jamestown Foundation China Brief*, September 13, 2005.

41. Liu's views are also analyzed by Frank Zhou, "China's Changing Military Ideology," posted on the World Affairs Web page bulletin board, May 3, 2006, http://www.worldaffairsboard.com/world-affairs-board-pub/11791-chinas-changing-military-ideology.html.

42. "Chinese Minister of Defense Arrives Here," *KCNA*, April 6, 2006, http://www.kcna.co.jp/item/2006/200604/news04/05.htm.

43. For an estimate of 65 million deaths, see Stephane Courtois, Nicolas Werth, Jean-Louis Panne, Andrej Paczakowski, Karel Bartosek, and Jean-Louis Margolin, translated by Jonathan Murphy and Mark Kramer, *Black Book of Communism: Crimes, Terror, Repression* (Cambridge, MA: Harvard University Press, 1999); for an estimate of 70 million deaths, see Jung Chang and Jon Halliday, *Mao: The Unknown Story* (New York: Anchor Books, 2006), p. 3; for an explanation of the importance of the latter work see Arthur Waldron, "Mao Lives," *Commentary*, October–November 2005.

44. Li-Fu Chung, "Mao's Dark Side Darker Than Chung Has Shown," *Taipei Times*, October 12, 2006, p. 8.

45. "China Angered by U.S. 'Victims of Communism' Memorial," *Kyodo*, June 14, 2007.

46. Gordon Chang, *The Coming Collapse of China* (New York: Random House, 2001); Arthur Waldron, "The Chinese Sickness," *Commentary*, July/August 2003; Susan Shirk, *China: Fragile Superpower* (New York: Oxford University Press, 2007). Michael Ledeen has written that China may be viewed as the first "successful" fascist state, combining relative economic freedom with hard authoritarian rule, reinforced by expansionist foreign policies and mass propaganda of historic resentment; see his "Beijing Embraces Classical Fascism," *Far Eastern Economic Review*, May 2008, http://www.feer.com/essays/2008/may/beijing-embraces-classical-fascism.

47. *Xinhua*, July 31, 2006.

48. Yingling Liu, "China's Aging Population Puts Pressure on Weak Pension System," *World Watch Institute*, August 15, 2006, http://www.worldwatch.org/node/4425.

49. David Barboza, "A Rare Look at China's Burdened Banks," *New York Times*, November 16, 2006.

50. Elizabeth Economy, "China vs. Earth," *The Nation*, May 7, 2007.

51. He Fan and Qin Donghai, "China's Energy Strategy in the 21st Century," *China and the World Economy*, No. 2, 2006, p. 96.

52. Richard McGregor, "750,000 a Year Killed by Chinese Pollution," *Financial Times*, July 2, 2007.

53. Carin Zissis, "China's Environmental Crisis," *Council on Foreign Relations*, February 9, 2007, http://www.cfr.org/publication/12608/chinas_environment.html?breadcrumb=%2F.

54. Ahmad Lutfi, "Uyghur Separatism and China's Crisis of Credibility in the War on Terror," *Jamestown Foundation China Brief*, February 4, 2004; "China's Islamic Awakening," *Jamestown Foundation China Brief*, May 13, 2004.

55. Richard Spencer, "Monks Reveal Brutal State Crackdown," *Telegraph*, February 19, 2007.

56. "Hundreds Protest in China over Jailed Monk," *Radio Free Asia*, July 31, 2007, http://www.rfa.org/english/news/2007/07/31/tibetan_monk/.

57. Statistics from Shirk, p. 56, drawn from her correspondence with Murray Scott Tanner and from a report by Public Security Minister Zhou Yongkang's report to the 2005 People's Political Consultative Congress, reported in *Reuters*, July 27, 2005.

58. Edward Cody, "Chinese Use Tear Gas on Villagers, Dispute Over Dike Sparks Unrest After 3-Month Lull," *Washington Post*, April 15, 2005, p. A10.

59. "Mobilized by Mobile," *Economist*, June 21, 2007.

60. Christopher Bodeen, "Thousands of Ex-soldiers Riot in China," *Associated Press*, September 11, 2007; "Former Soldiers Riot at China University," *Agence France Presse*, September 14, 2007.

61. Chris Buckley, "China Says Suffers 'Massive' Internet Spy Damage," *Reuters*, September 12, 2007.

62. Arthur Waldron, "How Would Democracy Change China?" *Orbis*, Spring 2004, pp. 255–257; "Democracy, Hu Needs It?" *Economist*, June 28, 2007.

63. Richard Spencer, "China Promises Socialism for 100 Years," *Telegraph*, February 28, 2007, http://www.telegraph.co.uk/news/main.jhtml;jsessionid=JYPVUNRZAHNPJQFIQMFCFF4AVCBQYIV0?xml=/news/2007/02/28/wchina28.xml.

64. In mid-2006, leftists who favor retaining strict Party control produced an eight-DVD series of lectures on the fall of the Communist Party of the Soviet Union that was viewed as critical of Jiang Zemin's "three represents" theory to broaden CCP membership and appeal. But this also sparked vigorous debate from the other side with argument

in favor of greater Party reform, even democratic reform; see "China: Lessons From CPSU Demise Reflect Policy Debate," *Open Source Center Analysis*, July 15, 2007.

65. "China Says Will Allow Nothing to Spoil the Party," *Reuters*, September 6, 2007.

66. "Chinese, Russian Special Forces hold Counter-terrorism Drill," *Agence France Presse*, September 4, 2007.

67. Bill Gertz, "FBI Calls Chinese Espionage 'Substantial,'" *Washington Times*, July 31, 2007.

68. "China's New Spy Chief a Specialist on U.S., Japan and Economic Espionage," *East Asia Intel.com*, September 5, 2007.

69. Nicholas Eftiamides, *Chinese Intelligence Operations*, Annapolis: Naval Institute Press, 1994, pp. 32–37; Steven Engleberg, "Spy for China Found Suffocated in Prison, Apparently a Suicide," *New York Times*, February 22, 1986.

70. Chitra Ragavan, "China Doll," *U.S. News and World Report*, November 2, 2003; U.S. Department of Justice, Office of the Inspector General, *A Review of the FBI's Handling and Oversight of FBI Asset Katrina Leung, Unclassified Summary*, May 2006; Sonya Geis, "FBI Officials Faulted in China Spying Case," *Washington Post*, May 25, 2006, p. A13.

71. Huo Zhongwen and Wang Zongxiao, *Sources and Methods of Obtaining National Defense Science and Technology Intelligence*, reported in Bruce Gilley, "China's Spy Guide," *Far Eastern Economic Review*, December 23, 1999, pp. 14–16.

72. Department of Defense, *Report to Congress Pursuant to the FY2000 National Defense Authorization Act: Annual Report on the Military Power of the People's Republic of China*, p. 36.

73. Ken Timmerman, "China Shops," *American Spectator*, May 1995.

74. Report on the Select Committee on U.S. National Security and Military/Commercial Concerns with the People's Republic of China, Submitted by Mr. Cox of California, Chairman, Part 1, Washington, USGPO, 1999, p. 42.

75. U.S. Department of Justice, "Undercover Investigation Leads to Federal Charges Against Nine Defendants for Illegally Shipping Arms" (Press Release), February 27, 2003, http://www.usdoj.gov/usao/cac/pr2003/036.html.

76. Paul D. Moore, "China's Subtle Spying," *New York Times*, September 2, 1999.

77. Paul D. Moore, "How China Plays the Ethnic Card," *Los Angeles Times*, June 24, 1999.

78. Interagency OPSEC Support Staff, "Section 3, Adversary Foreign Intelligence Operations," *Operations Security Intelligence Threat Handbook*, April 1996, revised May 1996, http://www.fas.org/irp/nsa/ioss/threat96/index.html.

79. Dinner meeting, February 2004. This is also a largely unnoticed example of the asymmetry in U.S.-China relations. It is very unlikely that a U.S. scholar, much less a U.S. government analyst, could know of Hu Jintao's reading list, obtain a post at a Beijing area university to produce classified analysis of China's leadership to be read by American political leaders, and publish critical opinion articles for Chinese newspapers.

80. "How The Communist Regime Uses Chinese Students Associations in Other Countries to Further Beijing's Interests," *Chinascope*, June 19, 2007, http://www.chinascope.org/news/us-china-relations/941.

81. "Chinese Students Running Industrial Spy Network Across Europe: Report," *Agence France Presse*, May 11, 2005; Damien McElroy, "China Aims Spy Network at Trade Secrets in Europe," *Telegraph*, July 3, 2005, http://www.telegraph.co.uk/news/main.jhtml?xml=/news/2005/07/03/wchin03.xml&sSheet=/news/2005/07/03/ixnewstop.html; Tim Luard, "China's Spies Come Out from the Cold," *BBC*, July 22, 2005.

82. Madelina Hubert and Jason Loftus, "Ex-envoy Details Regime's Overseas Scheme," *Epoch Times*, June 7, 2007, http://en.epochtimes.com/news/7-6-7/56236.html.

83. "How the Chinese Communist Regime Uses Student Associations in Other Countries to Further Beijing's Interests," *Chinascope*, June 19, 2007, http://www.chinascope.org/news/us-china-relations/941.

84. According to one report, Chinese students attending a mid-April 2008 counter-rally in Minnesota told of receiving $350 from the "Chinese government" to attend the counter-rally. See Phurbu Thinley, "China Salaries Overseas Chinese for Anti-Tibetan Protests," *Phayul* [Saturday, April 19, 2008 21:25], http://www.phayul.com/news/article.aspx?id=20795&article=China+salaries+overseas+Chinese+for+anti-Tibetan+protests.

85. Bill Gertz, "China Devoted to Weakening 'Enemy' U.S.: defector says," *Washington Times*, June 27, 2005; "Canada: Zhang Jiyan Exposes the Persecution of Falun Gong by the Chinese Embassy in Canada (Photos)," *Clearwisdom.net*, April 5, 2007, http://www.clearwisdom.net/emh/articles/2007/4/5/84242.html.

86. "United States: Falun Gong Practitioners in Houston, Texas, Condemn CCP Violence and Criminal Activities," *Clear Harmony*, February 13, 2006, http://clearharmony.net/articles/200602/31409.html.

87. China maintained unofficial contacts with the Taliban and with Osama bin Laden, in part to gain access to captured U.S. weapons or to modern U.S. weapons retained following their insurgency against the Soviet Union; see "p.c.," "Chinese With the Saudi Shaykh Too: They Are Studying the United States' Weapons," *La Repubblica*, October 11, 2001, p. 11, in *FBIS EUP20011011000048*.

Chapter 3

1. *Jeifangjun Bao*, December 13, 2004, mentioned in "OSC Analysis: China: Debate Suggest Difference over 'Sea Power' Concept," *Open Source Center*, August 9, 2007.

2. "Hu Jintao to Meet Chairmen of Taiwan Businessmen's Associations on 25 December" *Wen Wei Po*, December 23, 2003.

3. Accounts of this pressure, including petitions signed by many PLA officers, were reported in the Hong Kong press in the early 1990s. While noting his inability to verify these reports, John Garver agreed with the general proposition that PLA was placing great pressure on Party leaders to affect foreign policy during this period; see John W. Garver, "The PLA as an Interest Group in Chinese Foreign Policy," in Lane et al., op. cit., Chapter 11.

4. Bates Gill and Martin Kleiber, "China's Space Odyssey: What the Antisatellite Test Reveals about Decision-Making in Beijing," *Foreign Affairs*, May/June 2007.

5. Michael R. Gordon and David S. Cloud, "U.S. Knew of China's Missile Test, but Kept Silent," *International Herald Tribune*, April 23, 2007, http://www.iht.com/articles/2007/04/23/asia/23missile.php.

6. Ashley Tellis, "China's Military Space Strategy," *Survival*, Autumn 2007, pp. 43–44.

7. Mohan Malik, "Multilateralism Shanghaied," *International Assessment and Strategy Center Web Page*, July 14, 2006, http://www.strategycenter.net/research/pubID.115/pub_detail.asp.

8. "Latest Poll Shows Strong Support for Independence," *Taipei Times*, November 29, 2006, p. 1.

9. Jiang Zemin, "Continue to Promote the Reunification of the Motherland," *Web Page of the Foreign Ministry of the People's Republic of China*, January 30, 1995, http://www.fmprc.gov.cn/eng/ljzg/3568/t17784.htm.

10. "Vice Premier Highlights Sacred Mission for All Chinese," *People's Daily*, August 22, 2004, http://english.peopledaily.com.cn/200208/22/eng20020822_101876.shtml.

11. "Independence Means War: Army Paper," *People's Daily*, March 2, 2000.

12. Shirk, p. 187.

13. Ross Munro, "Taiwan: What China Really Wants," *National Review*, October 11, 1999.

14. Peng Guangqian and Yao Youzhi, *The Science of Military Strategy, English Edition* (Beijing: Military Science Publishing House, 2005), pp. 442–443.

15. For background on the new PLAN nuclear ballistic missile submarine and naval base at Sanya, on Hainan Island, see Richard D. Fisher, Jr., "China's Naval Secrets," *The Wall Street Journal*, May 5, 2008, p. 13.

16. Hiroki Fujita, "China's Policy Toward Taiwan To Promote Division on the Island—Hu Jintao's True Intention, Movements Behind KMT Chairman Lien Chang's Planned Visit to China, and When Will Be the Dangerous Year?" *Tokyo Foresight*, May 1, 2005, pp. 40–42, OSC Translation.

17. Number from U.S. Department of State, "Background Notes: Taiwan," 2007, http://commercecan.ic.gc.ca/scdt/bizmap/interface2.nsf/vDownload/BNOTES_0276/$file/BNOTES_0276.TXT.

18. DoD PLA Report, 2005, p. 43.

19. China's use of political and economic pressures is explored in DoD, PLA Report 2005, Chapter 6; Joel Wuthnow, "The Integration of Cooptation and Coercion: China's Taiwan Strategy Since 2001," *East Asia*, Fall 2006, pp. 22–45; author, "Unconventional Options," in Steve Tsang, ed., *If China Attacks Taiwan, Military Strategy, Politics and Economics* (New York; Routledge, 2006).

20. John Negroponte, Deputy Secretary of State, Interview by Naichian Mo, Phoenix TV, August 27, 2007, http://www.state.gov/s/d/2007/91479.htm; Thomas J. Christensen, Deputy Assistant Secretary of State for East Asia, *Speech to the U.S.-Taiwan Business Council, Defense Industry Conference*, September 11, 2007, Annapolis, MD.

21. Clarissa Oon, "China Praises U.S. for Opposing Taiwan Vote," *Straits Times*, August 30, 2007.

22. "Taiwan Has 'Urgent' Need to Buy United States F-16s," *Central News Agency*, September 12, 2006.

23. "China's Hu Asks Bush to Warn Taiwan Away from Dangerous Behavior," *Associated Press*, September 6, 2007.

24. Philip Dine, "Rep. Skelton Foresees Trouble over Taiwan," *St. Louis Post-Dispatch*, September 5, 2007, http://www.stltoday.com/stltoday/news/stories.nsf/washington/story/97ECE96977DBA1EF8625734D000F3695?OpenDocument.

25. Jiang Zemin, "Continue to Promote the Reunification of the Motherland," January 30, 1995, http://www.fmprc.gov.cn/eng/ljzg/3568/t17784.htm.

26. China's record of nuclear and missile proliferation and its impact is reviewed in several recent volumes: Gordon Corea, *Shopping For Bombs, Nuclear Proliferation, Global Insecurity, and the Rise and Fall of the A. Q. Khan Network* (Oxford: Oxford University Press, 2006), pp. 44–46; Gordon Chang, *Nuclear Showdown: North Korea Takes on the World* (New York: Random House, 2005), pp. 124–136; Bill Gertz, *The China Threat, How the People's Republic Targets America* (Washington DC: Regenery, 2000), Chapter 6; Evan S. Mederios and Bates Gill, *Chinese Arms Exports, Policy, Players and Process*, (Carlisle, PA: Strategic Studies Institute, U.S. Army War College, 2000); Edward Timperlake and William C. Triplett II, *Red Dragon Rising: Communist China's Military Threat to America* (Washington DC: Regenery, 1999), Part II.

27. John Mearsheimer, "Why We Will Soon Miss the Cold War," *Atlantic Monthly*, August 1990, pp. 35–50.

28. For more on China's geostrategic motivations for proliferation, see Mohan Malik, "The Proliferation Axia: Beijing-Islamabad-Pyongyang," *Korean Journal of Defense Analysis*, Spring 2003, pp. 77–83; Haesook Chae, "China's Little Korea Secret," *Los Angeles Times*, February 25, 2003; "Why China Is Not Helping Disarm North Korea," *Center for Security Policy Security Forum*, February 25, 2003; Thomas Woodrow, "China Opens Pandora's Nuclear Box," *China Brief*, Volume 2, Issue 24, December 10, 2002, http://china.jamestown.org/pubs/view/cwe_002_024_001.htm; and Justin Bernier, "China's Strategic Proxies," *Orbis*, Fall 2003, pp. 629–643.

29. Prasun K. Sengupta, "Pakistan's Strategic Forces Unraveled," *Tempur*, May 2007.

30. Ibid.; Prasun K. Sengupta, "Dr. Khan's Second Walmart," *Force*, April 2006, pp. 9–11; Rajat Pandit, "Pak Missile Is Made in China," *Times of India*, August 12, 2005.

31. Thomas L. Friedman, "China Stalls Anti-Atom Effort on Korea," *New York Times*, November 15, 1991; Nicholas D. Kristof, "China Opposes U.N. over North Korea," *New York Times*, March 24, 1993; Ann Devroy and Daniel Williams, "China Resists U.N. Resolution on North Korea, U.S. Aides Say," *Washington Post*, March 30, 1994, p. A20; Paul Lewis, "China Shields North Korea on Atom Issue," *New York Times*, March 30, 1994.

32. President Bush, Chinese President Jiang Zemin Discuss Iraq, N. Korea, White House Office of the Press Secretary, October 25, 2002, http://www.whitehouse.gov/news/releases/2002/10/20021025.html.

33. David Sanger, "In North Korea and Pakistan, Deep Roots of Nuclear Barter," *New York Times*, November 24, 2002.

34. Bill Gertz, "China Assists North Korea in Space Launches," *Washington Times*, February 23, 1999, p. 10.

35. Table,"North Korean Missile Imports and Technical Assistance from China, Updated 21 January 21, 2003," *Center For Nonproliferation Studies, Monterey Institute*, http://www.nti.org/db/profiles/dprk/msl/ie/NKM_EichinGO.html.

36. Thomas E. Ricks and Jackie Calmes, "Reports That China Aided North Korea on Missiles Complicates Trade Issues," *Wall Street Journal*, March 15, 1994, p. A3.

37. John R. Bolton, "Pyongyang's Upper Hand," *Wall Street Journal*, August 31, 2007.

38. Michael Sheridan, "A Tale of Two Dictatorships," *Sunday Times*, September 16, 2007, http://www.timesonline.co.uk/tol/news/world/asia/article2452356.ece.

39. "Iran Nuclear Update—2003," *The Risk Report, Wisconsin Project*, September–October 2003, http://www.wisconsinproject.org/countries/iran/nuke2003.htm; Center for Nonproliferation Studies, "China's Nuclear Exports and Assistance to Iran," http://www.nti.org/db/China/niranchr.htm.

40. China's nuclear, missile, and military relationships with Iran is reviewed by this author; see "China's Alliance with Iran Grows Contrary to U.S. Hopes," *International Assessment and Strategy Center Web Page*, May 20, 2006, http://www.strategycenter.net/research/pubID.109/pub_detail.asp.

41. "Iran after Obtaining Maraging Steel to Build Nuclear Bomb Casing," *Reuters*, July 28, 2005; "Iran Took Chinese Beryllium for Nuclear Weapons," *Pravda*, September 1, 2005.

42. Sengupta, "Pakistan's Strategic Forces Unraveled," op. cit.

43. "Visiting Chinese Military Delegation Meets Iran's Army Commander," *Fars News Agency*, August 17, 2005.

44. Bolton, op. cit.

45. The dangers to the world posed by Russia's and China's proliferation are eloquently presented by Gordon G. Chang, "How China and Russia Threaten the World," *Commentary*, June 2007, pp. 24–29.

46. *China's Endeavors for Arms Control, Disarmament and Non-Proliferation*, Information Office of the State Council of the People's Republic of China, Beijing, September 2005, http://english.people.com.cn/whitepaper/arms/arms.html.

47. "China's Proliferation and the Impact of Trade Policy on Defense Industries in the United States and China," Prepared Statement of The Honorable David Sedney, Deputy Assistant Secretary of Defense for East Asian Affairs, testimony before the U.S.-China Economic and Security Review Commission, Thursday, July 12, 2007, p. 2.

48. William R. Hawkins, "Chinese Realpolitik and the Proliferation Security Initiative," *Jamestown Foundation China Brief*, February 1, 2005.

49. James A. Baker III, *The Politics of Diplomacy, Revolution, War and Peace* (New York: G.P. Putnam & Sons, 1995), p. 593.

50. Jim Mann, *About Face* (New York: Alfred A. Knopf, 1999), p. 271.

51. Relayed to this author in a November 2007 conversation.

52. "Project 640: Missile Defense Program," *China Defense Today Web page*, January 26, 2007, http://www.sinodefence.com/army/surfacetoairmissile/missiledefence.asp.

53. Author, "China Increases Its Missile Forces While Opposing Missile Defense," *Heritage Foundation Backgrounder No. 1268*, April 7, 1999, http://www.heritage.org/ Research/MissileDefense/BG1268.cfm.

54. "China Renews Claim over Islet Claimed by South Korea," *AHN*, August 3, 2007.

55. Author conversations with South Korean officials in 1997 and 1998; also see "S Korea Refuses Participation in TMD," *Jane's Defence Weekly*, March 17, 1999, p. 16.

56. "S. Korea Looks to Buy Second-Hand Missiles from Germany," *Agence France Presse*, September 30, 2006.

57. Richard Halloran, "South Korea's President Talks Tough about U.S. Military Presence," *Taipei Times*, March 21, 2005.

58. In 2002, Asian officials began explaining to this author the PLA's intention to build an underground submarine base on Hainan Island. In 2004 a PLA General confirmed to this author that a base was being built, but said it was not an underground base. However, Google Earth satellite imagery made available in late 2005 and early 2006 confirmed that indeed, there was a new *underground* submarine facility at the new base. In 2006 one Asian source estimated the new underground facility might be able to accommodate up eight submarines. For further background see Fisher, "China's Naval Secrets."

59. Renato Cruz De Castro, "China, the Philippines and U.S. Influence in Asia," *American Enterprise Institute Asian Outlook*, July 5, 2007.

60. Communication with this author, April 2007.

61. "China, Thailand Stage Combined Training of Special Troops," *Xinhua*, July 16, 2007; Wendell Minnick, "Military Exercise Warms Up Sino-Thai Relations," *Defense News*, August 8, 2007.

62. Mohan Malik, "Australia, America and Asia," *Pacific Affairs*, Winter 2006–2007, pp. 587–591; "The China Factor in U.S.-Australia Relations," *Jamestown Foundation China Brief*, June 9, 2005.

63. "Australia Weighs Joining U.S. Japan on Missile Defense," *Associated Press*, June 5, 2007.

64. "China Warns Australia on Taiwan Stance," *The Age*, March 8, 2005, http://www.theage.com.au/news/Breaking-News/China-warns-Australia-on-Taiwan-stance/2005/03/08/1110160778362.html.

65. For an examination of the pressures driving Japan and Australia to consider nuclear weapons, see Robyn Lim, "Taking Offense," *The Australian*, October 10, 2006.

66. David Winning, "China's Reliance on Oil Imports Reaches Record," *Wall Street Journal*, August 16, 2007.

67. *Xinhua*, July 3, 2007.

68. BMI Forecasts, *The China Oil and Gas Report*, summary viewed at http://www.wtexecutive.com/cms/content.jsp?id=com.tms.cms.section.Section_ bookstore_chinaoilgas.

69. He and Qin, op. cit.

70. "Demand for Natural Gas on Rise in China," *SinoCast China Business Daily News*, April 25, 2007.

71. Daniel Griswold, "The Competition for World Resources: China's Demand for Commodities," *CATO Speeches and Transcripts*, February 8, 2007, http://www.freetrade. org/node/682.

72. United Nations Commission on Trade and Development, *The Iron Ore Market, 2006–2008*, *May 2007*, http://www.unctad.org/infocomm/Iron/covmar07.htm.

73. Ibid.

74. "Overseas Food Not China's Staple," *Danmex China Business Resource Web page*, April 26, 2007, http://www.danmex.org/spansk/tekst.php?id=393.

75. Interview, Singapore, May 2007.

76. *ITAR-TASS*, August 11, 2007.

77. Author, "Puzzling War Games," *Asian Wall Street Journal*, August 22, 2005; "Peace Mission," *Asian Wall Street Journal*, August 15, 2007.

78. "Malabar 2007: India, United States, Japan, Australia, Singapore Begin Massive 5-Day Naval Exercises," *India-Defence.com*, September 3, 2007, http://www.india-defence. com/reports-3519.

79. "Japanese PM calls for 'Arc of Freedom' Democratic Alliance," *Taipei Times*, August 23, 2007.

Chapter 4

1. *China's National Defense in 2006*, http://news.xinhuanet.com/english/2006-12/ 29/content_5547029_23.htm.

2. "Taiwan President Sees Military Balance with China Slipping," *Associated Press*, February 7, 2007.

3. *Zhongguo Jisuanji Bao (China Infoworld)*, January 4, 2001, in *FBIS, China Information Technology Report #14*, March 23, 2001, CPP20010323000156.

4. Peng Guangqian and Yao Youzhi, eds., *The Science of Military Strategy (Zhanluexue)* (English Edition) (Beijing: Military Science Publishing House, 2005) (Chinese Edition from 2001); Wang Houqing and Zhang Xingye, eds., *The Science of Campaigns (Zhanyixue)* (Beijing, National Defense University Press: 2000); Gao Yubiao, ed., *Textbook of the Science of Joint Campaigns (Lianhe Zhanyi xue jiaocheng)*, (Beijing, Military Science Publishing House: 2001). These texts plus many supporting Chinese sources are assessed in David M. Finkelstein, "Thinking about the PLA's Revolution in Doctrinal Affairs," and Jianxiang Bi, "Joint Operations: Developing a New Paradigm," in James Mulvenon and David Finkelstein, eds., *China's Revolution in Doctrinal Affairs: Emerging Trends In the Operational Art of the People's Liberation Army"* (Alexandria, VA: Center for Naval Analysis and RAND Co. 2005), Chapters 1–2.

5. Office of Naval Intelligence (ONI), *China's Navy 2007* (Washington, DC: Office of Naval Intelligence, March 2007), p. 23.

6. Ibid.

7. Finkelstein, "Thinking about...," op. cit., pp. 11–12; ONI, op cit., pp. 23–34.

8. Office of the Secretary of Defense, *Annual Report to Congress, Military Power of the People's Republic of China 2007*, p. 12, hereafter called "DoD PLA Report 2007."

9. "India and China: Building International Stability," Lt. Gen. Zhang Qinsheng, Deputy Chief of the General Staff, People's Republic of China, Sixth IISS Asian Security Summit Shangri-La Dialogue, Singapore, Saturday, June 2, 2007, http://www.iiss.org.uk/conferences/the-shangri-la-dialogue/plenary-session-speeches-2007/second-plenary-session–lt-gen-zhang-qinshen.

10. DoD PLA Report 2007, pp. 12–13.

11. Peng Guangqian and Yao Youzhi, eds., *The Science of Military Strategy* (English First Edition) (Beijing: Military Science Publishing House, 2005), p. 426.

12. Ibid.

13. DoD PLA Report 2007, p. 13.

14. For a succinct history of recent PLA doctrinal evolution, see Nan Li, "New Developments in PLA's Operational Doctrine and Strategies," in Nan Li, Eric McVadon, and Qinghong Wang, "China's Evolving Military Doctrine," *Issues and Insights, Pacific Forum CSIS*, Vol.6, No.2, December 2006.

15. Zhang Huacheng and Zhang Guochao, "Experimental Joint Training of Army-Air Tactical Corps in Shenyang War Theater Kicks Off," *PLA Daily*, April 19, 2007, http://english.chinamil.com.cn.

16. "PRC: Second Artillery Uses Technology to Strengthen Forces and Missile Strike Capability," *Zhongguo Xinwen She*, August 23, 2007, Open Source Center translation.

17. *China's National Defense, 2006*, op. cit.

18. Ibid.

19. Ibid.

20. *China's National Defense, 2004.*

21. The political and military-cultural inhibitions of Chinese leaders to use airpower are explored in Jacqueline Newmyer, "China's Airpower Puzzle," *Policy Review*, No. 119, June–July 2003.

22. *China's National Defense*, op. cit.

23. Information Office of the State Council of the People's Republic of China, "China's National Defense in 2006," December 2006, Beijing.

24. "Xinhua Overview of White Paper on 'China's National Defense in 2002,'" *Xinhua*, December 9, 2002, in *FBIS CPP20021209000077*.

25. Danny Gittings, "General Zhu Goes Ballistic," *Wall Street Journal*, July 18, 2005.

26. *Ta Kung Pao*, January 20, 2008, relayed in "China Rethinks No-First Use of Nuclear Weapons: Policy 'Not Unlimited, Without Conditions,'" *East-Asia Intel.com*, January 30, 2008.

27. Peng and Yao, op. cit., p. 305.

28. The possibility that the PLA's possession of tactical nuclear warhead armed missiles may signal Beijing does not intend to uphold its "No First Use" policy is also noted by Ta-chen Cheng, "China's Nuclear Command, Control and Operations," *International Relations of the Asia Pacific*, Vol. 7, No. 2, May 2007, pp. 155–178.

29. DoD, PLA Report, 2005.

30. Chinese books examining the military requirements for space power include the following: Bao Zhongxing, *The Initial Design for the Creation of a Space Force* (Beijing: NDU

Press, 1988); Li Daguang, *Space Warfare* (Beijing: Military Science Press, 2001); Jia Junming, *On Space Operations* (Beijing: NDU Press, 2003); and Yuan Zelu, *Space Warfare of the Joint Campaign* (Beijing: NDU Press, 2005). For U.S. reviews of this literature see Michael P. Pillsbury, *An Assessment of China's Anti-Satellite and Space Warfare Program, Policies and Doctrines*, Report submitted to the United States China Economic and Security Review Commission, January 19, 2007; "China's Military Strategy for Space," Statement of Mary C. FitzGerald, Research Fellow, Hudson Institute, before the U.S.-China Economic and Security Review Commission, China's Military Modernization and its Impact on the United States and the Asia-Pacific, March 30, 2007; Kevin Pollpeter, "The Chinese Vision of Military Space Operations," in James Mulvenon and David Finkelstein," *China's Revolution in Doctrinal Affairs* (Alexandria: Center for Naval Analysis and RAND Co., 2005), Chapter 9.

 31. Peng and Yao, op. cit., p. 286.

 32. Larry M. Wortzel, "Will China Construct a Great Wall in Space?" *Defense News*, July 9, 2007.

 33. Interview, November 2004.

 34. Chin Chien-li, "PRC Is Preparing for Form[ing] a Space Force," *Chien Shao*, No. 173, July 1, 2005, pp. 52–55.

 35. Ibid.

Chapter 5

 1. *Xinhua*, July 15, 2000.

 2. "PRC's High Technology Research, Development Plan 863 Discussed," *Guojia Gao Jishu Yanjiu Fazhan Jihua*, January 1, 2000 in *FBIS CPP20000721000161*.

 3. Michael Pillsbury, "China's Aspirations for Assassins' Mace Weapons: A View from Open Sources," National Defense University, October 30, 2001, p. 5.

 4. Michael Pillsbury translated a groundbreaking range of PLA literature on the RMA, which he compiled in an edited volume, *Chinese Views of Future Warfare* (Washington, DC: National Defense University, 1997), and then analyzed in chapter 6 of *China Debates the Future Security Environment* (Washington DC: National Defense University, 2000), pp. 259–304.

 5. General Mi Zhenyu, *China's National Defense Development Concepts* (Beijing: PLA Press, 1988), in Pillsbury, pp. 361–381.

 6. Drawn from Ch'en Huan, "The Third Military Revolution," *Contemporary Military Affairs*, March 11, 1996, in Pillsbury, ed. *Chinese Views of Future Warfare*, pp. 389–398.

 7. Major General Wang Hongguang, Commandant of the Armored Forces Engineering Academy, "Giving Birth to a New Ground Army," *Beijing Guofang*, January 15, 2001, in *FBIS CPP20010306000249*, January 15, 2001.

 8. The following abstracts of articles were viewed on the ILib (www.ilib.com/cn) and VIP (http://www.cqvip.com/) data bases in April and May 2008, indicating possible PLA research for land-based and naval laser weapons: Liu Shu Ying and Shao Yuan Pei, "Tactical Laser Weapons Against Cruise Missiles," *Modern Defense Technology*, No. 1, 2001; Tan Sheng, "High-Energy Laser Weapons Development and Application," *Infrared and Laser Engineering*, No. 3, 2002; Huang Yong and Liu Jie (Institute of Combat Systems, Naval Academy of Armament, Beijing), "Analysis on Kill Mechanism and Characteristics of High Energy Laser Weapon," *Optical and Optoelectronic Technology*, No. 5, 2004; Xu Huizhong, "High Energy Laser Weapons for Anti-Aircraft Defense," *China Aerospace*, No. 9, 2004; Hu Zhi-qiang and Yang Hui (Jiangsu Automation Research Institute of CSIC,

Lianyungang), "Research on a Model of Shipborne Laser Weapon System," *Command, Control and Simulation*, No. 3, 2006; Li Yong ,Wang Min Le, and Zhang Jun (The Second Artillery Engineering College, Xi'an), "Damage Evaluation of High-Energy Laser Weapon on a Ballistic Missile," *Infrared and Laser Engineering*, No. 5, 2006; Wang Hui (China Aerospace Group Third Academy), "Laser Weapons and Cruise Missile Protection Technology," *Electronic Technology Digest*, No. 5, 2006; He You Jin, Li Nan, and Song Li Tong (Navy Engineering College, Yantai), "Aircraft Carrier Laser Weapons Against Incoming Missiles," *Shipboard Electronic Countermeasures*, No. 6, 2006.

9. Annual Report on the Military Power of the People's Republic of China, Report to Congress Pursuant to the FY2000 National Defense Authorization Act, June 2000.

10. DoD PLA Report, 2002, p. 33.

11. See article by Guo Jin of the China Aero Space Chanchun Institute of Optics and Fine Mechanics in *Guangxue Jingmi Gongcheng [Optics and Precision Engineering]*, February 1996, pp. 7–14, in *FBIS–CST–96–015*, February 1, 1996, Internet; Ding Bo, Xi Xue, and Yan Ren, "Beam Energy Weaponry, Powerful Like Thunderbolts and Lightning," *Jeifangjun Bao*, December 25, 1995, p. 7, in *FBIS–CHI–96–039*, February 27, 1996, pp. 22–23.

12. Zhang Yujun, Liu Wenqing, Zhang Xinjia, Zhang Zhaohui, Jiang Geyang, Song Binchao, Zhou Bin, and Wang Fengping, "Lidar High Accuracy Target Tracking," *Hefei Liangzi Dianzi Xuebao (Chinese Journal of Quantum Electronics)*, October 1, 2001, pp. 455–461, in *FBIS CPA20020304000210*, March 4, 2002.

13. Du Zhufeng, Huang Tiexia, and Lu Yimin, "Calculation of Communication Capability in Submarine Laser Communications," *Journal of Huazhong University Science and Technology*, Vol. 25, No. 8, August 1997, pp. 63–65, in *FBIS CHI-98-064*, March 5, 1998; "Calculation of Signal Energy Transmission in Submarine Laser Communications," *Journal of Huazhong University Science and Technology*, Vol. 25, No. 8, August 1997, pp. 66–68, in *FBIS CHI-98-064*, March 5, 1998.

14. Brian Hsu, "Defense Sector Warns of Laser," *Taipei Times*, December 22, 2003, http://www.taipeitimes.com/News/taiwan/archives/2003/12/22/2003084494.

15. "China's Laser Weapon Revelation: Attacks Against Stealth Aircraft and Missiles," *Qianlong.com*, accessed on February 5, 2008, http://bbs.mil.qianlong.com/thread-1287260-1-1.html.

16. Mark A. Stokes, *China's Strategic Modernization: Implications for the United States* (Carlisle, PA: Strategic Studies Institute, U.S. Army War College, 1999), p. 201.

17. Ye Jian, "Armchair Strategy: Using a Bomb to Deal with Aircraft Carrier," *Jiefang Ribao*, February 12, 2000.

18. Stokes, p 201.

19. Ibid.

20. Edward Timperlake and William C. Triplett III, *Red Dragon Rising* (Washington DC: Regnery, 1999), p. 131; evidence of PRC familiarity with HPM weapons technology is seen in Luo Ji, Tian Qingzheng, and Jiang Haozheng, "Analysis and Tests of Non-Lethal Microwave Warhead," *Binggong Xuebao*, May 1, 2001, pp. 173–177, in *FBIS CPP20010829000160*.

21. Lin Zheng, Proceedings of 1996 Conference Sponsored by the Journal *Fire Control & Command and Control*, October 1996, pp. 16–21, in *FBIS-CST-97-012*.

22. Ibid., p. 113.

23. Peng Kai-lei, "PLA Has Developed Heavy-Duty Microwave Weapons in a Bid to Improve Weapons and Equipment of its Airforce," *Wen Wei Po*, October 15, 2002, in *FBIS CPP20021015000055*.

24. For this point the author thanks a friend who attended Dubai's biannual International Defense Exhibition in March 2001.

25. Craig Covault, "Hypersonic Strategy Sets Stage for 'Next Great Step,'" *Aviation Week and Space Technology*, March 26, 2001, p. 28.

26. For a useful overview of U.S. efforts see David Baker, "Global Hyperstrike," *Air International*, October 2001, pp. 208–212.

27. Craig Covault, "China's Scramjet Ambitions," *Aviation Week and Space Technology*, September 3, 2007, p. 29.

28. The following abstracts were listed on the ILib (www.ilib.com/cn) and Wanfang (http://www.wanfangdata.com.cn/) data base during April and May 2008, indicating Chinese research in the area of hypersonic vehicles and hypersonic weapons: Zhao Lifeng, Wang Xun, Liu Xiao Bing Liu and Zhang Shu Zheng, "Performance Simulation and Conceptual Investigation of Turbo Ramjet Engine in Transition Period," *Thermal Engineering Physics*, No. 1, 1999; Zhang Xinyu, "Progress and Development Trends of Air-Breathing Hypersonic Engines," *Mechanical Progress*, No. 3, 2001; Yao Wen Xiu, Lei Mai Fang, Yang Yao Dong, and Wang Fa Min, "An Aerodynamic Research Experiment on a Hypersonic Waverider Vehicle," *Journal of Astronautics*, No. 6, 2002; Luo Shibin, Luo Wen Cai, and Wang Zhenguo, "Analysis of the Sensitivity of Hypersonic Cruise Vehicle Airframe/Propulsion System Integrated Design Parameters," *National Defense Scientific and Technical University Journal*, No. 4, 2003; Zhou Fengqi and Yan Yi, "Variable Centroid Control Scheme over Hypersonic Tactical Missile," *China Science*, No. 6, 2003; Jia Liu, Lei Mai Fang, Tao Wen Xiu, Wang Fa Min, "Stability and Transition of Hypersonic Boundary Layer Flow," *Computational Physics*, No. 1, 2004; Jia Liu, Yao Wen-xiu, Lei Mai Fang, and Wang Fa-min, "Forebody Compressibility Research on a Hypersonic Vehicle," *Applied Mathematics and Mechanics*, No. 4, 2004; Zhang Dong-jun, Wang Yan Kui, Tang Xue Ying, Zhang Dongjun, Wang Yan Kui, and Deng Xue Ying, "Aerodynamic Configuration of Hypersonic Vehicle Based on Waverider Body Design," *Journal of Beijing University of Aeronautics and Astronautics*, No. 2, 2005; Xu Yongqin and Shuo Tang, "Attack-Defense Countermine of Analysis on Hypersonic Weapon," *Guided Bombs and Arrows Journal*, No. 2, 2005; Zhu Yun Ji and Shi Zhong-Ke, "Several Problems of Flight Characteristics and Flight Control for Hypersonic Vehicles," *Flight Mechanics*, No. 3, 2005; Xu Hua-song and Gu Liang-xian, "The Application of Uniform Experimental Design to Configuration Design of Hypersonic Aircraft," *Guided Bombs and Arrows Journal*, No. 2, 2006; Zhu Daming, Chen Min, Tang Hai Long, and Zhang Jin, " 'Over-Under' Concept Hypersonic Turbo-Ramjet Combined Propulsion System," *Journal of Beijing University of Aeronautics and Astronautics*, No. 3, 2006; Li Huifeng, Chen Jindong, and Li Na Ying, "Research on Midcourse Navigation of Hypersonic Cruise Air Vehicles," *Modern Defense Technology*, No. 6, 2006; Xu Hua-song and Gu—, "Nozzle Afterbody Design of Hypersonic Flight Vehicle," *Aviation Dynamics Reported*, No. 2, 2007; Gu Liang-yin, Xu Honglin and Song Jiang Yong, "Study about Hypersonic Cruise Missile Combat Engagement Simulation," *Flight Mechanics*, No. 3, 2007; Author unknown, "A New Concept and Preliminary Study of a Variable Hypersonic Inlet with Fixed Geometry Based on Shockwave Control," *China Science Series E (English)*, No. 5, 2007; Luo Jinling, Xu Min , and Liu Jie, "Research on Lift and Drag Characteristics for the Integrated Configuration of Hypersonic Vehicle," *Journal of Astronautics*, No. 6, 2007.

29. Covault, "China's Scramjet Ambitions," p. 30.

30. *PLA Pictorial*, October, 1997, p. 11. This author was able to briefly observe General Liu's delegation at the 1997 Moscow Air Show.

31. Brochure, "Hypersonic Flying Testbed," Raduga State Machine Building Design Bureau.

32. "Leninets Company and Chinese Government Delegation Sign Agreement to Participate in Creation of Hypersonic Flying Apparatus," *Vedmosti*, April 23, 2001, in *Roy's Russian Aviation Resource*, www.royfc.com/news/apr/2301apr02.html.

33. Nikolai Novichkov, "Russia in the Forefront of Aerospace Technology," *Military Parade*, May–June 1994, pp. 68–71.

34. "Western Intelligence Seeks Proof of Chinese Hypersonic Test Flight," *Air and Cosmos*, February 23, 2007, p. 8, translated by Open Source Center.

35. The photo appeared with an article about a high Chinese Academy of Sciences official visiting a hypersonic propulsion laboratory, viewed on December 12, 2007, http://military.china.com/zh_cn/bbs2/11053806/20071216/14552048.html

36. Bill Sweetman, "Skat-A Preliminary Filleting," *Ares Blog Web Page*, August 23, 2007, http://www.aviationweek.com/aw/blogs/defense/index.jsp?plckController=Blog& plckBlogPage=BlogViewPost&newspaperUserId=27ec4a53-dcc8-42d0-bd3a-01329aef79a7& plckPostId=Blog%3a27ec4a53-dcc8-42d0-bd3a-01329aef79a7Post%3a09d50d0d-b5b6-472d-bae4-0866741109ea&plckScript=blogScript&plckElementId= blogDest.

37. Interviews, Taipei, 2005 and 2006.

38. Andrei Chang, "An Jian UCAV—PLA Air Force 4th Generation Fighter," *Kanwa Defense Review*, August 10, 2007.

39. Guo Fu and Qian Jiang, "The Submarine Robot Searches the Dragon's Palace," *Jiefangjun Bao*, December 7, 1997, in *FBIS*, March 18, 1998.

40. "Deep Sea Robot Created for Use in Mining," *Xinhua*, May 22, 1997, in *FBIS*, FTS19970522000806.

41. Conclusion based on interviews with U.S. and Taiwanese officials.

42. Carolyn Meinel, "For Love of a Gun," *IEEE Spectrum*, July 2007, http://www.spectrum.ieee.org/jul07/5296.

43. Ibid.

44. Ch'en Huan, op. cit., p. 394.

45. Tung Yi, "China to Produce Ultra-Speed Electric Gun Soon," *Sing Tao Jih Pao*, January 15, 2001, p. A32, in *FBIS*, January 19, 2001.

46. Document listing rail-gun tests in China, the United Kingdom, and the United States, imaged in "The Electric Guns on the Mainland," bulletin board post on FYJS, http://www.fyjs.cn/bbs/read.php?tid=126177. Retrieved February 5, 2008.

47. Tung Yi, op. cit.; Space weapon employment of rail guns is also mentioned in "The Electric Guns on the Mainland."

48. Meinel, op. cit.

49. *People's Daily*, June 6, 2005, http://english.people.com.cn/200506/10/eng20050610_189657.html.

50. Zhao Xiangdong, "Put On Military Uniform—Military Applications of Nanotechnology and Impact," *Guofang (National Defense)*, March 2006.

51. Sun Bailin, "Nanotechnology Weapons on the Future Battlefield," *National Defense*, June 15, 1996, in Pillsbury, *Chinese Views of Future Warfare*, p. 416.

52. Xiao Yongli and Zhang Chen, "2mm-Diameter Electromagnetic Motor for Micro-Helicopter," *Beijing Cao Jishu Tongxuan (High Technology Letters)*, April 1, 2001, pp. 79–81, in *FBIS*, CPA20010601000131.

53. Sun, op. cit., p. 417.

54. Wu Dongwan and Ban Dingjun, "Mysterious Military-Application Biotechnologies," *Beijing Kexue Shibao (Science Times)* July 25, 2000, p. 3, translated by *FBIS*, *CPP20000804000134*.

55. Ibid.

56. Cao Benyi, "Future Trends in Stealth Weapons," *Modern Weaponry (COSTIND)*, No. 11 (November 8, 1992), in Pillsbury, *Chinese Views of Future Warfare*, p. 357.

57. David A. Fulghum, "Counterstealth Tackles U.S. Aerial Dominance," *Aviation Week and Space Technology*, Feburary 5, 2001, p. 56.

58. Possible Chinese military-academic literature on China's research into stealth materials, shaping, stealth for engines, and plasma stealth was viewed in abstract form during April and May 2008 on the China National Knowledge Infrastructure and ILib data bases. These articles are listed in note 79 in Chapter 6.

59. Brochure, 23rd Institute.

60. Interview, Moscow Air Show, August 2001.

61. Steven Ashley, "Warpdrive Underwater," *Scientific American*, May 2001, p. 72.

62. Rupert Pengelley, "Grappling for Submarine Supremacy," *Jane's International Defence Review*, July 1996, p. 53.

63. Robert Karniol, "China Buys Shkval Torpedo from Kazakhstan," *Jane's Defence Review*, August 26, 1998. p. 6.

64. Interview, Taipei, December 2001.

65. "Russia, China to Maintain Arms Trade Level," *ITAR-TASS*, December 17, 2003.

66. Robert Thomson, "China Welcomes Soviet Overtures," *Financial Times*, August 14, 1986, p. 1.

67. "China Lays Down Russian Arms, Military-Technical Cooperation Slows, *Kommersant*, May 7, 2007.

68. "New Russian-Chinese Joint Space Projects Outlined," *ITAR-TASS*, August 28, 1999.

69. "Yeltsin, in China, Eager to Expand Military Ties," *Agence France Presse*, December 17, 1992.

70. Veronica Romanenkova, "Russia Ready for Space Cooperation with China," *ITAR-TASS*, May 18, 1995.

71. "New Russian . . . ," op. cit.

72. "'Russian Sources' Comment on Sino-Russian Space Commission," *Agence France Presse*, November 3, 2000, *CPP20001103000109*.

73. "Russia: Official Notes Progress in Space Cooperation with China," *ITAR-TASS*, September 24, 2003, in *FBIS*, *CEP20030924000200*.

74. Anatoly Perminov, Head of the Federal Space Agency, "Russia and China: Good Prospects for Space Cooperation," *Military Parade*, September/October 2006, p. 48.

75. DoD PLA Report, 2002, p. 45.

76. "Chinese Delegation Brings over 100 High-Tech Projects to Russia," *ITAR-TASS*, August 1, 2002, in *FBIS CEP20020801000209*.

77. Ibid.

78. "Russia, China Sign Military Technology Cooperation Protocol for 2004," *ITAR-TASS*, December 17, 2003, in *FBIS CEP20031217000230* .

79. "Analysis of Russia-China Military-Technical Cooperation," *Moskovskiye Novosti*, August 20, 2007, Open Source Center translation.

80. Chin Chung-tien, "Momentum of China-Russia Cooperation in Arms Sales is Hard to Stop," *Ta Kung Pao*, September 13, 2007, OSC Translation.

81. Nikita Petrov, "Russia's Navy Gets Ambitious," *RIA Novosti*, July 31, 2007, http://en.rian.ru/analysis/20070731/70008268.html.

82. "Govt. Commission to View Fifth Generation Air-Defense System," *RIA Novosti*, February 26, 2007, http://en.rian.ru/russia/20070226/61246667.html.

83. "Production of Strategic Bombers Could Resume," *Agentstvo Voyennykh Novostey*, August 21, 2007.

84. Interview, Dubai Air Show, November 2007.

85. "Russian Arms Exports to China in Collapse—Report," *AFX News Ltd*, January 29, 2008; Nikita Petrov, "Russia-China Military Relations at Low Point," *RAI Novosti*, May 27, 2008, http://en.rian.ru/analysis/20080527/108566309.html.

86. *Narodna Armiya*, Kiev, November 21, 2003, Global News Wire—Asia Africa Intelligence Wire, BBC Monitoring International Reports, December 4, 2003.

87. Interview, IDEX, February 2005. "Ukrainian Radar Designer . . . ," op. cit.

88. Prasun K. Sengupta, "Pakistan's Missile Forces Unravelled," *Tempur*, May 2007, pp. 92–94.

89. Jim Krane, "U.S. Aid to Israel Subsidizes a Potent Weapons Exporter," *Associated Press*, June 19, 2002.

90. Douglas Barrie, "Chinese Tonic: The Chinese Air Force is Picking up the Pieces of Israel's Lavi Fighter Programme," *Flight International*, November 9, 1994; Jim Mann, "U.S. Says Israel Gave Combat Jet Plans to China," *Los Angeles Times*, December 28, 1994, p. A1; Charles Bickers and Nick Cook, "Russia, Israel Helping China Build New Fighter," *Jane's Defence Weekly*, November 25, 1995; Andy Chuter, "Israel/Russia Compete to Arm F-10 Fighter," *Flight International*, October 15, 1997, p. 9; David Isenberg, "Israel's role in China's new warplane," *Asia Times*, December 4, 2002.

91. Jim Mann, "US Says Israel Gave Combat Plane Plans to China," *Los Angeles Times*, December 28, 1994, p.A1; Larry Wortzel, "U.S. Commits to Security of Its Allies," *Taipei Times*, March 15, 2001.

92. Robert Hewson, "Chinese J-10 'Benefitted from the Lavi Project,'" *Jane's Defence Weekly*, May 16, 2008; Bill Gertz, "Israel-China Link," *The Washington Times*, May 23, 2008.

93. "Final RFP for Chinese AEW Follow-On Program Expected," *Journal of Electronic Defense Electronics*, April 1, 2000.

94. "IAI Sells Harpy Drones to China," *Flight International*, November 5, 2002, p. 5.

95. Opall, op. cit.

96. Bill Gertz, "CIA Suspects Chinese Firm of Syria Missile Aid," *Washington Times*, July 23, 1996, p. A1.

97. The original story was "Iran Buys Israeli Fighter Jets," *Kommersant*, October 23, 2007, http://en.rian.ru/analysis/20071023/85174001.html, and the author had received confirming reports noted in the author's "Chengdu J-10 Fighters for Iran," International Assessment and Strategy Center Web, October 28, 2007, http://www.strategycenter.net/research/pubID.171/pub_detail.asp.

98. "China Denies Reports It Will Sell Fighter Jets to Iran," *Associated Press*, October 25, 2007.

99. Richard D. Fisher, Jr., "Foreign Arms Acquisition and PLA Modernization," in James R. Lilley and David Shambaugh, eds., *China's Military Faces the Future* (Washington, DC: American Enterprise Institute and M. E. Sharpe, 1999), pp. 92, 113–114.

100. Bert Herman, "Tank Flap Splits Germany Coalition," *Associated Press Online*, October 25, 1999.

101. "Xinhua Carries 'Full Text' of China's EU Policy Paper," *Xinhua*, October 13, 2003, in *FBIS CPP20031013000072.*

102. "Europe's Companies . . ." op. cit.

103. Paul Betts and Justine Lau, "EADS Moves to Boost Ties with China Aerospace," *Financial Times*, October 21, 2003, p. 31.

104. Interview with Astrium official, November 2000.

105. "Latest China-South Africa Military Cooperation," *Kanwa Defense Review*, October 15, 2004, p. 14.

106. Chang, "An Jian UCAV" op. cit.

107. Interview, IDEX 2007.

108. Author, "China's Emerging 5th Generation AAMs," *International Assessment and Strategy Center Web Page*, February 2, 2008; illustrations of the PL-10 copy of the A-Darter first viewed on the CJDBY Web page on January 4, 2008, http://bbs.cjdby.net/viewthread.php?tid=445336&extra=page%3D1.

109. *Jane's Sentinel: China and Northeast Asia, 2002*, p. 121.

110. Jon Grevatt, "China Draws Up Industry Reforms in Bid to Raise Competitiveness," *Jane's Defence Weekly*, July 4, 2007.

111. Accounts of such challenges for the PLA are found in Kenneth W. Allen, "People's Republic of China People's Liberation Army Air Force," *Defense Intelligence Agency*, DIC-1300-445-91, May 1991, p. F-32.

112. Interviews, Zhuhai Air show, November 2002 and Moscow Air Show, August 2003.

113. Ibid.

114. Interview, Zhuhai Air Show, November 2002.

115. "Flow's Avure Technologies Signs Chinese Order," *PRN Newswire*, May 1 2003.

116. United States General Accounting Office, "Export Controls, Sensitive Machine Tool Exports to China," November 1996, pp. 5, 10–13, http://www.gao.gov/archive/1997/ns97004.pdf. China's late models of five-axis machine tools and reports of nine-axis tools can be viewed at "ICAM and Dalian Machine Tools Sign Strategic Marketing Agreement," ICAM Web page, September 7, 2007, http://www.icam.com/news_events/press115.php; and http://www.b2bchinasources.com/China-Manufacturers-58/5-Axis-Machining-Centers.html.

117. "The First Aircraft Institute of AVIC-I Chooses PLM Solutions from IBM and Dassault Systemes for Regional Jet Program; Chinese Aircraft Developer Cites Earlier Success Using PLM Solutions as Reason for Choice of CATIA(R) V5 and ENOVIA(TM) to Design New Commercial Jets," *Market Wire*, October 9, 2003.

118. Huang Tung, "'Xiaolong,' New Model of Chinese-Built Foreign Trade-Oriented Fighter Plane," *Kuang Chiao Ching*, October 16, 2003, pp. 72–73, in *FBIS CPP20031023000106.*

119. "China to Resume Jumbo Aircraft Production," *Xinhua*, March 11, 2006, http://english.people.com.cn/200603/11/eng20060311_249701.htm.

120. "China's Large Aircraft Dream to Come True by 2015: NPC Deputy," *Xinhua*, March 11, 2006, http://english.people.com.cn/200603/10/eng20060310_249535.html.

121. Nicholas Ionides and Leithen Francis, "China Starts Study into 150 Seater," *Flight International*, March 23, 2004.

122. *Xinhua*, December 30, 2007.

123. A good review of the obstacles is in Richard Aboulafia, "China's Jet 'Dream,'" *Wall Street Journal*, June 7, 2007, http://online.wsj.com/article/SB118116404804526904.html?mod=opinion_main_featured_stories_hs.

124. "China Mulls Building Own Large Aircraft," *Iran-Daily*, June 14, 2005, http://www.irandaily.com/1384/2298/html/ieconomy.htm.

125. Michael Mecham, "Staking a Claim in Civil Production," *Aviation Week & Space Technology*, November 4, 2002, p. 59.

126. Interview, Zhuhai Air show, November 2002.

127. Pierre Sparaco, "Chinese Puzzle," *Aviation Week and Space Technology*, April 16, 2007, p. 55.

128. William Dennis, "ARJ21 Looks West," *Aviation Week and Space Technology*, September 29, 2003, pp. 19–20; "Regional Jets," *Flight International*, September 16, 2003, p. 46.

129. Liu Haoting, "Barron's Guide to Airbus' China Plan," *China Daily*, May 16, 2007, http://www.chinadaily.com.cn/cndy/2007-05/16/content_873163.htm; Robert Wall, "Made in China," *Aviation Week and Space Technology*, April 14, 2008, p.64.

130. Liu Hasting, op. cit.

131. Leithen Francis, "AVIC 1 Separates Its Military and Civil Arms," *Flight International*, September 4, 2007, p. 15.

132. Xin Dingding, "Large Aircraft Firm to Be Launched in March," *China Daily*, January 8, 2008; "China Unveils New Jumbo Jet Company," *Agence France Presse*, May 11, 2008.

133. "China's New Jumbo Jet Firm Not Threat to Boeing, Airbus—State Media," *Agence France Presse*, May 12, 2008.

134. "China's Leading Aircraft Maker Sets Up Financial Unit," *People's Daily.com*, April 8, 2007, http://english.people.com.cn/200704/08/eng...408_364738.html.

135. Bruce Stanley, "Chinese Firm May Invest in Airbus Parts Factories," *Wall Street Journal*, June 21, 2007.

136. The following abstracts were viewed on the ILib (www.ilib.con/cn) and the CNKI (http://www.cnki.com.cn/) data bases and may indicate Chinese research in the areas of high-thrust-to-weight-ratio engines with supercruise capability for future fifth-generation fighters: Zhu Li, Zhang Chun, and Chan Tai Kwong (4th Dept.; Beijing University of Aeronautics and Astronautics), "Performance Related Key Technologies and Difficulties for Engines with a Thrust to Weight Ratio of 15," *Air Dynamics Reported*, No. 1, 2001; Jiang Yi Jun (Gas Turbine Establishment of China; Chengdu), "Technical Approaches to Aeroengines with Thrust-Weight Ratio 12~15," *Aviation Dynamics*, No. 2, 2001; Tang Di Yi and Ye Tu Qiu, "Study on Non-Augmented Supersonic Cruise in 4th Generation Engines," *Air Dynamics Reported*, No. 3, 2001; Zhou Lun and Tao Yuan, "The Summarization of Grade 10 Thrust to Weight Ratio Engines," *Shenyang Institute of Aviation Industry Journal*," No. 1, 2003; Wu Xue-hui, Cheng Bang-qin, and Tao Zeng-yuan (The Engineering Institute; Air Force Engineering University Xi'an), "Technical Improvement Scheme Analysis of Thrust-Weight Ratio 10 Aeroengine," *Aviation Dymamics*, No. 1, 2005; Guo Qi, Li Zhao Qiang, and Lu Chuan Yi, "Turbofan Engines for Fourth Generation Fighters," *Gas Turbine Test and Study*, No. 2, 2005.

137. Thrust-to-weight ratio mentioned by retired Major General Xu Guang Yu on Hong Kong Phoenix TV, November 21, 2007, as transcribed on the CJDBY Web Page, http://bbs.cjdby.net/viewthread.php?tid=429227&extra=page%3D1.

138. "Taihang Engine of Innovation, The Development of National Defense Industry Wisdom," *China Aviation Industry Corporation 1 Web Page*, February 21, 2008, http://www.avicone.com/Article_Show.asp?ArticleID=745.

139. Lan Tian, "AVIC-1 Committed to China's Aviation Growth," *China Daily*, October 31, 2006, http://www.chinadaily.com.cn/cndy/2006-10/31/content_720434.htm.

140. Yang Yun Qian, "Major '863' Project, R0110 Heavy Gas Turbine Briefing," China Aviation Industry Corporation 1 Web page, February 27, 2007, http://www.avicone.com/Article_Show.asp?ArticleID=763.

141. Salyut Web page, November 2, 2006, http://www.salut.ru/ViewTopic.php?Id=337; "China to Be Armed with Gas Turbines," *Kommersant*, November 3, 2006.

142. Interview, Singapore Air Show, February 2008.

143. "China Plans to Procure 500 RD-93 Aircraft Engines from Russia," *AVN-Interfax*, April 20, 2005.

144. "WS13 (Taishan)." http://www.fyjs.cn/bbs/read.php?tid=134979, accessed April 5, 2008.

145. "Russia Forbids Export of JF-17 Fighters with RD-33 Engines to Third Parties," *ARMS-TASS*, January 23, 2007; "Chinese Fighter Jets to Reach Pakistan," *Kommersant*, April 24, 2007; "Russian Engines to Fly to Pakistan," *Kommersant*, August 4, 2007.

146. Douglas Barrie and Jason Sherman, "China Seeks British Engine," *Defense News*, July 2-8, 2001, p. 1; "Chinese Speys Being Delivered," *Air Forces Monthly*, August 2004, p. 1.

147. Interview, IMDEX, Singapore, May 2007.

148. "First China-Made 8,530-TEU Container Ship Delivered," *Xinhua*, September 10, 2007, http://en.bcnq.com/china/2007-09/10/content_6093983.htm; "Everything Ship-Shape in Huge Chinese Project," *Xinhua*, May 1, 2007, http://www.china.org.cn/english/news/209827.htm.

149. He Lin, Institute of Noise and Vibration, Naval University of Engineering, Wuhan, "Development of Submarine Acoustic Stealth Technology," *Ship and Science Technology*, Volume 28, Supplement No. 2, 2006, pp. 9–17.

150. "China Develops Stirling AIP Technology for Submarines," *Jane's Navy International*, March 22, 2007.

151. Liang Li Bing, "Heart Give Impetus to Dreams, China Shipbuilding Heavy Industries Group New Application Engine," *Sina.com*, January 31, 2008, http://mil.news.sina.com.cn/p/2008-01-31/0733483714.html.

152. "Laboratory of Fuel Cells," Web page of the Dalian Institute of Chemical Physics, accessed on January 31, 2008, http://www.english.dicp.ac.cn/04rese/08/01.htm.

153. The following articles are indicative of China's effort to develop closed-cycle diesel engines: Huang Hua, Tang Ying, and Li Jian, "AIP Closed Cycle Diesel and Water Management Systems," *Wuhan Shipbuilding*, Vol. 6, No. 6, 1999; Zhang Weidong and Guo-Jun Chen, "Investigation on Simulation of the Performance of Closed-Cycle Diesel Engines," *Chinese Internal Combustion Engine Engineering*, Vol. 22, No. 3, 2001, pp. 6–10; Chen Xin-chuan, Xu Ding-hai, and Ao Chen-yang (all at Navy Equipment Demonstration Research Center, Beijing), "The Simulation of MWMTBD234V8 Diesel Engine Under the Closed Cycle Condition," *Journal of System Simulation*, Vol. 13, No. 2, 2001, pp. 219–243; Guo-Jun Chen (Navy Engineering University, Ships and Power Institute, Hubei Province, Wuhan), Deng Xianqun (South China University of Technology, Institute of Chemical Engineering, Guangdong, Guangzhou), and An Chang (Navy Engineering University, Ships and Power Institute, Hubei Province, Wuhan), "Closed Cycle Diesel Rotating Bed Absorber Gas Pressure Drop Model," *Chemical Engineering*, Vol. 25, No. 4, 2004, pp. 8–12; Lu Yi-qun, Zhang Wen-ping, and Cao Jian (all at Harbin Engineering University, the Institute of Power and Nuclear Engineering, Heilongjiang, Harbin), "PLC-Based Control Systems Closed Cycle Diesel," *Applied Science and Technology*, Vol. 32, No. 10, 2005, pp. 59–61.

154. Zhang Weidong, Zhang Zhen-Shan, and Shen-Gong (all at Navy Engineering University, Hubei Province, Wuhan), "AIP Technology for Unmanned Submarine," *Ship Science and Technology*, Vol. 25, No. 5, 2003, pp. 31–33.

155. "Type 022 *Houbei*," *Jane's Fighting Ships*, Internet edition, February 12, 2008.

156. "Comparison of the Newest Cross-Strait Missile Fast Boats," *Ping-ch'i Chan-shu T'u-chieh (Illustrated Guide for Weapons and Tactics)*, September 2007, in Open Source Center, *CPP20071214103001*.

157. Cheng Gang, Zhang Rijun, and Wu Tianmin, "This Year Is the 80th Anniversary of the Birth of the Chinese Military's Communications Corps, and the Tidal Wave of Military Transformation Has Caused Changes to Occur in the Traditional Battlefield Role of the Communications Corps. Informatized Warfare Has Bestowed upon Them a Whole New Position. Take a Look—'Information Pioneers' Run onto the Future Battlefield," *Jiefangjun Bao*, July 26, 2007, p. 3, OSC translation.

158. Bill Gertz, "China's Military Links Forces to Boost Power," *Washington Times*, March 16, 2000, p. A1.

159. Regional Integrated Electronic System ("Qu Dian")—Project 995," *Sinodefense Web page*, January 27, 2007, http://www.sinodefence.com/electronics/c3i/qudian.asp.

160. Report based on January 5, 2008 CCTV program on digital upgrading of an armored unit, posted on FYJS Web site on January 7, 2008, http://www.fyjs.cn/bbs/read.php?tid=122133.

161. "China Tests Real Time Data System," *Agence France Presse*, September 19, 2007.

162. Briefing distributed by China Aerospace Corporation, November 2006.

163. Office of the Secretary of Defense, *Military Power of the People's Republic of China, 2008*, p. 27.

164. Interviews, Moscow Air Show 2003; Zhuhai Air Show 2002 and 2004.

165. Interview, Zhuhai Air Show 2004.

166. Long Le Hao, "New Progress in Space Technology, New Generation of Carrier Rocket," an article likely written in 2002, available at http://www.esun2000.com/articles/space-tech.pdf.

167. Johnathon Weng, "China expands space reconnaissance power rapidly," *Jane's Defence Weekly*, June 14, 2007.

168. Ibid.

169. Interview, May 2007.

170. The following articles suggesting China's research to develop missile early warning satellites were viewed on the China National Knowledge Infrastructure and ILib data bases in April and May 2008: Yan Zhi Wei, Chen Jing, and Li Han Ling, "A Mission Analysis and Planning Simulation Environment for Space Early Warning System," *Journal of System Simulation*, No. 6, 2004; Zhang Ping, Yin Dong-Yun, Wu Yi, and Tong Li, "The LOS (Line of Sight) Measurement Error Characteristic Research for the Space Early Warning System," *China Space Science and Technology*, No. 6, 2004; Yu Ze, Zhou Yin-ching, Chen Jie, and Li Chun Sheng, "Research on Constellation Design for Space-Based Radar Early Warning System," *Journal of Astronautics*, No. 1, 2006; Shi Lei, Zhang Tao, Li Jun, and Wei An, "Simulation System of Signal/Data Processing for Space Early-Warning," *Computer Simulation*, No. 2, 2006; Guo Gao Bei, Ying Long Wang, and Zeng Hui, "Sensor Scheduling for Missile Early-Warning Satellite Based on Genetic and Simulated Annealing Algorithm," *Electro-Optic and Control*, No. 4, 2006.

171. Estimate of total satellites based on data gathered from the respective Web pages of these companies.

172. One recent report noted that a Western intelligence official had stated that China was made a partner in Galileo in part due to its successful espionage against the navsat program; see Damien McElroy, "China Aims Spy Network at Trade Secrets in Europe," *Telegraph*, July 3, 2005.

173. "China Speeds Up Space Development in Pursuit of Major Power Status," *Agence France Presse*, August 4, 2005.

174. The following journal abstracts were viewed on the Wanfang (http://www.wanfangdata.com.cn/) data base in May 2008, indicating possible Chinese research toward formation flying of small satellites: Chen Gu Cang, Wang Yuan Chin, and Wang Tian Xiang, "Distributed Small Satellite State of Space Radar Measurement Method," *Armament Command Institute of Technology Journal*, No. 8, 2005; Ma Tao, Hao Yun Cai, Ma Jun, and Zhou Sheng Li, "A Survey of Intersatellite Tracking and Sensing Techniques for Formation Flying Spacecraft," *Aerospace Control*, No. 3, 2005, pp. 91–96; Liu Yang, Yi Dong-yun, and Wang Zhengming, "Satellite Formation of the Baseline Study of High-Precision Measurement Method," *Journal of Astronautics*, No. 6, 2007, pp. 1643–1647.

175. Rui C. Barbosa, "China Launches Yaogan-II Satellite, 100th Success," NASA Spaceflight.com Web site, May 25, 2007, http://www.nasaspaceflight.com/content/?cid=5111.

176. China Aerospace Corporation, *China's Space Activities*, obtained at Zhuhai Air Show, November 2002.

177. The following articles indicating research regarding TDRSS satellite signals were viewed in abstract form on the China National Knowledge Infrastructure and ILib data bases in April and May 2008: Xiang Zhong, "Ka-Band Transmit/Receive Channel of TDRSS Ground Station," *Telecomunications Engineering*, No. 4, 2004; Yang Shizhong, Tang Chawowei, Zhang Hian, and Xie Fei, "TDRSS Forward Link and Return Link," *Telecommunications Engineering*, No. 3, 1997.

178. "Merkel's China Visit Marred by Hacking Allegations," *Der Speigel*, August 27, 2007, http://www.spiegel.de/international/world/0,1518,502169,00.html; Richard Spencer and Ben Quinn, "Chinese Hackers 'Raid Whitehall Computers,'" *Telegraph*, September 5, 2007, http://www.telegraph.co.uk/news/main.jhtml?xml=/news/2007/09/05/nhack105.xml; Gregg Keizer, "China Denies Its Military Hacked Pentagon Network," *Computerworld.com*, September 4, 2007, http://www.computerworld.com/action/article.do?command=viewArticleBasic&articleId=9034340&pageNumber=1; "France Latest to Accuse Chinese of Hacking," *Agence France Presse*, September 11, 2007; Patrick Walters, "China's Cyber Raid on Agencies," *Australian*, September 12, 2007, http://www.theaustralian.news.com.au/story/0,25197,22404058-601,00.html.

179. "Beijing Rejects German Accusation of PLA Hacking," *South China Morning Post*, August 27, 2007; Robert Boyles, "China Accused of Hacking into Heart of Merkel Administration," *Times*, August 27, 2007.

180. Shane Harris, "China's Cyber-Militia," *National Journal*, May 31, 2008. http://www.nationaljournal.com/njmagazine/cs_20080531_6948.php.

181. Kevin Coleman, "Cyber Threat Matrix," *DefenseTech.org Web page*, December 12, 2007, http://www.defensetech.org/archives/2007_12.html.

182. Office of the Secretary of Defense, *Annual Report to Congress, Military Power of the People's Republic of China 2006*, p. 36.

183. Major General Wang Pufeng, "The Challenge of Information Warfare," *China Military Science*, Spring 1995, in Michael Pillsbury, ed., *Chinese Views of Future Warfare* (Washington DC: National Defense University, 1997), p. 318.

184. Wei Jincheng, "Information War: A New Form of People's War," *Liberation Army Daily*, June 25, 1996, in Pillsbury, ed., op. cit., p. 411.

185. Lt. Col. Timothy Thomas, U.S. Army, retired, "China's Electronic Strategies," *Military Review*, May/June 2001, www-cgsc.army.mil/milrev/English/MayJun01/thomas.htm.

186. Coleman, op. cit.

187. Yang Liu and Wang Donghua, "Attention Should Be Given to the Information Territory," *People's Liberation Army Daily*, December 3, 2003, http://english.chinamil.com.cn/site2/columns/2004-09/11/content_11935.htm.

188. For an exploration of potential PLA information warfare capabilities, see William C. Triplett II, "Potential Applications of PLA Information Warfare Capabilities to Critical Infrastructures," in Colonel Susan M. Puska, ed., *People's Liberation Army After Next* (Carlisle, PA: U.S. Army War College and the American Enterprise Institute, August 2000), pp. 79–106.

189. Lt. Col. Timothy Thomas, U.S. Army retired, "China's Electronic Strategies," *Military Review*, May/June 2001, www-cgsc.army.mil/milrev/English/MayJun01/thomas.htm.

190. Chuang, op. cit.

191. Estimate of Andrew Yang, Taiwan's Council of Advanced Policy Studies (CAPS), in Glenn Schloss, "Mainland Cyber-soldiers," *South China Morning Post*, March 29, 2001.

192. Lt. Col. Timothy Thomas, U.S. Army retired, "China's Electronic Strategies," *Military Review*, May/June 2001, www-cgsc.army.mil/milrev/English/MayJun01/thomas.htm.

193. James Dunnigan, "China Attacks, No One Notices," *StrategyPage.com*, January 23, 2006, http://www.strategypage.com/htmw/htecm/articles/20060123.aspx.

194. James Dunnigan, "Chinese Cyber War Munitions Factories," *StrategyPage.com*, July 31, 2006, http://www.strategypage.com/htmw/htiw/articles/20060731.aspx.

195. "'Godfather of the Hackers' Reveals North Korea's Frightening Hacking Capabilities—Hacking into the CIA and the Pentagon Standard Fare, Even Breaking into Microsoft's Security System," *Gendai Koria*, May 6, 2006, pp. 20–32.

196. Manuel Cereijo, "Cuba and Information Warfare," http://www.amigospais-guaracabuya.org/oagmc207.php.

197. Ibid.

198. Aura Ang, "Chavez: China to Expand Oil Cooperation," *Associated Press*, August 22, 2006.

199. Frank Tiboni, "The New Trojan War," *FCW.Com*, August 22, 2005, http://www.fcw.com/article90262-08-22-05-Print.

200. Nathan Thornburgh, "Invasion of the Chinese Cyberspies, and the Man Who Tried to Stop Them," *Time*, August 29, 2005; Bradley Graham, "Hackers Attack Via Chinese Web Sites," *Washington Post*, August 25, 2005, p. A1.

201. Peter Warren, "Smash and Grab, the Hi-Tech Way," *Guardian*, January 19, 2006, http://technology.guardian.co.uk/weekly/story/0,,1689093,00.html.

202. "Computer Attacks Common for U.S. Business," *Reuters*, January 20, 2006; Bill Brenner, "FBI says Attacks Succeeding Despite Security Investments," *SecuritySearch.com*, January 11, 2006, http://searchsecurity.techtarget.com/originalContent/0,289142,sid14_gci1157706,00.html.

203. Robyn Wright, "State Dept. Probes Computer Attacks," *Washington Post*, July 12, 2006, p. 6.

204. Bill Gertz and Rowan Scarborough, "NDU Hacked," *Washington Times,* January 12, 2007; "The Secret Cyber War," *StrategyPage.com,* June 19, 2007, http://www.strategypage.com/htmw/htiw/articles/20070619.aspx.

205. Demetri Sevastopulo and Richard McGregor, "Chinese Military Hacked into Pentagon," *Financial Times,* September 3, 2007.

206. "FBI Fears Chinese Hackers and/or Government Agents Have Back Door into US Government & Military Computer Networks," FBI PowerPoint briefing slides, April 21, 2008, http://www.abovetopsecret.com/forum/thread350381/pg1.

207. Quoted in Bill Gertz, "Chinese Information Warfare Threatens Taiwan," *Washington Times,* October 13, 2004.

Chapter 6

1. See Ross H. Munro, "Taiwan: What China Really Wants," *National Review,* October 11, 1999, p. 47–48; Peng Guangqian and Yao Youzhi, eds., *The Science of Military Strategy (Translated Edition)* (Beijing: Military Science Publishing House, 2005), p. 443.

2. The dangers of North Korean disintegration have been a matter of concern for many years. A recent thoughtful analysis of its implications for the United State is in Robert D. Kaplan, "When North Korea Falls," *Atlantic Monthly,* October 2006, http://www.theatlantic.com/doc/200610/kaplan-korea; also see Claudia Rosett, "Let Them Eat Nothing," *New York Sun,* April 25, 2007, http://www.nysun.com/article/53139.

3. Bonnie Glaser, Scott Snyder, and John H. Park, "Keeping an Eye on an Unruly Neighbor, Chinese Views of Economic Reform and Stability in North Korea," *Joint Report of the Center for International Strategic Studies and the U.S. Institute for Peace,* January 3, 2008, pp. 18–20, http://www.usip.org/pubs/working_papers/wp6_china_northkorea.pdf.

4. "North Korea on Slippery Slope to Becoming Chinese Satellite State," *East-Asia Intel.Com,* January 23, 2008.

5. The first report appears to have been made by *Ming Pao* on November 20, 2007, which was then followed by protests, especially in Vietnam; see "Vietnamese Rally over Islands," *Agence France Presse,* December 10, 2007; "Whale and Spratlies," *Economist,* December 13, 2007.

6. "Domestic Stealth Warships and Sovremenniy class warships in attack formation," *Sina.com,* November 19, 2007, http://mil.news.sina.com.cn/p/2007-11-19/1711472447.html; "HK Phoenix TV Views PLA Exercise in Xiamen; US Naval Deployment in Asia," *Hong Kong Feng Huang Wei Shih Chung Wen Tai,* OSC Translation, November 28, 2007, CPP20071129715020.

7. This image appeared on Chinese websites on December 21, 2007, and was also copied by Jeffery Lewis on his blog *Arms Control Wonk* on January 6, 2008, http://www.armscontrolwonk.com/?pg=2.

8. Wu Xing Chen and Jeff Chen, "China's Nuclear Bases and Nuclear Capability," *Kanwa Intelligence Review,* July 20, 2007; these authors estimate the DF-5 inventory at eighteen to twenty-seven.

9. Bill Gertz, "China Tests Ballistic Missile Submarine," *Washington Times,* December 3, 2004, http://www.washtimes.com/national/20041202-115302-2338r.htm.

10. Bill Gertz, "China Expands Sub Fleet," *Washington Times,* March 2, 2007; *Kuang Chaio Ching,* February 15, 2007–March 15, 2007, No. 413, p. 80, translated by Open Source Center, February 16, 2007.

11. The following journal article abstracts indicating Chinese research regarding multiple warheads for ballistic missiles were viewed on the Chinese National Knowledge Infrastructure (CKNI) (http://www.cnki.com.cn/) data base in April and May 2008: Ding Bao-chun and Ye Ming-lan (Beijing Joint Information Technology Institute, Beijing), "An Optimal Controlling Method for Multiple Independently-targeted Reentry Vehicles," *Tactical Missile Technology*, No. 5, 2001; Zhang Yan, Tang Qiangang, Zhang Yi, and Kong Tiequan (Department of Aerospace Technology, National University of Defense Technology, Changsha), "Predicting Collision and Calculating the Nearest Distance During Missile Separation," *Tactical Missile Technology*, No. 4, 2003; Wang Chen and Wang Shi Cheng (The Second Artillery Engineering Academy, Xi'an), "The Estimation of Circular Error Probability of Multiple Independently Targeted Reentry Vehicles," *Journal of Ballistics*, No. 1, 2005; Wang Chen and Wang Shi Cheng (The Second Artillery Engineering Academy, Shanxi, Xi' an), "Analysis and Simulation of Control Stability of Multiple Independently Targeted Reentry Vehicles," *Computer Simulation*, No. 6, 2005. Wei Qiyong(Center of Research and Development, CALT, Beijing), "Influence of Using MIRV on Penetration Capability and System Effectiveness for Land-Based Strategic Missile," *Missiles and Space Vehicles*, No. 3, 2004; Wang Chen and Wang Shi Cheng (The Second Artillery Engineering Academy, Shanxi, Xi' an), "Analysis & Simulation of Control Stability of Multiple Independently Targeted Reentry Vehicles," *Computer Simulation*, No. 6, 2005; Zhang Hong-bo, Zheng Wei, Zhu Long-kui, and Tang Guo-jian (College of Aerospace and Material Engineering, National University of Defense Technology, Changsha), "Analysis of the Effectiveness of Multi-Target Penetration in Ballistic Missile Attack," *Journal of Astronautics*, No. 2, 2007.

12. *Report of the Select Committee on U.S. National Security and Military/Commercial Concerns with the People's Republic of China*, submitted by Mr. Cox of California, Chairman (U.S. Government Printing Office, 1999), Vol. 1, p. 186.

13. Bill Gertz, "China Tests Arms Designed to Fool Defense Systems," *Washington Times*, July 23, 2002, p. A1; Hiroyki Sugiyama, "Japanese Daily: China Tests Multiple Warhead Missile: New Missiles to be Deployed," *Yomiuri Shimbun*, February 7, 2003.

14. DoD PLA Report, p. 28.

15. Interview, May 2007.

16. "China," *Jane's Strategic Weapons Systems*, Internet Edition, posted January 10, 2008.

17. Interview, August 2005.

18. *Kuang Chaio Ching*, op. cit.

19. "China," *Jane's Strategic Weapon Systems*, op. cit.

20. Interview, May 2007.

21. Interview, December 2007.

22. The original article on the 640 Program likely appeared in the October 1999 issue of *Zhongguo Hangtian (China Aerospace)*, and was reported in *Kanwa News*, November 20, 1999. This history has subsequently been copied often on Chinese Web pages, such as under "640 original information" on the FYJS Web Page on July 14, 2006, http://www.fyjs.cn/bbs/read.php?tid=67857&fpage=16; also see "China's 1960s Ballistic Missile Defense Program," http://www.warsky.com/forum/htm_data/18/0803/248401.html; "On-Line Soldiers' 640 Works: The Chinese Exploration of a Missile Defense System," http://www.tianya.cn/techforum/Content/20/430.shtml.

23. Mark Stokes, *China's Strategic Modernization: Implications for the United States* (Carlisle: U.S. Army War College, September 1999), p. 188.

24. "Project 640: Missile Defense Program," *China Defense Today Web page*, January 26, 2007, http://www.sinodefence.com/army/surfacetoairmissile/missiledefence.asp; this illustrated review of the 640 Program was likely based on the original *Hangtian* article. Another brief acknowledgement of China's previous and potential current ABM programs is in "ABM Systems," *Jane's Strategic Weapons Systems*, Internet Edition 2008, January 10, 2008.

25. These academic technical articles indicating China's research into the areas of Anti Ballistic Missile Defense were listed in abstract form on CKNI (http://www.cnki.com.cn/) and ILib (www.ilib.com/cn) in April and May 2008 for the following subject areas: **Kinetic kill vehicles (KKV):** Li Shipeng and Zhang Ping, "Analysis of Solid Propellant Control Thruster Schemes for Small KKV," *Propulsion Technology*, No. 2, 1999; Hu Heng Zhang, Shen Yi, and Li Zhen Ying, "A New Optimal Guidance Law for Anti Ballistic Missile Kinetic-Kill Vehicles," *Engineering and Electronic Technology*, No. 12, 1999; Zhang Hong An and Guo Tong Yan, "Preliminary Discussion on Solid Propellant Kinetic Kill Vehicle," *Solid Rocket Technology*, No. 4, 2002; Song Bao Hua and Tang Shantong (Second System Design Department of the Second Research Academy of CASIC, Beijing), "Trajectory Tracking Guidance Law and Trajectory Simulation of Anti-Ballistic Missile," *Modern Defense Technology*, No. 4, 2005; Zhang Aiyu, "Simulation Modeling Research for Kinetic Kill Vehicle," *Control & Automation*, No. 12, 2005; Yang Rui, Xu Min, and Chen Shilu, "An Approximate But Fast Combined Ignition Algorithm for Attitude Control Thrusters System (ACTS) of Kinetic Interceptor (KI)," *Northwestern University Journal*, No. 1, 2006. **Antisatellite (ASAT) or anti-ballistic missile efforts:** Cheng Feng Zhou, Wan Zi Ming, and Chen Shi Lu (College of Astronautics, Northwestern Polytechnical University, Xi'an), "Terminal Guidance Analysis of Extra-Atmospheric Kinetic-Kill Vehicle," *Flight Dynamics*, No. 1, 2002; two authors unknown, "Error Analysis of Orbit-Transferring Velocity Increment on KKV in Space," *Equipment and Command Technology Academy Journal*, No. 3, 2004; Sun Xing, Wan Zi Ming, and Cheng Chu Zhi, "Energy Required Analysis of Space Intercept Terminal Guidance," *Modern Defense Technology*, No. 6, 2005; Ning Hai Jun and Yu Yun Feng (Institute of Flight Control and Simulation, Northwestern Polytechnical University, Xi'an), "Terminal Guidance Simulation and Analysis of Extra-Atmospheric Terminal-Guidance KKV," *Journal of Projectiles, Rockets, Missiles, and Guidance*, 2005; Zhou Fengqi, Zhou Jun, and Li Ji Xin, "Simulation Analysis of the Influence of the Midcourse Guidance Error on Terminal Maneuverability Requirement of Exo-Atmospheric Kinetic Vehicle," *Guided Missile Journal*, No. 2, 2006; Chen Minghui, Lei Chen, Wu Ruilin, and Zhou Bozhao, "The Design of the Gain Scheduled Robust Attitude Control System of the Endoatmospheric Kinetic Interceptor," *Journal of Astronautics*, No. 3, 2007. **Anti-tactical ballistic missiles (ATBM):** Liu Qing Hong, Chen De Yuan, and Wang Zi Cai (Simulation Center, Harbin Institute of Technology, Harbin; Beijing Institute of Electronic System Engineering, Beijing), "Miss Distance Simulation for Kinetic Kill Vehicle Intercepting Tactical Ballistic Missile," *Acta Simulata Systematica Sinica*, No. 2, 2002; Liu Qing Hong, Chen De Yuan, and Wang Zi Cai (Simulation Center, Harbin Institute of Technology, Harbin; Beijing Institute of Electronic System Engineering, Beijing), "Effect of Seeker Performance on Guidance Accuracy for Using Hit-to-Kill Technology to Intercept Tactical Ballistic Missile," *Acta Simulata Systematica Sinica*, No. 10, 2002; Lian Ke, Wang Hou Jun, and Cao Jian (College of Automation Engineering of University of Electronic Science and Technology of China, Chengdu; Aerospace College of Northwestern Polytechnical University, Xi'an), "Research on Target Orientation Angle Measurement with Wireless Phase

Discrimination Method in Anti-TBM Aimed Warhead," *Journal of Electronic Measurement and Instrument*, No. 1, 2007. **Space- and ground-based early warning:** Yan Zhi Wei, Chen Jing, and Li Han Ling, "A Mission Analysis and Planning Simulation Environment for Space Early Warning System," *Journal of System Simulation*, No. 6, 2004; Zhang Ping, Dong Yi Yun, Wu Yi, and Tong Li, "The LOS (Line of Sight) Measurement Error Characteristic Research for the Space Early Warning System," *China Space Science and Technology*, No. 6, 2004; Yu Ze, Zhou Yin-ching, Chen Jie, and Li Chun Sheng, "Research on Constellation Design for Space-based Radar Early Warning System, *Journal of Astronautics*, No. 1, 2006; Liu Jun Min, Wang Jin, and Wang Yan Jun, "Effectiveness Analysis of Ballistic Missile Early Warning System in Ground Radar," *College of the Air Force Radar Journal*, No. 2, 2006; Shi Lei, Zhang Tao, Li Jun, and Wei An, "Simulation System of Signal/Data Processing for Space Early-Warning," *Computer Simulation*, No.2, 2006; Guo Gao Bei, Ying Long Wang, and Zeng Hui, "Sensor Scheduling for Missile Early-Warning Satellite Based on Genetic and Simulated Annealing Algorithm," *Electro-Optic and Control*, No. 4, 2006.

26. One informal Web data collection is titled "China's Ballistic Missile Defense Leading Research!" posted on the CJDBY Web Page on December 12, 2007, http://bbs.cjdby.net/viewthread.php?tid=386098&extra=page%3D1.

27. Interview, April 2008.

28. Interview, April 2007.

29. DF-3A and DF-21A numbers from *Jane's Strategic Weapon Systems*.

30. Interview, April 2006.

31. See Richard D. Fisher, Jr., "New Chinese Missiles Target the Greater Asian Region." *International Assessment and Strategy Center Web Page*, July 24, 2007, http://www.strategycenter.net/research/pubID.165/pub_detail.asp.

32. For examples of Chinese Web reporting on the "DF-25" see http://zaobao.com/special/newspapers/2007/07/hongkong070715b.html and http://military.china.com/zh_cn/top01/11053250/20070716/14222598.html.

33. "DF-25," *Jane's Strategic Weapon Systems*, June 23, 2006, and "China, Offensive Weapons Chart," *Jane's Strategic Weapon Systems*, March 6, 2007.

34. Max Hirsch, "Wu Slams China's Invasion Plans," *Taipei Times*, November 10, 2006.

35. Pentagon PLA Report, 2008, p. 56.

36. "MND Says PRC Missiles Could Down 20,000 Plus Taiwan Soldiers in Half Day Attack," *Taiwan Central News Agency*, March 29, 2006.

37. "CSS-6 (DF-15/M-9)," *Jane's Strategic Weapon Systems*, May 3, 2006.

38. Bradley Perrett, "Almost 1,000 Missiles Ranged Against Taiwan," *Aviation Week and Space Technology*, January 29, 2007.

39. Pentagon PLA Report, 2008, p. 56.

40. Interview, August 2005.

41. Aliya Samigullina, "Ukraine Armed Iran and China," *Moscow Gazeta.ru*, March 18, 2005; Douglas Barrie, "China Provides Cash for Israeli Cruise Missile," *Flight International*, May 17–23, 1995, p. 5; Peter Finn, "Secret Tapes Suggest China–bin Laden Link, CIA Casts Doubt on Missile Technology Deal," *Washington Post*, October 20, 2001, p. A17.

42. Prasun Sengupta, "Pakistan's Strategic Missile Forces Unveiled," *Tempur*, May 2007, pp. 91–94.

43. Doug Barrie, "Chinese Cruise Missile Portfolio Expands," *Aviation Week and Space Technology*, September 19, 2005, p. 43.

44. Interview, August 2005.

45. See Richard D. Fisher, Jr., "Taiwan Face a More Precise Foe," *Taipei Times*, November 12, 2006.

46. Douglas Barrie, "Power Play," *Aviation Week and Space Technology*, November 6, 2006, p. 26.

47. Andrei Chang, "An Jian UCAV—PLA Air Force 4th Generation Fighter," *Kanwa Defense Review*, August 10, 2007.

48. See author, "China's "New" Bomber," *International Assessment and Strategy Center Web page*, February 7, 2007, http://www.strategycenter.net/research/pubID.146/pub_detail.asp.

49. Image posted on the CJDBY Web page on September 14, 2007.

50. A Tu-16A, which the H-6 copies, can carry twenty-four 100-kg or 250-kg bombs in its internal bomb bay, up to a max payload of 9,000 kg. This analyst estimates an H-6K with more powerful D-30 turbofan engines could easily carry twenty-four 100-kg bombs in its bomb bay and thirty-six more on six wing-mounted bomb racks.

51. DoD PLA Report, 2005, p. 44.

52. "Russia's Rosoboroneksport Preparing 'Several Big-Ticket Contracts' with China," *Interfax-AVN*, December 24, 2006; "Beijing Preparing Major Arms Deal for Su-30MK2 Jet Fighters," *Moscow Times*, December 28, 2004.

53. Andrei Chang, "Development of China-Sukhoi Relations," *Kanwa Defense Review*, December 2006, p. 61.

54. "New Aircraft Radar Installed on Su-27KUB Fighter," *Interfax-AVN*, July 23, 2007.

55. Bill Sweetman, "Wide Angle View," *Ares Blog Web Page*, August 31, 2007, http://www.aviationweek.com/aw/blogs/defense/index.jsp?plckController=Blog&plckScript=blogScript&plckElementId=blogDest&plckBlogPage=BlogViewPost&plckPostId=Blog%3a27ec4a53-dcc8-42d0-bd3a-01329aef79a7Post%3ab967dc21-1763-4f29-802d-a091b5e6495f.

56. Sergey Sokut and Maxim Pyadushkin, "Taking Step-by-Step Approach to Fifth Generation Fighter," *Russia and CIS Observer/Archive*, No. 3/10, September 2005, http://www.ato.ru/eng/cis/archive/10-2005/defense/news1/?PHPSESSID=edd454556414ccd4d6e4151192a256c6.

57. David A. Fulghum, "F/A-22 Secrets Revealed," *Aviation Week and Space Technology*, May 23, 2004; David A. Fulghum and Douglas Barrie, "Directed Energy for Missile Defense," *Aviation Week and Space Technology*, September 4, 2005.

58. After an initial purchase of fifty-four Al-31FNs, the Chinese ordered 100 more in mid-2005, with reports this could grow to 300.

59. John Golan, "Piercing the Dragon's Veil, Sizing-Up China's J-10 Fighter," *Air Combat*, November 2006, p. 25; By comparison *Jane's All the World's Aircraft 2007* credits the J-10 with a maximum 555-km combat radius.

60. Henry Ivanov, "China Working on 'Super-10' Advanced Fighter," *Jane's Defence Weekly*, January 11, 2006.

61. Interview, Dubai Air Show, November 2007.

62. See Richard D. Fisher, Jr., "Xian JH-7A Advances, News Airshow China 2004,"*Air Forces Monthly*, January 2005, p. 21.

63. Yihong Chang, "China Deploys Upgraded JH-7A Fighter Aircraft," *Jane's Defence Weekly*, August 3, 2005, p. 6.

64. Hui Tong, "Q-5E/F," *Chinese Military Aviation Web Page*, http://cnair.top81.cn/q-5_jh-7_h-6.htm.

65. Piotr Butowski, *Russia and CIS Observer*, June 17, 2007.

66. Images of the PL-10 and "PL-13" viewed on the CJDBY Web site on January 4, 2008, http://bbs.cjdby.net/viewthread.php?tid=445336&extra=page%3D1. Other sources note that their designation is the PL-13 and PL-14, see Prasun K. Sengupta, "JF-17 Goes Stealthy," *Tempur*, February 2008, p. 83.

67. These data were included on the original image of the PL-10 made available on January 3, 2008.

68. "Latest China–South Africa Military Cooperation," *Kanwa Defense Review*, October 15, 2004, p. 14.

69. Rob Hewson, "China Hints at New Air-Launched Missiles," *Jane's Defence Weekly*, January 30, 2008.

70. While the exact range of the AIM-9X is a classified number, *Jane's Air Launched Weapons* credits it with a 10-km range. However, one other source notes it has been fired to ranges of 20–22 km by modified F-15C fighters; see Seymour Johnson, "Raytheon Plans Datalink for AIM-9X Sidewinder," *Jane's Missiles and Rockets*, October 2005, p. 14.

71. After over a decade's hiatus, this missile may be benefiting from new development funds from a foreign client. China's interest was indicated recently in Vladimir Karnozov, "The Chinese Line," Voenno-Promyshlennyy Kur'er, July 20, 2005.

72. Piotr Butowski, "Novator Offers a Redesigned KS-172S-1 AAM," *Jane's Missiles and Rockets*, March 1, 2004; Reuben Johnson, "Russia Develops K-100-1 for Su-35," *Jane's Defence Weekly*, July 11, 2007.

73. "After Brahmos, More Collaborations?" An IDC analysis with inputs by Sayan Majumdar, *Indian Defence Consultants*, April 12, 2004.

74. Robert Hewson, "Event Reveals Slowdown in Russian Missile Development," *Jane's Defence Weekly*, September 5, 2007.

75. Interview, May 2007.

76. Interviews, AeroIndia, February 2005 and Moscow Air Show, August 2005.

77. Novator's intention to reveal this new missile was told to this author at the October 2006 Euronavale show.

78. Office of Naval Intelligence, *Worldwide Challenges to Naval Strike Warfare*, February 1997, p. 19.

79. The following Chinese engineering technical articles were listed in abstract form on the ILib (http://www.ilib.com.cn/) data base in April and May 2008 and offer an indication of China's research to develop a fifth-generation (called fourth-generation in China) combat aircraft. These articles are listed in the following categories: **Stealth materials and airframe:** Author unknown, "Application of Technology of Radar Absorbing Coating Materials in Design of Thin Wing of Stealthy Aircraft," *Engineering and Electronic Technology*, No. 6, 2000; Fu, "Electro-Optic Stealthy Technology of Aircraft," *Electro-Optic and Control*, No. 1, 2002; Li Tian, "Fighter Development Requirements for Stealth and Aerodynamic Technology," *Hydrodynamic Experiments and Measurements*, No. 1, 2002; Zhang Wei and Xu Jian Xiang, "Study on Radar Absorbing Properties of Composite Filled with Electric Conductive Fiber," *FRP Composite Material*, No. 4, 2002; Ding Gui Fu and Ying Cao, "Applying Computer Aided Design in Radar Absorbing Materials," *Electronic Technology*, No. 1, 2003; Sang Jian Hua and Zhou, "The Electromagnetic Discontinuities of an Aircraft Surface with the Application of the Radar Absorbing Materials," *Aeronautical Materials Journal*, No. 2, 2003; Haifeng and Li-Ming Yang, "Analysis Of the Stealth Shaping Technology Used in F-117A Stealthy Aircraft," *Photoelectric Technology*, No.1, 2004; Luo Wan Shun Sheng, Yi Jie, and Zhou Yi Fan Zhou,

"Calculation and Experiment of Radar Cross Section (RCS) for Blended Wing Body Aircraft Configuration," *Nanjing University of Aeronautics and Astronautics Journal*, No. 4, 2005; Zhang Zhen Bang, Shen Wei Dong, Song Si Hong, and Cui Fang, "Application of Resin Matrix Composite in Stealth Technique," *Photoelectric Technology*, No. 4, 2005; Author unknown, "Analysis of the Requirements for Structural Corrosion Prevention and Control of the Fourth Generation Fighter," *Environmental Engineering*, No. 3, 2006; Cui Fang, Shen Wei Dong, Zhang Zhen Bang, and Wang Pei Wen, "Research on Methods to Carry Out Multiple Stealth by Electro-Optic Stealthy Coatings," *Infrared*, No. 6, 2006. **Plasma stealth:** Ling Yong Shun, "Plasma Stealth Technology and the Possibility of Applying It to Aeroplanes," *Journal of the Air Force Engineering University (Natural Science)*, No. 2, 2000; Li Shang Sheng and Jiang Yonghua, "Plasma Stealth Technology and a Method of Detection for Anti-Stealth Technology," *Guided Missiles Journal*, No. 4, 2000; He Li Ming and Tang, "Principles and Key Techniques for Aircraft Stealth by Using Plasma," *Mechanical Science and Technology*, No. 1, 2003; Lu Ai Long Lu, Lu Gen Sou, Hou Xin Yu, and Xu Jia Dong, "Effects of Magnetized Plasma Density on Aircraft Stealth," *Shanxi Normal University (Natural Science)*, No. 3, 2005; Kong Yong, Wang Xiao Nian, and Wu Da Wei, "Discussion of Techniques for Plasma Stealth," *Aerospace Electronics Confrontation*, No. 4, 2005; Zuo Hong, He Li Ming, Yu Lan Dan, and Feng Shi," The Plasma Infrared Radiation Stealth of the Turbojet Nozzle," *Guided Missiles Journal*, No. 1, 2006; **Phased array radar:** Jiang Xing Zhou, Wang Yong-Liang, and Tang Zi Yue, "Space-Time Clutter Model and Analysis for Airborne Radar with Conformal Phased Array Antenna," *Engineering and Electronic Technology*, No. 2, 2001; Wang Yan, "Research on Key Technology of DBF [Digital Beam Forming] Phased Array Radar," *Engineering and Electronic Technology*, No. 4, 2001; Tang Zhen Fu, "New Threat in the 21st Century: Airborne Multifunctional Radiofrequency System," *Modern Defense Technology*, No. 5, 2001; Zhang Zhong-hua and Chang Sun Xiao, "Optically Controlled Phased Array Antenna," *Telecommunications Technology*, No. 2, 2004; Meng Shu Qian, "An Overview of Digital Array Radar Development," *Radar Science and Technology*, No. 3, 2004; Yin Ji Kai, "Study on Digital Multi-beam Transmit Antenna," *Radio Engineering*, No. 5, 2005; An Tao, Han Chun-lin, and He Zi-shu, "X-band Optically Controlled Phased Array Radar Rechnology," *Optical Communication Technology*, No. 2, 2006; Tu Zheng Lin and Yan Chun-Hua, "Intelligent Antenna and Adaptive Digital Beam Forming Technology," *Electronic Countermeasure Ships*, No. 5, 2006; Huang Yu Nian (Beijing Institute of Applied Physics and Computational Mathematics, Beijing) and Liu Shu Ying (Beijing Institute of Electronic System Engineering, Beijing), "Active Electronically Scanned Array Radar and High Power Microwave Weapon," *Information and Electronic Engineering*, No.5, 2006. **Avionics:** Tu Ze, Leixun and Hu Rong, "Development of Integrated Avionics Systems of Next Generation," *Avionics Technology*, No. 4, 2001; Cui Jian and Li Zheng, "Next Generation Avionics Optical Data Bus," *Optical Communication Technology*, No. 7, 2005; Bai Lin Jian, Zhang Ping Dong, and Liu Peng, "Conception of Integrated Avionics System of the Fourth Generation Fighter," *Firepower and Command and Control*, No. 5, 2006. **Fifth-generation engines:** Zhu Li, Zhang Chun, and Chan Tai Kwong, "Performance Related Key Technologies and Difficulties for Engines with a Thrust to Weight Ratio of 15," *Air Dynamics Reported*, No. 1, 2001; Jiang Yi Jun, "Technical Approaches for Aero-engines with a Thrust-Weight Ratio 12 to 15," *Air Dynamics Reported*, No. 2, 2001; Tang Di Yi and Ye Tu Qiu, "Study on Non-Augmented Supersonic Cruise in 4th Generation Engines," *Air Dynamics Reported*, No. 3, 2001; Zhou Lun and Tao Yuan, "The Summarization of Grade 10 Thrust to Weight Ratio Engines," *Shenyang Institute of Avi-*

ation Industry Journal, No. 1, 2003; Guo Qi, Li Zhao Qiang, and Lu Chuan Yi, "Turbofan Engines for Fourth Generation Fighters," *Gas Turbine Test and Study,* No. 2, 2005. **Engine thrust vectoring:** Ding Kai Feng, "A Study on the Cooperation Between the Thrust Vectoring Nozzle and the Aeroengine," *Air Dynamics Reported,* No. 1, 2000; Cai Yuan Hu and Qiao Wei Yang, "A Study of Two-Dimensional Thrust Vectoring Nozzle with Secondary Flow Injection," *Air Dynamics Reported,* No. 3, 2001; Lu and Fan Sai Ji, "Real-Time Mathematical Model for a Turbofan Engine with a Thrust-Vectoring Nozzle," *Propulsion Technology,* No. 5, 2001; Gao Yang, Guo Zhi Wei, and Bai Guang Chen, "Elastodynamic Analysis of Axisymmetric Vectoring Exhaust Nozzle," *Aeroengine,* No. 1, 2006; Wang Yu Xin, Wang Yi Ming, and Li Yu Dong, "Load Deformation Compensation of the Axisymmetric Vectoring Exhaust Nozzle," *Air Dynamics Reported,* No. 10, 2007. **Engine stealth:** Wang Yong Sheng and Wen Feng Li, "An Experimental Investigation of Combining Stealth Device in the Air Duct of a Turbofan Engine," *Air Dynamics Reported,* No. 1, 2004; Zhang Dong Mei, Shu Chun Ting, and Hung Sheng Zhao, "A Study of the Application of Infrared Stealthy Technology to an Aircraft Turbofan Engine," *Infrared,* No. 11, 2006; Zhang Bo, Luo Ming, Wei and Xu Cai, "Experimental Investigation of the Infrared Suppressing Characteristics of a Rectangular Nozzle with a Large Aspect Ratio," *Air Dynamics Reported,* No. 12, 2007.

80. See Richard D. Fisher, Jr., "Chengdu News," *Air Forces Monthly,* October 2005, p. 22.

81. Russia is also considering a lower-cost fifth-generation fighter design to complement its larger PAK-FA design; see Alexey Komarov and Douglas Barrie, "A Lighter Contender," *Aviation Week and Space Technology,* January 24, 2005, p. 30.

82. The following article abstracts were viewed on the ILib (http://www.ilib.com.cn/) and CNKI (http://www.cnki.com.cn/) data bases in April and May 2008 and offer an indication regarding China's research toward building unmanned combat aerial vehicles (UCAVs): Yao Zong Xin, "Predicting the Prospect of Applying Adaptive Wing Technology Based on Smart Material and Structure to Uninhabited Combat Air Vehicle (UCAV)," *Aircraft Design,* No. 4, 2001; Xu Yun Feng, "Technology Status and Perspective of UCAV," *Aviation Science and Technology,* No. 5, 2002; Liu Sung and Ming Tong, "Cooperative Attack Action of Multi-UCAV Team," *Flight Mechanics,* No. 2, 2003; Yang Long and Xiao Guang, "A Model Framework of Situation Awareness for Uninhabited Combat Air Vehicle," *Flight Mechanics,* No. 3, 2003; Cao Ju Hong and Gao Xiao Guang (Northwestern Polytechnic University; Xi'an), "Agent-Based Design for Multi-UCAV Intelligent Command and Control Cooperative System," *Firepower and Command and Control,* No. 5, 2003; Fan Yong and Li Wei Min (AFEU Missile Institute, Sanyuan), "Combat Effectiveness Analysis Models Research of Unmanned Combat Aerial Vehicle Based on Probabilistic Method," *Defense Technology,* No. 6, 2003; Gao Xiaoguang, Fu Xiao-Wei, Song Shaomei, "Trajectory Planning for Multiple Uninhabited Combat Air Vehicles," *Systems Engineering Theory and Practice,* No. 5, 2004; Gong Xi Ying and Zhou Zhou (College of Aeronautics, Northwestern Polytechnical University, Xi'an), "Combat Effectiveness of Analysis an Unmanned Combat Air Vehicle," *Flight Mechanics,* No. 3, 2006; Long Tao, Zhu Huayong, and Shen Lin Cheng, "Negotiation-Based Distributed Task Allocation for Cooperative Multiple Unmanned Combat Aerial Vehicles," *Journal of Astronautics,* No. 3, 2006.

83. Chang, "An Jian UCAV . . . ," op. cit.

84. "China's "New" Bomber," op. cit.

85. See Richard D. Fisher, Jr., "New Build H-6s, News, Airshow China 2004," op. cit.

86. Interview, May 2007.

87. In August 2005 Asian sources told this author that Russia and China were in negotiations over the sale of both bombers to the PLA.

88. "Analysis of Russia-China Military-Technical Cooperation," *Moskovskiye Novosti*, August 20, 2007, *Open Source Center* translation.

89. "Putin Decided for a Stealth Bomber Replacement," *Avion News*, January 23, 2008, http://www.avionews.com/index.php?corpo=see_news_home.php&news_id=1084886& pagina_chiamante=index.php.

90. Ed Cody, "China Now Test Flying Homemade AWACS," *Washington Post*, November 13, 2004, p. A19.

91. The original A-50 was delivered from Israel without Phalcon radar in 2001, after U.S. pressure ended the deal in 2000. The second Chinese AWACS modified Il-76 was first reported in early November 2005; see Hui Tong, "KJ-2000," *Chinese Military Aviation*, http://cnair.top81.cn/y-8x_sh-5_a-50i.htm.

92. DoD PLA Report, 2005, p. 32.

93. Lyuba Pronina, "Report: $900M Arms Deal Is Close," *Moscow Times*, August 20, 2004.

94. "Chinese Purchases of Russian Weapons at Saturation Point," *Agence France Presse*, October 13, 2006; *Vedmosti*, October 13, 2006; also see "Almaz Antey Running At Full Capacity," *Kommersant*, August 25, 2007.

95. Duncan Lennox, "SA-10/20 'Grumble' (S-300/S-300PMU/Buk/Favorit/5V55/ 48N6)," *Jane's Strategic Weapon Systems*, Internet version, February 21, 2005.

96. Interview, May 2007.

97. James O'Halloran, "Almaz/Antei S-400 Triumf (Triumph) (SA-20) low-to-high altitude surface to air missile system," *Jane's Land Based Air Defence, Internet edition*, March 14, 2005.

98. Interview, IDEFL, Moscow, August 2006.

99. This is the author's conclusion based on a 2002 converation with a German submarine industry source.

100. Interview, November 2006.

101. Zhang Weidong, Zhang Zhen-Shan, and Shen-Gong (all at Navy Engineering University, Hubei Province, Wuhan), "AIP Technology for Unmanned Submarine," *Ship Science and Technology*, Vol. 25, No. 5, 2003, pp. 31–33.

102. "CIA Report Reviews Weapons Proliferation Trends," http://www.cia.gov/cia/ reports/721_reports/jan_jun2003.htm.

103. DoD PLA Report, July 28, 2003, p. 27, http://www.defenselink.mil/pubs/ 20030730chinaex.pdf .

104. Interview, IDEX, Abu Dhabi, February 2005; it is also possible the new PLAN "Aegis" radar system may have benefited from U.S. Aegis radar system technology stolen by the "Chi Mak" spy ring; see Bill Gertz, "Four Arrests Linked to Chinese Spy Ring," *Washington Times*, November 5, 2005; Greg Hardesty, "Spy Suspects Blended In, The FBI Believes Four In-laws Were Involved in Stealing Information from an Anaheim Defense Contractor to Deliver to China," *Orange County Register*, November 11, 2005.

105. Interview, IMDEX Singapore, May 2007.

106. Doug Barrie, "Chinese Cruise Missile Portfolio Expands," *Aviation Week and Space Technology*, September 19, 2005, p. 43.

107. Ibid.

108. "About Catamaran Type Multi-Purpose Light Frigate," *Shipborne Weapons*, May 2008.

109. DoD PLA Report, 2006, p. 5.

110. Ibid, p. 44.

111. Prasun Sengupta, "China Offers Type 071 LPD to Malaysia," *Tempur,* January 2007.

112. At the May 2007 IDEX show in Singapore, a Chinese source confirmed to this author the existence of the Type 081 LHD program. The construction projection comes from Prasun Sengupta, "China Commences Building a Helicopter Landing Deck," *Force,* November 9, 2006.

113. Interview, Defexpo, New Delhi, January 2008.

114. Interview, Euronavale, Paris, October 2006. A September 2007 Russian report suggested negotiations for purchase may be completed in 2008; see *Interfax-AVN,* September 3, 2007.

115. Number derived from Stephen J. Phillips, editor, *Jane's High Speed Marine Transportation 2003–2004,* (Coulsdon: Jane's Information Group Ltd., 2003).

116. *2006 National Defense Report,* op. cit., p. 65.

117. The potential placement of artillery rockets in the Type 022 to support amphibious landings was suggested by James C. Bussert, "Catamarans Glide Through Chinese Waters," *Signal,* December, 2007, http://www.afcea.org/signal/articles/templates/Signal_Article_Template.asp?articleid=1433&zoneid=222

118. Norinco brochure.

119. Christopher Foss, "Driving Force: Wheeled Armoured Fighting Vehicles," *Jane's Defence Weekly,* September 12, 2007.

120. Christopher Foss, "Large-Caliber 'Super Tank' Being Developed by China," *Jane's Defence Weekly,* April 23, 2003.

121. Vladimir Shavarev, "KBM's Positions on the Global Arms Markets," *Arms Show News, IDELF Official Daily Magazine,* August 2, 2006.

122. Ibid.; Nikolai Novichkov, "KBM Hopes to Largely Expand its Exports to the Indian Market," *Arms Show News, IDELF Official Daily Magazine,* August 3, 2006.

123. Interviews, Defexpo, New Delhi, January 2006 and IDEX, February 2007.

124. Prasun K. Sengupta, "Mi-17 Delivers on the Rise in Southeast Asia," *Tempur,* July 2008, pp. 87–88.

125. Indications of a co-production agreement began appearing on Chinese military-issue Web sites after the 2007 Beijing Airshow, but such reports were downplayed to the author by Russian sources at the November 2007 Dubai Airshow. Nevertheless, such cooperation was reported in "China Starts Producing Mi-17I Helicopters—Paper," *RAI-Novosti,* May 12, 2008, http://en.rian.ru/russia/20080512/107127123.html.

126. Interview, IDELF Moscow, August 2006.

127. Interview, Dubai Airshow, November 2007.

128. Interviews, Zhuhai Air Show, November 2004, and IDEX, February 2005.

129. Interview, Dubai Air Show, November 2007.

130. Agusta officials readily acknowledge "past" support for this program.

131. First revealed in model form at the 2002 Zhuhai show, this Z-11 version first flew in December 2004.

132. *Military Balance 2004–2005.*

133. See Richard D. Fisher, Jr., "International Defense Exhibition Land Forces 2006: Highlighting Growing Russia-China Airborne Troops Cooperation," *International Assessment and Strategy Center Web Page,* October 1, 2006, http://www.strategycenter.net/research/pubID.121/pub_detail.asp.

134. Interview, IDEX, Abu Dhabi, February 2005.

135. DoD PLA Report, p. 24.

136. *Directory of Military Personalities, November 2002.*

137. Richard M. Bennett, *Elite Forces* (London: Virgin Books Ltd., 2003), p. 47.

138. As told to Dennis Blasko, op. cit., p. 13.

139. *Jane's Sentinel: China and Northeast Asia,* 2002, pp. 76–80.

140. Bennett, p. 48.

141. Ibid.

142. DoD PLA Report, 2002, p. 24.

143. Bennett, p. 48.

144. Susan M. Puska, "Rough but Ready Force Projection: An Assessment of Recent PLA Training," in Andrew Scobell and Larry M. Wortzel, eds., *China's Growing Military Power: Perspectives on Security, Ballistic Missiles, and Conventional Capabilities* (Carlisle, PA: Strategic Studies Institute, U.S. Army War College, 2002), p. 242; Glen Schloss, "PLA 'Dragons' Take Their Cue from U.S. Elite," *South China Morning Post,* March 4, 2002.

145. Author interview, June 2001.

146. Schloss, op. cit.

147. "Taiwan Would Have to Fight Alone: NSB," *Central News Agency,* April 26, 2007, http://www.chinapost.com.tw/news/archives/taiwan/2007426/108078.htm.

148. Xu Bodong, "PRC Military Strategic Expert Interviewed on Solution to Taiwan Question," *Ta Kung Pao,* May 13, 2002.

149. Bill Gertz, "China Sub Stalked U.S. Fleet," *Washington Times,* November 13, 2006.

150. Norman Friedman, "Back in the Surveillance Game," *US Naval Institute Proceedings,* January 2007, 90–91.

151. For an insightful overview of China's naval mine warfare effort see Andrew Erickson, Lyle Goldstein, and William Murray, "China's Undersea Sentries," *Undersea Warfare,* Winter 2007, pp. 10–15.

152. Interview, Defexpo, New Delhi, January 2006.

153. These abstracts of journal articles viewed on the CNKI (http://www.cnki.com.cn/) and VIP (http://www.cqvip.com/) data bases in May 2008 offer an indication of China's research toward antiship ballistic missiles: Li Xin-qi, Tan Shou-lin, and Li Hong-xia (The Second Artillery Engineering College, Xi'an), "Precaution Model and Simulation Actualization on Threat of Maneuver Target Group on the Sea," *Intelligence Command and Control Systems and Simulation Technology,* No. 4, 2005; Li Xin-qi; Bi Yi-ming, and Li Hong-xia (The Second Artillery Engineering College, Xi'an), "Movement Forecast Model and Precision Analysis on Maneuvering Targets on the Sea," *Firepower and Command and Control,* No. 4, 2005; Tan Shou-lin, Zhang Da-qiao (both at Second Artillery Engineering College; Xi'an), and Xie Yu (National Defense Science and Technology University, Changsha), "Research on Terminal Homing Guidance of Ballistic Missile Attacking Aircraft Carrier," *Command and Control and Simulation,* No. 5, 2006; Du Wei (Defense Technology Key Laboratory of Electronics, Academy of Equipment Command) and Li Zhi (Information Equipment Architecture Research, Technology, Huairou, Beijing), "Research on the Design of Ballistic Missile Anti Aircraft Carrier Simulation System," *Computer Engineering and Applications,* Vol. 29, 2006.

154. See author, "China's Missile Threat," *Wall Street Journal,* December 30, 1996, p. A12.

155. Tang Wei, Ma Qiang, Zhang Yong, and Li Wei, "A Study On Conic Maneuverability of a Biconic Vehicle with Flaps," *ACTA Aerodynamica Sinica,* March 2006; and "Aerodynamic Design Configuration for Elliptical Cross Section Vehicle with Flaps," *ACTA Aerodynamica Sinica,* June 2006; Chen Hong Bo, Yang Di, "De-Orbit Operations

Study of Reentry Vehicle," *Flight Dynamics*, June 2006; Chen Gang, Zu Min, Wan Zeming, and Chen Sheru, "Maneuver Reentry Trajectory Optimization with Inner State Constraints," *Journal of Solid Motor Rocketry*," Vol. 29, No. 2 (2006); "Pershing II Missile and Warhead Preliminary Analysis," *Missiles and Space Vehicles*, No. 1, 1994.

156. Office of Naval Intelligence, *Worldwide Maritime Challenges*, 2004, p. 22.

157. Ibid.

158. Author interviews.

159. Interview, Singapore, October 2004.

160. "Qi Faren: Anti-Satellite Technology Can Be Used to Attack Aircraft Carrier," *Ming Pao*, March 26, 2007, OSC Translation, March 26, 2007.

161. These abstract journal articles viewed on the ILib (http://www.ilib.com.cn/) data base in April and May 2008 indicate China's research in developing combat Sky Wave over-the-horizon radar: Su Wei Min and Ni Jin Lin, "Guo Development of Sky Wave Over-the-Horizon Radar," *Aviation Journal*, No. 6, 2002; Guo Xin and Ni Jin Lin, "Ship Detection with Sky Wave Over-the-Horizon Radar with Short Coherent Integration Time," *Electronics and Information Journal*, No. 4, 2004; Kong Yong, Meng Xiangzhong, Wang Zhi, and Qu Yongqing, "Combat Efficiency Evaluation for Sky Wave Over-the-Horizon Radar Based on ADC Modeling," *Fire Control Radar Technology*, No. 3, 2005; Kong Yong, Wang Xiao Nian, Dai Cai Bin, and Wang Zhi, "A Model for Evaluating Sky Wave Over-the-Horizon Radar Combat Efficiency," *Equipment Command Institute of Technology Journal*, No. 1, 2006; Liang Yi and Wang Zhong, "Refraction Effect in Troposphere on OTH Radar Signal," *Chengdu Institute of Information Engineering Journal*, No. 1, 2007.

Chapter 7

1. Office of the Secretary of Defense, *Annual Report to Congress: The Military Power of the People's Republic of China 2005*, pp. 12–13.

2. David Shambaugh, "China Engages Asia: Reshaping the Regional Order," *International Security*, Winter, 2004–2005, p. 85; Michael D. Swaine, "China's Regional Military Posture," in David Shambaugh, ed., *Power Shift, China and Asia's New Dynamics* (Berkeley: University of California Press, 2005), pp. 270–273; *Chinese Military Power*, Report of an Independent Task Force sponsored by the Council on Foreign Relations, Maurice R. Greenberg Center for Geoeconomic Studies (Harold Brown, Chair; Joseph W. Prueher, Vice Chair; Adam Segal, Vice Chair) (New York: Council on Foreign Relations, 2003), pg. 36.

3. Philip Bowring, "The Spirit of Zheng He," *International Herald Tribune*, August 5, 2005.

4. Edward Dreyer, *Zheng He: China and the Oceans in the Early Ming Dynasty, 1405–1433* (New York: Pearson Longman, 2006), p. 163.

5. *Jeifangjun Bao*, December 13, 2004, mentioned in "OSC Analysis: China: Debate Suggest Difference Over 'Sea Power' Concept," *Open Source Center*, August 9, 2007.

6. "Interview with Lt. General Liu Yazhou of the Air Force of the People's Liberation Army," *Eurasian Review of Geopolitics*, January 2005.

7. Tao Shelan, "Military Expert: In China's Peaceful Development It Is Necessary to Uphold the Dialectical Strategic Thinking of Making the Country Rich and Building Up Its Military Strength," *Zhongguo Xinwen She*, May 16, 2006.

8. This debate among Chinese government analysts responsible for advising Chinese leaders on determinations of "Comprehensive National Power" is revealed and reviewed

in Michael Pillsbury, *China Debates the Future Security Environment* (Washington DC: National Defense University Press, 2000).

9. *People's Daily*, December 27, 2006; David Lague, "China Airs Ambition to Beef Up Naval Power," *International Herald Tribune*, December 28, 2006; Mark Magnier and Mitchell Landsberg, "Chinese Focus on Navy Leaves Big Political Wake," *Los Angeles Times*, December 31, 2006.

10. *Xinhua*, December 27, 2006.

11. Cited in OSC Analysis, op. cit.

12. Zhang Wenmu, Center for Strategic Studies at the Beijing University of Aeronautics and Astronautics, quoted from *Huanqiu Shibao*, January 12, 2007, cited in OSC Analysis, op. cit.

13. Zhan Huayun, "The Impact and Inspiration of the Maritime Security Environment on Strategy," *Modern Navy*, August 2007, OSC translation.

14. Ibid.

15. OSC Analysis, op. cit.

16. *Xinhua*, July 30, 2007.

17. Ibid.

18. *Interfax-AVN*, July 30, 2007.

19. "Pilots Show Their Skills in Russia," *Zhongguo Xinwen She*, August 14, 2007.

20. "Russian TV Offers Insight into Peace Mission Military Drill," *Rossiya TV*, August 25, 2007, OSC Translation.

21. Vladislav Tyumenev, "Lessons From Rosboronexport," *Expert Online*, December 3, 2007, http://eng.expert.ru/printissues/expert/2007/45/goskorporacii/; Dimitry Kozlov, "Ul'yanovsk Aircraft Plant to Produce Basic Il-76 Models," *AviaPort.RU*, April 1, 2008.

22. Reports about final numbers of Il-76/78s vary. See "China Buys 38 Military Transport Aircraft From Russia for $850M," *MosNews*, September 8, 2005, http://www.mosnews.com/money/2005/09/08/chinabuysaircraft.shtml; Dimitry Kozolov, *AviaPort Ru*, December 12, 2005, http://www.royfc.com/cgfi-bin/today/acft_news.cgi. The 2006 Department of Defense PLA Report notes that "40" will be purchased.

23. *Interfax-AVN*, June 21, 2007; "Ilyushin Co. to Construct Aircraft for China," *Kommersant*, December 27, 2006.

24. "Russia May Not Profit from Il-76 Deliveries to China," *Kommersant*, May 14, 2007.

25. "Il-76 Issue Effects Russia-China Military Cooperation," *Kanwa Asia Defence Monthly*, September 2007, p. 11.

26. Frederick A. Johnsen, *Lockheed C-141 Starlifter, Warbird Tech Series*, Vol. 39, (North Branch, MN: Specialty Press, 2005), pp. 6–9..

27. "Upgraded C-5M Debut," *Flight International*, May 23–29, 2006, p. 4.

28. *Interfax-Ukraine*, September 4, 2002.

29. Interview, Defexpo, New Delhi, January 2006.

30. Robert Hewson, "All-Chinese Special Missions Platform Makes Appearance," *Jane's Defence Weekly*, December 14, 2005.

31. Interview, IDEX, Abu Dhabi, February 2007.

32. Ibid; for a later report on the AVIC-1 proposal, see Jonathan Weng, "China Details Heavy Transport Plan," *Jane's Defence Weekly*, August 22, 2007.

33. Communication with author, February 26, 2007.

34. Interview, Defexpo, New Delhi, January 2006.

35. Robert Sae-Liu, "China Approaches Ukraine for Heavylift Aircraft," *Jane's Defence Weekly*, September 29, 2004.

36. Andrew Doyle, "Volga-Dnepr Calls for Resumed Antonov An-124 Production Ahead of its 2007 IPO," *Flight International,* April 11, 2006; Vladimir Karnozov, "Companies Unite to Study Ruslan Production Restart," *Flight International,* March 9, 2004.

37. Interview, IDEX, Abu Dhabi, February 2007.

38. "An-124-300 Proposal Could Double Ruslan Range," *Flight International,* July 1, 2003.

39. Interview, Dubai Air Show, November 2007.

40. Andrew S. Erickson and Andrew R. Wilson, "China's Aircraft Carrier Dilemma," *Naval War College Review,* Autumn 2006, http://www.nwc.navy.mil/PRESS/REVIEW/2006/autumn/art1-a06.htm.

41. "Report: China Plans to Build Carrier," *Associated Press,* March 10, 2006.

42. Chua Chin Hon, "First, China Unveils This Fighter Jet . . . Now, It Says It Can Build an Aircraft Carrier, Military News Barrage Comes Ahead of Japan, US Talks on Taiwan," *Straits Times,* January 10, 2007.

43. "Building of Aircraft Carrier Owed to Strategic Needs," *People's Daily Online,* April 25, 2007, http://english.peopledaily.com.cn/200704/25/eng20070425_369725.html.

44. Al Pessin, "US Commander Calls China's Interest in Aircraft Carriers Understandable," *VOA News,* May 12, 2007, http://voanews.com/english/archive/2007-05/2007-05-12. voa5.cfm?CFID5169304599&CFTOKEN543041392.

45. Jeff Chen and A. Buistlov, "China Building Aircraft Carrier, Purchasing Sub-System from Russia," *Kanwa Intelligence Review,* July 24, 2007.

46. Liu Huaqing, *The Memoirs of Liu Huaqing* (Beijing: People's Liberation Army, 2004), chapter 17, *FBIS CPP20060707320001001.*

47. Ibid.

48. Ibid.

49. Bruce Gilley, "Flying Start," *Far Eastern Economic Review,* March 11, 1999, p. 24.

50. Nayan Chanda, "No Cash Carrier," *Far Eastern Economic Review,* October 10, 1996, p. 20.

51. Ibid.

52. Christie Manbar (as transliterated), France, translated and edited by Dan Jie, [China's Early Stage Conception of Aircraft Carrier(s)], *Shipborne Weapons,* July 2005, pp. 18–21, cited in Erickson and Wilson, op. cit.

53. Ji Mingzhou, "I Set Sail with the 'Charles de Gaulle,'" *Naval & Merchant Ships,* November 2005, pp. 18–22, cited in Erickson and Wilson, op. cit.

54. Nikita Petrov, "Russia's Navy Gets Ambitious," *RIA Novosti,* July 31, 2007, http://en.rian.ru/analysis/20070731/70008268.html.

55. In their expansive academic review of the carrier issue, Ian Storey and You Ji concluded, "[N]o firm evidence exists that China intends to refurbish, build or buy an aircraft carrier. The prospect of a Chinese carrier remains subject to a great deal of rumor and speculation." See their "China's Aircraft Carrier Ambitions, Seeking Truth from Rumors," *Naval War College Review,* Winter 2004, p. 77.

56. See Bernard D. Cole, *The Great Wall and the Sea, China's Navy Enters the Twenty-First Century* (Annapolis MD: Naval Institute Press, 2001), p. 148.

57. "Suspicion Over Tight Security Around 'Casino' Aircraft Carrier in China," *Agence France Presse,* May 12, 2002.

58. "Building Aircraft Carrier in Shanghai Denied," *Xinhuanet,* June 16, 2005.

59. Report to Congress Pursuant to the FY2000 National Defense Authorization Act, Annual Report on the Military Power of the People's Republic of China, July 28, 2003, p. 25, http://www.defenselink.mil/pubs/20030730chinaex.pdf.

60. Images of this model were viewed and downloaded by the author in August 2003.

61. Yihong Chang and Andrew Koch, "Is China Building A Carrier?" *Jane's Defence Review*, August 11, 2005.

62. Ibid; author interview with Asian military sources, November 2005.

63. Jeff Chen and A. Buistlov, "China Preparing Aircraft Carrier," *Kanwa Asian Defence Monthly*, September 2007, p. 17.

64. These articles indicating Chinese research on aircraft carrier technologies were listed on the ILib (http://www.ilib.com.cn/) Chinese academic research data base as of April 2008: **Automatic carrier landing:** Gao Qing Wei,Guo-Rong Zhao, and Liu Tao, "Carrier-Based Aircraft Integrated Electronic Display and Automatic Landing Guidance System Simulation,"*Journal of the Navy Aeronautical Engineering Institute*, No. 4, 2005; Dai Shi Jun, Yang Yi Dong, Yu Yong, Shi-jun, and Yu Yong, "Thrust Integrated Control Using H_∞ Syntheses in Automatic Carrier Landing System," *Journal of Nanjing University of Aeronautics and Astronautics*, No. 1, 2002; Cao Dong, Yang Yi-dong, Yu Yong, and Fan Yan-ming, "Automatic Carrier Landing System with Gust-Rejection Capability," *Harbin Industry University Journal*, No. 2, 2004; Guo Dong and Lin Yan, "Reduced-Order H_∞ Controller Design of a Longitudinal Automatic Carrier Landing System," *Information and Electronic Engineering*, No. 5, 2006. **Carrier aircraft arresting issues:** Hu Meng, "Arresting Dynamics Research of Carrier Aircraft," *Journal of the Air Force Engineering University*, No. 5, 2000; Zhou Hao, Zhang Zhi Wei, Song Jin Chun, Cao Chu Hua, "Arresting Performances Simulation Research on Aircraft Arresting System," *Aviation Technology*, No. 3, 2002; Sheng Xian Ho, Cao Chu Hua, Zhang Zhi Wei, and Song Jin Chun, "Hydraulic System Design and Performance Simulation of Aircraft Arresting System," *Northeastern University Journal*, No. 10, 2002; Song Jin Chun, Zhang Zhi Wei, Zhang Fu Bei, Song Jin Chun, and Wang Yan, "Study on the Electro-Hydraulic Proportional Controlled Aircraft Arresting System," *Aviation Journal*, No. 4, 2005. **Deck motion issues:** Yu Yong Yang, "Deck Motion Prediction Technique Based on Kalman Filtering Theory," *Data Acquisition and Processing*, No. 4, 2002; Shi Ming, Qu Xiang, Ju Qu, and Wang Meng Hui, "The Influence and Compensation of Deck Motion in Carrier Landing Approach," *Flight Mechanics*, No. 1, 2006. **Carrier landing control issues:** Zhang Yong and Zhang Dong Kwong, "Precision Flight Path Control for Carrier Based Aircraft Landing Approaches," *Aircraft Design*, No. 1, 2006; Yang One, Shi Jun, Yu Yong, and Fan Yan Ming, "The Control Scheme for Resisting Air Wake Disturbance for Carrier Landing," *Journal of the Navy Aeronautical Engineering Institute*, No. 1, 2003; "Precision Flight Path Control in Carrier Landing Approach," *Flight Mechanics*, No. 1, 2000. **Special features of carrier aircraft:** Li Xing and Wang Xiao Hui, "Overview of Three-Proof Design on Carrier-Based Aircraft," *Environmental Engineering*, No. 4, 2006; Wang Qian Sheng, "Critical Technologies in Carrier-Based Aircraft Design and Development," *Aircraft Design*, No. 2, 2005; Peng You Mei, "Technical Features for Ship-board Aircraft Engine," *Gas Turbine Test and Study*, No. 2, 2005. **Carrier deck coatings:** Zheng Dong Jin, "Development and Progress in Nonskid Coatings for Aircraft Carrier Decks," *Ship Science and Technology*, No. 5, 2003.

65. See Richard D. Fisher, Jr., "2005: A Turning Point for China's Carrier Ambitions," *International Assessment and Strategy Center Web page*, January 8, 2006, http://www.strategycenter.net/research/pubID.87/pub_detail.asp.

66. "Chinese Interest in Su-33," http://www.redorbit.com/news/technology/294831/russian_industry_shows_its_stuff.

67. Konstantin Lantratov and Alexandra Gritskova, "China Lands on Russian Carrier," *Kommersant*, October 23, 2005; "China Buying Russian Fighter Jets," *Prensa Latina*, October 24, 2006, http://www.plenglish.com/article.asp?ID=%7B409520EE-81B8-4DF6-9CDF-6079C7A632CE%7D)&language=EN; also see Siva Govindasamy, "Beijing Lines Up Naval Fighter Deal," *Flight International*, October 31–November 6, 2006, p. 16.

68. Wendell Minnick, "Russian Arms Dominate at China Airshow," *Defense News*, November 6, 2006; Piotr Butowski and Bernard Bombeau, "Modernized Su-33K for Beijing," *Air and Cosmos*, December 2006, pp. 32–33.

69. Analysis of Russia-China Military-Technical Cooperation," *Moskovskiye Novosti*, August 20, 2007, Open Source Center translation.

70. "Russia Will Build Nuclear Powered Aircraft Carriers—Navy Command," *AVN-Interfax*, June 23, 2007.

71. Office of the Secretary of Defense, Annual Report to Congress, *Military Power of the People's Republic of China*, May 23, 2006, p. 32, http://www.defenselink.mil/pubs/china.html.

72. "China Buying . . .," op. cit.

73. Interview, Moscow Air Show, August 2005.

74. For more detail on the history of the Su-33's development see Andrei Fomin, *Su-27, Flanker Story* (Moscow: RA Intervestnk, 2000), pp. 111–162; Yefim Gordon and Peter Davidson, *Sukhoi Su-27 Flanker, Warbird Tech Series Volume 42* (North Branch, MN: Specialty Press, 2006), pp. 53–64.

75. "Sukhoi Markets New Multi-Role Fighter at Chinese Air Show," *RIA Novosti*, October 31, 2006, http://en.rian.ru/russia/20061031/55256972.html.

76. *Interfax-AVN*, September 13, 2007.

77. Interview, Dubai Air Show, November 2007.

78. For more data on the design, performance, and upgrade potential of the Su-33 see Dr. Carlo Kopp, "The Flanker Fleet—China's Big Stick," *International Assessment and Strategy Center Web page*, May 3, 2006, http://www.strategycenter.net/research/pubID.106/pub_detail.asp.

79. "Russia to Deliver Aircraft Equipment to China's Navy," *Finmarket Agency*, April 27, 2006; Wendell Minnick, "Chinese Eye Russian Warplanes," *Defense News*, May 15, 2006. The PLAN operates about a dozen Ka-28 helicopters for antisubmarine, antiship, and rescue missions.

80. Interview, IMDEX Naval Exhibition, Singapore, May 2007.

81. Prasun K. Sengupta, "Spotlight on China's LPDs, LHDs and Carriers," *Tempur*, July 2008, p. 93.

82. Ibid.

83. Paul Lewis, "China Seeks Helicopter Carrier," *Flight International*, November 26–December 2, 1997, p. 18.

84. Interview, London, May 2005.

85. Gerald Segal, "Renew U.S. Ties with a Changing Chinese Military," *International Herald Tribune*, July 18, 1992.

86. "Summit on Cannibal Island," *Time*, January 15, 1979, http://www.time.com/time/magazine/article/0,9171,919982-1,00.html.

87. This aircraft was profiled in "Harrier in Beijing," *Binqi Zhishi (Ordinance Knowledge)*, March 2002, pp. 22–24. Apparently, a Western aircraft restoration specialist arranged for a trade of a retired British Harrier for World War II–era aircraft held by the Museum.

88. Chinese books examining the military requirements for space power include Bao Zhongxing, *The Initial Design for the Creation of a Space Force* (Beijing: NDU Press, 1988); Li Daguang, *Space Warfare* (Beijing: Military Science Press, 2001); Jia Junming, *On Space Operations* (Beijing: NDU Press, 2003); Yuan Zelu, *Space Warfare of the Joint Campaign* (Beijing: NDU Press, 2005); for U.S. reviews of this literature see Larry M. Wortzel, *The Chinese People's Liberation Army and Space Warfare, Emerging United States-China Military Competition* (Washington, DC: American Enterprise Institute, October 2007); Michael P. Pillsbury, *An Assessment of China's Anti-Satellite and Space Warfare Program, Policies and Doctrines*, Report submitted to the United States China Economic and Security Review Commission, January 19, 2007; "China's Military Strategy for Space," Statement of Mary C. FitzGerald, Research Fellow, Hudson Institute, before the U.S.-China Economic and Security Review Commission, China's Military Modernization and its Impact on the United States and the Asia-Pacific, March 30, 2007; Kevin Pollpeter, "The Chinese Vision of Military Space Operations," in James Mulvenon and David Finkelstein," *China's Revolution in Doctrinal Affairs*, (Alexandria, VA: Center for Naval Analysis and RAND Co., 2005), chapter 9.

89. Mark Wade, "Shuguang-1," *Encyclopedia Astronautica Web Page*, http://www.astronautix.com/craft/shuuang1.htm; Brian Harvey, *China's Space Program, From Conception to Manned Space Flight* (Chichester, UK: Praxis Publishing, 2004), Chapter 9.

90. "China Reveals Deadly Threat to First Flight," *Agence France Presse*, August 13, 2007.

91. Minnie Chan, "PLA Argues for Space Race," *South China Morning Post*, April 27, 2007, http://china.scmp.com/chitoday/ZZZ7I1TPVoF.html.

92. "China's Space Activities in 2006," Information Office of the State Council of the People's Republic of China, October 2006, Beijing.

93. Rao Radhakrishna, "Manned Indian Mission Could Take Off in 2014," *Flight International*, August 14, 2007, p. 27.

94. "NASA Agrees Sale of X-43A Airframe Blueprints to Japan," *Flight International*, October 17, 2006, p. 35.

95. Cited in Christopher Stone, "Chinese Intentions and American Preparedness," *Space Review*, August 13, 2007, http://www.thespacereview.com/article/930/1.

96. Yuan Guoxiong, Bai Tao, and Ren Zhang, "A Hybrid Reentry Guidance Method for Space-Based Ground Attack Weapon System," *Zhanshu Daodan Kongzhi Jishu*, September 1, 2005, Open Source Center *CPP20060104424006*.

97. The Shenlong space plane was first revealed on Chinese Web pages on December 11, 2007, in a likely tribute to the "father" of China's space program, Qian Xueshen, whose birthday was the same day. For this author's analysis, see "Shenlong Space Plane Advances China's Military Space Potential," *International Assessment and Strategy Center Web Page*, December 17, 2007, http://www.strategycenter.net/research/pubID.174/pub_detail.asp; and " . . . And Races Into Space," *Asian Wall Street Journal*, January 3, 2008, also available at http://www.strategycenter.net/research/pubID.175/pub_detail.asp .

98. The following article abstracts viewed on the ILib (www.ilib.com.cn/) and VIP (http://www.cqvip.com/) data bases during April and May 2008 indicate China's research toward the development of trans-atmospheric vehicles: Zhang Zi Yan, "Reusable Space Vehicle Flight Control," *Journal of Beijing University of Aeronautics and Astronautics*, No. 12, 2003; Zhou Yu Xiao, Zhang Zi Yan, and Ming Xiao, "Longitudinal Flight Control and Guidance Law Design for Trans-Aerosphere Vehicle During Climbing Phase," *Nanjing University of Aeronautics and Astronautics Journal*, No. 2, 2005; Yang, Yang Yi

Dong, and Shu Juan, "Predicted Trajectory Design for Space Shuttle Terminal Area Energy Management Phase," *Journal of Astronautics*, No. 6, 2005; Chen Jian-qiang, He Xin, Zhang Yi-feng, and Deng Xiao-gang (China Aerodynamics Research and Development Center, Mianyang, Sichuan; Department of Modern Mechanics, Uniersity of Science and Technology of China, Hefei, Anhui), "The Numerical Study on RCS Interaction for Trans-atmospheric Vehicle," *Aerodynamics Journal*, No. 2, 2006; Yin Zhizhong (Department of Training, Academy of Equipment Command and Technology, Beijing) and Li Qiang(Company of Postgraduate Management, Academy of Equipment Command and Technology, Beijing), "Analysis of Near Space Vehicle and Its Military Application," *Journal of the Academy of Equipment Command & Technology*, No. 5, 2006; Zhou Yu-xiao (Research Institute of Unmanned Vehicle, NUAA, Nanjing), Zhang Zi-yan (Chengdu Aircraft Design and Research Institute, Chengdu), and Ming Xiao (Aerospace Institute, NUAA, Nanjing), "Conceptual Study on Flight Control Laws for a Trans-Aerosphere Vehicle in Climbing Phase," *Flight Mechanics*, No. 1, 2006; He He-tang, Zhou Bo-zhao, and Chen Lei (College of Aerospace and Material Engineering, National University of Defense Technology, Changsha), "Aerodynamic Configuration of Trans-Atmospheric Vehicle Based on Waverider Research," *Journal of National University of Defense Technology*, No. 4, 2007.

99. This author first discovered this image at the 1996 Zhuhai Air Show.

100. This photo was seen in an article on Military.China.com, http://military. china.com/zh_cn/bbs2/11053806/20071216/14552048.html. This photo also reveals what may be a model of the new JL-2 SLBM, with a blunt nose cone, perhaps indicative of multiple warheads. The photo also contains a flying body with a thin, sharp delta wing, perhaps indicating a Chinese hypersonic test vehicle.

101. Mark Wade, "China," *Encyclopedia Astronautica*, http://www.astronautix. com/articles/china.htm.

102. Liu Huanyu, Dalian Naval Academy, "Sea-Based Anti-Satellite Platform," *Jianchuan Kexue Jishu*, February 1, 2004.

103. "China Drums Up Nationalistic Sentiment As Manned Space Mission Nears," *Agence France Presse*, October 13, 2003.

104. Veronika Romanankova and Viktor Gritsenko, "Russo-Chinese Space Cooperation," *Tass*, October 17, 1996; Mark Wade, "Project 921," *Encyclopedia Astronautica*, http://www.astronautics.com; "Russia Helped China Prepare for First Manned Space Mission," *Agence France Presse*, October 12, 2003.

105. Sven Grahn, "Shenzhou-3 Notes"; Craig Covault, "Chinese Milspace Ops," *Aviation Week and Space Technology*, October 20, 2003, p. 26.

106. Sibing He, "Space Official in Beijing Reveals Dual Mission of Shenzhou," *SpaceDaily.com*, March 7, 2003.

107. Mark Wade, "Shenzhou-Divine Military Vessel," *DRAGON SPACE*, October 2, 2003, http://www.spacedaily.com/news/china-03zd.html.

108. Li Tung-mei and Wu Yung-chiang, "Chinese Academy of Sciences Successfully Develops Shenzhou Spacecraft-Mounted Infrared Camera with a Resolution of 1.6 Meters," *Ta Kung Pao*, October 12, 2003, in *FBIS CPP20031013000062*.

109. Cheng Ho, "China Seeks Russian Help with Own Space Station," *www.SpaceDaily.com*, March 7, 2000; "Sino-Russian Space Station Cooperation," *www.SpaceDaily.com*, March 22, 2000.

110. Qian's early interest in space planes, which influenced first the late 1950s U.S. DynaSoar military space plane program and then the Space Shuttle, is relayed by Mark

Wade, "Tsien Space Plane 1949," and "Chinese Manned Spacecraft," *Astronautics.com*, http://www.astronautix.com/craftfam/chicraft.htm

111. Department of Justice, "Former Boeing Engineer Charged with Economic Espionage in Theft of Space Shuttle Secrets for China," press release, February 11, 2008, http://www.usdoj.gov/opa/pr/2008/February/08_nsd_106.html.

112. Wade, op. cit.

113. Rob Coppinger, "First RLV by 2020?" *Flight International*, October 17, 2006.

114. *Wen Wei Po*, December 1, 2006.

115. "Why Does China Want To Probe Moon?" *People's Daily Online*, February 7, 2007, http://english.peopledaily.com.cn/200702/07/eng20070207_348107.html.

116. "Ouyang Ziyuan and Academicians: Why Explore the Moon," *Sina Technology*, June 4, 2007, http://tech.sina.com.cn/d/2007-06-04/17281544569.shtml

117. Ibid.; "Why Does China Want . . .," op-cit.

118. Alexander Chebotarev, Director General of the Special Design Bureau of the Moscow Power Engineering Institute, "Hardware Reliability and Quality Are in Skillful Hands," *Military Parade*, September/October 2006, p. 53.

119. Mark Wade, "China," *Encyclopedia Astronautica Web page*, http://www.astronautix.com/articles/china.htm; "Chinese Lunar Base," http://www.astronautix.com/craft/chirbase.htm.

120. See *National Defense Science and Technology*, December 2007, p. 16.

121. "China's Laser Weapon Revelation: Attacks Against Stealth Aircraft and Missiles," *Qianlong.com*, accessed on February 5, 2008, http://bbs.mil.qianlong.com/thread-1287260-1-1.html.

122. Xu Ke-hua, Ma Jing, and Tan Li Ying, "Analysis for the Feasible Lunar-Earth Laser Link," *Optical Communication Technology*," No. 5, 2005, this abstract viewed on www.ilib.com./cn http://www.ilib.cn/A-gtxjs200505005.html

123. China's record of proliferation in Pakistan and North Korea is well documented in William Triplett, *Rogue State* (Washington DC: Regnery, 2004).

124. Jim Mann, *About Face* (New York: Alfred A. Knopf, 1999), p. 271.

125. "US Assures Taiwan Its Interests Not to Be Traded to China," *Agence France Presse*, September 30, 2003.

126. For an examination of potential Pakistani upgrades for their JF-17 see Prasun K. Sengupta, "JF-17 Goes Stealthy," *Tempur*, February 2008, pp. 81–83.

127. Reuben F. Johnson, "Pakistan Considers Mix of Chinese, French Weapons for Its JF-17s," *Jane's Defence Weekly*, December 5, 2007; "France Confirms Talks with Pakistan on High-Tech Systems for Fighter Developed with China," *Associated Press*, February 26, 2008.

128. Jon Grevatt, "China's JF-17 Draws Interest from Asia, Africa," *Jane's Defence Weekly*, March 5, 2008.

129. Kelly Hearn, "China's 'Peaceful' Invasion," *Washington Times*, November 20, 2005.

130. "Venezuela Poised to Take Over As Top Latin American Arms Buyer," *Newtown CN (SPX)*, November 15, 2005; http://www.spacewar.com/news/milplex-05k.html.

Chapter 8

1. Department of Defense, *Quadrennial Defense Review Report*, February 6, 2006, pp. 29–30.

2. Dr. Carlo Kopp, "Sukhoi Flankers, The Shifting Balance of Regional Airpower," *Airpower Australia* Web page, August 11, 2007, http://www.ausairpower.net/APA-Flanker.html; "Battle of the Fighters, Flanker V Raptor," *Air International*, March 2007, p. 21.

3. Roger Thompson, *Lessons Not Learned: The U.S. Navy's Status Quo Culture* (Annapolis: Naval Institute Press, 2007); see "Appendix: USN Ships That Have Been Theoretically Destroyed," pp. 185–186. In August 2007 a South African Type 209 submarine "sunk" six NATO warships during friendly exercises, including the U.S.S. *Normandy* CG-60, an Aegis radar-equipped cruiser; see "RSA Submarine 'Sinks' All NATO Ships During Naval Exercise Off Cape Coast," *Johannesburg SAPA*, September 4, 2007.

4. Bill Gertz, "Defenses on Subs to Be Reviewed," *Washington Times*, November 14, 2006.

5. The history of allied non-nuclear submarines "sinking" U.S. SSNs is also reviewed in Thompson, p. 24–34.

6. Rubin Bureau slide briefing, Defexpo, New Delhi, January 2006.

7. Tim Weiner, "Drive to Build High-Tech Army Hits Cost Snags," *New York Times*, March 28, 2005.

8. Major Daniel L. Davis, U.S. Army, "Flawed Combat System, FCS is Too Costly, Overly Complex and Potentially Dangerous," *Armed Forces Journal*, July 2005, pp. 37–39.

9. Nathan Hodge, "US Army Robots See Exponential Growth," *Jane's Defence Weekly*, August 22, 2007.

10. Kris Osborn, "'U.S. Wants 3,000 New Robots for War," *Defense News*, August 13, 2007, p. 1.

11. Peter LaFranchi, "Army Looks to Battle Unmanned Threat," *Flight International*, August 9, 2007.

12. Interview, Association for Unmanned Vehicles International Convention, Washington DC, August 2007.

13. It must be noted that many modern manned combat platforms reliant on sophisticated computer controls are also vulnerable to outside manipulation and compromise.

14. Jay Miller, *Lockheed-Martin F/A-22 Raptor, Stealth Fighter* (Hinkley, UK: Midland Publishing, 2005), p. 76.

15. For background on the A-12 debacle see James P. Stevenson, *The $5 Billion Misunderstanding*, (Annapolis: Naval Institute Press, 2001); Herbert L. Fenster, "The A-12 Legacy: It Wasn't an Airplane, It Was a Train Wreck," *U.S. Naval Institute Proceedings*, February 1999.

16. Jason Sherman, "Defense Department Eyes Further Cuts to Carrier Fleet," *Inside the Pentagon*, April 21, 2005, p. 1.

17. "U.S. Navy to Expand Fleet with Enemies in Mind," *New York Times*, December 5, 2005.

18. Congressional Budget Office, "Options for the Navy's Future Fleet," May 2006, http://www.cbo.gov/ftpdocs/72xx/doc7232/05-31-Navy.pdf.

19. David A. Fulghum, Michael Bruno, and Amy Butler, "The Plan Behind The Plan," *Aviation Week and Space Technology*, February 12, 2007, p. 23; Amy Butler, "On the Horizon," *Aviation Week and Space Technology*, March 5, 2007, p. 28.

20. Robert O. Work, "Numbers and Capabilities: Building a Navy for the Twenty-First Century," in Gary J. Schmidt and Thomas Donnelly, *Of Men and Materiel: The Crisis in Military Resources* (Washington DC: AEI Press, 2007), pp. 93–113.

21. For a more detailed treatment of the USAF's challenges see Loren Thompson, "Age and Indifference Erode U.S. Airpower," in Schmidt and Donnelly, op. cit., Chapter 3; Christopher Griffin, "Dual-Role Dilemma," *Armed Forces Journal*, September 2007, http://www.armedforcesjournal.com/2007/09/2952344.

22. Loren Thompson, "Two Decades of Decay," *Armed Forces Journal*, September 2007, http://www.armedforcesjournal.com/2007/09/2923793.

23. Julien E. Barnes, "Air Force May Shrink Its F-15 Fleet," *Los Angeles Times*, January 9, 2008, http://www.latimes.com/news/nationworld/nation/la-na-airforce9jan09,0,135 8206.story?coll=la-home-center.

24. Vago Muradian, "USAF Struggles with Budget Shortfall," *Defense News*, August 20, 2007, p. 4.

25. For a description of the challenges of the Air Force's aging inventory, see Jon Lake, "Fighting Tomorrow's Wars with Yesterday's Aircraft," *Air International*, May 2007, pp. 18–24.

26. David S. Cloud, "Army Finds Brigade Finds Itself Stretched Thin," *New York Times*, March 23, 2007.

27. Glenn Goodman, "Marine Corp Chameleon," *Defense Technology International*, January/February 2007, p. 21.

28. Gregg Jaffe and Jonathan Karp, "Pentagon Girds for Big Spending Cuts," *Wall Street Journal*, November 5, 2005.

29. Eric W. Hughes and Jon Houghtaling, "The Big Drop," *Air Combat*, March 2007, p. 20.

30. Alan Vick, David Oreletsky, Bruce Pirnie, and Seth Jones, *Striker Brigade Combat Team, Rethinking Strategic Responsiveness and Assessing Deployment Options* (Washington DC: RAND, 2002), pp. 18–29.

31. Ibid.

32. Lt. Col. Rick W. Taylor, "Logistics Risk in the Striker Brigade Combat Team," http://www.almc.army.mil/alog/issues/JanFeb04/LogisticsRiskintheStryker.htm.

33. "U.S. Admiral Defends Military Exercise near Guam," *Associated Press*, August 10, 2007.

34. Carlos Bongioanni, "Age Takes a Toll," *Stars and Stripes*, February 23, 2004.

35. David A. Fulghum, "Cruise Missile Killers Go to Okinawa," *Ares Blog Web Page*, August 23, 2007, http://www.aviationweek.com/aw/blogs/defense/index.jsp?plck Controller=Blog&plckScript=blogScript&plckElementId=blogDest&plckBlogPage= BlogViewPost&plckPostId=Blog%3a27ec4a53-dcc8-42d0-bd3a-01329aef79a7Post% 3a69c42fb8-9b4d-4ee8-b97d-a113bed0054c.

36. Bill Gertz and Rowan Scarborough, "Pacific Buildup," *Washington Times*, June 4, 2004.

37. James Brooke, "Looking for Friendly Overseas Base, Pentagon Finds It Already Has One," *New York Times*, April 7, 2004; Natalie J. Quinata, "Fighter Squadron Arrives on Guam," *Pacific Daily News (Guam)*, April 30, 2005; Audrey McAvoy, "U.S. Pacific Commander Says Taiwan A Factor in Guam Buildup," *Canadian Press*, April 16, 2007.

38. "U.S.-Japan Alliance: Transformation and Realignment for the Future," Security Consultative Committee Document by Secretary of State Rice, Secretary of Defense Rumsfeld, Minister of Foreign Affairs Machimura, and Minister of State for Defense Ohno, October 29, 2005.

39. Society of American Military Engineers, "Guam Military Buildup Program," May 3, 2007.

40. Robinson Duffy, "Eielson Fighter Squadron Gets New Name, Mission," *Fairbanks Daily News-Miner*, August 25, 2007, http://hosted.ap.org/dynamic/stories/A/AK_ FIGHTER_SQUADRON_AKOL-?SITE=AKFAI&SECTION=HOME.

41. Arthur Waldron, "Why Does America Cling to Failed China Policies?" *Family Security Foundation Web Page*, September 17, 2007,http://www.familysecuritymatters.org/ global.php?id=1343758

42. Vivek Raghuvanshi, "Australian Navy Chief, Indian Officials Discuss 5-Nation Exercise," *Defense News*, August 21, 2007.

43. John T. Bennett, "Pentagon Lacks Funds for ORS Plans," *Defense News*, August 20, 2007, p. 36.

44. The new Northrop Grumman E-2D uses a combined AESA and rotating radar with a reported 500+ km range to increase U.S. Navy defenses against cruise missiles; see David A. Fulghum, "New Threats, New Counters," *Aviation Week and Space Technology*, April 30, 2007, p. 50.

45. Such a capability was being explored in 2007 by the Defense Advanced Research Projects Agency (DARPA); see Peter LaFranchi, "Two Hours to Seek and Strike," *Flight International*, July 17, 2007, p. 18.

46. Amy Butler, "Leadership Crisis, Shortfalls Plague Airlift Community," *Aviation Week and Space Technology*, September 24, 2007, p. 76.

47. William Matthews, "U.S. House Panel: Cap DD(X) Buy at 2," *Defense News*, May 1, 2006.

48. Boeing "C-17B Advanced Intra Theater Airlift," brochure, obtained September 2007.

49. Robert O. Work, "Numbers and Capabilities: Building a Navy for the Twenty-First Century," in Gary J. Schmidt and Thomas Donnelly, eds., *Of Men and Materiel: The Crisis in Military Resources* (Washington DC: AEI Press, 2007), p. 99.

50. Kopp, op. cit.; Benjamin S. Lambeth, *American Carrier Airpower at the Dawn of the New Century* (Washington DC: RAND, 2005), p. 114.

51. For an explanation of the potential impact of UCAVs for the U.S. Navy, see Thomas P. Ehrhard and Robert O. Work, "The Unmanned Combat Air System Carrier Demonstration Program: A New Dawn for Naval Aviation?," *Center For Strategic and Budgetary Assessments Backgrounder*, May 10, 2007.

52. David A. Fulghum and Michael J. Fabey, "F-22: Unseen and Lethal," *Aviation Week and Space Technology*, January 8, 2007, p. 47.

53. Graham Warwick, "USAF Says Next Bomber Will Be Subsonic and Unmanned," *Flight International*, May 3, 2007; Sydney J. Freedburg, Jr., "Air Force's Commitment to New Bomber a Matter of Debate," *National Journal*, August 15, 2007.

54. Kris Osborn, "The Tank Is Back," *Defense News*, July 30, 2007, p. 11.

55. David Eshel, "Power Shields," *Defense Technology International*, March 2007, p. 30.

56. James Mann, *The China Fantasy: How Our Leaders Explain Away Chinese Repression*, (New York: Viking, 2007), p. 37.

57. Mann credits this formulation to Harvard University Professor Dr. Joseph Nye (p. 38) and Nye repeated this formulation in 2008; see Joseph S. Nye, "Taiwan and Fear in US-China Ties," *Taipei Times*, January 14, 2008. Also, in early 2007 former Pacific Command Commander Admiral Dennis Blair was quoted saying: "We can make them into an enemy who will try to expand in any way they can . . . and the way we do that is treat them like that now with the creation of a containment strategy on the lines of what was used to deal with the former Soviet Union. To say that China has grand ambitions in the world is simply completely premature and maybe wrong. You cannot conclude that they have this plan of building up their power to dominate Asia"; see Wendell Minnick, "'Habits of Cooperation,' Former PACOM Chief Calls for U.S., Chinese Militaries to Work More Together," *Defense News*, April 30, 2007.

INDEX

640 Program, 131, 279n.22, 280n.24
863 Program, 58, 81, 85, 87, 106, 114, 116, 204, 230

A-10 (Fairchild), 141, 240
Afghanistan, 1, 45, 47, 52, 59, 161, 162, 235, 236, 237, 238
AGAT, 141, 144
AHEAD(Advanced Hit Efficiency and Destruction), 97, 234
  Skyshield, 234
Airborne forces, 15th Airborne Army, 161, 176
  armor, 160, 176, 178, 234
  doctrine development, 173–176
  expeditionary mission, 53
  Peace Mission 2005, 64, 175
  Peace Mission 2007, 74, 173–174
  Taiwan, 124, 125
  Tiananmen, 24
Airbus, 103, 104, 147, 160, 183, 231
  AVIC-1 investment, 105
  Tianjin assembly line, 105
Aircraft carrier, 3, 4, 11, 12, 17, 61, 75, 90, 146, 184, 232, 292n.64

air wing, 188–94
  disinformation, 188
  French influence, 185, 186
  Russian technology, 92, 137, 186
  Ukraine, 93
Amphibious forces, 113, 125, 153–158
  Peace Mission 2005, 64, 173
Anti-Ballistic Missile (ABM), 3, 58, 78, 131–132, 229, 280n.25
  anti-ABM, 58–60, 132, 244
Antiship Ballistic Missile (ASBM), 2, 3, 76, 124, 125, 147, 148, 165, 167–168, 210, 222, 223, 288n.153
  for U.S., 246
Anti-Satellite (ASAT), ABM connection, 58, 76, 78, 131, 229
  air launched, 144, 202
  missile, 2, 41, 78, 131, 202
  laser, 82–83
  SC-19, 2, 131, 202, 228, 229, 243
  space based, 202, 207
  submarine launched, 205, 228
  U.S. concern, 201, 222, 228, 243–244
Anti-Tactical Ballistic Missile (ATBM), 249
Antonov, 160, 176, 180, 183

ANZUS Treaty, 62
Argentina, 212
ARJ21, 104, 105
Armor, infantry fighting vehicles,
    ZBD–2000("EFV"), 156, 158
    ZBD–97, 158, 21, 233
    ZLC–2000, 160, 161, 174, 176, 178, 183
    tanks, T–63A, 156, 158
    T–96, 113, 159, 210
    T–99 (ZTZ–99), 113, 159, 210
    wheeled combat vehicles, 158
    Arena-E, 159
    Reflex, 155, 159
    U.S., M1A2, 156, 159, 233, 237, 249
Artillery, 75, 82, 83, 86, 154,157, 194
    truck-mounted, 234
    PLZ–04 155mm, 234
    rocket, 134, 210, 234
Asia Pacific Space Cooperation Organiza-
    tion (APSCO), 202
Asymmetric Warfare, 2, 75, 81, 125, 144,
    163, 214, 218–225
Australia, 5, 18, 39, 42, 43, 46, 47, 62, 65,
    111, 118, 153, 186, 218, 223, 224, 226,
    240, 242
    missile defense of, 6, 58, 59, 62,132
Aviation Industries Corporation (AVIC)
    AVIC-1, 88, 103, 104, 105, 106, 136,
        141, 146, 160, 181, 183
    AVIC-2, 95, 103, 105, 160, 181, 183

B-1 (Rockwell), 35, 106, 239, 249
B-2 (Northrop Grumman), 35, 88, 146,
    236, 239
B-52 (Boeing), 135, 223, 239, 249
B-70, 35
Baker, James A., 56, 263n.49
Biotechnical Weapons, 87
Boeing, 36, 104, 105, 160
Bolton, John, 51, 53
Brazil, 53, 55, 114, 212, 227
Britain (United Kingdom), 32, 46, 94, 95,
    117, 118, 186, 197, 245
Burma (Myanmar), 6, 37, 61, 63, 218, 227
Bush Administration, 1, 10, 11, 13, 44,
    216, 244
    Iraq and China, 57
    Israel and China, 94

North Korea, 51, 56, 210
    space cooperation, 201
    Taiwan policy, 44, 45–46, 56, 148, 238,
        250
Bush, George W., 18, 28, 39, 51, 57, 62

C4KISR, 112–113
C-17 (Boeing), 35, 160, 117, 179, 181,
    182, 183, 237, 238, 240, 246
Cao Gangchuan, 22, 27, 90, 92, 200
CATIA, 103
Central Military Commission (CMC), 15,
    18, 23, 26, 71, 77, 79, 200
    combat experience, 19, 21
Chavez, Hugo, 58, 120, 212, 227
Chen Bingde, 19, 21
Chen Shui-bian, 45, 67
Chengdu Aircraft Corporation, 102, 103,
    104, 105, 117, 147, 204, 232
Chi Haotian, 7, 11, 22, 24
Chiang Kai-shek, 27, 28, 42
China Xinshidai, 21
Chinese Students and Scholars
    Association (CSSA), 39
Chung, Dongfan, "Greg," 35, 208
Clinton, Administration, 10, 11, 50, 51,
    94, 162, 236, 238, 239
Clinton, Bill, 45, 125
Communist Party, Chinese (CCP), 241, 251
    Foreign Liaison Department, 39
    relations with PLA, 15–16, 22–28, 76
    space, 199–200
    United Front Works Department
        (UFWD), 32, 33, 41, 125
    weakness, 4–5, 28–32
Cox Commission, 35, 38, 129
Cruise Missile, 96, 117, 124, 125, 184,
    210, 214, 219, 229, 234
    antiship, 52, 125, 167, 223
    Israel, 93
    land attack, 76, 77, 88, 124, 132, 133,
        134, 148, 191, 217
    Pakistan, 50
    Russia, 191
    Ukraine, 98
Cuba, 6, 37, 57, 120, 212, 227

Defense Intelligence Agency, 16

Defense spending, 16–17
Denel, 85, 96, 97, 144
Deng Xiaoping, 2, 9, 14, 20, 23, 58, 67,
    69, 76, 185
Destroyers (DDG)
    Luhai, 100, 107, 152
    Luhu, 11, 100
    Luyang I, 134
    Luyang II, 134, 152
    Sovremenniy, 90, 151, 153, 165, 166
    Type 051C, 152
Digital Soldier, 113
Doctrine, 7, 11, 20, 21, 66–68, 70
    Active Defense/offense, 68–69
    computer network operations, 118
    joint operations, 20, 71–73
    nuclear issues, 77–78, 222

Electronic Intelligence (ELINT)
Espionage, 8, 22, 34–39, 118, 121
    Chinese Americans, 164
    Ministry of State Security (MSS), 33,
        34, 37, 38, 39
    Second Department, 33, 37, 41, 68
    Third Department, 37
    U.S. response, 242–243
Eurocopter, 90, 160, 234
Europe, 17, 39, 47, 52, 81, 86, 146, 216,
    218, 228
    arms embargo, 90, 92, 94–95, 228
    arms technology sales, 89, 94–96, 104,
        105, 107, 113, 116, 153, 201, 211
    pressure versus Taiwan, 95

F-14 (Grumman), parts for Iran, 38
F-15 (Boeing), 60, 145, 221, 222, 223,
    232, 236, 239, 240
F-16 (Lockheed Martin), 12, 46, 60, 94,
    139, 140, 211, 212, 222, 223, 232, 238,
    239
F-22A (Lockheed Martin), 106, 109, 220,
    221, 223, 232, 233, 236, 237, 240, 242,
    249
F-35 (Lockheed Martin), 109, 145, 194,
    197, 198, 221, 232, 237, 247, 248
F/A-18 (Boeing), 166, 187, 190, 191, 192,
    194, 212, 222, 223, 232, 239, 247, 248
Falun Gong, 24, 31, 39

Fast Attack Craft (FAC), Type 022, 88,
    111, 153, 157
Fifth Generation Fighter, 60, 102, 103,
    106, 137, 145, 191, 223, 247, 249,
    273n.136
Ford, 34
France, 94, 95, 115, 118, 160, 185, 186,
    204, 211, 212
Frigates (FFG), Type 054, 88, 110, 151,
    152
Future Combat System (FCS), 85, 121,
    159, 224, 225, 233, 237, 246, 249

Germany, 36, 59, 86, 95, 97, 101, 115,
    118, 149, 150, 234
Gowadia, Noshir, 35, 88, 146,
Guam, 12, 26, 43, 44, 124, 125, 132, 147,
    218, 220, 221, 222, 231, 238, 239–240,
    246
Guizhou, Aeroengine Research Institute,
    107
    Aircraft Corporation, 85, 99, 177
Guo Boxiong, 19

H-6 (Xian), 12, 99, 152, 165
    ASAT, 202, 203, 205
    H-6K, 134, 136,138,146, 248
    tanker, 147
Hainan Island, Sanya naval base, 43,
    60–61, 127, 150
Harbin Institute of Technology, 188, 204,
    280n.25
Hezbollah, 47, 48, 52, 53, 54, 94, 210,
    216, 229, 243
Hill, Christopher, 51
Hongdu Aircraft Corporation
    L-15 trainer, 103, 141
    Q-5 attacker, 138, 141
Hu Jintao, 5, 9, 15, 18, 19, 20, 22, 24, 28,
    40, 41, 46, 62, 171, 172, 216
Huawei Co., 57
Humvee, 176, 178
Hypersonic Vehicles, 84–85, 86, 92, 208
    233, 268n.28
    U.S., 232, 245

IDEX (International Defense Exhibition,
    Abu Dhabi), 84, 88, 97, 99, 134, 234

India, 6, 7, 18, 41, 42, 43, 47, 62, 76, 107,
132, 145, 153, 189, 215
nuclear threat, 48, 50
Shanghai Cooperation Organization,
64, 65, 128, 226
space, 202
U.S. cooperation, 240, 242
Indonesia, 60, 61, 202, 212
Information Warfare (IW), 75, 83, 113
attacks against Taiwan, 121–122
attacks against U.S., 121
Computer Network Operations (CNO),
118–122
Informationization, 111–113
Iran, 18, 57, 218, 236
aiding terrorists, 229
arms sales, 38, 84, 93, 94, 153, 181
China's proliferation, 52–53, 215, 216,
250
military cooperation, 218, 231
secondary proliferation, 6, 47, 48, 53,
210, 215
Shanghai Cooperation Organization,
64, 128, 226, 231
space cooperation, 202
U.S. weapons, 38
Iraq, 1, 45, 47, 51, 62, 224, 235, 236, 237,
238, 249
insurgency and china, 52, 229
Saddam and China, 57, 210
U.S. versus Chinese aid, 57
Israel
military aid to China, 36, 89, 93–94, 96,
101, 103, 134, 141, 147, 148, 149
threat from China, 6, 47, 52, 53, 94,
210, 216, 226, 229, 243
Iveco Company, 34, 161

J-6 (Shenyang), as UCAV, 85, 146
J-7 (Chengdu), 12, 102
J-8 (Shenyang), 12, 100, 102, 138, 142,
J-10 (Chengdu), 12, 61, 91, 94, 100, 101,
103, 137, 140, 166, 232 233
exports, 94, 211, 212
Israeli influence, 94
J-10C, 140
J-10S, 138, 140
U.S. influence, 94

weapons, 141–142
J-11 (Shenyang), 102, 106, 137, 232, 233
carrier version, 190, 192
dispute with Russia, 92, 190
J-11B, 92, 101, 102, 137, 166
J-11BS, 102, 137
weapons, 138, 141
Japan, 5, 6, 7, 8, 14, 18, 27, 43, 51, 57,
103, 101, 117, 137
European Union, 95
larger forces, 62, 131, 226
maritime disputes, 41, 61, 125–126
military spending, 17
military threats, 133, 137, 144, 148,
150, 161, 166, 184, 218, 219, 222,
232, 233
missile defense, 57, 59, 132, 133
new military relations, 62, 65
space, 202
and Taiwan, 43, 44, 47, 60, 124,125, 218
U.S. alliance, 42, 218, 238–239, 240,
242, 245
JH-7 (Xian), 136
British help, 95, 100, 107
JH-7A, 12, 100, 137, 141, 148, 152,
165, 166, 174
weapons, 136, 138
Jiang Zemin, 9, 20, 23, 24, 41, 46, 51, 80,
81, 200, 205

Kamov
Ka-28, 151
Ka-29, 196
Keating, Timothy, 11, 13, 14, 58, 185
Khan, Abdul Qadeer (A.Q.), 58, 98, 215, 216
Kitty Hawk, U.S.S., 13, 14, 164, 186, 223
Korea, North
Chinese support/intervention, 40, 52,
62, 126–27, 177, 227
nuclear threat, 1, 6, 8, 50–51, 59
proliferation to, 6, 47, 48, 50–52, 216,
250
proliferation from, 51, 54, 63, 216
Six-Party Talks/ diplomacy, 6, 45, 51,
216
impact on Taiwan, 56, 210
Korea, South, 40, 41, 43, 51, 58, 59, 62,
110, 126, 127, 150, 159, 218, 233

missile defense, 59
Taiwan, 59–60, 132, 227
U.S. alliance, 235, 238

Landing Helicopter Dock (LHD), Type
    081, 110, 157, 158, 196–198
Landing Platform Dock (LPD), Type 071,
    61, 154, 157, 158, 194–196, 197, 211,
    212, 217
Landing Ship Tank (LST), 110, 154, 158,
    194, 196
Large Transport Aircraft, 17, 74, 76
    civilian, 103–105
    military, 181–183
Laser, communication
    weapons, 82–83, 87, 93, 131, 230,
        266n.8
    space weapon, 3, 79, 83, 165, 203, 208,
        209, 228, 229
    U.S., 239, 244, 249
Lavochkin, 91
Lawless, Richard, 10, 122
LCAC (Landing Craft Air Cushion), 157,
    196, 198
Lee Teng Hui, 11
Leung, Katrina, 35, 37
Liang Guanglie, 19, 21, 22
Liao Xilong, 19, 21
Libya, 48, 53, 215
Lin Biao, 22, 26, 76
Liu Daxiang, 104
Liu Huaqing, 20, 185, 186
Liu Yazhou, 27, 171
Luoyang Optoelectric Technology Devel-
    opment Center (LOEC), 136, 140, 141,
    142

Mak, Chi, 36
Malaysia, 41, 42, 60, 61, 63, 212, 227
Mann, James, 250
Mao Zedong, 8, 22, 28, 131, 199
Mars, 200, 202, 208
Masorin, Vladimir, 189
Mil Mi-17, 9, 160, 162
Mir space station, 207
Missile, Air-to-Air (AAM), 247, 249
    A–Darter, 97, 144
    AIM-9X, 144

AIM-120, 139, 142, 143n
CADE, 249
Helmet Mounted Display (HMD), 144
Infrared Search and Tracking (IRST),
    144
K-100/172, 144, 191, 223
PL-8, 141
PL-9, 141
PL-12, 137, 140, 141
PL-10, 144, 232
PL-13, 141, 223, 232
R-27, 141
R-77, 137, 141, 144, 191
R-Darter, 97, 144
Missile, Anti-Radiation (ARM), Kh-31,
    165, 191, 223
Missile, Intercontinental Ballistic (ICBM),
    DF-5 Mod 2, 128, 129, 132, 229
    DF-31, 31, 128, 224
    DF-31A, 128, 129, 131, 229, 244
    multiple warheads, 78, 129, 131, 132,
        133, 167, 222, 229, 244, 279n.11
    Russia, 129
    U.S., 129, 244
Missile, Intermediate/medium Range Bal-
    listic (IRBM/MRBM)
    DF–21, 2, 129, 133, 167, 203
    multiple warheads, 133
Missile, Short Range Ballistic (SRBM)
    B-611, 133, 135
    DF-11, 132, 133, 135
    DF-15, 71, 83, 132, 167, 222
    DF-15B, 135
    DF-15C, 135
    P-12, 133, 135
    WS-1/WS-2/2C/2D/WS-3, 134, 135
    nuclear armed, 78
Missile, Submarine Launched Ballistic
    (SLBM)
    JL-2, 128, 129, 131, 244
    multiple warheads, 129
Missile, Surface-to-Air (SAM), 147–148
    HQ-7, 151
    HQ-9, 101, 151, 152
    RIF, 152
    S-300, 76, 89, 90, 132, 147, 148
    S-400, 148
    U.S., Patriot, 36

Moon, 4, 17, 200, 202
 exploration, 209
 Russia cooperation, 91, 209
 military use, 3, 83, 208–209
 race with U.S., 200, 213, 229, 244
 Shenzhou circumlunar mission, 209
Mullen, Mike, 11
Munro, Ross, 42
Myasishchev, 246

Nanotechnology, 86–87
Nigeria, 212
Nixon, Richard, 2, 242
NORINCO (China North Industries Co.),
 21, 159
Novator
 air to air missiles, 143, 144, 191, 223,
 232
 Club cruise missiles, 144, 149, 153,
 156
Nuclear Weapons, control, 13

Pace, Peter, 11
Pakistan, Chinese arms sales, 210, 212
 Chinese missile aid, 49, 50, 58,132, 202
 Chinese nuclear aid, 42, 47, 49, 50, 51,
 209, 215
 Gwadar and China, 63
 Iran and, 53
 Libya and, 53
 North Korea and, 50, 51
 Saudi Arabia and, 54
 Shanghai Cooperation Organization
 and, 64, 65, 128, 226
 space cooperation, 50, 202
Peace Mission, 11, 226
 2005, 74, 146, 158, 176
 2007, 21, 22, 25, 26, 64, 74, 76,
 173–176, 177
People's Armed Police (PAP), 5, 27, 34
People's Liberation Army (PLA–Ground
 Forces)
 aviation, 160–161
 impact on foreign policy, 40–42
 leadership, 18–22
 modernization, 153–162, 233–234
 relations with Communist Party,
 22–28

People's Liberation Army Air Force
 (PLAAF)
 future power projection, 176–183
 modernization, 136–148
 roles and doctrine, 76
People's Liberation Army Navy (PLAN)
 future power projection, 183–199
 modernization, 148–153
 roles and missions, 75
Philippines, 34, 41, 47, 60, 61, 62, 127
Poly Technologies, 21
Power Projection, 25, 40, 62, 64, 69, 75,
 126, 163
 air projection, 176–183
 arms sales, 209–212
 maritime projection, 183–199
 new interests and doctrine, 171–173
 Peace Mission 2007, 173–176
 space projection, 199–209
 U.S. concern and reaction, 169–170,
 230–232
Precision Guided Munitions (PGM), 76,
 132, 138, 140, 141, 144, 211, 232, 249
Proliferation, 6, 8, 47–57, 215–216
 abjures responsibility, 56–57, 216
 Chinese leaders profit from, 56, 215
 Iran, 53–53, 216
 linkage to Taiwan, 56
 MTCR, 56
 North Korea, 50–52, 216
 Pakistan, 50
 secondary proliferation, 53–56, 250
 threat to China, 6, 57
 threat to India, 215
 threat to Israel, 94
 U.S. Proliferation Security Initiative, 56

Quadrennial Defense Review, 170, 214

Radio Frequency Weapons, 83–84, 163,
 223, 249
 against carriers, 83
 on missiles, 125, 133, 163
Raduga, 84, 134, 153, 191
Rail gun, 36, 86, 230, 246
Reagan, Ronald, 10, 45, 58, 244
Rolls Royce, 95, 100, 107, 141
Rumsfeld, Donald, 10, 235, 238

Russia, 3
    aircraft carriers, 189, 226
    arms/technology, 22, 25, 83, 84, 85,
        88, 89–93, 96, 100, 101, 103, 106,
        107, 108, 110, 116, 131, 132, 134,
        137, 140–153, 155, 157–161, 176,
        182, 183, 185, 186, 188–194, 197,
        199, 201, 205, 207, 223–224, 228,
        230, 232–234
    concerns, 41, 93, 102
    cooperation with China, 6, 64, 128,
        132, 226–227, 244
    PAP, 34
    Peace Mission/SCO, 25, 64–65, 74,
        128, 173–175

Salyut space station, 207
Satellites, Communication, 112, 115, 116
    BeiDou/Compass, 115, 116, 229
    CBERS, 114
    Data Rely, 117, 276n.177
    Early Warning, 116, 275n.170
    Galileo, 90, 95, 116, 201
    HuanJing HJ, 113, 114, 116
    JianBing, 114, 116
    Navigation, 90, 113, 116, 133, 136,
        157, 167, 175, 199, 210, 228, 229
    Russian assistance, 90, 91, 116
    Signals or Electronic Intelligence
        (SIGINT/ ELINT), 116
    Surveillance, 90,
    ZiYuan, 116
Saudi Arabia, 48, 50, 53, 54, 215
Sawyer, Ralph, 14
Second Artillery, 11, 20, 21, 68, 71, 74,
    76–78, 79, 112, 128–131, 200
Segway Company, 34
Sha Zukang, 13
Shanghai Cooperation Organization
    (SCO), 6, 63–65, 74, 128, 169, 173,
    226
Shen Dingli, 13
Shenyang Aircraft Corporation, 85, 97,
    102, 103, 104, 105, 145, 190, 208, 233
    Aeroengine Research Group, 106
    Commercial Aircraft Company, 105
    Shenyang-Liming Aeroengine Group,
        106

Shenzhou (Divine Vessel) space capsule,
    200
    military use, 114, 204, 205, 207
    Russian assistance, 205, 206
Shipbuilding, 97, 107, 110–111, 157, 188,
    231
Siberian Aeronautical Research Institute
    (SibNIA), 103
Singapore, 10, 42, 60, 61, 63, 65, 68, 107,
    171
South Africa, 96–97, 227
    AAMs, 144
    UCAV development, 85, 97, 145
South China Sea
    nuclear missile submarine bastion, 61,
        127
    sea lanes, 43
    Taiwan, 61
    territorial conflicts, 41, 60, 67, 123,
        124, 126, 127, 218
Southeast Asia Nuclear Weapons Free
    Zone Treaty, 61
Soyuz space capsule, 91, 205
Special Forces, 75, 112, 113, 124, 125,
    133, 150, 153, 160, 161–162
    mechanized, 162, 234
    versus U.S., 164, 222
Space Force, 79, 200
Space Plane, 3, 203, 204, 208
    Hermes, 204
    Shenlong, 204
Space Station, 91, 207–208, 228
    military use, 205, 208, 229
    Russian assistance, 207
Space Warfare, 3, 8, 79, 86, 203
Space Warfare (Li), 202
Stealth/Counter stealth, 12, 35, 82, 87,
    88, 90, 101, 107, 111, 140, 141, 145,
    146, 152, 153, 190, 204
Stryker Brigade Combat Team (SBCT),
    58, 177, 179, 223, 237, 238, 240, 249
Submarines
    Air Independent Propulsion (AIP),
        111, 150, 212, 224, 274n.153
    Kilo, 89, 90, 91, 149, 150, 153, 164,
        165, 199, 224
    Ohio class, 239, 246
    Russian assistance, 110, 150–151

Submarines (*continued*)
    threat to U.S. Navy, 223–224
    Type 035 *Ming*, 110, 149, 150, 164,
      224
    Type 039 *Song*, 11, 12, 61, 100,107,
      110, 149, 164, 211
    Type 091 *Han*, 149
    Type 093 *Shang*, 110, 149, 150, 184,
      199
    Type 094 *Jin*, 100, 127, 128, 129, 149
    Virginia class, 240
    Yuan, 100, 110, 111, 149, 150, 165,
      212, 224
Sudan, 5, 6, 58, 212, 227
Sukhoi Aircraft Corporation, 137, 190,
    223, 239, 247
    Su-25, 141
    Su-27, 11, 12, 71, 74, 91, 92, 102, 106,
      137, 141, 173
    Su-30, 137, 138, 212, 141, 144, 147,
      148, 166, 212, 233
    Su-33, 102, 137, 189, 190, 191, 192,
      231
    Su-33UB, 189, 190, 191
    Su-35, 137, 144
Sun Zi, 5, 7, 8, 14, 34
Supercavitating weapons, 88–89
Surrey Space Systems, 117
Sweden, 95, 103, 162
Syria, 47, 53, 54, 94, 212

Taijung, 125
Thailand, 60, 61, 202, 212, 227
Thermobaric Weapons, 84
Taiwan
    arms sales, 45, 46, 59, 148
    blocked satellite sale, 95
    challenge to China, 27, 28, 32, 124, 215
    Chinese rule of, 44, 46–47
    deterring U.S. military support,
      164–168, 222
    impact of fall, 60, 62, 64, 218
    military isolation, 61, 62
    threats to, 5, 6, 8, 9, 13, 13, 21, 26, 29,
      42–47, 67, 71, 77–78, 121–122,
      124–125, 133, 134, 137, 146, 147,
      148, 151, 154, 157, 159, 161,
      216–218

U.S. commitment to defend, 44, 46,
    214–215, 241–242
U.S. relations, 10, 45–46
Tiananmen Massacre, 10, 22, 23–24, 25,
    32, 34, 89, 90, 95, 102, 228
Tibet, 4, 5, 13, 24, 28, 30–31, 42, 69, 140
    Dali Lama, 13
    Hu Jintao, 9
    March 2008 protests, 30
Training, 25, 46, 64, 68, 73–74, 76, 113,
    137, 161, 162, 189, 194, 201
Transparency, 10, 13, 102
Tupolev
    Tu-22M3, 92, 146, 173, 248
    Tu-95, 92, 146
    Tu-154, 101
Turbofan engines, *Qinling* engine, 100,
    107, 108
    R0110 generator, 106
    Taishan, 107, 108, 190
    WS-10A *Taihang* engine, 106, 108, 190
    WS-15, 106
Turkey, 53, 55, 128, 202, 212

UCAS-D, 145, 148
Ukraine, and arms sales, 50, 64, 93, 96,
    134, 160, 176, 180, 183, 185, 188, 190
United States, alliances, 58–62, 238–240
    cyber attacks against, 121
    military challenge to, 213–234
    military reductions, 234–238
    deterrence requirements, 240–250
    economic relations, 17–18
    engaging PLA, 9–14
    espionage against, 34–39
    threats to critical infrastructure, 8, 118
    Taiwan Relations Act, 13, 44
    U.S. Congress, 11, 44, 82, 128, 170,
      201, 246
Unmanned Aerial Vehicle (UAV), 71, 83,
    85, 97, 117, 125, 127, 147, 167
    U.S., 191, 224, 225
Unmanned Combat Aerial Vehicle
    (UCAV), 85, 97, 145, 146, 233, 285n.82
Unmanned Ground Vehicle (UGV), 85–86
Unmanned Underwater Vehicle (UUV),
    85
Unrestricted Warfare, 7

Varyag (aircraft carrier), 12, 93, 185, 186, 187, 188, 189, 194, 231
Venezuela, 6, 58, 120, 212, 227
Victims of Communism Memorial, 28
Vietnam, 9, 21, 40, 41, 60, 61, 62, 76, 85
Vympel, 141, 142, 143, 144, 191

Wen Jiabao, 31, 45, 103
White Paper, arms control, 56
    PRC–EU relations, 95
    PRC National Defense, 18, 66, 75, 75–78, 160, 172, 201
Wu Bangguo, 189

Xian
    Aeroengine Group, 107
    Aircraft Industries Group, 103, 146
Xu Qiliang, 19, 20, 174

Y-8 (Shaanxi), 159, 160, 176, 180, 181, 211
    Airborne Early Warning (AEW), 101, 147,
    Command, 147
    Electronic Warfare (EW), Ground Mapping Radar, 136, 147

Y-8F600, 181
Y-8X, 180
Y-9 (Shaanxi), 160, 176, 180, 181, 211, 212
Yak-141, 197
Yakovlev, 103
Ye Jianying, 26
YJ-62 (C–602), 153, 165
YJ-63, 146

Z-8 (Change), 195, 196, 198
Z-9 (Harbin Aircraft Industry Group), WZ-9, 161, 174, 196
Z-10 (Chinese Helicopter Research and Design Institute), 160, 195, 196, 234
Z-11 (Change), 160, 196
Zhang Qinsheng, 3, 69
Zheng Bijan, 7
Zhuhai Airshow, 1996, 167
    1998, 88
    2002, 99, 102, 117, 132, 180
    2004, 141, 146, 207
    2006, 85, 88, 96, 97, 106, 113, 116, 117, 136, 137, 141, 145, 146, 147, 189, 191, 202, 207

About the Author

RICHARD D. FISHER JR. is a Senior fellow, International Assessment and Strategy Center, and the Director of its Project on Asian Security and Democracy (June 2004 to present). He has previously served as Asian Security Fellow with the Center for Security Policy, editor of the Jamestown Foundation *China Brief*, Senior Fellow with the Republican Policy Committee of the United States House of Representatives, and as Director of the Asian Studies Center of the Heritage Foundation. He received a BA (Honors) from Eisenhower College in 1981. His articles and reports have appeared in numerous journals and national newspapers and he as testified on Chinese military issues before the United States Congress.